Montanism was a prophetic movement of the second century CE, deriving from Montanus of Phrygia and two female prophets, Priscilla and Maximilla. It preached the outpouring on the Church of the Holy Spirit, and – despite winning the allegiance of the great North African theologian, Tertullian – was subsequently condemned as heretical.

This study of the movement is the first in English since 1878. It takes account of a great deal of scholarship of the nineteenth and twentieth centuries and refers to the epigraphical evidence. Dr Trevett questions some of the most cherished assumptions about Montanism. She covers its origins, development and slow demise, using sources from Asia Minor, Rome, North Africa and elsewhere, and pays particular attention to women within the movement.

The rise of Montanism was an important phenomenon in the history of the early church. This prophetic movement survived for centuries after its beginnings in the second half of the second century and posed a challenge to the developing catholic tradition. *Montanism* looks at its teachings and the response of other Christians to it. To an unusual degree Montanism allowed public religious activity and church office to women, and therefore bears interestingly on a number of contemporary issues and debates.

MONTANISM

MONTANISM

Gender, authority and the New Prophecy

CHRISTINE TREVETT

Lecturer in Religious and Theological Studies
University of Wales College of Cardiff

CAMBRIDGE
UNIVERSITY PRESS

Published by the Press Syndicate of the University of Cambridge
The Pitt Building, Trumpington Street, Cambridge CB2 1RP
40 West 20th Street, New York, NY 10011-4211, USA
10 Stamford Road, Oakleigh, Melbourne 3166, Australia

First published 1996

Printed in Great Britain at the University Press, Cambridge

A catalogue record for this book is available from the British Library

Library of Congress cataloguing in publication data

Trevett, Christine
Montanism: gender, authority and the New Prophecy
p. cm.
Includes bibliographical references and index.
ISBN 0 521 41182 3 (hardback)
1. Montanism–History. 1. Title.
BT1435.T74 1995
273'1.–dc2095-8503
CIP

ISBN 0 521 41182 3 hardback

I dedicate this book to the Revd Dr David Hill, my teacher in the University of Sheffield and a student of Christian prophecy, who will be forgiving of its conclusions.

Contents

ix

Preface

This study has been researched for and written between the years
1989 and 1994, sandwiched precariously between my university
teaching and administrative duties. A lot of it was done during two
terms of study leave in 1992–3. In those years too I took the
opportunity to make a third visit to western Turkey, to visit the area
where the beginnings of Montanism are usually located and to pass
through Cappadocia. In the summer of 1993 I gave a series of lectures
on 'Approaching the New Testament from the Second Century' for
the ninetieth year of the *Vacation Term for Biblical Study* series, held at
St Anne's College, Oxford, and the process of preparation helped me
to clarify some of my thinking about second-century Christianities.

I had some interest in Montanism already but would not have
ventured into wholehearted study of it at this stage without the
invitation from Alex Wright, of Cambridge University Press. I am
glad the invitation came, for Montanism has proved to be a fascin-
ating topic – hard to unravel but never dull. I have valued
particularly the brief to write about Montanism 'from a woman's
perspective' and as a result women figure large in this work.

Montanism cannot be a comprehensive study, however. More than
one volume is needed for that and only one is allowed me. We know
less about Montanism, even about its beginnings, than many writers
have liked to assume and what evidence we possess sometimes points
(in my opinion) in directions quite other than those scholars have
taken. There is much work still to be done; on the prophesying of its
founders, on the significance of its innovations, on the sites where
epigraphy has been discovered, on some of the ideas which (I suspect)
underline aspects of its teaching. What the present work aims to do is
to bring the reader up to date with scholarly thinking on Montanism
(which in its early form should be called the New Prophecy), to
challenge a number of prevailing assumptions about it and to fill a

remarkable gap. There has not been a study in English of Montanism since 1878.

I am grateful to the following: the staffs of the Humanities and Social Studies Library in the University of Wales at Cardiff and of the British Library, London; Cambridge University Press staff; those people who have kindly provided me with pre-publication copies of material, have read Syriac for me and so on (they are acknowledged in the endnotes). My thanks also to the many sharp-eyed members of the Religious Society of Friends (Quakers) in Britain who pointed me towards iconography relating to Perpetua and Felicitas. Thanks too to my fellow Late Antiquarians in Cardiff, for sanity and humour in the sometimes bizarre turmoil of modern British university life: Professor Humphrey Palmer, the Revd Gordon Jeanes, Dr Will Johnson, Dr Frank Trombley and Dr John Watt. Finally I thank my long-suffering husband and my growing son, who sometimes took advantage of the fact that he is now big enough to play in friends' houses!

CHRISTINE TREVETT

Department of Religious and Theological Studies
University of Wales at Cardiff
September 1994

Abbreviations

ABR	*Australian Biblical Review*
AFL	*Annales Faculté des Lettres*
An. Boll.	*Analecta Bollandiana*
ATR	*Anglican Theological Review*
BALAC	*Bulletin d'Ancienne Littérature et d'Archéologie Chrétienne*
BJRL	*Bulletin of the John Rylands Library*
CAH	*Cambridge Ancient History*, ed. J.B. Bury, S.A. Cook, F.E. Adcock and M.P. Charlesworth, 1923–39
CH	*Church History*
CIG	*Corpus Inscriptionum Graecarum*, ed. A. Boeck, Berlin 1828–77
CIL	*Corpus Inscriptionum Latinarum*, Berlin 1863–1909
Civ. Catt.	*Civiltà Cattolica*
DCB	*Dictionary of Christian Biography*, ed. H. Wace and W. Smith, London 1877
Down. Rev.	*Downside Review*
Exp. T.	*Expository Times*
GRBS	*Greek, Roman and Byzantine Studies*
HE	*Historia Ecclesiastica*
HTR	*Harvard Theological Review*
JAAR	*Journal of the American Academy of Religion*
JAC	*Jahrbuch für Antike und Christentum*
JBL	*Journal of Biblical Literature*
JECS	*Journal of Early Christian Studies*
JEH	*Journal of Ecclesiastical History*
JFemSR	*Journal of Feminist Studies in Religion*
JRS	*Journal of Roman Studies*
JSNT	*Journal for the Study of the New Testament*
JSNTSS	Journal for the Study of the New Testament Supplement Series

JSOTSS	Journal for the Study of the Old Testament Supplement Series
JSPSS	Journal for the study of the Pseudepigrapha Supplement Series
JTS	*Journal of Theological Studies*
LV	*Lumière et Vie*
MAMA	*Monumenta Asiae Minoris Antiquae*, Manchester 1928–39
Nov. Test.	*Novum Testamentum*
NTS	*New Testament Studies*
PG	*Patrologia Graeca*, ed. J.-P. Migne, Paris 1857–87
PL	*Patrologia Latina*, ed. J.-P. Migne, Paris 1844–64
REAug	*Revue des Etudes Augustiniennes*
Rev. Bib.	*Revue Biblique*
RivAC	*Rivista Archeologia Cristiana*
RQ	*Römische Quartalschrift*
RQCAK	*Rhomische Quartalschrift für Christliche Altentumskunde und Kirchengeschichte*
RScR	*Recherches de Science Religieuse*
SBAW	*Sitzungsberichte Bayerische Akademie der Wissenschaften*
SNTSMS	Society for New Testament Studies Monograph Series
SPAW	*Sitzungsberichte Preussische Akademie der Wissenschaften*
SSR	*Studi e Materiali di Storia della Religioni*
TDNT	*Theological Dictionary of the New Testament*, ed. G. Kittel and G. Friedrich, Grand Rapids 1964–76
ThQ	*Theologische Quartalschrift*
ThSt	*Theological Studies*
ThZ	*Theologische Zeitschrift*
TLZ	*Theologische Literaturzeitung*
TU	Texte und Untersuchungen
Vet. Chr.	*Vetera Christianorum*
Vig. Christ	*Vigiliae Christianae*
VT	*Vetus Testamentum*
ZKG	*Zeitschrift für Kirchengeschichte*
ZNW	*Zeitschrift für die neutestamentliche Wissenschaft*
ZWT	*Zeitschrift für wissenschaftliche Theologie*

CHAPTER I

Beginnings

1.1 THE STUDY OF MONTANISM

1.1.1 'One of the holiest men . . .'

Montanism and the Primitive Church (1878), Soyres' work, has been until now the only monograph in English on the history of Montanism, though recently there have been studies in English of oracles, inscriptions and testimonia. Towards the end of his work Soyres raised the question which many a student of Montanism has continued to keep in a recess of the mind:

was the 'Spirit' which Tertullian preached, and for which Perpetua died, the Father of lies, or was it the Spirit of God? [1]

In other words, was Montanism heresy or a much-maligned movement with the potential to be valuable grit for the pearl of the Church? Was Montanus, whose name was taken to designate the movement,[2] indeed 'one of the holiest men in the second century' (as the sermonising John Wesley maintained[3]) or was he that wretched little man (τὸ ἐλεεινὸν ἀνθρωπάριον; Epiphanius *Panarion* xlviii.11,9), the deceiving, corrupt, semi-pagan opportunist 'prophet' described in a number of ancient sources?

Montanus has mostly been regarded as a villain, though a few have conceded that, like the women Priscilla and Maximilla and some of those who followed them, he may have been only in ecstatically contrived error – like Edward Gibbon's whirling dervishes, mistaking 'the giddiness of the head for the illumination of the spirit'. This study will examine both the phenomenon of Montanism and its leading protagonists.

What was Montanism? Montanism was a religious movement emerging within Christianity of the second century. It was not a simple and single phenomenon but was long-lived. Indeed it was 'an

unconscionable time a-dying', languishing long in a depleted and
ailing state.[4] As late as John of Damascus' eighth-century day (*Haer.*
xlix) sectarian 'Pepuziani' (named after the Montanists' 'Mecca' at
Pepuza) may possibly have existed in the region of its beginnings,
though I doubt it.[5] Its death throes began in the fourth century and it
seems to have been left barely alive, so far as we can tell, after blows to
it in the fifth.

'Montanism' was a name applied by others to a prophetic
phenomenon. Cyril of Jerusalem (d. 386 CE) first used the term
Montanoi ('Montanists') in his exceedingly polemical *Catechetical
Lectures* (*Cat.* xvi.8), countering their claim to be 'Christians'. In the
same source he used the term Cataphrygian, the name we find most
frequently in our sources. The fifth-century *Codex Theodosianus* also
used the term 'Montanists' along with 'Phrygians', 'Pepuzites' and
'Priscillianists': the various designations were derived either from the
geographical hub of the movement (Phrygia and the town of Pepuza)
or from names of Prophets associated with it (Montanus/Montanists;
Priscilla/Priscillianists; Quintilla/Quintillianists).[6] Epiphanius and
others refer to some (more or less probably) related groups which
stem from a later period of Montanism. These are described in terms
of their allegedly aberrant eucharistic and ritual practices. They
included Artotyrites ('bread and cheesers') and Tascodrougites
('nose-peggers').

The first 'Montanists' called themselves none of these things. They
talked of 'The New Prophecy' or perhaps at first of 'The Prophecy'.
This is suggested both by the language of the Anonymous in Eusebius
HE v.16,4 ('this new thing. . . not prophecy', contrast the form in
v.16,14) and by the words of Serapion of Antioch in *HE* v.19,2
('so-called new prophecy').[7] In this study I shall write of 'The (New)
Prophecy' too and of the Prophets (capital P) when speaking of the
first six decades or so of the phenomenon (i.e. chronologically
speaking up to and including the work of Hippolytus and Apollonius).
Then I shall use the familiar, if anachronistic, term 'Montanism'. I
make an exception with the person of Tertullian. His views should
always be suspected of being less than truly representative of the
Prophecy ('Tertullianists' was another name given to such believers),[8]
but, since his writings tend to be divided as a matter of course into
pre-, proto- or truly Montanist, then against my own strictures (viz.
that the proper term for this early period is (New) Prophet) I shall call
him Tertullian the Montanist.

The New Prophecy believed in the outpouring of the Spirit and the appearance of a new, authoritative prophecy which brought fresh disciplinary demands to the churches. Women were prominent as leaders and the Prophets clashed with catholic representatives on matters such as the nature of prophecy, the exercise of authority, the interpretation of Christian writings and the significance of the phenomenon for salvation-history. The New Prophecy – later Montanism – spread and diversified, despite some catholic success in countering it. It was hard to kill. It represented, as Robert Eno observed in his 1971 study of 'Authority and Conflict in the Early Church', 'a fundamental type of conflict'.

1.1.2 *The sources*

There is much we do not know about the New Prophecy and later Montanism. We are forced to interpret the remaining fragments of a history which was written by the winners and in this we meet serious historical limitations on patristic scholarship. Recognising the limitations, we must take account of *much* of the available material, for the writer can afford to ignore none of the evidence, excepting that late kind which merely parrots the descriptions of earlier and better-known anti-Montanists. 'There is nothing to be gained from reading through this tittle-tattle', Campenhausen concluded in *The Formation of the Christian Bible* (233), dismissing loftily Eusebius' early anti-Montanist Anonymous source. But when the task is to glean what may be gleaned, then we must use what there is, recognising that primary and secondary sources have been coloured with the brush of the authors' prejudices.

Evidence from the Montanist side includes Prophetic oracles, available now in collection and translation into modern languages through the work of Hilgenfeld, N. Bonwetsch (in Lietzmann's *Kleine Texte*, 1914), Labriolle, R.M. Grant, Kurt Aland, David Aune, also in the *New Testament Apocrypha* edited by E. Hennecke and W. Schneemelcher, and most recently (and usefully for the English-speaking reader) in Ronald Heine's *The Montanist Oracles and Testimonia* (1989; omitting ninety-six of the texts which Labriolle cited). Some of these oracles are of questionable authenticity. Some seem not to be strictly 'oracles' at all (see below, 3.1.2; 4.3.1–4) and they have sometimes been too readily dismissed as trivial, lacking in the *gravitas* of scriptural pronouncements or meaningless. I disagree. Such judgements are unworthy of serious scholarship, for they fail (among

other things) to take account of the fact that the material has come to
us in attenuated form, subject to redaction, wrenched from the
saying's original context and used in the propaganda war which was
being waged. In the present study I shall use sayings as appropriate,
numbering the oracles according to Aland's scheme and cross-referring
to Heine's study. A tabulated list appears in 3.1 note 8.

Then there is Montanist epigraphy. This is much debated, not least
about whether some of it is Montanist or not. It has been increasingly
available since the publications of W.M. Ramsay and his three
students W.H. Buckler, J.G.C. Anderson and (most notably) William
Calder. Elsa Gibson and recently William Tabbernee have examined
the most important discoveries too and as I write this, at the end of
1993, Tabbernee's study of 'Montanist Regional Bishops: New
Evidence from Ancient Inscriptions' has just been published and
*Montanist Inscriptions and Testimonia: Epigraphic Sources Illustrating the
History of Montanism* will be forthcoming in 1996. This is in part the
outcome of his mammoth Ph.D. study of 'The Opposition to
Montanism from Church and State'. The epigraphy is a significant
addition to the available resources, for it was not available to most of
the earlier commentators on Montanism. It relates to the later stages,
however, and like the oracles I shall cite it as appropriate throughout.

Also from the Montanist side and from North Africa there is (i)
defence of the New Prophecy by the remarkable and idiosyncratic
apologist Tertullian (see 2.3.2) and (ii) the writing of the Redactor of
the *Passio Perpetuae et Felicitatis*. Incorporated in the latter is the
witness of Perpetua herself (4.5).

The bulk of the evidence is from the anti-Montanist side. At worst it
is hostility of a vicious and highly imaginative kind and at best there
are relatively civilised descriptions of strongly held differences of
view. Considering the number of centuries and geographical areas
through which the influence of Montanism percolated, the witnesses
to it are few enough and, as Soyres wrote, 'some of them do not
survive cross-examination'.[9] This makes Montanism an interesting
and difficult phenomenon to study.

I shall not refer to all the material in Labriolle's *Sources* though I
will use a great deal (a) from the second and third centuries, viz.
Eusebius' early anti-Montanist sources, the early source of Epiphanius,
the writing of Hippolytus, Tertullian, Origen and others; (b) some
important fourth- and fifth-century witnesses which include Epiphanius (again), Didymus of Alexandria and the *Dialexis* (this last a

dialogue between an orthodox and a Montanist believer), Pseudo-Tertullian, Filastrius of Brescia, Augustine and others, plus (c) some later testimonia relating to the final throes of Montanism.

1.1.3 What writers have said

Patristic studies are 'often like a walk through excavated ruins', offering 'the mutilated remains of past glory'.[10] For Montanism only partial edifices can be recognised and this is also true about the communities of its catholic opponents. Yet metaphorically speaking, at least, the ruins of Montanism have been excavated regularly and variously interpreted.[11] Yet there have been fewer studies of the New Prophecy and later Montanism than of (say) Ignatius of Antioch or of Gnosticism, of emerging catholicism or 'Jewish-Christianity'. That is odd, given that studies of the second century Church or of the sweep of church history to Nicaea or Chalcedon make reference to Montanism as a potent force in shaping catholic developments.

Karlfried Froehlich wrote of this lack of interest in Montanism in 'Montanism and Gnosis' in 1973. Kurt Aland had explained it, he said, in his useful essay 'Bemerkungen', and it was due to belief that *there was no more to say.* The evidence had been picked over and something approaching a scholarly consensus had been reached about Montanism's distinctive features. Nevertheless, Montanism has not been neglected in the last few decades. Short studies have appeared with great regularity up to the present and I shall be citing a large number of items. Interest in Montanism is no less lively than in the nineteenth century, though it is not at the forefront of church historians' thinking.

Turning to the research of the nineteenth century, Bonwetsch provides a good beginning. In *Die Geschichte des Montanismus* (1881) Bonwetsch discussed findings on Montanism to his day, moving from the catholic Baronius and Tillemont in the seventeenth century,[12] through eighteenth-century critics including Arnold and Wernsdorf, Walch (*Entwurf einer vollständigen Historie der Ketzereien*, Leipzig 1762) and Mosheim, who was chancellor of Göttingen University, friend of the Hanoverian court and pioneer in the 1760s of a new kind of objective Church history writing. Important nineteenth-century studies which had preceded Bonwetsch's own included those of Neander and Ritschl, F.C. Baur, Réville, Renan, Schwegler, Georgi and Soyres.[13] Bonwetsch's own examination of Montanism proved stimulating and comprehensive. Klawiter has reviewed the nineteenth-century discussions in his Ph.D. study,[14] and included the two important articles in English (i) by Harnack ('Montanism', which appeared first in the ninth edition of *Encyclopaedia Britannica* vol. xvi, 774ff.) and (ii) by G. Salmon ('Montanus' in *DCB* iii). Zahn, Voigt and Hilgenfeld had written in the closing decades of that century too, addressing the causes, sources for and development of Montanism. Our debt to German-speaking scholars is obvious. But what were they saying about Montanism?

The New Prophecy was often portrayed as a form of primitive, 'original' Christianity revived (or perhaps surviving with minority status) and involved in a desperate struggle to preserve legitimate but decaying elements of the tradition in the face of developing catholicism and ecclesiastical organisation. Here was 'the lost Pentecostal springtime of the Church' as Whale put it, or 'le plus remarquable de ces retours fort naturels vers l'esprit apostolique'.[15] This has been a view particularly associated with Protestant scholarship but certainly not exclusive to it.

For F.C. Baur the catholic Church had emerged as synthesis out of tensions between Pauline and Petrine (Hellenistic and Judaic) kinds of Christianity. The work of Baur's pupil Schwegler (*Der Montanismus und die christliche Kirche des 2. Jahrhunderts,* 1841) proved an important if controversial contribution to the nineteenth-century debate. Indeed Bonwetsch saw in Schwegler's work the opposite extreme to Neander (*Allgemeine Geschichte der christlichen Religion und Kirche* and *Antignostikus*), who had overvalued the significance of Montanus himself and understood Montanism as a reaction against Gnosticism's perversion of Christianity. At the hands of Schwegler Montanism was a name *invented* to cover certain second century and later modes of thought, and the question of Montanus' very existence might be raised. Montanism was legalistic *Judenchristentum* and Schwegler looked to Ebionism for explanation, positing a stand versus gentile Christianity.

Ritschl took issue with this view in an 'epoch-making' (Bonwetsch) work (*Die Entstehung der altkatholischen Kirche,* second edn, 1857). The root of Montanism was not Ebionism, he maintained, but catholic *Heidenchristentum* should be examined. Montanism's enthusiasm betrayed the influence of gentile Christian, even pagan, practice, which for Ritschl certainly did not derive from the legitimate prophecy of the Hebrew Bible and the Christian Church. As for its opposition to a developing (and non-apostolic) catholic form of church order, the fact was that it was not itself apostolic. Still neither its chiliasm nor its legalism divided it from the beliefs of the Church catholic, he thought.

Some felt that the Jewishness of Montanism had been overstressed but Baur had wondered where the many 'Jewish' elements in Montanism would have derived from, if not from Judaism. Like Harnack he took note of the parallel rise of monarchical episcopacy and he saw in Montanism a more ancient and Jewish form of Christianity which was now in opposition to a hierarchical, Hellenised form. It is clear, then, that J.M. Ford's attempt (in 1966) to explain Montanism as a 'Jewish-Christian' phenomenon was far from new. Long ago Gregoire for one had looked at the possibility of elements having been borrowed from a Palestinian kind of Judaism, a generation after the disastrous Bar-Cochba revolt. Intransigence against Rome was still in the air, he suggested.[16]

Nineteenth-century scholars had also examined Montanist eschatology, looking for the roots of its rigorism;[17] had questioned whether Tertullian was a good source for the Prophecy, and had acknowledged the possibility that it had been a bastion against Gnosticism. Réville, Soyres and Renan should be mentioned in these respects, as also Augustus Neander's work *Antignostikus* (ET by J.E. Ryland, London 1887). In the writings of Renan and Harnack we see interest in conflicts of culture and in the political dimension of apocalyptic thought. This last aspect of the study of the Prophecy's beginnings has been developed in the twentieth century in the work of Schepelern and Kurt Aland, and most recently in studies by W.H.C. Frend. Hilgenfeld (*Die Glossalie in der alten Kirche*, Leipzig 1850, and *Die Ketzergeschichte des Urchristentums*, Leipzig 1884), on the other hand, had studied the Prophecy in terms of an attempt to reinstate a more original, charismatic form of ministry.

The same questions are still in the air. Klawiter's thesis has asked whether Montanism was a prophetic reform movement of protest against secularisation and spiritual decline in catholic circles (so Baur and Campenhausen), or whether it was perhaps the revolution of martyrs in political revolt against Rome. This latter view, more clearly expressed in the twentieth century, was presupposed in some nineteenth-century comments on the Prophecy's apocalyptic eschatology (e.g. Renan). Writers are still asking whether the Prophecy was revival or unacceptable innovation; whether Tertullian's North African Montanism was at all like 'real' (Asia Minor) Montanism and so on.[18] There are no definitive answers, though in some respects we are now better served with evidence.

Pierre de Labriolle has been an unsurpassed chronicler of Montanism. No student of it dares to ignore the work of this Roman Catholic who saw in the Prophecy something bigger than a purely local Phrygian reaction against the catholic Church. In *La Crise Montaniste* (1913) and *Les Sources de l'Histoire du Montanisme* of the same year Labriolle gave a comprehensive overview of what was known of Montanism in Rome, North Africa and the East, and the sources and analysis took the reader from its beginnings to the destruction of its sites. Labriolle ventured as far as John of Ephesus, who launched a major attack on the Montanists, but he did not include the evidence of Michael the Syrian (see 5.2–5.3) or of those epigraphic sources which were available (thanks to Ramsay) even in 1913. There is still excellent meat in his Introduction to the sources, which considered their possible dependence one upon another. As for what Labriolle thought, he believed that the apparent revivalism of the Prophecy was misleading. What it offered was not truly primitive Christianity at all. Despite its return to prophecy, its apocalyptic turn of mind and its rigorous refusal to betray the faith, it could not be. For Montanus (Labriolle believed) taught that the Paraclete was incarnate in the prophetesses Priscilla and Maximilla and in himself.[19]

The twentieth century has brought more systematic study of the Prophecy's possibly pagan roots, though the attempt to parallel the Prophecy and later Montanism with elements in pagan Phrygian practice is not new. It can be traced back at least to the work of Neander in 1827. Bonwetsch, Schwegler, Hilgenfeld and Harnack, among others, drew attention to parallels with Phrygian paganism, especially with the cult of Attis-Cybele, and towards the end of the century the British scholar W.M. Ramsay took up the theme in his study of *The Church in the Roman Empire*. There he had contrasted the Prophecy's insistence on a local, Phrygian church polity (not uninfluenced by the society and native cults of Phrygia) with the unifying ideal of the Roman church.[20] Nevertheless, the work of Harnack, Schwegler and Labriolle had already served to dampen enthusiasm for Phrygian pagan parallels when in 1929 Wilhelm Schepelern undertook a comprehensive study of the topic. This was under the title *Der Montanismus und die phrygischen Kulte*.

That title has misled some writers (who seem not to have read the book) into thinking that Schepelern found the roots of the Prophecy in Phrygian paganism. This was not so. He recognised that *ecstatic* prophecy had been a key factor for the catholics' condemnation and certainly there were parallels to be examined with the cult of Attis-Cybele. Similarly the honouring of pagan priestesses was examined as a possible clue to the position of women in Montanism, and the most striking parallels with Montanist practice were found to be the lamenting virgins in congregational worship (as described by Epiphanius) and rites which involved the pricking of infants with needles. Yet the sources concerned were late. They could not tell us about the roots of the Prophecy. Its immediate dependence, he concluded, was not on Phrygian paganism. Its roots lay in the kind of Christianity which looked to Johannine sources and especially to the Revelation.[21] Kurt Aland was even more uncompromising about its Christian origins. In 'Der Montanismus und die kleinasiatische Theologie' (a resumé of his 'Bemerkungen') he declared that Montanism was 'eine Bewegung rein christlichen Charakters'. Scholars since have endorsed this view. Aland stressed the importance of the *Asian* theological setting for the Prophecy.

Interest in pagan parallels with the Prophecy seems to have diminished in recent decades, though the study by Greville Freeman is less critical of the sources than was Schepelern and there is an unpublished 1980 dissertation by B.W. Goree on 'The Cultural Bases of Montanism', more sympathetic than most writers to dependence on Phrygian paganism.[22] W.H.C. Frend's valuable study, *Martyrdom and Persecution in the Early Church*, has combined the Jewish, Christian apocalyptic and native rural Phrygian strands in examining the Prophecy's beginnings, and in 'Montanism: A Movement of Prophecy and Regional Identity' he expressed the view that Prophetic rigour and ecstatic utterances probably had owed more to Phrygian paganism than Schepelern allowed. A. Daunton-Fear's article on 'The Ecstasies of Montanus' linked Montanus' form of prophesying with the cult of Apollo, but such views are now rare. Goree's dissertation began by expressing regret that for the preceding half century scholars of Montanism had lost interest in examining a possible pagan background for it. Avid readers, I suggest, *could* find references to Phrygian pagan influence in writings since the 1930s (E. Evans in *Tertullian's Treatise Against Praxeas*, Knox in *Enthusiasm* and Greenslade in *Schism in the Early Church*, to cite but a few) but such claims in my view have tended to be inadequately defended assertions.

The Prophecy, in the opinion of most scholars of the present day, was *Christian*. I would not struggle to deny that elements of local Phrygian religious practice may have fed into the Prophecy during its long life and been Christianised, but we should distinguish between its *Phrygian* Christian character and a real connection with paganism.[23]

For many, of course, the Prophecy/later Montanism was synonymous with revolt – against emerging catholic authority and catholic pragmatism ('worldliness' to some); the Spirit against the letter; the prophet against the bishop or the fanatic against the sober teacher. As early as 1729, in Arnold's *Unparteyische Kirchen und Ketzerhistorie*, it was being portrayed as the genuine world-denying piety of godly Christians, rudely attacked by the opposition. Many catholic writers over the centuries have also seen it as a form of opposition but have not graced it with the mantle of *legitimate* protest. Rather it was a heinous threat to the truth of the Church catholic or to Christian orthodoxy. Of whatever century, and whether catholic or protestant, writers have tended to treat Montanism with a sideways glance at the Reformation.

Montanism's rise as critic, irritant, or even heresy is sometimes regarded as a watershed for the young Church.[24] It rose alongside the growth of episcopal authority and certain forms of Gnosticism. Hence the history of ecclesiology and of doctrine has tended to be understood with reference to these two (Montanist and Gnostic) aberrant and abhorrent forces. Adolf von Harnack represented one angle on this view though he gave Ritschl the credit for 'first discerning the true significance of the Montanistic movement'.[25] The Church, he said, 'marched through the open door into the Roman state' and Montanism was among the forces (the 'warning voices') raised against secularising tendencies. In turn it fell prey to arrogance and legalism.[26] Gnosticism and Montanism (so Harnack and Ritschl too)[27] were the two movements whose defeat made the catholic Church. Given such 'twinning' in terms of influence, it is interesting that we rarely encounter attempts to twin Montanism and Gnosticism genetically. Instead Montanism is usually assumed to have been at odds with, rather than influenced by, Gnosticism. There has been one dissenting voice, however.

Froehlich made a spirited attempt to link the two. The consensus view, he said, still owed much to a 'triangular theory' of church history and the Hegelian view which went back to F.C. Baur and was popularised by Harnack. This, which had marked a lot of Roman Catholic historiography, maintained that the second-century Church faced danger on three fronts: from Gnosticism, paganism and Montanism. Protestant scholarship, Froehlich went on, offered only variation on the theme, with Montanism, the catholic tradition, Marcionism, paganism/Hellenisation, Gnosticism and so on, appearing in various combinations and systematisations in different works by Protestants. There was some support for the assumption about the antignostic character of Montanism but he attempted to undermine 'the speculative constructions of Christian history', to show Montanism's close affinities with Gnostic thought. He made an impression upon Francoise Blanchètiere, at least, who concluded ('Le Montanisme originel', 1979, 19) that

Fondementalement, la 'nouvelle Prophétie' est d'abord un renouveau spirituel à coloration apocalyptique et même encratiste, non sans quelque parente avec certaines idèes gnostiques.

Tabbernee ('Opposition', 558) disagreeed, however, and I too shall argue that the Prophecy was hostile to Gnostic thinking.

1.1.4 Is Montanism worth the effort?

The study of Montanism, says Klawiter, has been dominated by desire to know how the ancient catholic Church evolved. So the presentation of Montanism has depended on whether the writer considered that evolution valid.[28] But we should also note that some of the partisans have wondered whether Montanism is worth the study at all. English speaking scholarship of the outspoken kind has accused students of gullibility, of taking too seriously a movement of 'coarse revivalism': Christianity

perverted by fear of learning and speculation . . . opposed to . . . the dignified traditionalism of the sub-Apostolic church.

Church historians had exaggerated its importance, for Montanism, 'if the wayward genius of Tertullian had not lent energy to its propaganda', would have made no more than 'a small ripple' on Christendom's surface.[29] In France even Labriolle thought that Montanism (never as great a threat as Gnosticism to the Church) had suffered from over-dramatisation.

Edward Gibbon, of course, had offered a different perspective. Convinced of the rightness of his picture of 'gloomy and austere' second-century Christians who 'with caution and reserve' offered 'frequent predictions of impending calamities', Gibbon wrote of that

same Church censuring the Prophets 'for discharging too freely the
dangerous secret'. Here then was a domestic struggle, in which the
catholics turned on the New Prophecy with a venom and level of
accusation which matched what the Church itself had suffered.[30]

Nevertheless, there are many in Christian churches today –
charismatics and those who fear their influence, feminist commentators
and others – who look on the New Prophecy/Montanism as more
than a matter of antiquarian interest. Montanism was once a reality
in Cappadocia. In May 1993 I was in Cappadocia and found myself
in conversation with a British member of the charismatic House
Church movement while we both waited in the heat to be let into a
church dedicated to Basil the Great. The man was familiar with
Montanism and for him the issues he thought it represented (as well as
the dangers he had read of) deserved to be expressed, for they were
alive and kicking. Similarly feminist reclaimers of the history of
Christian women have seized on the Prophecy, sometimes with scant
knowledge of its history and implications but conscious that here was
a phenomenon in which (unusually in Christian history) women were
prominent. The study of Montanism has always been moulded by the
concerns and the confessional stance of writers.

So here is a confession: I stand in the Protestant camp, heir to a
seventeenth-century radical Puritanism to which Montanism has
sometimes been compared. I'm sure some readers will think that it
shows. But Montanism merits study not because it can continue to
provide ammunition in centuries-long wars of words about authority,
charisma, women's ministry and more. It deserves study not least
because in the present century new fields of scholarship (decipherment
and interpretation of new-found epigraphy, study of the phenomenon
of ancient prophecy both Christian and otherwise, the sociology of
religion and psycho-history) are bringing fresh insights to bear on
what we think we know of it. Frend does regret in several of his
writings that there are not systematic surveys and excavations of sites
where epigraphy was discovered, as happened with Donatism. And
this is a gap to be filled. Nevertheless, a lot of new work has been done
on Montanism and it is right that for the first time in English since
1878 Montanism should have an airing.

1.1.5 More on methodology
The subject index at the end will allow the reader to trace oracular
and epigraphic items. The index of scholars' names will give access to

bibliographical details which do not appear in the final bibliography (for no nineteenth-century or earlier works will be included, for example). What is to be done about Tertullian? Tertullian's evidence poses particular problems (2.3). One could treat Tertullian's Montanist writings as being maverick about Montanism or more generously see them as evidence only for the (second-phase) phenomenon in North Africa. One might disregard all he has to say. Yet on certain matters his is the only available evidence and since my purpose in chapter three, in particular, is to examine what may be known of the New Prophecy's teachings, such gaps are to be avoided. Consequently the evidence of Tertullian will be discussed, but always with acknowledgement of its possible shortcomings.

The distribution of the Prophecy creates difficulties too. Even in its first few decades it was not confined to a single area but we know something of it in Rome and in Africa as well as in Asia Minor and beyond. It was not the same in all of these places, though writers of the past have sometimes collated information and then assumed unjustifiably a uniformity of belief and practice. Klawiter was rigorous in his separation of these different settings for the Prophecy and this was a proper reminder to students about assumptions we should not make. It is right, then, that in chapter two these settings are considered separately. Nevertheless, when in chapter three the Prophecy's *content* is described, evidence from all three settings will be brought together, albeit giving due recognition to possible variations in practice. Chapters four and five take us beyond the early third century and into the realm of sources which are more scattered and at times more suspect.

The death of the prophetess Maximilla (*c.* 179–80 CE) is usually taken to mark the end of the first phase of the Prophecy, since she is assumed to have been the last of the Prophetic Trio (Montanus, Priscilla and Maximilla) to die. Hence some would differentiate rigidly between first and second 'phases'. I have not found it possible to do so. There are far too many unknowns to be able to state with certainty that what we hear must have been characteristic of *either* the pre-179 CE Prophecy *or* that which was true of (say) Asia Minor only after that date. Moreover I am not wholly convinced that Maximilla was the last of the Three to die (see 1.3,3–4; 4.1–4.2), a doubt which must alter any understanding of the Prophecy's 'phases'. While it is clear from early and later sources on the subject that the activity of the Three marked a time of special dispensation of the Spirit, and therefore that change would have come about after their deaths, it seems to me possible that this 'first phase' (if it is marked by all or some of the Prophets being alive) might well take us into the third century, to the time when Apollonius was writing. A better point of distinction, I think, is the catholic rejection of the Prophecy. This seems to have started in the decade of the 170s and was complete by the time the Eusebian Anonymous wrote (*HE* v.16,9–10; v.16,17) in the 190s. The Prophecy would have undergone self-appraisal and probably modification after the events concerned.

Careful (and feminist) readers may object that although I consider the possibility that Montanus was not the Prophecy's founder (4.2), yet I do not consider the women and their teaching until chapter four, and have chosen to place Montanus and his oracles at the head of chapter three (the section on the early stages of the Prophecy). I have done this firstly because Montanus, rightly or wrongly, *is* regarded as the eponymous villain and secondly because studying him illustrates well some of the problems of our sources. In any case (thirdly), study of the leading women (Priscilla and Maximilla) and of women in general in Montanism is best reserved for its own section (chapter four). A significant proportion of this work is given over to women in Montanism and the work is unique in that respect at least. This is so not just because of a need to redress an imbalance which exists in much church history writing (and such an imbalance is obvious to me) but because the sources for the history of Montanism are remarkable not least for the fact that *women* figure in them with much greater regularity than do men. This is not to be ignored.

The fact that the Prophecy won the heart and mind of so great a Christian thinker as Tertullian and inspired much of the Christianity of the new North African church gave it a higher profile in Christian history than otherwise it might have enjoyed.[31] As a result it figures in every book on the history of second- and third-century Christianity, in studies of the charismatic movement, in feminist Christian claims about an original and more egalitarian Gospel-order, in studies of the dynamics of millenarian movements, in analyses of 'the sect', in writings on the clericalisation of women, on the development of the Christian canon of Scripture and on trinitarian controversy. It has encouraged comparisons with other 'revolutionary Millenarians and Mystical Anarchists' of the Middle Ages,[32] with seventeenth-century Antinomians and Quakers,[33] and with a great range of groups up until the present century, taking in Novatianism and the followers of

Joachim of Fiore, Flagellants and Quietists, Mormons and Seventh-day Adventists on the way.

From Montanus to James Nayler, from Muggleton to Evan Roberts, the list could be extended almost indefinitely . . . Chronologically considered, the head and front of the offence is Montanism.[34]

I am wary of such comparisons with later phenomena, though occasionally they are thought-provoking. It is not self-evident, for example, that the New Prophecy was a millenarian movement and the case must be argued (see 3.3.1–3). Making Montanus a type for the likes of Joachim of Fiore or Joseph Smith begs the question of whether Montanus was the key figure in the Prophecy at all (see 4.2), and seventeenth-century Antinomians, in my opinion, seem little like Montanists. Unlike Whale (who offers no justification), I would not compare Montanus with James Nayler.[35]

The present study will confine itself to the early centuries of Christian history and will try to avoid such comparisons. Yet it is a measure of the powerful sway which the mythology of Montanism holds that such comparisons continue to be made. Montanism is assured a place in the history of religion, if only as a bogey within a lot of Christian historiography.

1.2 THE GEOGRAPHY OF THE PROPHECY: ARDABAU, PEPUZA AND TYMION

1.2.1 Phrygian beginnings
Montanus was said to have started his prophesying in Ardabau. Pepuza and Tymion, named 'Jerusalem' by the Prophets, were where the followers of the Prophecy gathered. Pepuza soon overshadowed Tymion and there catholic officials and exorcists came to challenge the phenomenon. Later Pepuza lent its name to one branch at least of Montanism, the so-called Pepuzites. Ardabau was described as belonging in Phrygian Mysia but Pepuza and Tymion were assumed to be Phrygian locations.

Paul travelled in the Phrygia–Galatia region (Acts 16:6; 18:23). The significance of 'Galatia' is much disputed,[36] but in this instance at least south Galatia, including Iconium, was intended. Paul did not actually preach in Asia on his second missionary journey (see Acts 16:6–8,11 cf. 18:23; 20:5; 2 Cor. 2:12) and on the third journey (Acts

18:23) we learn only that he travelled, strengthening existing converts. Paul had planted and/or encouraged churches on a route which led from Ephesus past Hierapolis, Colossae and its sister church Laodicea, up towards southern Galatia. Thereafter Christianity probably moved into central Phrygia from churches in the regions mentioned and then further north into the Tembris valley and to towns such as Traianopolis on the Hermus valley route. We do not know how.[37]

If Paul passed by the site of Pepuza on his poorly documented travels we do not know of it. The epitaph of Abercius Marcellus, influential Christian of the late second century and presbyter in the area of Phrygian Hieropolis/Hierapolis, shows that Paulinists had indeed made inroads there but Philip, his daughters and various Johns were remembered in that region too (Eusebius *HE* iii.31 (Polycrates); iii. 39,4 and 9 (Papias); v.8,4f. (Irenaeus)). We should not assume that Paul's influence had been uppermost and we should not forget the 'open door' which existed from the Seer's church in Philadelphia to the world beyond (Rev. 3:8).

Paul tended to concentrate upon the educated urban synagogue-goers, as Acts 13–19 illustrates.[38] If we assume, then, that neither the enigmatic Ardabau nor Pepuza/Tymion were large urban sites in Paul's day,[39] and that unlike Sardis or Apamea or Acmoneia (modern Ahat) they did not have significant Jewish populations,[40] then probably the Christians of the Prophecy's beginnings could not boast of direct contact with the apostle Paul as part of their churches' heritage. Nevertheless they were familiar with the apostle's writings, as we shall see (3.9.1 *et passim*).

Rome annexed Phrygia before the end of the first century BCE, its western sector becoming part of the province of Asia, its eastern being subsumed into Galatia. Thereafter Cotiaeon (modern Kütahya), Synnada and Philomelium, all of which figure in this study, were on the Asian side. Pliny the Elder in his *Naturalis Historia* listed some of the early so-called *conventus juridicus* districts: in his day Laodicea, Synnada and Apamea-Cibotos enjoyed conventus status; Philomelium did later; in Asia, Smyrna, Ephesus and Miletus, at least, did so. The actual number of these and their significance at different times is debated, however.

The degree and speed of Christianisation in Phrygia should not be overestimated. My colleague Frank Trombley has looked at literary sources and found a slow adaptation to the new religion among local

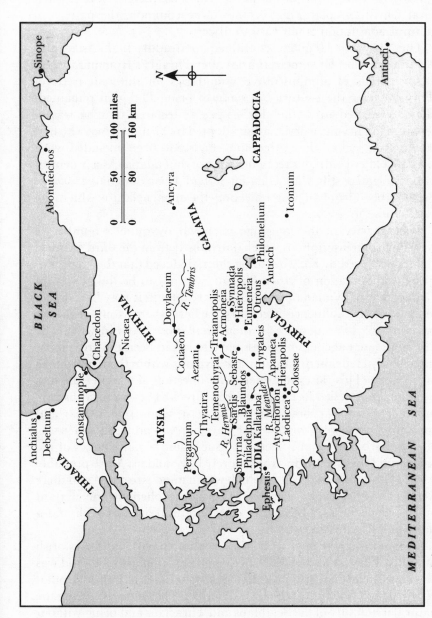

Map of Asia Minor

cultures of Asia Minor. But until the fourth century, of course, when
rural Christian epigraphy becomes more common, the pattern of
cultural adaptation is not easy to discern.[41]

The Phrygian language continued to straddle both Asian and
Galatian divides for some centuries after Phrygia's Romanisation.[42]
Despite shifts of administrative boundaries for different parts of
'Phrygia' over the centuries, a sense of being Phrygian remained.
Hierax, referred to in the *Acts of Justin*, declared that he was of
Iconium in Phrygia, a designation adopted by Firmilian too, who had
attended a synod there. Iconium had not been included with
Lycaonia after Hadrian's reorganisation of the Galatia–Asia provinces
but, associated still with Galatia, it had been designated *colonia*.
Presumably Firmilian was reflecting the nomenclature which the
locals chose to adopt.

The tenacity of the language is shown by quite a number of
Neo-Phrygian inscriptions which date mostly from the third century.
Calder, followed by Klawiter and others, deduced that the Phrygian-
speaking population of *Asian* Phrygia was not to be found west of
Cotiaeon or of Synnada by about 250 CE, though it may have had a
more extensive influence a century earlier, when Montanism was
beginning.[43] The inference is, then, that those areas in which the
Phrygian language had been less tenacious had been the areas more
successfully Hellenised. The ethnic Phrygians within them now spoke
only Greek. This raises the interesting question of whether the first
Prophets prophesied in Phrygian or in Greek. They were accused of
unintelligibility but some of those, at least, who came to hear and
confront them were of towns where Phrygian was probably still in use.
Had a 'barbaric' tongue been the issue, some of our sources of the
second and third centuries would surely have told us. More probably
it was glossolalian enthusiasm which was in mind (see 3.2.3) and there
were, of course, pagan parallels with such a phenomenon. Extant
oracles from the early centuries of Montanism are in Greek and a
subsequent Latin translation.

'Phrygian' could be a near synonym for 'slave' and for boorish
hill-billy. Phrygia harboured religious groups of many kinds and was
known to have 'une certaine ardeur de mysticisme', as Labriolle put it
(*La Crise*, 10). Socrates (*HE* iv.27) described Phrygians as lacking the
natural irritability of the Scythians and Thracians and being without
the penchant for sensual pleasures notable among Orientals. They
deplored vice and were unimpressed by the circus and the theatre.

Here, wrote Lightfoot in his study of *St Paul's Epistles to the Colossians and to Philemon* (third edn, London 1879, 98), was a part of the world for 'the mystic, the devotee, the puritan'. It was apposite that in Phrygia Montanism had its beginnings.

1.2.2 Pepuza and Tymion

Where were these 'Jerusalem' towns of the earliest Prophecy? Pepuza has been variously identified with modern Dumanli, Suretli or Bekilli in the Çal Ovasi region.[44] In *Byzantion* vol. 6 in 1931 Calder announced with confidence that the 1930 expedition by the American Society for Archaeological Research in Asia Minor had confirmed the conclusions of Radet and Ramsay ('The New Jerusalem of the Montanists'), for epigraphy and other finds in the region of Bekilli and Uçküyu had convinced him that Pepuza and Tymion had been around these two sites of ancient habitation. Travellers had discovered among other items the probably fifth-century marble slab and basin inscribed

† Μοντανου προτο διακονου †

– a witness to the continued use of the name of Montanus among some Christians. Yet, while not ruling out the Çal Ovasi region, Elsa Gibson has suggested that Pepuza and Tymion lay further south-east, in the Dazkiri plain,[45] for this seemed to accord better with Hierocles' later list of bishoprics. Pepuza of Phrygian Pacatiana (see n. 48 and text below) figured in that list, which probably belongs to the period of Justinian (527–65) and was reliant upon information from the time of Theodosius II. The arrangement of cities in it could also be taken to imply that Pepuza was south of Acmoneia and north of Eumeneia (Isikli), also to the east of Philadelphia (modern Alaşehir). Ramsay first located Pepuza 'on the high road from Eumeneia to the cities of the Sandyklu valley'. Then he inferred from Hierocles' list a situation in southern Banaz-Ova near the edge of the Eumeneian plain.[46] Strobel located Pepuza a little further to the north, in the plain of Kirbasan, which is separated by a ridge from that of the plain of Bekilli.[47]

Doughty travellers – Radet, Ramsay, Calder, Buckler, Haspels and others – forded rivers on horseback, sought alternative routes to well-worn mountain passes and took to horse and cart, making impressions of many inscriptions they encountered or excavated on the way. The student of Montanism owes them a great debt. Yet still not one of the places (Pepuza, Tymion or Ardabau) is locatable with certainty.

We do have some snippets of information about later Pepuza, however.

(1) Following Diocletian's reorganisation at the end of the third century a town called Pepuza found itself, with Laodicea, Colossae, Hierapolis and Ancyra, within the division of Pacatiana.[48] This was then the western region of Phrygia.

(2) In the Byzantine era this Pepuza was a major town in its region but it had had no bishop at the Council of Nicaea (perhaps because of its known Christian heterodoxy).

(3) When Epiphanius (d. *c.* 402 CE) wrote the *Panarion* (xlviii.14) the *polis* Pepuza was already razed, he said; ruined and a desert. Calder, in his study of 'Monuments of the Great Persecution' (363) suggested that Pepuza was that town Eusebius referred to in *HE* vii.11, the population of which was destroyed.[49] But Pepuza appears in other ancient sources (see 4 and 5 below) and in any case Epiphanius (not always a reliable source) may have been exaggerating or wrong about Pepuza's destruction.

(4) Philostorgius of Borissus in Cappadocia wrote of someone called Aetius being exiled to Petuza (*sic*) *c.* 356 CE (*HE* iv.8). If this were not a piece of 'grim humour', as Calder posited (and Philostorgius, too, is not noted for his accuracy or objectivity), then Pepuza must have existed at that time, not very long before Epiphanius wrote.

(5) We hear of Pepuza again when Theophylactus, the superior of a monastery in Pepuza, was listed among those at the second Council of Nicaea in 787 CE.

The site of this Pepuza may only be surmised. It seems to me significant that Montanist teaching was related to that of the Revelation. It was related to the teaching and promises of the letter to Philadelphia in that work, so it is not improbable, then, that the site of Pepuza lay within Philadelphia's sphere of influence and a spot east of Philadelphia does accord with the consensus of scholars' opinions. Karahalli, Bekilli, Süller and several other Turkish towns and villages mentioned are clustered within ten miles of one another, at least as the crow flies, off the road north to Uşak which one takes off the Denizli–Dazkiri highway. These are undistinguished places, as doubtless were Pepuza and Tymion. Certainly the critics of

Montanism were not impressed. The area would accord, too, with what we know of the travels of the first opponents of the Prophecy, for Pepuza must have been accessible for those who came to challenge it, from Otrous (Zoticus), Cumane (Zoticus), Hierapolis (Apolinarius), Apamea (Julian) and Hieropolis/Hierapolis (Abercius Marcellus) (*HE* v.16,5 and 17 cf. v.16,2ff.).[50]

Most scholars locate Pepuza/Tymion on a plain and the detail of the *plain* becomes significant when we consider that the name Ardabau (see 1.2.3), the location, allegedly, of Montanus' first prophecies, may recall a site which in turn was associated with a plain named in 4 Ezra. If Ardabau and Pepuza were not in the same region (and the Anonymous' claim that Ardabau was in 'Phrygian Mysia' may be unreliable as well as vague), then a *Hijra* of sorts must have occurred, when a decision was made to transfer activity to Pepuza and Tymion. The choice of a plain site (if such this was) might have been out of reverence for apocalyptic promises. There are very many plains to choose from between Philadelphia (Alaşehir) and Cappadocia!

I reject Kraft's suggestion that Pepuza and Tymion stood either side of a mountain (cf. the expectation of Rev. 21:10),[51] and there is little to be said of Tymion (τύμιον), which occurs only in association with Pepuza and then only in Eusebius *HE* v.18,2. Like Pepuza it was one of the 'little towns' of Phrygia (*HE* v.18,2). Like Ardabau it does not appear in epigraphic and historical sources. Radet and W. Ruge ('Pepuza' and 'Tymion' in A. F. Pauly (ed.), *Real-Enzyklopädie der Classischen Altertumswissenschaft*, Stuttgart 1937, xix and xx) suggested Dumanli as the site of Tymion.

1.2.3 Ardabau

Ardabau is on even shakier ground. The 'Phrygian-Mysia' of Eusebius *HE* v.16,7 could indicate a site anywhere between Philadelphia and Dorylaeum (Eskisehir) in the Tembris region. Ramsay pre-empted all subsequent identification of Ardabau with the region round the modern village of Kallataba, only about fifteen miles up the Hermus valley from modern Alaşehir (Philadelphia).[52] He had considered two sites: (i) north east of Philadelphia/north west of Appia, between Aezani and (non-Galatian) Ancyra to the west (Ardabau should not be placed too much south-*east* of Inegöl, Ramsay declared); and (ii) Kallataba, his final choice, 'in the open plain'. The Kallataba mentioned by Herodotus, he observed, was where the tamarisk tree provided the staple industry. Whereas such trees flourish in the neighbourhood of Inegöl, this is not so in the mountain passes.[53]

Ramsay, it should be said, tended to revise his opinions when on his travels. If (after some revision) Pepuza was to be in the Banaz Ova (*Cities and Bishoprics* ii, 569f.), then Ardabau was in the Katakekaumene. Ramsay's choice of Kallataba, east of Philadelphia, was in fact not too far distant from where some sited Pepuza, i.e. between this Kallataba/Ardabau and Eumeneia. Calder agreed,[54] again placing Pepuza further to the east. Haspels concurred.[55] But Ramsay's identification is, as Labriolle wrote, 'pure hypothèse',[56] and most writers are rightly undogmatic in locating the sites. Knox,[57] of course, never to be hindered by lack of evidence, confidently asserted that Ardabau was over the Mysian border, 'not far from Mount Ida' and that Pepuza 'looks across the river-valley' towards the southern slopes of Mount Dindymos. This region is the south west border of the flat plain of Altintas (the Tembris area, not the Altintas near modern Akşehir), Mount Dindymos being the Murat Daği.

Strobel was next to examine the area thoroughly, noting inscriptional evidence associated with cult activities, similar-sounding names and the most likely identification of the 'Phrygian-Mysia' described by the Anonymous. Ardabau, he suggested, might have been the site of ancient Atyochorion, a few miles north-west of modern Akkent. Akkent, in turn, has been identified with ancient Dionysopolis (though Strobel demurred on this point).[58] So too has Uçküyü, between ancient Blaundos and the territory of the Hyrgaleis.[59] But following Drew-Bear's study,[60] Strobel opted for the region of modern Çal (south of Akkent, south-south-west of Süller). This, he concluded, and not Uçküyü, was the site of ancient Dionysopolis.[61] Atyochorion (Ardabau?), not far distant, was a centre for priestly activity. This places Ardabau north-west of Akkent and in close relation to (and west of) posited sites for Pepuza, viz. Bekilli/Karahalli/Süller. Like most writers (myself included) Strobel believed the two places could not have been very far distant from one another. I tend to identify Pepuza with the region around modern Bekilli, though it must be said that this option is not more defensible than a number of others.

1.2.4 The significance of Pepuza/Tymion and Ardabau

Only the Eusebian Anonymous names the village Ardabau (*HE* v.16,7) as the place where Montanus first displayed his frenzied and ecstatic prophetic behaviour.[62] Was this a local place name or was 'Ardabau' as much symbol as geographical designation – much as were the 'Jerusalem' towns (Pepuza and Tymion) of the New Prophets' community (*HE* v.18,2 (Apollonius))? A similar-sounding place name occurs in the apocalyptic and millenarian work 4 Ezra and the passage concerned will be discussed in due course. If Ardabau, like Jerusalem, *was* more symbol than local nomenclature, then (i) Montanus may have chosen the site precisely because of reminiscences which its actual local name evoked, or (ii) the Prophets gave to that (otherwise unnamed) place the title 'Ardabau', much as Pepuza and Tymion came to be termed 'Jerusalem'. There is a third option, one which writers do not mention, viz. that Ardabau and Pepuza Tymion (called Jerusalem) were one and the same geographical reality, referring at different times in the history of the early Prophecy to the same place.

I do not advocate this third option, but think it deserves consideration. This region was not a very great distance from the prophetic church of Philadelphia. The Seer had told Philadelphian Christians that they would bear the name of God's holy city, new Jerusalem, and the name of God himself (Rev. 3:12f.), and Philadelphia had been where the prophetess Ammia had lived (*HE* v.17,3–4), she who figured in the prophetic succession to which the Prophets appealed. The Prophets had established themselves in that area (like the Christians of the Philadelphian conventicle in the Apocalypse) as communities beloved of Christ and uncompromising in loyalty. 'Jerusalem' aptly described them. 'Ardabau', echoing 4 Ezra (indeed possibly reflecting a more widespread speculation of which we know nothing), may well have done the same, while also saying something of the geography of that place where Montanus first prophesied.[63] Hence it is not impossible that what could be called on one occasion 'Ardabau' (in 4 Ezra a place of promise of a city and a place of prophecy) might be 'Jerusalem' at another time, particularly when responding to questions about what was happening and why. Jerusalem (rich in symbolism) may have become the preferred title because its significance was more readily understood by a greater number of Christians but we should remember that 'Jerusalem' was not a single entity for the Prophets, it might be the name given to two places at once, viz. Pepuza *and* Tymion (*HE* v.18,2).

I would say that east of Philadelphia was the *region* in which God was at work and where 'Jerusalem' Christians dwelt – or so the Prophets believed, heirs of the promise which no longer belonged to

the 'synagogue of Satan' (Rev. 3:9).[64] Perhaps they were awaiting the
fulfilment of the prophetic 'I' saying 'Behold I come quickly' (Rev.
3:11). Indeed it may have been to just that region, to the east of
Philadelphia, that some of Philadelphia's Christians of the past had
'gone out' in time of peril (cf. Rev. 3:12). Many commentators
interpret this as signifying escape from the effects of earthquakes in
the town.[65] Not too far distanced for contact, Christians who were not
unlike the type which had once responded to the prophetic Seer in
Philadelphia now continued the study of Jewish and Christian
writings, kept the liveliness of their hope and kept, too, their certainty
of communication from the Lord through prophecy.

The view of the Prophets' community-consciousness expressed
above is tied to belief in the importance for them (a) of teaching in the
Revelation (which had local associations) and (b) of being, as
community, 'Jerusalem'. This latter, in turn was related to promises
in the letters to the seven churches of the Apocalypse (see 3.3.3). The
apocalyptic tradition must have been strong in the communities
which the Seer addressed (Ephesus, Smyrna, Thyatira, Sardis,
Laodicea, Pergamum and Philadelphia), just as it was strong for
bishop Papias and his community in Hierapolis.[66] It is hard to believe
that such a spirit, associated with minority and disaffected groups,
would have failed to penetrate beyond the major towns. Like the
Revelation, contemporary Jewish apocalypses such as 2 Baruch and 4
Ezra itself also maintained what Frend calls the 'phrenetic hostility to
the pagan world'.[67] It was Christians and not Jews who preserved and
modified such sources and 4 Ezra, in particular, is of interest for it is
there we find a name akin to Ardabau.

The Jewish apocalyptic 4 Ezra does not predate Domitian's reign.
It is synonymous with chapters of the apocryphal 2 Ezra (Esdras) but
appears in an expanded form in Latin which provides a Christian
framework.[68] We find in the Christian expansions of 4 Ezra many of
the same concerns as characterise the Asian canonical Apocalypse.[69]
Its setting is probably Asia (15:46ff. and 16:1ff.), which is as corrupt
as Babylon (Rome) itself (15:46, cf. Rev. 14:8; 17:4f.). Harlotry
(idolatry), persecution and food sacrificed to idols are concerns, as
they are in the Apocalypse (15:46; 15:52; 16:68f.). 4 Ezra was much
concerned with theodicy, law and the end times. 5 Ezra's (Christian)
readers would 'believe with the spirit' the things it said, though they
had not seen 'with bodily eyes' (1:37, cf. John 20:29), while Jews had
rejected God and 'Ezra' (of 5 Ezra) had turned to the gentiles (cf. 5

Ezra 1:35f.; 2:10f.). Those who confessed the Son of God in the world would stand as a great singing multitude upon Mount Zion, to receive a crown and palm (12:42–8, cf. Rev 7:9; 14:1 and 5 Ezra 2:42–5).[70] There was but a short time to the consummation of history (5 Ezra 1:33f.; 2:13, cf. 4 Ezra 4:44). The restoration which the work promises has a this-worldly colour and 4 Ezra is genuinely chiliastic.[71]

4 Ezra was available in Greek translation before the closing decades of the second century and it may be echoed in the *Epistle of Barnabas* 12:1 (// 4 Ezra 5:5a, cf. too 4 Ezra 5:35 // Clement *Stromateis* iii. 16). I shall suggest in this study that 4 and 5 Ezra offer useful parallels for the interpretation of teachings and events in the early New Prophecy. These include the vision of Christ in female form who tells of the promised Jerusalem descending,[72] and the practice of fasting and xerophagy.[73] Its promises could certainly have been known to Asiatic Christians of 'prophetic' type well before the Eusebian date of 172 CE for the start of the Prophecy.[74] Moreover there are faint echoes of 4 Ezra in the Montanist *Passio Perpetuae*. At this point, however, it is Ardabau and 4 Ezra which concern us.

4 Ezra promises an inheritance of 'a city built and set on a plain', full of good things (7:6). The path to the site is narrow and precipitous, fraught with danger, and inheritance is ensured only to those who pass through the danger (cf. Rev. 3:11f. in the letter to Philadelphia). The city is, however, promise and not reality, just like the Jerusalem promised in the Revelation: 'the time will come when . . . the city which now is not seen shall appear (7:26).[75]

This promise is fulfilled (10:27). A city of vast foundations appears on a site where no foundation had existed (11:53, cf. 13:36 of the heavenly Zion).[76] The site for this Zion was a field, rich in flora.[77] The name of the field (with a number of variants including Ardab and Ardaf) was Ardat.[78] Montanus and others may have heard in the village name *Ardabau* an echo of 4 Ezra. Alternatively they may have chosen to award the name to *the place where revelations came* (as they had come to Ezra); where individuals had that experience which transformed them into prophets (or Prophets) and the knowers of secrets. For in 4 Ezra the vision at Ardat is 'pivotal', as Stone notes (*4 Ezra*, p. 28). Thereafter Ezra comes to be acknowledged as a prophet and fully an eschatological Seer (12:37ff.; 12:42; 14:23 (likened to Moses)). Maybe, too, the geography of the area where Montanism began was not inconsistent with the description in 4 Ezra: i.e. a plain approached by a precipitous path, hazardous to the unwary – 'fire on

the right hand and deep water on the left' (4 Ezra 7:6) – like the
psalmist's description of a journey to a place of rest (LXX Ps. 65:12).
The geography of the region of Turkey east of Alaşehir, with its basins
and massifs, plains and long ascents, offers plenty of scope for
identification.

This 'Ardabau', then, would have been a backwater, sparsely
populated, a place with little history of habitation. But it would have
been there that Montanus first intimated the coming of a greater
glory which was presaged in prophecy.[79] Strobel recognised that
'Ardab', close to Pepuza, represented a place of expectation, a
location which owed much to prophetic and literary association.[80]

1.2.5 Findings
Montanus first prophesied east of Philadelphia and not many miles
distant from Pepuza. 'Ardabau' probably lay between the two
geographically. Knox saw Montanus as the child of his surroundings
– other writers associated natural geography with fanaticism, hellish
landscapes and earthquakes, such as bred the extravagancies of
Gnosticism and the wildness of Montanism.[81] The truth was probably
far less dramatic. The Prophecy arose in a region where apocalyptic
speculation was commonplace. It made the language and promises of
that speculation its own. Ardabau and Pepuza-Jerusalem, wherever
they were precisely, were examples of that process of adoption. But
there was more to the Prophecy than apocalyptic speculation and
more to its vision than could be confined in the plains and mountains
(far from hellish) of the area of its birth.

1.3 THE DATE OF THE PROPHECY

The evidence for the date of the Prophecy's beginnings is notoriously
confused and contradictory. Writers usually begin by outlining the
Eusebian and Epiphanian options and I shall start with the former
(accepted by Labriolle and followed by Barnes, D.H. Williams,[82]
Frend[83]). This dated its beginnings around the year 172 CE. Having
then looked at Epiphanius, however, this chapter will present a case
which does not opt simply for either of them.

1.3.1 Eusebius
In the *Chronicon*, the first of Eusebius' works (relying on the Armenian
and Jerome's edition in Latin)[84], he dated the start of the Prophecy in

the twelfth year of Marcus Aurelius (171–2 CE), and the persecution of Christians of Lyons and Vienne in the seventh of Marcus Aurelius' reign (166–7). Hence the martyrdoms would have *predated* rather than post-dated the outbreak of the Prophecy. In *HE* iv.27, Eusebius again set the Prophecy' beginnings in the middle of Marcus Aurelius's reign (161–80 CE), i.e. *c.* 171–2. He was not consistent in dating the Gallic martyrdoms, however. In *HE* he gave the year 177 (not 167 as previously), the date generally accepted as correct,[85] there indicating that the martyrs, *not for the first time*, had submitted a judgement on false teaching (*HE* v.3,4). If the Prophecy is in mind then its beginnings must have preceded events in Gaul.

The *Chronicon* also suggested that Apolinarius became bishop of Hierapolis in the year 171 CE. Probably *after* having written treatises on other subjects he then wrote against the Prophets (*HE* v.27) and at a time when the Prophecy was still in an early stage of growth. Most writers assume that this too dates it in the 170s.[86] When Eusebius wrote of addresses to the emperor by Melito and Apolinarius (*HE* iv.27,1, cf. iv.26,1f) he did indeed write of *the* emperor.[87] That may indicate that Apolinarius was writing *between the years 169 (February) and 176 (November)*, when there was no co-emperor (neither Lucius Verus (161–169) nor Commodus (176–192)). Apolinarius' anti-Prophecy writings would have been penned a short time after its beginnings, Labriolle observed, while the *Chronicon* says his accession to the episcopate happened in 171 CE. Hence Eusebius probably took the year 172 (an almost midway point between 169 and 176) as a plausible date for the Prophecy's origins.[88]

Eusebius gives other clues to chronology. He mentions other kinds of aberrant teaching, associating the rise of the Prophecy with the activity of Tatian and the Encratites (*HE* iv.28–9 cf. Irenaeus *Adversus haereses* i.28.1). Tatian's teaching emerged *after* the martyrdom of Justin his mentor, i.e. in the 160s (v.29,3) and in the *Chronicon* Eusebius had given 172–3 CE as the time of Tatian's coming east and apostasy to Encratism; i.e. the twelfth year of Marcus Aurelius. Thus it paralleled closely the outbreak of the Prophecy. In the *HE*, as we have seen, Eusebius had claimed only that Tatian's Encratism post-dated the death of Justin (which was in the mid 160s). This last is not at odds with the Prophecy becoming significant in the years after 170 CE, but it may also indicate that the *beginnings* of the Prophecy had been earlier.

On Eusebius' evidence we have at least a broad base for the

Prophecy's rise, between *c.* 165 and 177 CE, and his own preference is for the 170s CE.

1.3.2 Epiphanius

Epiphanius is not consistent. In his clearest statement on the matter he placed the Prophecy's beginnings in the nineteenth year of Antoninus Pius (138–161 CE) and thus in the year 157 (*Pan.* xlviii.1,2). This date was accepted by Pearson, Dodwell, Neander and Harnack, and more recently is accepted by G.S.P. Freeman-Grenville, Robert Eno and Aland among others.[89] But Epiphanius is self-contradictory to an extent Eusebius is not and his evidence is at odds with Eusebius. It runs as follows:

(a) *Pan.* xlviii.1,2 dates the Phrygian heresy to around the year 157. It does not tell us whether he was reckoning from the conversion of Montanus, from the first inklings of prophetic activity in the region or from the beginnings of serious confrontation with the catholic authorities.

(b) Earlier in the *Panarion* Epiphanius had told his readers that the Prophecy arose contemporaneously with Encratism. So too had Eusebius (see 1.3.1 above). Epiphanius made the Prophets contemporaries of Marcion too (*Pan.* xlviii.1), though they arose somewhat later than either Marcion or Tatian. Tatian (*Pan.* xlvi.1,6f.) founded his school in Mesopotamia after Justin's martyrdom, he said (thus far he is not much removed from Eusebius), but that martyrdom had been in the *twelfth* year of Antoninus Pius, i.e. in 149–50 CE (cf. *Pan.* xlviii.1,2 where encratism comes after Hadrian's time). This is, of course, at odds with Eusebius' reckoning. As for the Marcionites (Eusebius *HE* iv.10–12, cf. Irenaeus *Adv. haer.* i.24f.; iii.3,3f.; Justin *I Apol.* i–xxvi), he tells us that Marcion came to notice in the 140s (in the *Chronicon* Eusebius knew that Justin's *Apology* named Marcion). Marcion, of course, was a well-travelled survivor and probably was still active in Tertullian's day (*De praescr. haer.* xxx) but clearly Epiphanius is leaning towards the decade of the 140s, in this part of his evidence at least. So while Eusebius and Epiphanius are not at odds in associating the Prophecy with the rise of other unacceptable groups, they conflict in dating that rise. So far as the alignment with Encratism is concerned, Epiphanius' date is simply incorrect, given what we know of the date of Justin's martyrdom.

(c) Epiphanius' other markers cause only greater confusion. In *Pan.* xlviii.2, for example, he suggests the clearly impossible date of 85

CE for the end of Maximilla, allowing 290 years from her time to his own writing in 375 CE.[90] His statements on the Alogi (3.9.6) also contain elements of the bizarre. Let us turn to these.

(d) In *Pan*. li.33 he refers to the book of Revelation, notably to (i) the warning of Revelation 22:19 and (ii) the address to the church in Thyatira in Rev.2:18. The Alogi in their day argued the falsity of this prophetic address, he told his readers, since no true church existed in Thyatira. That church had succumbed to the New Prophecy 93 years after the Ascension though catholics regained their hold there (and he mentioned a space of 112 years). We know how Epiphanius reckoned the length of the Lord's life (*Pan*. li.26–9), and his arithmetic would put Thyatiran conversion to the Prophecy in the early 120s (Didymus of Alexandria also pointed to an early date, writing of the Prophecy which came 'more than a hundred years after the Ascension').[91]

Epiphanius' chronology at this point would surely put its inception in the reign of Trajan! (That of Didymus at least takes us into the 140s.) He goes on, however: Thyatira's *return* to the catholic fold would have been *either* in the decade of the 230s *or* perhaps in the 260s, depending on whether Epiphanius' 112 years are taken to mean *before* his own writing in 375 CE or after the church's fall to the Prophecy.

The date in the 120s has seemed improbable and in any case it contradicts what Epiphanius wrote in *Pan*. xlviii.1. Emendations of the text have been suggested, notably by Holl and Calder. Both of these proposed a lacuna in the text and that we should reckon the 93 years backwards from the year 263 (that being 112 years before Epiphanius was writing). This would bring us to the familiar date of 172. Such a conjecture cannot be verified as the evidence stands, and in 'Opposition' Tabbernee argued for Thyatira's lapse between the years 223 and 335, when it would have returned due to the impact of Constantinian legislation. If emendation had brought the right date, of course, then Epiphanius was telling us of a successfully proselytising, established New Prophecy movement at just the same time as Eusebius portrayed the rise of Apolinarius of Hierapolis as a combative bishop against it. In this respect, at least, an element of near reconciliation between the accounts of Eusebius and Epiphanius would be possible. Still 172 (the Eusebian date) could not be the date of the Prophecy's *beginnings*. These would have predated 172 if Thyatira fell to it in that year.[92]

1.3.3 *The Anonymous*

The writing of the Eusebian Anonymous predated 215–16 CE, for an epitaph modelled on that of Abercius Marcellus of Hierapolis may be dated to that year (this is Hierapolis/Hieropolis of the Phrygian Pentapolis). Ramsay subsequently discovered the original Abercius gravestone inscription in the region of hot sulphurous springs just two to three miles south of Synnada – 'built into the wall of one of the bathing houses'. It may be dated before the end of the second century. Abercius, it would seem, was alive when the Anonymous was writing (*HE* v.16,3).[93]

We have a *terminus a quo* of sorts for the Anonymous' writing if we take *HE* v.16,19 where it says it was more than thirteen years since the death of Maximilla. These had been years of freedom from warfare and persecution, a period generally taken to fall in the reign of Commodus (176–92 CE, cf. Eusebius *HE* v.21,1).[94] Hence the Anonymous would have been writing *c.* 192–3, thirteen or so years after the death of Maximilla in 179–80. She may have been the last of the Three to die - though in my view this is less certain than is generally assumed. Her death is not recorded (cf. *HE* v.16,13 and 19, and see 5.5.2 and 1.3.5 below). It is possible that Maximilla was the Prophecy's most notable figure for several years, either after the deaths of the other two or while Priscilla was still alive,[95] but we cannot be certain of that (see 1.3.4 below). If she *was* the last of the Three to die and was dead by the year 179, then taking the Eusebian date of 172 for its origins the Prophecy would have taken root, made impact, spread and been condemned officially in a very short time indeed (172–9CE).[96] This is *too* short a time for the liking of quite a few scholars. Unfortunately the Anonymous' other clue is of no use to us. Gratus was proconsul of Asia when Montanus arose in Ardabau (*HE* v.16,7) but Gratus' proconsulship cannot be dated.[97]

1.3.4 *Apollonius*

Apollonius said he wrote his anti-Montanist treatise forty years after Montanus took it upon himself to prophesy (*HE* v.18,12). One at least of the Prophetesses was still alive (*HE* v.18,4 and 6) and this evidence opens up a number of intriguing options. If our date for the Anonymous is correct (192–3 CE), and forty years are counted from the dating given by Epiphanius (156–7 CE) we come to the date 196–7[98] which makes Apollonius post-date the Anonymous in writing by several years and puts him in the decade of the 190s. Yet the

Anonymous assumes the Prophets are dead, or at least in the case of Priscilla he makes no reference to activity at the time he was writing. Apollonius writes as if Prophets are alive, referring to one of the Prophetesses and to her contemporaries. I do not think this precludes belief that Apollonius' witness post-dated that of the Anonymous and, if Eusebius' date of 172 CE were correct, then Apollonius might have been writing as late as *c.* 212.

The Prophetess known to Apollonius may have been a later one who had achieved prominence after the Anonymous wrote (see 4.1.1; 4.3.3 on Quintilla, though I do not think it was she). In any case we need not assume that Priscilla was dead. The Anonymous nowhere referred to her death and she may even have been alive when Tertullian wrote. Maximilla's well-known statements that there would be no prophet (or prophetess) after her own death (*Pan.* xlviii. 4–6, see 3.3.4) has led to the assumption that she was the longest surviving – yet such a prediction on Maximilla's part need not preclude Priscilla being alive. Possibly Priscilla was alive *but no longer prophesying* when Maximilla made the statement. For all we know, the fine clothes and gifts which Apollonius decried may have been marks of respect to an aged 'virgin' (Priscilla), still in the heart of the Prophetic community in the first decade of the third century.(*HE* v.18,3–4). When Epiphanius' anonymous source was writing (cf. Hippolytus *Refutatio omnium haeresium* viii.19,1) all three Prophets were dead (*Pan.* xlviii.2,1). We need not assume, then, that the reference to a living Prophetess precludes Apollonius' writing post-dating that of the Eusebian Anonymous. In fact it may have done so by more than a decade, so that his work is evidence for the Prophecy in the East post-200 CE.

If the Eusebian date of 172 CE is accepted as a starting-point, then (adding the exact forty years) Apollonius would indeed have been writing *c.* 212.[99] Barnes found confirmation for this decade in the fact that Tertullian wrote in opposition to Apollonius in a seventh book added to the six of the (non-extant) *De ecstasi*, specifically to counter Apollonius (Jerome *De viris illustribus xl; liii*). Since Tertullian in this case was writing (Barnes concluded) after 213 CE, then Apollonius wrote *c.* 210. Barnes assumed that knowledge of Apollonius's views reached Carthage only after the first six books were in circulation, and hence that they were recently published.

If we do not take the year 172 as a starting point, and do not treat Apollonius' chronology in too literal a way, then the alleged forty-year

gap between the appearance of Montanus and the writing of
Apollonius could be interpreted in a number of ways: even to reach a
date in the 140s for the Prophecy's beginnings, if we (i) took it for
granted that *Maximilla* (died 179–80?) and not Priscilla or some other
was the Prophetess referred to by Apollonius in *HE* v.18,4,6,12, and (ii)
worked backwards forty years from her death. Montanus, then, would
have been active some years before the year 157 which Epiphanius
posited (see note 90). On the other hand, if we concede an early-third
century date for Apollonius' writing, still some flexibility of arithmetic
must be allowed, 'forty years' being a suspiciously round figure. The
fact is that any number of dates for the Prophecy are possible which do
not match exactly either 156–7 or 171–2 CE. In the rest of this chapter I
shall make a case against the Eusebian date and one in favour of the
decade of the 160s as the decade of the Prophecy's rise.

1.3.5 A case against Eusebius

Many permutations of the evidence are possible, each one of which
will choose to disregard some claims and lay great store by others.
Pace Barnes, who dislikes harmonization, I think that there is more to
be said for harmonisation of the witness of Eusebius, Epiphanius and
others so as to give due weight to the decade of the 160s in the
Prophecy's history.

This is not new. Other writers have looked to the first half of the
reign of Marcus Aurelius as an important decade in the history of the
Prophecy. Salmon suggested that Epiphanius *and* Eusebius were
correct but that they referred to different events in the movement's
early stage, viz. beginnings and formal condemnation by the catholics.
Fischer in his study of 'Die antimontanistischen Synoden' did much
the same,[100] and more recently Tabbernee (in 'Opposition') dated
the Prophecy's beginnings *c.* 163–6 CE. I would not rule out the
possibility that its first stirrings were in the late 150s; but more
defensible still, I think, is the claim that it was alive and energetic in
the decade of the 160s.

First some general observations in support:

(i) *Starting from Tatian*, if Tatian did fall away from the catholic
tradition in the mid 160s (Eusebius *HE* iv.29, cf. Irenaeus *Adv. Haer.*
i.26),[101] then the date for the rise of Montanism (rather than its
beginnings), if this was indeed contemporaneous with Tatian's
apostasy, may be taken back at least to the mid 160s.[102]

(ii) *Starting from the matter of prophetic succession*, if the claims of Alcibiades (probably Miltiades) and the Anonymous are to be believed (Eusebius *HE* v.17,3–4), then we should look to a pre-172 date for the beginning of Montanus' prophetic activity. The reasons need to be explained at some length. The idea of succession in prophecy was known among Jews (Josephus *Contra Apionem* i.8), but it appears first in Christian writings with the New Prophets. The succession had taken in the prophets Agabus, Judas (Barsabas) and Silas (see Acts 11:28; 15:22, 27, 32; 21:10), went through the daughters of Philip in Hierapolis, Ammia and Quadratus, and then to Maximilla and Priscilla (seemingly not to Montanus, see 4.2.2). We know of Maximilla, at least, that she had a sense of having been divinely commissioned (Epiphanius *Pan.* xlviii.13,1). What can be said of those listed?

Judas (surnamed Barsabas, Acts 15:22) and *Silas* are associated closely with the mission of Paul and with the letter of Acts 15:23 to the gentile Christians of Antioch. With Paul, Silas had passed through Phrygia and Galatia (Acts 16:6). *Agabus* was a Jerusalem prophet of famines and imprisonments who knew Philip's daughters in Caesarea (Acts 21:8f.). Did he, I wonder, like the daughers of Philip, come to be closely associated with the region around Hierapolis (*HE* iii.21,4; iii.39,9; v.24,2)? As for the less locatable *Judas Barsabas*, we should note that a certain *Barsabas called Justus* was also associated with the circle around Philip's daughters, according to the witness of Papias (*HE* iii, 39, 9). He is here identified with the man who 'lost out' in the lot which fell on Matthias (Acts 1:23), though his later experience, according to Philip's daughters and Papias, included miraculous good health after swallowing poison. Has there been a confusion between Judas and Justus in our anti-Montanist sources? The former has little to do with the region of Montanism's beginnings but Barsabas Justus takes his place easily in that circle which valued prophecy, ongoing evidence of the miraculous (including the resurrection of a corpse) and a line of descent from the Apostles themselves. The prophetic succession was a very Asian affair and it was surely being argued on grounds of local association. *Ammia*, next in the succession according to *HE* v.17,3 (but contrast 17,4), came from Philadelphia. Finally comes *Quadratus*, linked with the prophetic daughers of Philip (*HE* iii.37,1) and with other transmitters of tradition and evangelists of 'first rank in the Apostolic succession'.

Here was a man of 'apostolic orthodoxy' (*HE* iv.3,1), an apologist to
the emperor Hadrian (117–38 CE) who knew of miraculous cures and
resurrections among Christians of time past. Jerome (*De vir. ill.* xix;
Ep. lxx.4, cf. Eusebius *HE* iv.23,3) wrongly identified him with
Quadratus who was later bishop of Athens. Quadratus probably
lived in Asia Minor. Is it possible to assign dates to these people so as
to calculate a date for the appearance of the Three?

The words of the Anonymous about the failure of the prophetic gift
(*HE* v.17,4) suggest that no great time-lapse was expected between
the end of one kindling of prophetic activity and the start of another.
We know that Papias of Hierapolis was a younger contemporary of
Philip's daughters (*HE* iii.39,2 and 7) and that they must have been
alive (and prophesying if Luke is to be believed) in the decade of the
60s CE, and probably at the time he was writing. Philip's daughters
may bring us into the second century, to be succeeded in fame by the
enigmatic Ammia, of whom we know nothing beyond the fact that
catholics and Prophets alike acknowledge her as a prophet. We have
no date for Ammia and it is not impossible that Quadratus, rather
than Ammia, had been the next famous prophetic figure to emerge
after Philip's daughters.

We are on firmer ground with Quadratus only if he is indeed the
apologist who wrote an open letter to the emperor Hadrian in
response to harassment of Christians. This is usually dated in the mid
120s, and Quadratus (as stated above) was described by Eusebius as a
prophet (*HE* iii.37,1). Writers tend to assume that a single Quadratus
was intended and Eusebius tells us that many Christians of his own
(fourth-century) day possessed copies of Quadratus' (orthodox)
work. It is not remarkable that one who was of 'Prophetic' tendency
should be sufficiently honoured to have his writings studied by the
faithful. The same thing happened to Tertullian. But it may be that
Eusebius' observation on the sound 'apostolic' nature of the work
designed to calm reservations. In any case, if it did not bridge the gap
from the first decade of the second century to the time of Ammia, then
the activity of Quadratus may well take us up to Montanus' time.
'The Montanist women' (i.e. Priscilla and Maximilla), wrote the
Anonymous, succeeded Quadratus and Ammia (*HE* v.17,4).

Chronologically it may be true that fame as prophets (rather than
Prophets) had belonged to the women *in Philadelphia* before ever
Montanus himself became infamous and gathered them into his circle
(see 4.2). In any case, if Quadratus flourished in the decade of the
120s and was *succeeded* by Ammia, the start of the activity of the Three

could certainly have been in the 160s if not earlier. If Quadratus and not Ammia was last in the succession before Montanus' time, then it is even more probable that the 170s is too late for the start of the Prophecy.

I have a suspicion about Quadratus but no proof. He, I think, was last in the succession of prophetic exemplars which the Prophets cited. His death (in the region of Ardabau-Pepuza, east of Philadelphia, or perhaps in Philadelphia itself?) may even have been one of a number of factors underlying a surge of interest in prophecy in the region. The name of Quadratus may figure in a late source about the Montanists, and it is this which arouses my suspicions.

According to Michael the Syrian's *Chronicle* (Bk IX.33), John of Ephesus, under emperor Justinian I (527–65 CE), destroyed the mighty reliquary of the Montanists at Pepuza (cf. too John of Ephesus HE iii.20 and 32 for Montanist activity). This was not the first such attempt on their most sacred shrine. A few decades previously, bribery alone had protected their most sacred relics from the attention of the local bishop. The bishop had had the remains exhumed but accepted a bribe so that other bones were substituted for those of the Three. He had made a pretence of destroying them and the bones of one other person. The person's name was variously rendered as *Crites* or *Qrytys*.

As Gero's study has shown, the traditions about Montanism in the work of Michael the Syrian vary in nature and reliability. Michael is in part dependent upon Eusebius, as can be seen in Bk VI.6 where also we learn that 'sickness' (plague? see 1.3.7 below) coincided with the period of Montanism's beginnings. J.-B. Chabot's edition of *Chronique de Michel de Syrien Patriarch Jacobite d'Antioche* (Paris 1899–1905) gives the salient passages in vol. II/ii, 269ff. (cf. IV, 323 (1910)) and, while he transliterated the Syriac name in the *Chronicle* as *Crites*, he also noted *Qratis* as an alternative from Pseudo-Dionysius. Labriolle's *Les Sources*, on the other hand, did not include the *Chronicle* of Michael, though he did use the J.S. Assemani edition (*Bibliotheca Orientalis* ii, 1821) when citing John of Asia's treatment of the Montanist relics in the *HE* (a source itself related to the Pseudo-Dionysius *Chronicon*). Assemani had rendered the Syriac qr'tys as reference to an otherwise unheard of Montanist woman called *Carata*. Labriolle altered this, however, and conjectured that the name should in fact be *Cratis* (adding (?)). Michael the Syrian, on the other hand, referring to qrytys, had assumed (as the rest of the text shows) that this was a male associate of Montanus.

Assuming that the person concerned *was* male, then it seems to me that neither a bowdlerisation of the name Theodotus (Eusebius *HE* v.16,14) nor yet Alcibiades (v.3) is the person referred to (options which Strobel cites). *It must be Quadratus*[103] (but contrast Tabbernee, 'Trophies'), whose importance as one of the precursors in the Montanist prophetic succession seems to have been overlooked by commentators. As immediate predecessor of the Three, had Quadratus' remains also been laid to rest (we do not know when) reverently in Pepuza? This man had been a prophet, defender of the veracity of 'primitive' Christian experience, apologist for Christians and heir of the Asia Minor tradition. Should we regard Quadratus, who died perhaps in the 150s, as the grandfather of 'Montanism'?

(iii) *Working from the argument that the 170s was the decade of acute confrontation with the Prophecy*, I would note the following: first, in 177 CE Gallic Christians had knowledge of Christians' difficulties in Asia and Phrygia. The martyrology from Gaul suggests this, though the language is less explicit than we might like. Probably at the request of catholics in Asia (but quite possibly in response to approaches from the Prophets too), the faithful in Gaul ventured a view on the situation for the sake of Christian peace (*HE* v.3,4) and sent comment to bishop Eleutherus in Rome (*HE* v.3,4; see too *HE* v.4,1 and below 2.2.2). The document of martyrdom was forwarded to Christians in Asia and Phrygia, who were presumed to have an interest in the matter (*HE* v.1,2). Perhaps the Prophets had already made their own approaches to Rome; possibly Asian catholics, troubled at the course of events, had requested a response from recognised spiritual 'high-flyers', namely the martyrs among the catholics in Gaul. We do not know. But by 177 the teachings of the Phrygian Prophecy (here associated with the names of Montanus, Alcibiades and Theodotus) had taken hold among 'many' in the East (*HE* v.3,4), and time has to be allowed for the growth of its influence and for the development of such a degree of concern in the catholic camp, for confrontations and exorcisms (*HE* v.16,16–17,20; v.18, 13, and see below 4.3.3–4.3.5), gatherings and excommunication. The period 172–7 is too short a time, I think, especially since writers who accept the limited time-span are also assuming that all three of the Prophecy's chief exponents met their deaths before 179 CE.[104]

Yet Thraseas was suffering martyrdom at about the same time as the catholic-Prophecy confrontations, at least according to Apollonius (*HE* v.18,13; v.24,5 (Polycrates)). Polycrates sandwiched the name of

Thraseas between that of Polycarp the martyr on the one hand, and on the other Sagaris (martyr of Laodicea, *HE* iv.26,3) and Melito of Sardis (cf. Polycrates' similar order in *HE* v.24,4–5). So the death of Thraseas, therefore (here simultaneous with catholic action against the Prophecy), is probably best located earlier than Eusebius' date for the Prophecy, for the martyrdom of Sagaris (under the proconsul Servillius (Sergius) Paulus) would have been in 167–8 CE or possibly 164–5.[105] In any case, if catholic clergy *were* travelling to Pepuza, engaging in face-to-face debates and attempting exorcisms at the latest before the early 170s, then the start of the phenomenom must have been earlier.

Apollonius wrote approximately four decades after the troubled time when Montanus had put his mind to prophesying. The balance of probability must lie with Apollonius writing in the first decade of the third century, since it was then that his writings became known to the Carthaginian apologist, probably at a late stage in Tertullian's defence of the Prophecy (see 1.3.4 above). I accept this third-century dating, even though a date in the 190s for Apollonius would put back the start of the Prophecy to a time close to Epiphanius' date for it, and would better suit my argument. It means, however, that Apollonius had not been a witness of the events concerned. His knowledge was of the Prophecy of the following generation. Even assuming, then, that he was correct about the time of Montanus' activity, it is still possible that that activity is to be dated in the 160s, given that Apollonius may have been writing in (say) *c.* 205 CE. We need not assume *either* that the 'forty years' is exact *or* that his work was very recently penned when Tertullian in Africa gained access to it. Any time from *c.* 160 would be a plausible interpretation of his witness. Indeed, Jerome (*De vir. ill.* xl) says that Apollonius flourished under Commodus (180–92) and Septimius Severus (192–211), which (taking the forty years literally) would give us a possible spread from 140 to 171 CE for the Prophecy's beginnings. From all the evidence thus far there is nothing improbable in dating the *start* of the Prophecy earlier than the 172 CE given by Eusebius. The next task is to ask whether there existed a climate in Asian Christianity and a background of circumstances which would have given rise to the Prophecy in a particular decade.

1.3.6 Prophecy and 'proto-Montanism'

Catholic attention was on prophecy (*HE* v.18,12), with the sect publishing its teachings on prophecy (*HE* v.3,4, presumably some time after the start) and Apolinarius countering the error of false prophets and innovations which were 'sprouting' (*HE* iv.27). The language is vague but does not allow us to think this was something which had only just appeared when he wrote in the 170s.[106] Though the vigour and ecstasy of the New Prophecy probably were elements unusual in Asian Christians' experience, the fact was that prophecy itself was not. Prophecy and apocalyptic, from the canonical Hebrew Scriptures onwards, had been associated with challenge: to the *status quo*, to abandonment of 'true' religion, to priesthood and court. The Prophecy, I shall argue, arose in an area and among Christians who were already thoroughly familiar with aspects of its challenging message (3.2–3.10) and for that reason we do not have to wait until the decade of the 170s for its appearance.

Some years ago I argued that the seeds of the Prophecy had been semi-dormant in the East for decades before the Prophecy emerged. It was not just in the Apocalypse that we find the kinds of concerns which marked the Apocalypse-loving Prophets (prophecy itself, visionary experience, celibacy, the interpretation of Scripture, witness even unto death, a church order which laid great weight by prophets and 'little ones' and made no mention of bishops). They were present even in the letters of Ignatius of Antioch, written to Asia little more than a decade after the Apocalypse and written (in the cases of Ephesus, Smyrna (two letters) and Philadelphia) precisely to those areas which the Seer of the Apocalypse had addressed. At first sight this must seem a remarkable thesis.

Most readers are familiar with Ignatius as the champion of monepiscopacy, or even of full-blown episcopacy of the monarchical kind, as the father of the catholic tradition (he was the first to use the phrase 'catholic church', *Smyrn*, viii), mentor of Polycarp and admirer of the church in Rome. Certainly it was not the Syrian bishop's *own* outlook that was in general 'proto-Montanist'. Rather it was the outlook of the people who were at odds with him and other bishops in Asia. The debate pre-111 CE between the emerging catholic hierarchy and these 'other' Christians (some of them clearly *within* catholic congregations) involved precisely those things which re-emerged in the catholic–Montanist debate decades later.

What were they? They included Scripture and the nature and content of 'the Gospel' (*Phld.* vii-viii); the importance of visionary and other charismatic gifts, not least for a bishop, so that he might retain his credibility (*Eph.* v.1f.; xx; *Trall.* iv; *Phld.* vii (cf. 1 Cor. 2:6ff.;

15:24ff.; Gal. 4:3 *et passim*) and especially *Pol.* ii.1f.); celibacy (*Pol.* v); prophecy (*Phld.* vii) and failure to participate fully in the life of congregations *gathered round their bishops* (*Eph.* v.2–vi.1; cf. *Eph.* ii–iii; *Phld.* vi.3; viii–ix; *Pol.* vi). As for the question of martyrdom, Ignatius was on the road to his death, though not anxious to be praised for that, I have argued that he had given himself up to the authorities. Ignatius had his differences with certain Christians in Asia, but even those who did not share his outlook in other respects went to visit him in his imprisonment.[107]

I have been arguing for more than a decade that Ignatius was opposing (what he regarded as) false teaching on more than one front. Lines of demarcation are not always easy to draw, yet it seems to me that his letters to Asia witness to the discomforting presence of just the kinds of Christians whose descendants would have welcomed the Prophecy. Most significant of all, *Philadelphia* was where he met strongest opposition, and that town is a common factor linking the Apocalypse, the Ignatian letters and Montanism. According to his letters there were difficulties for Asian bishops in other churches too, notably in Ephesus and Smyrna. It does not seem to me coincidental that these were places to which the Seer had addressed letters.

Montanus' bid for the public sphere half a century or so later must have come in relation to something *which already existed*. Was he part of a tolerated prophetic conventicle whose relations with catholic clergy had been relatively unstrained up to this time (though, like Ignatius, the local clergy must have muttered annoyance at times, given that there was serious (docetic and Gnostic) error to be countered in the region)? That is an option I favour. Was Montanus now seeking to usurp the rights of clergy while still a member of a catholic congregation, or was he instigating schism (using Tertullian's dictum) because of envy of bishops? I doubt that that was the initial intent (see below, 3.10), but we have few details. I have argued already that the Prophecy must have begun its life *within* the Church, for subsequently it was driven out of it (*HE* v.16,10). There is every cause to think that the Prophets saw their task as renewal in the Church (this will become apparent in chapters two and three of this study), but inevitably their increased insistence on the voice of the Spirit (which encouraged rigour and tended to 'bind' rather than 'loose', see below, 3.4–3.8) was bound to be seen as a threat to catholic clerical authority. As Frend put it memorably in his study of *The Rise of Christianity* (p. 255), 'the orthodox clergy ran scared'. But there was a ready market for the

Prophecy's message and catholic Christians in Phrygia, Galatia, Asia
and elsewhere would not have succumbed to the Prophecy had not
some of them been ill at ease with aspects of life in their churches. It
could not have grown to wreak havoc (as catholic observers saw it) in
the churches of Thyatira – which succumbed utterly – and Ancyra –
which was thoroughly infected with it – according to Epiphanius
(*Pan.* li.33) and Eusebius (*HE*. v.16,3).

So Montanus' circle was probably within but already somewhat
alienated from some things in emerging catholic traditionalism,
though the degree of difference between the Prophets and the
catholics at the outset must not be overestimated. *Charismata* were in
churches of the day (*HE* v.3.4),[108] and there were many around, said
Eusebius, who thought of themselves as prophets. How comfortably
they were integrated into catholic congregations is another matter, of
course, and the Anonymous had an opinion on this. Those 'prophetic'
types who encouraged Montanus were already far in understanding
from 'the true faith' (*HE* v.16,8). Irenaeus warned his co-religionists
against looking for the chance to drive prophecy from the Church
(*Adv. haer.* iii.11,9). Evidently prophecy, whether ecstatic or not, was
not a comfortable phenomenon to have in the midst.[109] Like
Tertullian later, its proponents must have been critical and restless
Christians, prophesying Christian women among them.[110] At some
point there was a 'shift'.

Like Montanus, Priscilla and Maximilla 'upgraded' their role as
relatively conventional Christian prophets when they experienced
(they said) a fresh outpouring of the Spirit. The women abandoned
their husbands and became part of the circle which included
Montanus (see below, 3.5 and 4.1–2), prophesying in ecstasy and at
what seemed to the catholics to be inappropriate moments. What
seems to have started as revivalist outpourings with demands and
promises attached – challenging the lives of listeners, condemning
some and praising others (*HE* v.16,9) – next turned to condemnation
of unreconstructed catholics and the tradition of which they remained
uncritical (*HE* v.16,9). Sectarian 'schism' described the situation (*HE*
v.16,6). Time must have elapsed before opposition was formalised,
then concerted, but during the decade of the 170s attitudes on both
sides hardened. Apolinarius wrote his anti-Montanist works; Abercius
Marcellus wished the Anonymous would record his confrontations
with the Prophets (*HE* v.16,3). Melito had composed (now lost)
works on prophecy and the Apocalypse (*HE* iv.26,2). Catholic

Christians convened on several occasions (*HE* v.16,10).[111] Eleutherus, bishop of Rome, first acknowledged the phenomenon and then withdrew from that position (see below, 2.2.2). In the end the Asian bishops decided on excommunication. 'I am driven away', said Maximilla, 'like a wolf from the sheep . . .' (*HE* v.16,17).[112] By the end of the decade she was dead.

If the 170s was the decade of acute confrontation, then the 160s, I suggest, was the decade of the rise of the Prophecy proper, out of a milieu which already harboured the seeds, the *proto-Montanism* of Asia Minor. What I here label 'proto-Montanism' was not just that *kleinasiatische Theologie* which certainly made fertile the ground in which the Prophecy flowered.[113] Nor can 'proto-Montanism' be so general as to allow almost any date and place to fit it, for the Prophecy, when it emerged, must have been more than a heightened awareness among onlookers of things which were Christian Asian-Phrygian commonplaces for some. I cannot agree with J. Massingberd Ford in her 'Note on Proto-Montanism in the Pastoral Epistles' that 'a first-century date would be possible' for Montanism of this kind.[114] Then it would not have been 'the Phrygian heresy' of which the catholic writers tell us, for there *was* novelty within it (if less than is sometimes assumed), and novelty brought condemnation. If the problematic term 'proto-Montanism' *is* to be used, then I think it should point to the rigorous, prophetic, women-tolerating Christians around centres such as Hierapolis and Philadelphia. Perhaps, too, it was known in Philomelium. Christians in Smyrna sent to Philomelium an account of the martyrdoms (which accorded with the Gospel) in their city. Had Philomelium's hardline Christian faction spawned Quintus, 'of late come from Phrygia', who in Smyrna had encouraged others to a martyr's death, given himself up and then played the coward at the sight of the beasts (*M. Pol.* iv)? A date in the 150s for Polycarp's death aligns it closely with Epiphanius' date for the start of the Prophecy, but *M. Pol.* must be used with caution, given that the martyrdoms may have happened post-165 CE (the alternative date). Also the martyrology as we have it may have been subject to anti-Montanist additions (2.2.1 below).

J.M. Ford treated the New Prophecy as 'a Judaeo-Christian group' which 'broke off from the Church and still later became heretical'. In essence the movement existed before the time of the Three (hence she wrote of 'proto-Montanism'), but 'it was only in his day that it became a separate movement'.[115] In 3.10 I shall disagree with Ford's view of Montanism and certain kinds of Judaism but taken in its most general sense I can envisage a kind of 'proto-Montanism' such as she posited, albeit I would want to locate it more precisely. Like her I see the kind of Christianity which mothered Montanism as existing *within the wider Church*, until the time of Montanus and the events which separated them. The twists which turned this phenomenon into the New Prophecy were (a) outbreaks of ecstatic and unconventional behaviour and (b) the explanations given for them. What we need to establish is the balance of probability about the decade in which the smouldering tendencies of 'proto-Montanism' in this region would have burst into flame.[116] I believe the decade of the 160s provides the setting.

1.3.7 'Signs of the times' and the decade of the 160s

For Christians in the East who were versed in apocalyptic speculation (and the Prophets were) or minded against compromise with a hostile world, there were certainly events in the 160s which would have hardened resolve and caused them to look to the 'promises' they cherished. There was plague. Galen the physician returned from Rome to his native Pergamum in 166 CE, for plague, whether smallpox, bubonic plague or typhus is disputed, had been carried by returning soldiers through all the provinces between Mesopotamia and Rome and was then devastating the capital. The most pessimistic scholars have written of the death of half the population of the Mediterranean world – probably too high a reckoning, but things were bad. Galen wrote of abscess of the lungs, fever and pustules (*Methodi Medendi* xii) and Aristides wrote of its effect in the provinces (*Oratio* xxxiii.6). Soon Galen was appointed to imperial headquarters at Aquileia, where experts in medicine and apotropaic rites were in demand. Invaders threatened from the north. This brings us neatly to wars.

The decade of the 160s brought not only warfare against the Parthians but around 166–7 CE, just as triumph over the Parthians was achieved, there came that invasion of Italy by the Slavs and Germans from the north which demanded the services of Galen.[117]

Marcus Aurelius' reign had started with the social upheaval caused by earthquakes (cf. Eusebius *HE* iv.13,4) and with the governor of Cappadocia at war in Armenia in a vain attempt to stem the Parthian advance. The plague had not disappeared completely when his reign ended. Inevitably financial problems accompanied the demands which such plague, disaster and warfare brought. The emperor raised money by sale of his own treasures and, of course, by further taxation. But Asia Minor was a particular target for taxation and the ill feeling was great, occasioning revolts. Social and religious nonconformists would not readily be tolerated in harder times or when natural disaster struck. The harassment of Christians in the 160s should not cause surprise.[118] Tertullian put it succinctly just a few decades later:

If the Tiber floods to the walls, if the Nile floods not the fields, if the sky stands still, the earth shakes, if there is famine or plague immediately [comes the cry] 'The Christians to the lion!' (*Apol.* xl.2, cf. Augustine *Civitate Dei* ii.3.)

The number of Christians making addresses to Marcus Aurelius shows that they had cause to fear. Certainly they – Miltiades (*HE* v.17,5), Apolinarius and Melito (*HE* iv.26,1) – did so in terms suggesting that here was a cultured and just man,[119] but they were conscious of injustices to Christians as well as seeking a peacable coexistence with the authorities. These were, of course, the very Christians who were opposing the Prophecy! To them, probably, as to the pagan populace, we may surmise, the New Prophecy would have seemed troublesome not least because, with its noisy, crowd-attracting phenomena, its rigorism and unpragmatic approach to persecution, it was not capable of a low profile.[120] Nevertheless, we must not overestimate the significance of the Prophecy itself in triggering fear and hatred of Christians. Christians had their enemies already.

The emperor Marcus Aurelius (161–80) did not suffer *damnatio memoriae* at the hands of Christians. On the contrary Eusebius appealed to the writings of Apolinarius and Tertullian to show the emperor's gratitude for the prayers of Christians and his unwillingness to persecute them (*HE* v.5.5f.).[121] Yet the truth about Christian suffering under Marcus and the co-emperor Lucius Verus (161–9) was quite different and Eusebius was not unaware of it.[122] It seems reasonable to assume that (i) Carpus, Agathonike and Papylus were martyred in Pergamum under Marcus; that (ii) under Marcus, Justin in Rome met his death after trial by the *praefectus urbi* (one Q. Junius Rusticus, the man who had instructed Marcus Aurelius in Stoicism) and that others had been martyred too. By the next decade Melito, well acquainted with the situation in Asia, was addressing himself to Marcus, deploring new decrees and the brigandage of the mob. Even if local dignitaries rather than the emperor himself were to be blamed for the extent of suffering, the suffering was real (see *HE* iv.15,1–48; iv.16–17; iv.26,3–11).[123] With good communications between churches within the empire and the reality of an undercurrent of pagan and Jewish dislike of Christians, the first part of Marcus' reign would not have been comfortable for them.

It is true that the Antonines had brought stability, security within the empire and a new-found freedom to travel unmolested. Even Aristides of Smyrna and Athenagoras attested to this. Irenaeus, native of the East but domiciled in Gaul, concurred (*Adv. haer.* iv.30,3; but see iv.33,9). There could be no legislating for occasional troubling incursions from outside, of course, or the ravages of plague and earthquake. Nor did those of the less prosperous classes, the slaves and people in the countryside, lead lives of ease and satisfaction. In the towns, even with improved roads and sanitation and the splendour of public buildings, there could still be discontent. In Ephesus bakers went on strike,[124] and on the religious front the chosen Encratism of Justin's pupil Tatian

illustrates the underlying forces of alienation and discontent that sometimes existed below the calm surface of the Greco-Roman city-states of the Antonine era.[125]

Tatian's change of heart had come in the 160s.

Phrygia was exceptional only in degree. Despite the success of Hellenisation in the East its relative isolation would have ensured both a strong sense of independence and of that alienation which must have led some of its inhabitants to Christianity in the first place.[126] In such a setting, sufficiently removed from the highways of power to encourage a sense of being 'different' but not out of touch with the wider world, the Prophecy could well have broken out of its conventional Christian prophetic mould in the first part of the reign of Marcus Aurelius. The 'signs of the times', viz. hostility to the faithful, warfare and plague and a growing disillusionment with the relationship of the churches to 'the world', would have fanned its embers into flame.

Events in the 170s would have done nothing to convince the Prophetic faithful of the cessation of that warfare which they believed (as did most Christians) must presage the end (Epiphanius *Pan.* xlix.1; Tertullian *De fuga* ix. 4). The legate of Syria was putting down an Egyptian revolt in the year 172 (Eusebius' date for the start of the Prophecy), which may in fact have been the year when catholic

opposition to the Prophecy hardened noticeably. On the Danube
that same year natural forces relieved the water-starved soldiery,
defeating the Quadi. Two years later Cappadocia was the setting for
the halting of legate Avidius Cassius' revolt. Speculation about the
nearness of the end was not confined to Phrygian Christian Prophets.
The *Augustan History* (*Marcus Antoninus* xiii,6) tells of an unidentified
man who used to climb a fig tree on the Campus Martius. There he
would predict the coming of fire from heaven and the end of the
world. It would come, he predicted, should he fall from the tree.
There was talk of turning into a stork. When he did fall (or so it is
alleged) he released a stork and was promptly arrested. To judge from
the Prophecy's rapid success in Asia and beyond, not a few Christians
agreed that God-given change was in the air and had been for some
time.

CHAPTER 2

The New Prophecy to Hippolytus and Tertullian

2.1 THE PROPHECY IN ASIA MINOR AND BEYOND

Chapter two of this study will look at the early stages of Montanism in the three centres of which we know most: Asia Minor, Rome and Carthage. This will take us up to at least the second decade of the third century – to the time of Apollonius in Asia Minor, to Hippolytus in Rome and to Tertullian in Carthage.

The Prophecy had also reached other places. In the period in question we hear of it from writers associated with Egypt, viz. Clement of Alexandria and Origen (Clement *Strom.* iv.13.93.1; cf. vii.17.108.1 (*Phrygian* heresy); Origen *De princ.* ii.7.3). The former (the elder of the two) lived in Caesarea of Cappadocia from 202 CE, though formerly in Alexandria where he had been head of the Catechetical School. Origen had replaced him in that rôle. Their testimony confirms: (a) that *prophecy* itself was important in the debate with the catholics (Clement proposed to argue with them and others in a work *Concerning Prophecy*); and (b) that Prophets used the term 'psychics' as one of denigration of the catholics (Clement). It confirms too (Origen) that they had distinctive teaching about the Paraclete (cf. *In Matthaeum* xv,30) and were zealous in religious obligations ('per ostentationem acrioris observantiae') including abstinence from foods and forbidding of marriage. But both writers were probably dependent on sources from elsewhere. Origen had been in Rome a few years prior to writing *De principiis* (*c.* 225 CE), though his reference to Agabus and the daughters of Philip in his commentary on Matthew (xxviii) suggests knowledge of a debate about prophecy such as we know from Asia (Eusebius *HE* v.17,3 [Anonymous]). It may be that much the same case for prophetic forebears had been made in Rome, of course. It is possible that the Prophets had enclaves in Alexandria at this time (cf. 2.1.3 below, on

Syria) but we may not assume this from the little Origen and
Clement have to say.[1]

2.1.1 The Asian sources

The sources for the Prophecy in Asia may be dealt with quickly:

(1) The earliest possible reference to it (though not by name) may
well be in the Asian *Martyrdom of Polycarp*, with its insistence on
martyrdom which was in 'accordance with the Gospel' and its
unflattering references to the Phrygian Quintus who showed zeal for
martyrdom. This was not the monopoly of followers of the Prophecy,
but the *Martyrdom of Polycarp* was indeed addressed to Christians in
Philomelium, where presumably the readers would understand the
significance of the document's strictures about voluntary death. We
may not rule out the possibility (putting it no more strongly) that
'Phrygian' in this document is more than a simple geographical
designation.

The *Martyrdom* is dated either in the 150s[2] or the 160s,[3] as noted
above in 1.3.6. The former, if correct (156 CE), would date the start of
the Prophecy in the time of Antoninus Pius and would mean that
Epiphanius had opted for the right decade at least (see above 1.3.2).
A date for the *Martyrdom* in the 160s (under Marcus Aurelius), if it
presupposes the existence of the Prophecy, would also not be at odds
with what was said in 1.3.[4]

(2) Eusebius provides our second set of Asian sources, from
Apollonius (who was considered in 1.3.4) and the Anonymous
(1.3.3) – men of note in the catholic churches of Asia Minor who
had had direct contact with the followers of the Prophecy in its first
half-century. The Anonymous claimed some success in routing its
influence in Galatian Ancyra and he has been variously (and
speculatively) identified with Apolinarius, Apollonius (since the
time of Rufinus of Aquileia, *HE* v.15), Abercius Marcellus (Eusebius
HE v.16,3), Rhodo (Eusebius *HE* v.13; Jerome *De vir. ill.* xxxvii
and xxxix) or Asterius Urbanus (Eusebius *HE* v.16,17, see n. 5
below).

Eusebius more than once mentioned Claudius Apolinarius, bishop
of Hierapolis (*HE* iv.27; v.16,1; v.19,1), but he was not able to
provide anti-Prophetic extracts. Similarly he mentioned a certain
Miltiades (quoted by the Anonymous, *HE* v.17,1) who opposed and
was opposed by the Prophets (cf. v.28,4). The source (hostile to
Miltiades and not Alcibiades) which the Anonymous quoted in that

instance included sayings of the Prophets themselves,[5] but unfortunately Eusebius chose not to repeat them.

(3) Finally there is the early and most probably Asian anti-
Montanist source preserved in Epiphanius' *Panarion* xlviii.1 (or
2)–13. This section of the anti-Montanist work is taken to be different
in date and provenance from the rest and Epiphanius used both oral
and written sources (xlviii.15). Separately R.A. Lipsius and H.G.
Voigt argued that the material concerned dated from the late second
or early third century,[6] and its content points to its being Asian in
origin. In this instance the sometimes imprudent and interfering
Epiphanius has preserved a useful source, especially for the recovery
of Montanist oracles. Already it contained anti-Prophecy exegesis
and scriptural citation.[7]

Who were on the Prophecy's side? There were the Three, of course,
with Alcibiades and a man called Themiso. Themiso had been an ally
of Maximilla in particular (cf. *HE* v.16,17) and he was probably the
leading male figure in Pepuza after the death of Montanus (who is
assumed to have died first of the Three). Then there was Miltiades –
evidently a leader, whose name seems to have been adopted for one
faction among the Prophets (*HE* v.16,3) – plus Alexander and
Theodotus (Eusebius *HE* v.3,4; v.16,14). Theodotus was a remarkable
man – θαυμαστός, opined the Anonymous, tongue in cheek perhaps
(*HE* v.16,14 (cf. 1 Pet. 2:9 and Matt. 21:42; Rev. 15;1)), an ecstatic
who experienced heavenly ascent and who was furthermore the first
financial officer of the Prophecy.[8]

The Three and others who followed after them were vilified by
rumour and in writing about their teachings and for acceptance of
money and gifts (*HE* v.18,4 (Apollonius)).[9] There is little even-
handedness in the Asian accounts and Bauer expressed his disgust
with them, dismissing them as 'caricature'.[10] These Asian sources are
the products of some decades after the beginnings of the Prophecy, of
course, and they reflect a hardened attitude against it. Matters had
deteriorated to the level of personal abuse. Perhaps the debate had
been on a higher and more objective level in the writings of Melito
and Apolinarius, and we owe Eusebius' use of these 'low specimens'
only to an accident of finding them in Pamphilus' library. We do not
know. Perhaps, too, some of the rumours were true.

Maybe some in the movement got rich (*HE* v.18,4 and 11) and this
seemingly counter to the kind of teaching about prophets which the
Didachē preserved.[11] The *Didachē* had said that a prophet should not

ask for money (xi.6 and 11; cf. *HE* v.18,4; v.18,7, quoting Matt. 10:9f.), though (giving the Prophets every benefit of doubt) perhaps we should understand what was happening in terms of the *Didachē*'s teaching elsewhere. A *settled* prophet, said the Didachist, might be furnished with the first-fruits of viticulture, agriculture and baking, of money, clothing and 'of all your possessions' (*Didachē* xiii). The Prophetess decried by Apollonius had received gold, silver and expensive clothes (*HE* v.18,4), which suggests there must have been some wealthy loyalists of the Prophecy in Asia Minor (*HE* v.18,7 says as much). Some people are corrupted by easy gain and Apollonius in *HE* v.18,11 tells of gifts, usury, worldly or even pagan attire (unless his description of Alexander is deliberately and scurrilously contrived to be reminiscent of the likes of Peregrinus Proteus (see below, 3.1.1) and is not to be believed). Theodotus and Themiso were criticised too: the former for claiming spurious confessor ('martyr') status, the latter for daring to pen a general epistle (*HE* v.18,5 (Apollonius) – 'an official Montanist manifesto', Turner suggested).[12] In addition his ecstatic excesses, and abuses in revenue collection, were condemned (*HE* v.16,14; cf. v.18,2). Money and gifts loom large in the attacks in Asia Minor. The Prophecy must have been successful in attracting monetary support and probably the catholic side was outraged not just by the success of the Prophecy and the gullibility, as they saw it, of those Christians who succumbed to it (rich and needy alike, v.18,7) but also at the threatened loss to their own coffers!

The Prophecy in Asia Minor was not a rustic phenomenon for long. The urban Apolinarius had dismissed Pepuza and Tymion as little places (*HE* v.18,2) but news of the early Prophecy spread fast, due perhaps to the work of its *salaried* ministers (*HE* v.18,2). The writings of the likes of Themiso probably helped too, as did the collectors of the Prophets' sayings (e.g. Asterius Urbanus, *HE* v.16,17). Tabbernee believes that inscriptions from Temenothyrai in north-west Phrygia show the church there to have been Montanist *by the early third century* and of course rural Phrygia continued to be a stronghold for Montanism (5.1–5.3 below; cf. Epiphanius *Pan.* xlviii.14).[13] But the Prophecy/Montanism is not to be dismissed as simply or *primarily* a rural phenomenon.

2.1.2 Encounter and confrontation
The Prophets first made their mark in the areas round about: in Phrygia, in the towns of Cumane, Otrous and Hierapolis/Hieropolis.

The last was a town of note where Apolinarius wrote in opposition (Eusebius *HE* iv.27). Influential people from those places encouraged condemnation, or even travelled to challenge them (Eusebius *HE* v.16,3–5). But some of the confrontations did not take place in the 'Jerusalem' centre of Pepuza, but rather in those towns and villages to which Prophetic missionaries had taken the news. Feeling ran high in Apamea on the Meander, for example, another important centre where at one point Julian had been the catholic spokesman (v.16,17). It must have run high in Eumeneia, too, to the north of Apamea and not twenty miles from Cumane. In the latter town some catholic martyrs (one at least from Eumeneia) refused to associate with followers of the Prophecy who suffered the same fate as their own Christians (*HE* v.16,22). This sad incident may have occurred *after* Christians 'in many places in Asia' had considered the implications of this New Prophecy and had rejected it (*HE* v.16,10).

The Anonymous had not realised what was happening until he visited Ancyra in Galatia. There he found the church a-babble with it, probably both infiltrated by the Prophecy and full of talk about it (v.16,4). He felt that on that occasion the victory had been his, but the Anonymous knew that sober presbyters and conservative bishops were proving helpless against its unrestrainable enthusiasm and the message it preached. Silence could not be imposed (which is probably the meaning of *HE* v.16,8, where the Greek is troublesome). Then at some point, over in Lydian Thyatira to the west, the Prophecy took firm hold (Epiphanius *Pan.* li.33). Such successes were not achieved overnight but over decades, and it looks as though the catholic response was sporadic for a time and ill co-ordinated.

So the Prophecy was not a small affair for Christians in Asia Minor. There were crowds at its meetings (*HE* v.16,8), although the Anonymous insisted that but few of the Phrygians were taken in by it (*HE* v.16,90). Other evidence contradicts that claim.[14] Catholic teachers in Phrygia and elsewhere found themselves hampered by partisans for the Prophets (*HE* v.16,8; v.18,13; v.19,3). The inexorable *spread* of its influence, as much as the facts of the Prophecy itself, troubled the catholic side. In Gaul, where the martyrs knew of it in 177 CE, Irenaeus was aware that prophecy had become a bone of contention among some catholics (*Adv. haer.* iii.11,9). Irenaeus had a finger on the pulse of the Christianity of Rome and Asia Minor, as well as that in Gaul.

2.1.3 Beyond Asia Minor

To the east there was Serapion, bishop of Antioch (*c.* 190–209 CE). He knew the work of Apolinarius against the Prophets and he was himself a man committed to orthodoxy in those writings which churches used (Eusebius *HE* vi.12). He condemned the Prophecy in his epistle to Caricus and Pontius (Eusebius *HE* v.19,1–2), two individuals otherwise unknown to us. *Pace* Faggiotto's assertions in *L'Eresia* we have no reason to assume they were bishops with Montanist leanings.

Serapion said the Prophecy was loathed throughout the Christian world (cf. Jerome *De vir. ill.* xli and the *Chronicon Paschale* ccxl) and as proof of the universality of that hatred he included with his letter the writing of Apolinarius, together with some appended (mostly episcopal) signatures.[15] There were, according to Eusebius, 'a large number' of these but Eusebius tells us only of a 'martyr' (confessor, for he was very much alive), one Aurelius Cyrenaeus, who prayed for the good health of the recipients – and, this banality apart, seems not to have said anything. There was also the signature of Aelius Publius Julius, bishop of Thracian Debeltum. Thrace, like Antioch, is sufficiently far distant from Pepuza to be interesting.

The bishop of Debeltum was against the Prophecy too. He attested that a blessed (deceased?) man called Sotas had wanted to cast out Priscilla's demon, and this in (Thracian) Anchialus (surely not in Cilician Anchialus). Those sympathetic with the Prophets had prevented the action. Priscilla in Anchialus? It is usually assumed that Priscilla's base was Pepuza. Had the Three themselves (as well as lesser loyalists) carried on an itinerant prophetic ministry to drum up enthusiasm for Christian life of the appropriate 'Jerusalem' community standard? Perhaps so. Apollonius told of a confrontation with Maximilla in *Pepuza* (*HE* v.18,13) and that may have been worth saying not least because not all such confrontations *were* in the Prophetic capital. If Sotas really heard Priscilla in Anchialus, then perhaps[16] we should envisage a degree of itinerant activity before the leading exponents of the Prophecy were able to settle at its hub in Pepuza. Maximilla may have been less itinerant than Priscilla. In any case in the second phase of the Prophecy it was *in Pepuza* that there were received in abundance those dues which settled prophets might expect.

The *Libellus Synodicus* of Pappus refers to a Holy Synod convened in Anchialus (called wrongly *Achilus*) with Sotas and a dozen other bishops present. Theodotus and the women had been condemned, it claimed. The account is to be taken with a large pinch of salt, like the description of another provincial synod in Hierapolis, with Apolinarius and twenty-six other bishops – there to condemn Montanus, Theodotus and Maximilla.[17] Later writers had read Serapion's account too!

As for Syria, I wonder whether Serapion had merely *heard* about the Prophecy or whether its tentacles had reached Syria too. It may have been in its infancy there. Contacts between Asia Minor and Syrian Christians were good. Ignatius of Antioch had assumed that Asian catholics would make personal contact with the church of Antioch (*Phld.* x.1–2; *Smyrn.* xi.2; *Pol.* vii, cf. viii.1), and ambassadors between churches covered long distances. The Prophecy which had reached Rome (see 2. 2 below) could certainly have reached the third greatest city of the empire, and fast. At the latest by the first decade of the third century Serapion (and presumably his church) had certainly *read* what at least one Asian had had to say on the matter. He was conscious of the views of Christians elsewhere and had formed a strong opinion about the Prophecy. It was a negative one. Perhaps he *had* encountered it personally. Or maybe he had just come to be wary of enthusiasm. I wonder whether Serapion had known that Syrian bishop referred to in the *Commentary on Daniel* attributed to Hippolytus (iii.18). The foolish bishop had trekked with his congregation into the desert – women, children and all – to await the coming of Christ.[18]

And had the Prophecy reached Pontus when a visionary bishop (referred to in *Comm. Dan.* again) had his flock sell its possessions and expect God's imminent intervention? We need not assume so. Those things regarded as rigours and enthusiasms peculiar to the New Prophecy were in fact little removed from what might be found among other Christians (as chapter three will show). They only go to show how relatively commonplace among the faithful were many of the Prophets' concerns. So, for example, when the Prophecy was on the rise, perhaps before Apollonius, Hippolytus or Tertullian had had the opportunity to notice its rigorous response to the pleasures of marriage and food, we find Dionysius of Corinth penning catholic epistles in an interfering way (though Eusebius offers a soothing description). They went to churches in Pontus, to Amastris in Bithynia and to the island of Crete, to the Lacedaemonians, the Nicomedians, the Athenians, to bishop Soter in Rome, to the Christian woman Chrysophera and presumably to others, and they were about encouragement to receive the penitent and to avoid over emphasis on chastity (Eusebius *HE* iv. 23). There is nothing to indicate that all the places concerned abounded with Prophets, though refusal of penance and sexual continence were of interest to the Prophets. It only goes to show that many a Christian community *might* have proved fertile ground for its seeds.[19]

Around Lyons and Vienne were Christian communities with orientals in the midst. They had individuals among them with a proclivity for asceticism (*HE* v.3,2f.) and they believed in the imminent coming of the Lord, foreshadowed by persecution (v.1,5). They used the word *paraclete*, perhaps deliberately and in the context of a wider debate known to them (v.1,10; cf. v.3,3 on the Holy Spirit), and the individual with whom that word was linked was also praised in terms of Revelation 14:4. These Gallic Christians saw in the person of Blandina the martyr that in Christ there was neither slave nor female (v.1,17f.; cf. Gal. 3:28f.).

These Christians knew others in Asia and Phrygia who shared with them a common faith and hope of redemption (v.1,3). They valued witness unto death but refused to accord the term 'martyr' to any who had not paid the final penalty (v.2,2ff.). They preferred to 'loose' rather than 'bind' and forgave the lapsed (v.2,5) – unlike some, the document may imply (see below, 3.6 and 3.8). Without once mentioning the Prophecy the martyrology from Gaul gives the impression that here were Christians who shared some of the concerns which we associate with the Prophets. But they did not want an extension of rigorism, a hierarchy of spiritual attainment or any causing of offence to, or dissent among, the Christian brethren. Orientals who had settled in Gaul may have carried the Prophecy there, or else ambassadors of the Three may have travelled that far.

It may also have reached many points west and east of which we know nothing. Kurt Aland is rightly cautious about tracing its spread, for scholars have been overreliant on lists of heresies as evidence of Montanism's existence in a given area. Montanism soon acquired a fixed place in such lists. And while in the East the laws against heretics seem to suggest that Montanism continued as a reality down to the fifth century and beyond[20] one has to suspect that in many places writers habitually condemned Montanists without ever having encountered one. Yet what has been outlined above shows that the impact of the Prophecy was considerable and that it

moved within little more than a decade to being more than a local
Phrygian affair.

2.1.4 *Reaction and response*

After some hesitancy and disarray the catholic side closed ranks.
Anti-Montanist writings were passed from one province to another
(including to Rome, to Syria and possibly to Gaul). Clergy supported
one another in their attempts to trounce the Prophets and their
followers. Montanus had arranged gatherings in Pepuza but the
catholics were convening elsewhere to assess the threat. Prophylactic
letters were circulated, like that from Serapion, warning any who
might not know otherwise that here was a phenomenon which had
already been widely condemned. The development of catholic
ecclesial structures and of solidarity between churches, increasingly
in evidence throughout the second century, now came into its own.[21]
The Christians in Gaul, on the other hand, just wanted *peace* in the
churches.

'Montanus', opined Ramsay, represented 'the old school of
Phrygian Christianity', quite unlike the ordered, traditional, hierarchical Church 'which was making Christianity a power in the
world'.[22] This is a half-truth. The New Prophets were averse neither
to organisation nor to apostolic tradition and they had made their
mark first *within* the Church. This was more than 'indignant
regression towards primitive mentality', wrote Whale, for in any case
'this mentality had never died out in the Church'.[23] It was claiming
(via the prophetic work of the Paraclete) to bring something new and
would not allow the catholic side, in any case, to lay claim to a
monopoly of insight about what 'apostolic' tradition entailed.
Christians were built upon foundations laid by apostles and prophets,
as the New Testament Ephesian letter had said (cf. 2:20). It was not a
matter of one *or* the other and, while apostolic succession might be
appealed to, there was prophetic succession also (Eusebius *HE*
v.17:1–5 cf. *Didachē* xi, 3ff.). Here were some of the roots of the
argument which Pacian of Barcelona would look back on later, for
Montanists, he asserted, had raised questions and created dissension
about everything – apostles and prophets, pardon and penitence, and
the very meaning of 'catholic'. Phrygia was an obvious place for such
tendencies to bubble over, but for their part the Prophets hoped to fire
the world-wide Church. Their forays in all directions, to Thrace, to
Syria, to Gaul, to Rome and to Africa, are indicative of that.

2.2 THE PROPHECY IN ROME

2.2.1 The move to Rome

The Prophecy moved West. By the 170s it was known in Rome and then become mixed up with the Monarchian controversy. Prophecy itself was not foreign to Roman Christians (see Romans 12:6; the language of Ignatius' letter to Rome;[24] and Hermas *Mandates* xi) but in Rome they debated the place of the Paraclete in the Prophecy. There were arguments about Scripture too, as Irenaeus, Hippolytus and Tertullian tell us. Some of these had overtones of rivalry between Asiatics and Romans.

Little has been written about the Prophecy in the capital.[25] There is some epigraphy for Roman Montanism but it stems from a later time and so it will be referred to in chapter five. In the present section I shall consider (i) episcopal response to the Prophecy in Rome; (ii); the evidence of that prolific writer, scourge of heretics and first 'anti-pope' Hippolytus, and (iii) teaching about the Paraclete.

2.2.2. Episcopal response to the Prophecy in Rome

The most often-quoted piece of evidence about the Prophecy in Rome is the Proclus (Montanist) versus Gaius (catholic) debate. The latter, said Eusebius, was an orthodox man (*HE* ii.25,6; vi.20,3).[26] This clash of theological heavyweights took place during the episcopate of Zephyrinus (*c.* 199–217 CE), who was no great theologian. Indeed he was an untutored simpleton and a tool in the hands of that *bête noire* Callistus, in the opinion of Hippolytus at least (*Refut omn. haer.* ix.11,1). But the early years of Zephyrinus' episcopate coincided with an outbreak of intense persecution and eschatological speculation. This may well have brought the Prophecy to the attention of Roman Christians once again, so it was under Zephyrinus that the presbyter Hippolytus took up the cudgel against the Prophecy and in Zephyrinus' time that Proclus and Gaius were at odds. Proclus was a leader for the Prophecy in Rome at this time. Montanus and Maximilla were dead, of course. Probably Priscilla was too. A third generation of Prophets had been born and the Prophecy had a foothold in many places.

The details of the Proclus–Gaius debate indicate that there was jockeying over apostolic authority. The latter appealed to the sacred relics of the Apostles Peter and Paul (Eusebius *HE* ii.25,6–7; vi.19,3). The Asians, for their part, could point to the relics of Philip's daughters and John in the East (*HE* v.24). During the Quartodeciman controversy Polycrates of Ephesus had also made this claim in an epistle to the unsympathetic Victor, Zephyrinus' predecessor. Now Proclus was doing the same to Gaius (*HE* iii.31,2–5; v.24). A view of Christianity was at stake which could appeal (Proclus thought) to both Asian and apostolic precedent, for there were many Asiatics in Rome and that fact was probably not lost on Rome's catholic leaders. Chadwick put it succinctly when describing the lasting tensions between West and East – 'Rome has got the bones'.[27] As a result of the tensions, some time pre-217 CE, in Zephyrinus' episcopate, catholics in Rome rejected the Prophecy.

But by that time, I suggest, Rome had been familiar with it for some years and official opposition was not new. To show this we have to return to the episcopate of Eleutherus, the predecessor of Victor.

Eleutherus, bishop in Rome from 174 to 189 CE, had received letters of embassy from the martyrs in Gaul in the year 177. Problems arising from the Prophecy were probably in mind (1.3.5 and 2.1.2 above) and Asian Prophets may already have made their own approaches to churchmen in the capital. It may have been Asian catholics who had asked the Gallic Christians for their view, so that both sides were canvassing sympathy and the good offices of the Roman bishop. Teachers of all kinds gravitated to Rome – from Peter and Paul through Polycarp, Justin and Hegesippus to Cerdo, Marcion, Valentinus and Abercius Marcellus. Hence Eleutherus' discussions with Irenaeus (who had been an ambassador on this matter) probably concerned a phenomenon which was already a reality in the city.

Irenaeus and the Christians in Gaul wanted no hastiness. They wanted 'peace' in churches, though it is clear that aspects of the Prophecy's rigour went too far for their own tastes. It is often assumed that Eleutherus proved unsympathetic to the Prophecy, despite the intervention from Gaul, but we cannot be certain of this. Nor should we assume from Tertullian's report about an *unnamed* bishop that it must have been predecessors of *Victor* (i.e. including Eleutherus) who had been hostile to it (*Adv. Prax.* i). Victor may not have been the bishop concerned. If Eleutherus *had* been hostile (perhaps aware of the potential for tensions between Asiatic followers of the Prophets and other Roman Christians), then the more sympathetic response ascribed usually to Victor his successor seems odd indeed. Such liberalism does not accord with what we know of Victor on another occasion.

Victor, we should remember, was faced with differences of opinion about the date for celebrating Easter. These separated churches of the West and the East (Asia Minor again) and would certainly have impinged upon the mixed Christian community in Rome. Victor, having taken steps to ensure that many Christians were on his side (Eusebius *HE* v.23 describes synods in Rome, Palestine, Corinth, Pontus and elsewhere) was firm to the point of being autocratic (*HE* v.23–6). He sought to excommunicate those who did not agree with him and again the irenic Irenaeus tried to mediate from Gaul (*HE* v.24,11). What peaceful coexistence there may have been of Asiatic and other Christians in Rome was now surely shattered. There followed the schism of Blastus, of Quartodeciman persuasion, as Eusebius and Pseudo-Tertullian tell us.

Victor's action contrasted with that of Anicetus (predecessor of Eleutherus), who had discussed the same matter with Polycarp. On that occasion Polycarp travelled to Rome on behalf of Asian Christians and in a spirit of compromise the bishops seem to have agreed to differ (*HE* v.24,14ff.). We should not assume that Rome was seeking to impose its practice on Asia, rather that it had been hoping for uniformity of practice in its own territory. Asiatic Christians in Rome may have appealed to Polycarp for support, however, so as to retain autonomy on this matter in their own enclaves.

At a later date Victor behaved quite differently, so it is hard to credit that it was the determined Victor who recognised the claims of the Prophecy, if only briefly (Tertullian *Adv. Prax.* i),[28] and contrary to the practice of those who preceded him (i.e. Eleutherus, for one).

We know most of this from Tertullian's treatise on the Trinity, *Adversus Praxean*. This deals with the Trinity-in-unity and Praxeas' destruction of the truth in his defence of the unity of God. 'Praxeas', perhaps a derogatory description rather than a proper name,[29] had been first to import to Rome from Asia that heresy which came to be known as Monarchianism, Patripassianism and Sabellianism.[30] Tertullian described Praxeas as a person of restless disposition, a proud confessor (albeit he had spent little time in prison, Tertullian maintained) and a man who subsequently repented of his theological error. But this was not before the harm had been done and the 'tares' of wrong doctrine had been sown everywhere among the 'psychics' (*Adv. Prax.* i). It was Tertullian's purpose to expose and refute that wrong doctrine, while openly declaring his allegiance to the Prophecy (*Adv. Prax.* i; ii; viii; xiii). Praxeas was implacably hostile to it.

Tertullian accused Praxeas of resisting and destroying the gifts of God (prophecy no doubt intended) and of having organised false accusations against the Prophets and their communities. He had done this so as to dissuade an unnamed bishop of Rome from his willingness to acknowledge the Prophecy – a bishop, Tertullian claimed, who had not only recognised the prophetic gifts of Montanus, Prisca and Maximilla, but had already penned a pacific letter to churches in Asia and Phrygia. Praxeas' activities had led him to recall that letter and to withdraw his recognition of the prophetic gifts since it allegedly ran counter to the response of the bishop's predecessors (*Adv. Prax.* i).

The train of events as Tertullian described it made of Praxeas the villain in terms of both Patripassian heresy and opposition to prophecy. It has given us one of Tertullian's many memorable descriptions. Praxeas, he declared, had 'put to flight the Paraclete and crucified the Father'. Pseudo-Tertullian names Praxeas last in his list of heretics (*Adv. omn. haer.* viii), as a man condemned by Victor, but this tells us nothing about the date of Praxeas' opposition to the Roman view of Prophecy. It says more of the Patripassian/Monarchian controversy which raged in Victor's time and beyond. Who then was the Roman bishop who was friendly to the Prophecy and then disavowed it under Praxeas' influence?

I think it was probably not the tough-minded Victor in the decade of the 190s. The prophecy was widely condemned by that time and according to Praxeas had previously been criticised in Rome.[31] Other pointers suggest that his predecessor Eleutherus was the peace-bestowing bishop.

It was Eleutherus (174–89 CE) who had been sent letters by the churches of Vienne and Lyons just as the Gallic Christians, ambassadors for the *peace* of the churches, sent word to Asia and Phrygia (*HE* v.3,4; v.4). The letters *of peace*, sent to the East from a bishop (unnamed by Tertullian) in Rome, probably had come from that same bishop, Eleutherus. Irenaeus' sympathy towards charismatics is apparent in his work. Given his irenic tendencies, it seems unlikely that he would have counselled Eleutherus to condemn the Prophecy. The martyrs in Gaul also betray characteristics which align them with the Prophets (not least the language used about Alcibiades, Vettius Epagathus and Alexander the Phrygian suggests this) and,[32] although (indeed because) they were not as rigorous and unforgiving as the Prophets in Asia and Phrygia (see below, 3,3; 3,5), it is hard to believe they would have said the Prophets should be anathematised. Eleutherus, I suggest, responded positively to the embassies and wrote the 'letters of peace'. But that could not be the end of the matter. It was only about the year 178–9 CE.

Asian catholic Christians had probably started to gather to discuss the Prophecy before such letters from Rome were received (Eusebius *HE* v.16,10). They were condemning it while elsewhere there were signs of sympathy! It may well have been the receipt of Eleutherus' decision, together with the deaths of some of the Prophecy's leading protagonists, which spurred Christians in the East into stronger action. Apolinarius was already writing his treatises against the Prophecy (*HE* iv.27; v.16,1; v.19,1). Abercius Marcellus began to badger the Anonymous to put something in writing (*HE* v.16,3). Praxeas, we may surmise, then went to Rome to counter Prophetic propaganda armed with a dossier of complaints against the Prophecy. Eleutherus' short-lived appeasement came to nothing. In any case the independent Asiatics probably did not take kindly to what might have seemed ill-informed Roman interference in their affairs. Praxeas was himself an Asian and determined *anti*-Montanism was as much a product of the East as was the Prophecy itself. If Tertullian is to be believed, Praxeas in Rome presented the Asian catholics' case with vigour.

Rome revised its position and went along with their view. It was not that Asia needed Rome's approval or condemnation, just as it was not a matter of Rome seeking good relations with Asia against her better judgement. It was a case of acting in the light of fresh evidence. Opinions had hardened in Asia Minor in the 170s. The Prophecy had already been driven out of some places. What had so troubled the brethren in Asia might well become reality in the capital too - even if as yet there was no cause for anxiety in Rome.

The question remains, of course, if Eleutherus was the irenic bishop, who were those predecessors who had not been favourable to the Prophecy? The answer might be Anicetus (bishop 155–66 CE) and his circle (Eusebius *HE* iv.14; iv.19,1; v.24,16)[33] but more likely it was Soter and his (*HE* iv.19,1; iv.22,3 (Hegesippus); v.1,1). These two had been bishop from 155 to 166 and 166 to 174 CE respectively. There is some very weak corroborative evidence for this in the account of Praedestinatus, a late and not reliable source. Praedestinatus claimed that bishop Soter wrote against the Prophecy and that Tertullian then contradicted Soter's view of it (i.26). The

Praedestinatorum haeresis i.86 suggests, however, that Soter condemned the Tertullianists – an indication of how far awry the chronology of this document is. The truth may be that no one in Rome had *condemned* the Prophecy officially before Zephyrinus. Rather the point Praxeas was making was that previous Roman bishops had given it no comfort.

Such a reading of events matches my belief that the decade of the 160s CE was an important one for the rise of the Prophecy and that the end of Antoninus Pius' reign, or the first part of Marcus Aurelius', saw its beginnings (1.3 above). The Prophecy must have predated Eusebius' year of 172 CE because knowledge of it was in Rome already before that date – though it had not enjoyed the approval of the catholic authorities.

Other commentators have read matters differently. Tertullian's account (of Praxeas) has been taken to indicate an official condemnation of the Prophecy before its temporary reprieve under the unnamed bishop. Some have treated the reference to the embassy from Gaul as an indication that there was need for removal of an existing excommunication and for greater understanding of the Prophets' position. I do not think this was so.[34] It seems to me more probable that no recognition had been given to the Prophecy, though it had had no formal condemnation. After all, had the matter been treated very seriously in Rome, it seems improbable that a successor in the see would have needed to be reminded of what predecessors had done.

Whether this was the case or not, Tertullian reported: (a) that the bishop who bestowed his peace promptly withdrew it; and (b) that this had come about under pressure from accusers of the Prophecy. The accusations carried to Rome may well have been in the form of copies of the anti-Prophecy treatises being written in Asia at the time. The Prophecy in Rome must have been a small and a quiet affair (the accusations about unacceptable *manner* of prophesying do not seem to have surfaced in Rome; cf. 3.2.1–3.2.3 below). This was not so in the East by the 170s. No doubt the Asian writers and Praxeas, their ambassador, indicated as much.

2.2.3 *The evidence of Hippolytus*[35]
Hippolytus, writing in the third century, tells us of debate about Scripture and authority. We also learn from him that the Prophecy was not monolithic in his day. In Rome more than one form of it

existed, and this in a Christian community which was already diverse.

Rome had an abundance of Asians, not a few of whom were to be found in Christian communities. They were one among many ethnic minorities there. The diversity of teachings which resulted from this mix was problematic for catholic Christians like Hippolytus, who found himself opposing Theodotus the Adoptionist of Byzantium, the Smyrnean Noetus, and (according to the twelfth-century Jacobite Dionysius bar Salibi) at another time opposing Gaius, who had taken on Proclus the Montanist. The Roman Christian community comprised groups 'representing the various races and the various provinces of the empire'. Incoming teachers of heresies and heads of schools brought ever-new divisions and conflicts. This is the view of La Piana, who wrote that about the end of the second century the Christian community of Rome seemed in the process of complete disintegration.[36]

This is an exaggeration, I think, but there *were* many changes and novelties. Catholic Roman Christianity was becoming Latinised; it was trying to deal with personal antipathies within its boundaries and was seeking to exert its influence on the liturgical and other practices of Christians elsewhere. There was need not to alienate an already hostile populace and an intelligentsia which was suspicious of orientals and others allied to antisocial cults. All things considered, Hippolytus was measured in his response to the Prophecy. Roman Christianity wanted no further sources of difficulty.

Hippolytus was already a man of significance. He commented on the Prophecy as on other aberrations,[37] especially on new and strange fasts (*Refut. omn. haer.* vii.19; x.25f. cf. *Comm. Dan.* iv.20) derived from the teaching of the Three. He complained too of excessive respect for Priscilla and Maximilla but like Tertullian and Epiphanius he asserted the trinitarian orthodoxy of (the main body of) the Prophets (*Refut. omn. haer.* viii.19; cf. Epiphanius Pan. xlviii.1; Filastrius *Div. haer. lib.* xlix; Tertullian *De virg. vel.* i-ii; *De jej.* i).[38] Had the Prophecy been tainted with Gnosticism, then Hippolytus, no less than Tertullian, would certainly have recognised and written of it.

What he said of the Prophets followed on his words about the Quartodecimans. Possibly he knew of Quartodeciman tendencies among them. These can scarcely be described as heterodox in any case. Nevertheless, in one respect the Prophets had strayed into bad company. Both Hippolytus and Pseudo-Tertullian, the author of *Adversus omnes haereses*, knew that one group among the Prophets in

Rome was heterodox. Perhaps less than half a century after the
Prophecy's first sparks there was no longer uniformity of doctrine;
'sed horum non una doctrina est' wrote Pseudo-Tertullian. One
group in Rome (leader unnamed) espoused the Monarchianism of
Noetus of Smyrna (so Hippolytus *Refut omn. haer. x.26*), while Pseudo-
Tertullian wrote of Aeschines leading a group which held that Christ
was both the Father and the Son (*Adv. omn. haer.* vii; cf. 5.2.1 below).
Proclus, who debated with Gaius in Zephyrinus' time (Eusebius *HE*
vi.20,3), represented the other and orthodox strand of Prophetic
teaching in Rome.

Monarchianism was not a novelty but was 'widely distributed in
the second-century church'.[39] Moreover, it was growing at the turn of
the third century. Origen (who had heard Hippolytus discourse) and
Tertullian had to take up arms against it, the latter becoming the
most eloquent promoter of a right understanding of the Trinity. It
was certainly not the sole preserve of people in the Prophecy and
when Hippolytus was writing it was probably not the norm within
it.[40] We may wonder why Tertullian said nothing of such Prophetic
proclivities. Perhaps he was ignorant of what was happening in Rome
in that respect (see below, 2.3.2; 2.3.4). In any case there is no cause to
disbelieve the account of Hippolytus.

Hippolytus was a determined upholder of tradition, the scourge of
Zephyrinus and his presbyter (later bishop) Callistus, and a man who
wrote a treatise (now lost) on spiritual gifts.[41] Hippolytus defended
the Fourth Gospel and the Apocalypse against those (anti-Montanists?) who denigrated them (3.9.6 below),[42] though here was a man
who decried excessive reverence for the utterances of Priscilla and
Maximilla and who was scathing about the visions (and the
cabbage-eating) among followers of the Prophecy (*Refut. omn. haer.*
viii.19; x.25–26). Hippolytus, I suspect, (like Irenaeus) was wise
enough to know that prophetic babies should not be thrown out with
the bathwater of Prophecy. Hippolytus is an important witness for
Rome. His evidence will appear again in chapter three on the
Prophecy's teachings.

2.2.4 *The Paraclete*
Early sources do not mention explicitly that there was debate about
the Paraclete in Asia (see below 3.2.5). This has led to speculation
that emphasis on John's Paraclete passages was the product of a later
stage of the Prophecy and of Rome. Hence the Roman Prophecy

would have been unlike that in Asia Minor. I do not see matters that way. It seems to me that such paucity of references in Eastern sources is not because there was no perceived relation between the Prophets/ Prophecy (on the one hand) and the Paraclete's work (on the other). Instead it was because of an *assumed* relation between Christian prophecy and the presence of the Paraclete, such as would have existed for generations in Asian Christian circles. It would not have sparked the kind of discussion which arose in Rome.

In Rome probing questions *were* asked about the links between this contemporary revelation and preceding ones; about the authority conveyed in the Prophecy and its writings and about the Christian literature to which its loyalists appealed. It was in the process of clarification that the Prophecy underwent doctrinal developments.

Ronald Heine has tried to isolate the distinctively *Roman* developments in teaching about the Paraclete and revelation, claiming that Phrygian Montanists had not appealed to Johannine Paraclete passages,[43] only Roman.[44] His case runs as follows:

(i) It is assumed that the Prophets used John 14–16 to defend their prophetic activity and that Montanus declared himself the Paraclete.[45]

(ii) Yet the earliest sources about Phrygia give 'no indication' of appeal (p. 2) to the Paraclete passages, which were 'of little or no significance' (p. 10) to the early Montanists. In Phrygia the discussion concerned *false prophecy and ecstasy* (see below 3.2). Clear evidence of debate about the Paraclete comes in sources from Rome and North Africa. Tertullian got his knowledge of Montanism from Rome and is not, in any case, a sound guide to the beliefs of the early Prophecy.

(iii) A related Roman question was whether there could be contemporary prophets (i.e. after the time of the Apostles).

(iv) The passages which do identify the Three with the Paraclete are suspect and became significant, in any case, during later controversy about the Trinity.

Fridh made some not dissimilar points many years ago and there is much in Heine's view that I agree with. Nevertheless, I am unconvinced by Heine's conclusion about the non-use of John's Gospel in the Asia Minor Prophecy, and hence by his conclusions on the Paraclete. Here are my observations:

With regard to (i) and (iv), it is true that we have (one instance from

Epiphanius apart, see below) no early case of direct reference to the
passages concerned. It is also true that we must question the
identification of Montanus with the Paraclete on the basis of certain
oracles (3.1.2; 5.2.1 below) and Eusebius' statement (*HE* v.14 cf. 4.2
below). *With regard to (ii)* we have seen (and will see in 3.2; 4.1) that
the emphasis in Asia Minor was indeed on the questionable validity of
the prophecies, as Heine claims. Heine is right about (iii), but I am
not convinced that Tertullian knew of the Prophecy *only* from Rome.
After all, he is credited with having opposed Apollonius' work
(Jerome *De vir. ill.* xl and below 1.3.4–5; 2.1.1) and seems ignorant of
certain Roman developments in the Prophecy. Heine has to
acknowledge that debate about Paraclete *and* about ecstasy (the
latter he attests a feature of *Phrygian* opposition to Montanism)
feature in Tertullian's writing.

In my view Heine dismisses too quickly the role of the Fourth
Gospel's Paraclete teaching in the East. He refers only in passing (p.
14) to the incidence of *paraclete* language in the report from the
martyrs of Gaul (Eusebius *HE* v.1,10; v.3,4; v.4,1f.) and in this (sent
east as well as west) there may well have been a deliberate echoing of
language which was meaningful to the Prophets: e.g. the 'paraclete'
language of the document may have been included to illustrate to the
Romans that such language might *validly* be used of an individual
(and hence that the 'paraclete' question *was* a live issue in Rome).

The only incidence of use of a Johannine Paraclete passage in
Epiphanius' early source comes in *Pan.* xlviii.11. There John 16:14
occurs as a point scored *against* the Prophets by the writer. It was not
made by the Prophets themselves. Heine thinks that is significant, but
then that is true of much else in our sources. We are almost always
dependent on reading behind the polemic to determine what points
had first been made by the Prophets. From this passage it seems to me
at least as plausible that the Prophets in Asia Minor referred to the
Paraclete promises as it is plausible on the basis of *HE* v.18,14 (from
an opponent) and Epiphanius *Pan.* xlviii.10,1f. (an opponent again)
to conclude that they were appealing to the language of the
Apocalypse on other counts.[46] I do not think (as does Heine) that this
passage constitutes 'silence' about the issue on the part of this early
source.[47] Instead I assume that the language is a response to an
alleged claim of Montanus himself.

Had Montanus not claimed that the Paraclete had come, there
would have been no need for comparison between the promised

Paraclete which glorifies *Christ* and the figure of Montanus, whose prophetic words ('I am the Lord God . . .' *Pan.* xlviii.11.1) seemed self-glorifying (*Pan.* xlviii.11,6). Why is there reference not just to *fulness* of deity in the Lord (cf. Col. 2:9; *Pan.* xlviii.11,7) but also to fulness granted to *all* the prophets (cf. John 1:16), if there had been no Prophetic argument for a specific Paraclete dispensation manifested in prophetic gifts (cf. *Pan.* xlviii.11,5–6)? If I seem here to be devoting much space to an argument with Heine it is because it is an important argument. The teaching on the Paraclete in Asia, I shall suggest (3.2), was indeed central to the self-understanding (and others' under-standing) of the Prophecy – though it was different from what emerged later in the Prophetic Diaspora. The fact that relatively little is said about it in Asian sources was due to the fact that the association of Paraclete and prophetic activity was taken for granted in the region concerned.

Like Heine I believe that the crucial early source of Epiphanius was Asian (see 2.1.1). If it were not so, of course, but Roman (and reliance on the ubiquitous but lost *Syntagma* of Hippolytus has been posited), then much of Heine's analysis falls down. Moreover, it is now commonplace to observe likenesses between (a) this source of Montanist and anti-Montanist material (already subject to catholic redaction and comment) and (b) material (showing scriptural texts and exegetical positions) in Tertullian's writing. This latter represents what may well have been an unredacted form of that source.[48] If such a relation exists and Epiphanius' source is indeed Asian, then again we should not assume that all Tertullian's knowledge had been derived from Rome – including his knowledge of teaching on the Paraclete (2.3.2 below).

The Johannine teaching on the Paraclete and the relation of that teaching to Christian prophecy and revelation *would have needed discussion* in Rome but that would have been much less the case in Asia Minor (see below, 3.2.5).[49]

However, contemporary prophecy *was* being denied in Rome (see also 3.9.3 below). Heine is surely right to think that the Roman church 'did not argue with the Montanists about true or false prophecy', nor about rational versus ecstatic prophecy. It refused simply to grant the possibility of any prophecy after the Apostles.[50] It was in relation to *that* debate that the Paraclete passages were ransacked so that the enemies of the Prophecy could point to seemingly extravagant claims on the part of (some of?) the Prophets

(Hippolytus *Refut. omn. haer.* viii.19; cf. *Dialexis* (Heine *Oracles*, 228); Didymus *De Trin.* iii.41,2–3; Filastrius *Div. haer. lib.* xlix; Isidore of Pelusium *Etym. lib.* xx.8.5,27 (*PL* lxxxii,300)).[51]

The debate had to be taken back to the Johannine writings, so what was it the Fourth Evangelist had written? He had promised (John 15:26f.; 16:14) that the Paraclete, the Spirit of truth, would bear witness (cf. 1 Cor. 14:24f.) to Christ and glorify him (as Epiphanius observed, contrasting this promise with the Prophets' self-aggrandise-ment). So too would those Christians who received it glorify Christ. It would guide into all truth and convict the world of sin (John 16.:8f., 13; cf. 1 Cor. 14:24f.). It would make manifest meanings (of Scripture) hitherto not understood (John 16:13; cf. Acts 8:31) – and this is a theme found in Tertullian of course. It would tell of things to come (John 16:13). These were in fact the functions of prophecy – the things which Christian prophets of the past and the Prophets themselves had always been doing. Even in Rome Hermas and his like would have known that (but *The Shepherd* was to find itself marginalised in the debates about authoritative writings). When the need to clarify and justify in Rome became obvious, it was to prove less easy than the Prophets, products of an Asia Minor milieu, would have imagined. Consequently the teaching on the Paraclete and the relation of prophecy/the Prophecy to it underwent change in Rome. As aftermath to the argument it may have been in Rome that the so-called *Alogi* appeared, enemies of the Fourth Gospel (Irenaeus *Adv. haer.* iii.11,9), and it was there that Gaius came to deny the apostolic status of the Apocalypse (Eusebius *HE* iii.28,1f.; vii.25,1ff.). All such things will be discussed under 'Scripture' in 3.9.

Rome, then, was an important setting for the early Prophecy and there is some evidence for its survival there after the time of Hippolytus. This will be considered in chapter five, though there is nothing which takes us beyond the fifth century (5.3.2). We do not know whether Montanists were ever there in great numbers.

2.3 AFRICA AND TERTULLIAN

2.3.1 Tertullian the man

Studies of Montanism have too often ended as studies primarily of Tertullian. It is doubtful that he was wholly typical of it, however, though it is not new to say that. H.J. Lawlor's article in *JTS* in 1908

('The Heresy of the Phrygians') was written precisely to counter such faulty methodology. I suggest it is valid only to examine Tertullian's teaching and practice in each case, to try to work back and then to determine whether it might *also* have been true of the Asia Minor Prophecy. That is the practice adopted in chapter three of this study and it is there that the details of Tertullian's Montanism will emerge. But this is not an easy task, because Tertullian was surely capable of using and modifying the Prophecy to his own cherished ends and there is a lot we do not know about the Prophecy in Asia and in Africa.

I shall not examine the many theories which try to explain Tertullian's conversion to Christianity and subsequently to Montanist Christianity. I shall not chart systematically Tertullian's 'shifts' or argue for continuity in his understanding of the Church, of priesthood, of eschatology etc. Such questions *will* emerge from time to time in chapter three, but this is not a study of Tertullian. My interest in the man is to discover whether his version of the Prophecy bore much relation to that in Asia Minor.

He called it the New Prophecy ('nova prophetia' *Adv. Marc.* iii.24,4; iv..22,4; *De res. mort.* lxiii.3). New Prophecy corresponds to the title we find among catholic writers in the East.[52] It may well have been a self-designation by the Prophets themselves, who would have acknowledged that *innovation* was a necessary factor in its message. Tertullian did not fight shy of speaking of innovation. By the time it reached North Africa the Prophecy was probably well established and condemned already at gatherings in Asia Minor. So African Prophetism does represent a second phase and much of what we know of it in Africa has been filtered through the individualism of Tertullian himself. Fortunately he is not our only witness.

The *Passio Perpetuae* is an important source (considered at length in 4.5) and there are later references to Montanism in Augustine and less significant references in the Anonymous writer known as Praedestinatus (partly reliant on Augustine) and Optatus of Milev. But the fact that the New Prophecy won over the towering, brooding figure of the African Quintus Septimius Tertullianus gave it an impact on the writing of church history which otherwise it would not have had.

Here was a man of learning and strong opinion. By birth and education alike, Barnes observed, he 'belonged to intellectual circles in Carthage.'[53] He had not been born into a Christian family and I tend to the view that he was *a layman* and not a disaffected presbyter at odds with aspects of Rome's teaching,[54] *pace* Jerome in *De vir. ill.* liii:

Hic usque ad mediam aetatem presbyter fuit ecclesiae, invidia postea et contumeliis clericorum Romanae ecclesiae ad Montani dogma delapsus in multis libris novae prophetiae meminit.

Well read in both Greek and Latin sources, Tertullian was sharp of mind 'and extraordinarily skilled in the art of rhetoric'.[55] 'Quid Tertulliano eruditius, quid acutius', wrote Jerome (*Ep*. lxx.5) – what erudition! But what a troubled and troublesome man too. Pierre Labriolle in *History and Literature of Christianity from Tertullian to Boethius* wrote of 'tempestuous genius' and 'a passionate attachment to his own private judgement'. An 'explosive personality', wrote Klawiter[56] and in Fredouille's major study in 1972 there emerged a restless man of his time, never satisfied, spurred on by *curiositas* as far as that stubborn 'Tertullianism' with which his life ended. Johannes Klein, like Antonio Quacquarelli after him, wrote of a man beset with the need for the highest in moral character, doomed to disillusionment in the Roman world generally or in his native Carthage in particular, who turned to Christianity as his hope. Many similar things have been written. I have pondered most that memorable judgement of Nisters in his *charakterlogischer Versuch*, made in 1950, namely that Tertullian was not quite a psychopath, though paranoid![57] He may be right.

More kindly one might describe Tertullian the spiritual high-flyer as a Montanist by instinct. In many respects the move to the Prophecy must have been but a short step for him (see chapter three) and it served mainly to provide him with newly revealed witness to the kind of tradition which was in some respects commonplace among African Christians already. But we do not know because we are so ignorant of Christianity in Carthage before Tertullian. There had to have been *some* shift, however, for the Prophecy *was* 'new' and Tertullian's allegiance went beyond just defending Montanist teaching because of its 'spiritual' types whose desire for sanctification and love of discipline matched his own.

Tertullian may properly be described as a Montanist, I think. He did think in terms of 'us' (Prophetic types) rather than 'them', and I cannot agree with Quacquarelli who doubted the reality of a Montanist group in Carthage. However, Tertullian was perhaps not thoroughly acquainted with the details of what Prophetic Christianity was like in some other places.

We should not assume that a *schismatic* Prophetic community was formed apart from the catholics in Carthage. Tertullian the catholic Christian remained catholic in his thinking,[58] and the Prophecy in Asia Minor had been entirely orthodox theologically and was forced *from* the churches in that area. If Tertullian's knowledge of the Prophecy had stemmed primarily from the East (which does not exclude his also knowing about its progress from Roman sources), then catholic Christians in prophetically minded Carthage may have found it possible to live with it. It is only if we determinedly present the Asian Prophetic phenomenon as a frenzied aberration and Montanus as the claimed incarnation of the Paraclete that it becomes difficult to envisage a man like Tertullian succumbing to it and African Christians not driving it from their midst.[59] Tertullian's unquestionably Montanist treatises, albeit recognisable by allusions to the revelations of the Paraclete, still tell of doctrines and practices essentially the same as those in his undeniably catholic writings.[60] Tertullian the Montanist was Tertullian the Montanist catholic.

Passing over much of the considerable bibliography on African Christianity,[61] and on Tertullian himself,[62] I propose to state a position about only three things: (i) when and from what source did the New Prophecy reach Carthage?; (ii) Which of Tertullian's writings date from after his 'conversion' to it and so may be used in this study as evidence?; (iii) What was the relation of Prophetic Christians, including 'Tertullianists' to others in the churches of Carthage?

2.3.2 The Prophecy in Africa

African Christianity emerges suddenly in the year 180 CE with the appearance of Scillitan Christians before proconsul Vigellius Saturninus.[63] By the time Tertullian wrote to the proconsul Scapula (*c.* 212) he could reckon on very many Christians of all classes and ages in Carthage.[64] Christians were not popular, however. Though a proconsul might be tolerant (cf. *Ad Scap.* iv.3), the non-Christian populace of Carthage was not: betrayal and violence, invasion of Christian assemblies, desecration of Christian graves, attacks with stones and torches, mocking caricatures of the Christian God circulated for the heathen to laugh at (*Apol.* vii.4; xxxvii.2; *Ad nat.* I. xiv cf. *Apol.* xvi) – all such things were the stuff of local ill feeling wherever Christians existed in numbers. It was not that persecution of Christians was systematic, legally imposed or on a large scale, it was that it was an ever-present possibility, even without any imperial

edict being published. The church in Africa should probably not be
singled out as 'a church of martyrs' more than some others of this
time, but what little we know of it (the fate of the Scillitan Christians,
Tertullian's own writings and the *Passio Perpetuae*) speaks of a
Christian community which knew rejection.

W.H.C. Frend has reminded us often that Africa was 'different'
(my word, not his):

The christian mission there, whatever its source, had been confronted with
problems different from those encountered in the Greek-speaking world.
Roman Africa was ostensibly Latin, but beneath the outward form of
latinisation, the population retained much of the religious and cultural
heritage of Carthage.[65]

It was he who called its church 'a church of the Martyrs',[66] and it was
also a church of the Spirit. Certainly prophecy survived in Carthage
well into the third century in a way we do not hear of elsewhere, and
this despite the incidence of Montanism which in other places bred
wariness of prophecy.[67]

Some have argued, too, that in Carthage there was peaceable
coexistence between Christians and Jews, or at least closer relations
than we know of in the East.[68] Tertullian himself may well have been
attracted to the ethical demands of Judaism – though Christianity
(with its asceticism) won him eventually. But the question of whether
and how Tertullian had direct access to contemporary Jewish
writings and Jewish sages need not detain us. The 'Jewish' Christian
elements of Montanism (which is our concern) are explainable with
reference to its Christian origins (see 3.10 below).

So when did Montanism reach Carthage? We do not know. The
date of the (Montanist-edited) *Passio Perpetuae* – after 203 CE –
provides only a *terminus ante quem* (see 4.5 below). It may have been
present for a decade or two previously, unlikely though that may be.
The most widely accepted chronology of Tertullian's life has dated his
birth *c.* 160 (roughly contemporaneous with what I take to be the
beginnings of the Prophecy) and his conversion to Christianity *c.* 195.
All three of the Prophets were already dead by that time, according to
most scholars' reckoning, so when he learned of their utterances it
must have been through written sources. His death would have been
some time after 220. This chronology has been disputed, however,
most notably in the important study of Tertullian by Timothy
Barnes,[69] who is rightly conscious of how little we know about

Tertullian's life. Questionable inferences have been drawn from the scant evidence, he warns, and instead Barnes posits a *short* life for Tertullian, who would have been born *c.* 170. Discounting the inference from Jerome's long list of Tertullian's writings (*De vir. ill.* liii), which has suggested long life and lapse in middle age,[70] Barnes has dated Tertullian's extant works between the years 196 and 212, and his death (perhaps as a martyr the church preferred to forget!)[71] while in his forties. If Tertullian's conversion to Christianity was in the mid 190s, then we may wonder why (if the Prophecy was established in Carthage by that time) he was not attracted to it immediately. More probably it began to make its presence felt just after the turn of the century.

It is generally agreed that Tertullian had migrated to the Prophecy by the year 207 at the latest. Barnes suggests that it may have been a few years earlier, and it seems to me that his sympathies with it, what might be called his 'proto-Montanism', probably *predated* 207. The *Passio Perpetuae* was the product of a Montanist redactor (R^{Pass}) some time after the year 203 and the martyrs in that source (I argue in 4.5) were probably themselves of the Montanist circle (2.3.4 below). It seems improbable that Tertullian, who knew of and honoured these martyrs, would not have been in sympathy with them at that time. Perhaps it was the events associated with those deaths which 'shifted' Tertullian to more open acknowledgement of his sympathy.

As for how the Prophecy reached Africa, it has been popular to assert that it came via Rome (2.2.4 above). The church in Africa, it is maintained, had a filial relation with that of Rome, and this is a view which also allows critics to put Tertullian at another remove again from the original Prophecy. It assumes, of course (probably rightly), that the Roman Prophecy would not have been wholly like that of Asia Minor and encourages the argument that African (or Tertullian's) Montanist beliefs and practices must have been unlike happenings in Asia Minor too.[72] I have doubts about this. Tertullian (and presumably other African Christians) were well appraised of what was happening in the Greek-speaking East and they retained contacts with it. Even before his conversion to Montanism Tertullian was aware of conditions for Christians in the East. He wrote of the author of the Asian *Acts of Paul* (*De bapt.* xvii), he knew something of events among Christians in Bithynia, Asia and Cappadocia (in the Montanist *Ad Scapulam*).[73] Probably it was commonplace to know (*De cult. fem.* i.1) that Phrygians were good with the embroidery needle (as were Tyrians with dye) and according to Jerome he wrote the last book, *De ecstasi*, against the Asian anti-Montanist Apollonius. His probable knowledge of a source akin to what underlies Epiphanius *Pan.* xlviii also speaks of contact with traditions from the East. So I find myself at one with Douglas Powell in his study of 'Tertullianists and Cataphrygians'. African Montanism, he thought, orthodox in its theology, had derived from the Phrygian–Asian kind. Whether it also came to embody elements additional to it is another question, of course.

2.3.3 *Tertullian's Montanist writings*

Not all of Tertullian's writings have survived. Sadly for the student of Montanism his seven books *De ecstasi* are among the non-extant, but more than thirty writings are available to us. There is general agreement among students of Tertullian that his treatise about the martyrs (*Ad. mart.*), his Apology (*Apol.*) and writing on the shows (*De spect.*), as well as his writing on heresy (*De haer.*), the *Ad nationes* and *Against Hermogenes* (*Adv. Herm.*), stem from before his move to the Prophecy. So too writings on aspects of the Christian life: baptism (*De bapt.*), repentance (*De paen.*), prayer (*De orat.*) and patience (*De pat.*), and his writings addressed to women, viz. *To his wife* (*I and II Ad uxor.*) and *On the Dress of Women* (*De cult. fem.* i and ii), predate his Montanism, though the latter probably underwent a later reworking.

There has been debate about *De idololatria* (the work about Christian participation in society), as also about *De scorpiace*,[74] *De pallio*[75], *De carne Christi*[76] and the writing *Against the Jews* (*Adv. Jud.*). Fortunately these are not writings of great importance for our purposes.

The long work *Against Marcion* (*Adv. Marc.*) probably takes us into Tertullian's early Montanist years and if the preceding list were correct we would assume that the following writings were products of those years:

Against Valentinus (*Adv. Val.*)
On the Soul (*De anima*, post 203 CE)
The Soldier's Crown (*De cor. mil.*)
On the Veiling of Virgins (*De virg. vel.*)
On Flight in Persecution (*De fuga*)
Exhortation to Chastity (*De exhort. cast.*)
On Modesty (*De pudic.*)

On the Resurrection of the Flesh (*De res. mort.* in the present study)
On Fasting (*De jej.*)
Against Praxeas (*Adv. Prax.*)
To Scapula (*Ad Scap.*)
On Monogamy (*De monog.*).

Scholars' criteria for determining Montanist-phase writings are necessarily crude. Those which include references to 'Prophetic' concerns – viz. mention of any of the Three, citation of oracles, concern for the revelations of the *Paraclete* (rather than Holy Spirit) – are assumed to belong to Tertullian's Montanist period and they may also include we/you or our/your distinctions assumed to differentiate Montanist Christians from catholic ('psychic') ones.[77] I believe that Tertullian *did* ally himself formally with sympathisers for the Prophecy and so it remains to consider the relations between these and other Christians in Carthage.

2.3.4 Tertullianists and Cataphrygians

There is nothing to suggest schism in the church of Carthage during the early decades of the Prophecy's presence there. Later writers were of course critical of Tertullian's association with Montanism but we must bear in mind (a) that Montanism came later to be more clearly associated with heresy than it was in its first half-century or so, and (b) that schism in Africa may have been avoided *while Tertullian was alive*. Tertullian regarded himself as a catholic Christian (though wishing others in the Church showed themselves more 'spiritual')[78] and later catholics recognised him and Perpetua the martyr. Cyprian greatly respected Tertullian – he was favoured reading (cf. Jerome *De vir. ill.* liii),[79] while Perpetua had a church erected to her memory (see 4.5.2 below). Such things are hard to explain if the Prophetic faction had been condemned as heretical or had formally become schismatic.[80]

His writings tell of Tertullian's continued association with catholic co-religionists. In the Montanist *Ad. Scap.*, for example, he still seemed to be speaking for all right-thinking Christians.[81] It is clear, too, that, even while he was avowedly Montanist, catholic Christians were in association with him and seeking his opinion. 'Brother' Fabius of *De fuga* i.1 had not accepted the Paraclete and as Powell pointed out, the use of *frater* in *De exhort. cast.* xii.6 indicates that the widowed (and non-Montanist) Christian to whom the advice on second marriage was addressed was of 'one institution' with Tertullian.[82] Similarly *De anima* ix, the famous passage in a which a woman received a vision of the corporeal form of the soul (4.4.3 below), has been interpreted as evidence of the *separation* of Tertullian's Montanist co-religionists from the catholic group in Carthage. For it might be taken to suggest separate rituals,[83] and the *nos* of the passage to indicate 'we Montanists'. Conversely, of course, it has been taken to show that enthusiasts of the New Prophecy were *not* so separated, but were more probably an *ecclesiola in ecclesia*.[84] In the latter case loyalists of the Prophecy participated in the services (which services brought on the woman's visions) but also felt free to share their insights among themselves. (I am reminded of Ignatius' anguished complaints about small numbers claiming to raise a 'mighty prayer' apart from the wider congregation around the bishop (*Eph.* v) and about people who paid lip-service to bishops but in practice disregarded them and in his view held 'invalid' meetings (*Magn.* iv).)

The least that such passages show is that Tertullian was not radically estranged from the catholics of Carthage, for, as Neymeyr also noted in his study of teachers (p. 131), there was continued appeal to the learned Tertullian on biblical and theological questions. I would want to go further, however, and suggest that Tertullian, catholic by persuasion and enthusiastic, ascetic Christian by nature, in Carthage did not have to abandon the one in order to be the other. And if this is so, then the 'reconversion' of Tertullian to the True Church, which some have posited, is surely both unlikely (in that later writers would have gloated about it) and an unnecessary hypothesis. Eccentric though Tertullian was, difficult and uncompromising though he was, I think that *in his day* he neither regarded himself, nor was branded formally by the catholics, as anything so harsh as 'heretic'. He failed to win catholics to his position, of course, but it would have been for that purpose, I think, that he would have refrained from separating himself formally from the Church.

The now 'classic' presentation of such a view belongs to Douglas Powell in his 1975 study of 'Tertullianists and Cataphrygians', though more than a decade previously Joseph Moingt had argued against the necessity of schism. Moingt observed that rival clerical authority was not of concern to the Montanists and that in North Africa there was already Christian disunity (not least about penitential discipline). As for Powell, he concluded along the following lines:

there is no unambiguous statement of the excommunication of the Tertullianists by the Church, no more is there one of excommunication of the Church by Tertullianists . . . Mutual accusations of heresy undoubtedly formed part of the repudiation of the former *societas sententiae*;[85] but there is no hint that this involved also a repudiation of the *communio sanctorum* and a denial that the psychics were in the true Church at all (pp. 36f.).[86]

On the other hand, Augustine did seem in passing to suggest a split *within* the Prophecy in Africa (*De haer.* lxxxvi), with Tertullian activating his own 'Tertullianist' conventicles. Yet if Augustine, describing retrospectively, knew (a) of a category of 'Tertullianists' (simply a synonym for African Montanists), and (b) of condemnation *by Rome* of the Cataphrygian phenomenon together with its separation from the catholic fold, then we may just be seeing Jerome's *inference* about the situation in Tertullian's Carthage. We have no hint from elsewhere of any such division *within* the African Prophecy and I tend to the view (with Barnes, Fuller and Powell) that 'Tertullianists' are to be regarded simply as Montanists in Carthage.[87]

Like Powell, I think that what Tertullian knew did not include some of the aberrant prophetic doctrinal developments to which Hippolytus and others bear witness in Rome (see 2.2.3 above) – Tertullian would have been hostile to any such thing and I find it hard to credit that he would have ignored it for his own ends. Also, we do not find in Tertullian the kind of distinction between Holy Spirit and Paraclete which (it is posited) first came to the fore during catholic–Prophet debates in Rome.[88] He was not familiar (I shall argue) with the more realised eschatology of Montanism to which the later vision of Quintilla bore witness (see 3.3.1–2; 4.3.3) but, these things said, I do not think we can know·the whole truth on such matters. Certain kinds of modification may be assumed, of course. Tertullian was his own man. For example, women with the prophetic freedom accorded to Prisca (the form of the name Tertullian used) or Maximilla, or like those whose activities Origen abhorred (4.4.3(ii)), would not have functioned in any congregation over which Tertullian, even as a Montanist, had influence! But in other respects the degree of modification is not easy to be certain about.

If only we possessed the lost books *De ecstasi*, the last of which was supposedly written to refute Apollonius. With this we would know more clearly whether indeed, as I suspect, Tertullian, lover of the Prophecy, had been much more indebted to (probably written)

sources *from the East* than he had from the West – though his
knowledge may have been limited and access to it sporadic.[89] Had we
only *De ecstasi* we might learn more of the chronology of Asian writing
against the Prophecy and the accusations of Apollonius against its
followers – accusations of gluttony and greed, of empty claims of
'martyrdom', of criminal associations, of ornamentation and pencilled
eyelids – these things (abhorrent to Tertullian in his writings, most
notably in *De cultu feminarum*) would have provided fodder indeed for
his practised rhetoric. If we possessed *De ecstasi* it might even be that
Tertullian would show himself to have been at odds with developments
in the Prophecy in the East.[90] But we do not have it.

Lawlor may or may not have been right to say of Tertullian that
'his influence in determining the form of Montanism in Africa must
have been immense'.[91] One suspects it, of course. Powell may have
been right when he maintained (as I suspect too) that Tertullian's
departures from the *original* Prophecy were minimal (indeed that he
lacked knowledge of some of its subsequent developments *in the East*,
as well as in the West).[92] On the present state of the evidence we do
not know. What seems clear is that Tertullian's Prophetic *pneumatiki*
were a minority among Christians in Carthage. He wrote in terms of
numbers of bishops, of a crowd of psychics and of the chosen few
('pauci electi'; cf. Matt. 22:14).

CHAPTER 3

The Teachings of the New Prophecy

3.1 MONTANUS: THE MAN AND THE ORACLES

3.1.1 Montanus the man

Montanus has a native Phrygian name and first appears, enig-
matically, in the village called Ardabau, coming on the stage of
history like Melchizedek (Gen. 14:18f.), without details of ancestry or
birth (Heb. 7:3). He was dead by the time the Anonymous wrote and
that author did not believe the rumour that Montanus, like Judas
Iscariot, had hanged himself (*HE* v.16,15). The Anonymous had no
first-hand knowledge of events. It was reported that Montanus was a
recent convert to Christianity (*HE* v.16,7), but that may have been
said to discredit him. All we really know of Montanus from the early
sources is that (i) the mode of his prophesying was noteworthy, with
possession and ecstasy and strange manner of speech (*HE* v. 16,7; and
cf. Miltiades (not Alcibiades) in v.17,2f., see 3.2.2–3 below); that (ii)
he allowed marriages to be annulled and instituted new fasts (*HE*
v.18,2; cf. Hippolytus *Refut. omn. haer.* viii.19; x.25, and see 3.4–3.5
below), and that (iii) the small Phrygian towns of Pepuza and
Tymion were, at his instigation, known by the name 'Jerusalem'
(v.18,3, see 3.3.3 and 3.3.5 below). Then (iv) he won followers and
began to organise them: encouraging gatherings in the 'Jerusalem'
towns of Pepuza and Tymion, soliciting and collecting offerings from
the convinced and (perhaps for the first time in Christian history)
formally paying salaries to appointed teachers (*HE* v.18,2).

Points (ii), (iii) and (iv) are considered elsewhere in this study
(3.4–3.8), as also is the manner of prophesying which Montanus
employed. Nevertheless, the accusations against his *mode* of prophesying need discussing.

There was talk of possession (πνευματοφορηθῆναί), frenzy and false
ecstasy (ἐν κατοχῇ . . . παρεκστάσει), enthusiasm and strange speech

77

(ξενοφωνεῖν). The women (Priscilla and Maximilla) subsequently spoke like Montanus, namely madly (ἐκφρόνως), inappropriately (ἀκαίρως) and oddly (ἀλλοτριοτρόπως). This seemed strange stuff and later writers called him a former priest of Apollo or the idol (*Dialexis* in Heine *Oracles*, 123; cf. Didymus *De Trin.* iii.41,3), or of Cybele ('an emasculated man', Jerome *Ep.* xli.4). In the *Dialexis* the Montanist never denies that Montanus had once been a priest of an idolatrous cult – instead the debate revolves around the fact that Paul too had once been an enemy of the Church but became (as did Montanus) a chosen vessel. 'The Montanist' here may just be a literary device, however, allowing the Orthodox to make a case.

The Anonymous said nothing so explicit about Montanus but his language evokes descriptions in Lucian's satire on the pagan prophet Alexander of Abonuteichos (Ionopolis), the important Black Sea coastal resort.

Alexander prophesied under divine influence, spoke incomprehensibly and (cf. *HE* v.16,9) gave blessings. He too organised his cult with flair and was active in the 160s, probably during the plague of 166 when he used his itinerant (salaried?) prophets to circulate an oracle from Apollo which told of protection from the disease (Lucian, *Alex.* xxxvi). Klawiter considered Alexander briefly and also the ambitious Asiatic Peregrinus Proteus. Peregrinus was the subject of Lucian's other satire and unlike Alexander he was a man who flirted long with Christianity. Klawiter found 'striking' similarities between Peregrinus and the New Prophecy, 'if one reads between the lines'. Both were prophets and lawgivers (using the same term, νομοθέτης; *HE* v.18,2 (Apollonius). Both saw martyrdom as a means to transcendent glory (*De morte Peregrini* xii, xiv; Epiphanius *Pan.* xlviii.10,3) and Peregrinus was said to have suffered as a confessor in Palestine (cf. too Lucian's account of Peregrinus and things said of the Montanist Alexander by Apollonius, *HE* v.18,9ff.). Both were credited with suicide (*HE* v.16,13) – in a public holocaust at the Olympic games of 165 CE in the case of Peregrinus (cf. Athenagoras *Legatio* xxvi.3) – and there is 'remarkable similarity between the cultic understanding of his [Peregrinus'] person and the character of the New Prophecy'.[1]

The parallels are interesting enough, and in a racy chapter in *Pagans and Christians* Robin Lane Fox helps us put into perspective the likes of Alexander and his satirist Lucian. Such men are an important reminder of the hold of oracle religions. They indicate, too, that 'a streak of radicalism' and bloody-mindedness was attractive to people

(Christians among them) of the 150s onwards.[2] Nevertheless (*pace* Klawiter) I do not assume, with Klawiter, that the Prophecy should be understood much as the Apollo–Asclepius epiphany associated with Alexander of Abunoteichos. To understand the Prophecy as a movement which announced and embodied

the epiphany of the Father, Son and Spirit but in the context of a new iconography associated with the figures of Montanus, Priscilla and Maximilla,[3]

(as Klawiter seems to do) places the Prophecy at a greater remove than I would countenance from the forms of Christian prophecy which preceded it. Aune, on the other hand, thinks there was a deliberate attempt by heresiologists (Eusebius and his source) to paganise Montanus, and it has led scholars astray.[4] The Anonymous said Montanus had been deceived by the devil (*HE* v.16,7). There is no explicit reference to paganism, which is noteworthy in the light of later 'garbled rehashings . . . [and] gossipy hearsay'.[5] Neither at first was Montanus accused of 'procuring' harlots (Timothy of Constantinople in *De iis qui ad ecclesiam accedunt*),[6] nor of being 'truly deranged', without moral restraint or humanity (Cyril of Jerusalem *Cat.* xvi.8).

Hippolytus and Eusebius' Asian sources agreed that Montanus was revered (*Refut. omn. haer.* viii.19; x.25; *HE* v.16,8; cf. Epiphanius *Pan.* xlviii.3 and Tertullian *De jej.* i). And in Epiphanius (*Pan.* xlviii.11,5–6) we find the first association of Montanus and the Paraclete (see below, 3.2.5 and 4.2). Hippolytus is our earliest source to link the women and the Paraclete (*Refut. omn. haer.* viii.19). The accusation, however, was not that Montanus (already dead) had identified himself *as* the promised Paraclete. That accusation, like the others, came later – in Origen (*De princ.* ii.7,30); in Eusebius (*HE* v.14); in the *Dialexis*, in the mouths of the Montanist and the Orthodox;[7] as well as in Didymus (*De Trin.* iii.41, 1 and 3); in Basil of Caesarea (*Ep.* clxxxviii.1) and in Germanus of Constantinople (*Ad Antimum* v). In early sources Montanus seems to be just the mouthpiece of the Spirit.

He was both a recognised prophet and a considerable organiser. Both of these things troubled the catholic side, which claimed his prophecy was false and his attempts at organisation were the products of lust for power and gluttony among his loyalists (*HE* v.18,2 (Apollonius)). The accounts in Eusebius are not precise about chronology, however. We do not know whether the organisation (see too 4.2.1 below) *post-dated* the beginning of concerted catholic opposition, which was a reality when the Anonymous wrote.

3.1.2 The Oracles of Montanus

Certain of Montanus' claims were cited to show his blatant self-aggrandisement and heresy. However, these belong to late sources and reflect contemporary theological discussion on the nature of the Trinity rather than claims original to the Prophecy (see 5.2.1 below).

For example, in the *Dialexis* we read 'I am the Father and I am the Son and I am the Paraclete' (cf. Didymus *De Trin.* iii.41,1) or 'I am the Father and the Son and the Spirit' (or Holy Spirit elsewhere in this source). Aland lists these as 'doubtful' oracles nos. 1 and 2 and Heine also lists them as questionable. They should be seen against the background of later debate about the kinds of modalism to which Montanism increasingly fell prey. Not every oracle so attributed is to be regarded as a genuine utterance of the man, and those in the later sources are particularly suspect.[8]

Among the early material Epiphanius' unnamed source in the *Panarion* (xlviii) does preserve sayings, and certain unattributed oracles and reported teachings found in Tertullian's writings (genuine oracles 7–9 in Aland's 'Bemerkungen') may also have originated with Montanus (*De pudic.* xxi.7 on the forgiveness of sin; *De fuga* ix.4 and *De anima* lv.5 on flight in persecution). Most of the utterances preserved by Epiphanius prove to be explanations of the Prophecy's nature. They are the fragments of much longer utterances – really introductory formulae only, originally legitimising the Prophet as the source of the divine message. It is important to note that the message itself has not been preserved by the catholic side but instead we have just the language of self-designation and self-commendation.[9] Even when longer units of Prophetic material have been preserved the tendency has been to publish merely the saying, without attention to its context in the (anti-Montanist) writing. It is this, of course, which might offer clues to its setting in a wider debate but the truth is that this remaining material (including the oracles of the women Prophets) has received poor treatment in the past with some notable exceptions in recent decades. Utterances have been dismissed as worthless, as evidence of the shallowness or hubris of the Prophets and as a pointer to the extent to which the Three had lost touch with proper, biblical prophecy. There was no attempt to examine possible scriptural allusions, for example, because of the critic's assumption about the Prophets and their claims. Let us look at some of the material concerned.

The first in Heine's *Oracles* (no. 3 in Aland) was from Montanus, preserved by Epiphanius. It was a declaration that the speaker was not Montanus but 'the Lord God the Almighty (παντοκράτωρ), remaining among humankind'. Epiphanius also preserved related claims that *God* (or the Lord God, the Father) was the source of the utterances and was manifesting himself through the Prophet Montanus (*Pan.* xlviii.4–11). The formulae used here are of interest. As Aune points out it is unusual in early Christianity to have oracles in which speech is attributed to God. The *YHWH ᵉlohei-sabaoth* title occurs in Hosea 12:6; Amos 3:13; 4:13; 5:14 and the Apocalypse furnishes at least two further examples: Revelation 1:8 and 21:5ff. (and we should compare the παντοκράτωρ title in Rev. 4:8; 11:17; 15:3; 16:7,14 *et passim*).[10]

The words of Aland's oracle no. 4 dissociated Montanus and his teaching from the work of angelic figures or other envoys (πρέσβυς) of God (*Pan.* xlviii.11,9). The words are:

neither an angel nor an envoy but I the Lord God the Father have come'.[11]

Little of his speech survives but these words suggest charismatic exegesis of LXX Isaiah 63:9, with the promise of God's loving intervention. It was the function of the Spirit of truth, the Paraclete, to guide believers into understanding including (as Tertullian argued) understanding of the teaching of the Scriptures (John 16:13; cf. Acts 8:31); and this was associated in Asian minds with the practice of prophecy itself, I think (see 3.2.5). It should be remarkable to *fail* to find instances of Prophetic appropriation and 'charismatic exegesis' of scriptural material (though not expecting to find them, scholars have not looked for them). The use of LXX Isaiah 63:9 which is posited here may also provide clues to the context and content of Montanus' wider message.

Isaiah 62–6 tells of the deliverance *of Zion*, the condemnation *of idolatry and compromise* and the giving of *a new name*. A *Jerusalem* would be established in which all sorrow would be at an end and there was to be a new heaven and earth. It was precisely such language, of course, which fed the apocalyptic visions of John the Seer (Rev. 2:17; 3:12 (letter to Philadelphia); 21; 22:4) and of a chiliast like Papias. The *Sitz im Leben* of this utterance probably lies in exposition of the promises and requirements of God to his people.[12] The God of Isaiah 63:7–14 was the God who had put his Holy Spirit in the midst, the God of a people which had rebelled against and grieved that Spirit (LXX Isa. 63:10). The language and ideas of these chapters of Isaiah mirror concerns in the Prophecy itself.

Montanus appears from this passage as Prophet of the Spirit's presence and of the eschaton (LXX Isa. 63:5).[13] Churches needed reminding of these things, as also of God's promised vindication and of righteousness (LXX Isa. 63:1). Other Prophetic oracles, notably that of Maximilla on her role as interpreter of the covenant and present suffering (*Pan.* xlviii.13,1 Aland no. 15 and see 4.3.2 below), suggest that the Prophets *were* addressing de-spirited people and bringing comfort and promises (cf. *HE* v.16,9). Montanus would probably have had in mind God's promises and the maintenance of the proper quality of life in Zion, as he named the Pepuza and Tymion communities *Jerusalem*.[14]

Finally let us look at how Tertullian used the LXX of Isaiah 63:9. The Old Latin versions favoured by the Fathers, Groh reminds us, took the Greek aorist tense of the LXX ('saved') as matching the Hebrew prophetic perfect – so that it belonged, therefore, to the καὶ εἶπεν divine speech introduced in v. 8. For these Fathers, Isaiah 63:9 was God's prophetic speaking of his intention and with the Greek aorist rendered as a Latin future tense the words could be taken to refer to Christ himself. He would save his people (Irenaeus *Adv. haer.* iii.20,4; Cyprian *Test.* ii.7,1; cf. Tertullian *Adv. Marc.* iv.22,11). Tertullian interpreted the passage christologically, sandwiched between discussion of ecstatic prophecy (*Adv. Marc.* iv.22,4–12, citing Luke 9:33f. (not Acts 10:10 as in *Pan.* xlviii.7,3f.)) and discussion of the Law and prophets. The Isaiah text was here being linked with claims for ecstasy and the immediacy of revelation. Montanus, suggests Groh, had provided 'an interpretive citation' of Scripture, speaking in ecstasy and using a self-commendation form. Has Tertullian left us a clue about the real debate? Perhaps so. Montanus' utterance concerned not just the kinds of promises outlined in Isaiah and echoed in the Revelation but also the immediacy of revelation and the in-breaking of God's activity. Probably a great debate about Scripture, its promises and its interpretation was going on. We have been left with next to nothing of it. The *Panarion* of Epiphanius (xlviii) contented itself with cataloguing Montanus' seemingly scandalous personal claims and long arguments about ecstasy, offering no context for them. But Tertullian may have known the same early source without its anti-Montanist accretions and redactions (see above 2.2.4; 2.3.2).

Oracle no. 5 in Aland's collection (Epiphanius *Pan.* xlviii.4,1) is probably the best known of those attributed to Montanus:

Behold, the human being is like a lyre and I alight like a plectrum. The human being sleeps and I awaken; behold it is the Lord who changes (ἐξιστάνων) human hearts and gives to people a heart.

The claim that God/the Spirit worked upon a passive/sleeping recipient should be compared with the language of Tertullian *Adv. Marc.* iv.22; Hippolytus *De antichr.* ii; Pseudo-Justin *Cohortatio ad Graecos* viii; Clement of Alexandria *Paedagogus* ii.4 and especially Athenagoras *Legatio* ix. The last wrote of Moses, Jeremiah and others uttering in an ecstasy of thought as the spirit moved through them like breath into a flute. Then there is the 'wind through the harp' parallel in the *Odes of Solomon* (vi.1−2).[15] Are there any clues to the *Sitz im Leben* of Montanus' oracle?

Perhaps. First there must have been a need to defend the divine origin of the utterances against sceptics. Hence the claim that they were free from the interference of the human, passive prophet. Ecstasy (of heart) was also a God-given state. (Cf. the verb in Acts 8:9 of the negative effect of Simon Magus and in Luke 24:22 on the effect of the news from the women at the tomb.) This oracle is part of the propaganda of ecstasy. But Epiphanius not only denied that Montanus was a prophet (and hence denied the validity of the words); he also dissected the language, dismissing it as evidence of derangement ('I alight . . . I strike' etc. *Pan.* xlviii.4,2). He was implying (xlviii.4,4ff.) a considerable history of Montanist appeal to Scripture in defence of ecstasy, and he was trying to counter it (cf. xlviii.7,1−9,10). So he (or the source to which he had access) derided even 'the Lord changes hearts'. Such language was evidence of lunacy, he implied.

It was, of course, the language of Christian prophecy, of the conviction of wrongdoers, of seeing innermost secrets, of the Christ who through the prophets was the knower of hearts (Rev. 2:23; cf. 3:8; 3:15; 1 Cor. 14:24f.). According to Tertullian this was precisely the kind of gift which Marcionites lacked. The oracle was explanation of the change being wrought in individuals through the Prophecy, explained in terms of renewal and the promised covenantal relationship. The (new?) heart is reminiscent of Ezekiel 11:19f.; 18:31; 36:26

and Jeremiah 31:31ff. Covenant and promise were important features
in the Prophets' message, I think, and Maximilla declared herself an
interpreter of the covenant, promise and suffering (Epiphanius *Pan.*
xlviii.13,1).

Epiphanius' interest in ecstasy probably does reflect faithfully a
concern of both the first Prophets and the first anti-Prophets (3.2.2
below). Examples from Scripture were being cited at every opportunity and perhaps this oracle was originally part of an exposition on the
'sleep' of various biblical figures. The ἄνθρωπος would lead us to
Genesis 2:21ff. (cf. *Pan.* xlviii. 4,4 on Adam) and again there is a
parallel in Tertullian, not with the oracle proper but rather with the
scriptural passages used to prove that the human vessel of revelation
underwent an altered state.

The last oracle of Montanus to be considered is in *Pan.* xlviii.10,3
(Aland no. 6). Dismissively, as usual, Epiphanius introduced the
saying as something out of Montanus' self-styled 'Prophecy'. Heine
translated the passage as follows (p. 3):

Why do you call the more excellent man saved? (τὸ ὑπὲρ ἄνθρωπον
σωζόμενον) For the just (ὁ δίκαιος), he says, will shine a hundred times
brighter than the sun, and the little ones (οἱ μικροί) among you who are
saved will shine a hundred times brighter than the moon.

The second part of this passage is strongly reminiscent of Matthew
13:40ff. (cf. Dan. 12:3), where the righteous shine like the sun. The
μικροί δίκαιοι language is also characteristically Matthew's (cf.
10:40ff. ; 13:17; 18:6,10,14; 25:37,46), though not confined to that
Gospel, and the μικρός language of this oracle is particularly
interesting, I think.

Eduard Schweizer painted a picture of the Matthaean community
as one with ascetic charismatics, a community of 'little ones', just as in
the community which produced the *Apocalypse of Peter* (see 3.3.4
below). 'Little ones' were at odds with those who allowed themselves
titles such as 'bishop' and such Christians experienced visions and
auditions. G.N. Stanton has posited that 5 Ezra, too, is the product of
a similar circle in which prophecy and 'little ones' figured. For such
'Jewish-Christian' believers, he suggested, the events of the Bar
Cochba revolt were painfully recent, raising questions about how
Jerusalem was to be understood.[16] So perhaps in this utterance, too,
there may be small clues about the kind of Christian milieu from
which the Prophecy had sprung.

In Matthew's Gospel the context for this language is the explanation of the parable of the seed (Matt. 13: 37ff.). The harvest is the end of time (συντέλεια), using that same term which appears in Maximilla's oracle of the end of prophecy (no. 13, see 4.4.2 below). Good and bad will be separated and the righteous will shine like the sun in their Father's kingdom (cf. the face of the Lord in 17:2; Rev. 1:16; 10:1).

In the anti-Montanist source this seems at first less an oracle than it does a reminiscence of a debate between Montanus and a second party about salvation, though prophetic speech might take a variety of forms.[17] Presumably the *verba Christi* in the Matthaean parable are intended, though Matthew's 'hundredfold' is in the parable itself and not Jesus' explanation of it. It relates to the seed bearing fruit (13: 23) and not the brightness of the righteous. The explanation of Matthew's parable (like the Isaiah material referred to above) was in fact about precisely those things which commentators have taken to be special concerns of uncompromising and rigorous Prophets. It was about lack of staying power in time of persecution; about conformity to the world such as makes true discipleship impossible. The parable may well have figured in the paraenesis of the Prophets on discipleship.

So in this 'oracle' Montanus exercised the prophet's prerogative of creative use of Scripture (if we dare use such a word of Matthew's Gospel in his day), probably in treating of one of those 'promises' which the Anonymous had in mind (*HE* v.16,9).[18] It looks as though he conflated the Gospel promise to the righteous (which made no mention of the moon) with reminiscence of Revelation 21, which also told of the separation of the good from the bad. Revelation 21 will be referred to with regularity in this study – when discussing the Prophecy's eschatology, its possible millenarianism and its concept of community in particular. Revelation 21 contains the promise of the new heaven and new earth, of the end of suffering and the descent of the New Jerusalem. Neither sun nor moon would shine on the holy city, for God's glory would illumine it. Presumably the brightness of the little ones and righteous ones would be equally illuminating!

The kind of promise being made is clear enough. Less clear is the identity of the person in the opening sentence. Perhaps the Prophet was opposing a view of salvation more Gnostic than biblical. This would have merited an appeal to the promises, based on an understanding of discipleship which had apostolic authority.[19] Without more extensive testimony we cannot know for sure.

To sum up, then, it seems to me that the extant oracles preserve enough hints for us to say that Montanus the Prophet (the mouthpiece of God and the Spirit, he declared) was engaged in the interpretation and proclamation of Scripture and its promises for his own generation. Groh is right to argue that we need a thoroughgoing analysis of the Montanist material to search out scriptural citations and further Christian charismatic exegesis of the Old Testament.[20] Constraints of space mean that I can do little of this in the present study (but see chapter four on the women Prophets). Nevertheless I am convinced, not least on the basis of the language they used, that the Prophets were not part of an upsurge of pagan enthusiasm, neither was Montanus an opportunist, publicity-hungry half-convert. The Prophecy purported to be *Christian* prophecy and in its form and content arguably it was just that (cf. 3.2 and 4.3).[21] The catholic leaders *did* argue, of course, and struggled to discredit it, taking issue with the interpretations of religious writings which the Prophets brought forward (3.9) and pointing to faults and foibles in the Three and their successors. It is a pity that only remnants of their utterances remain and these presented in a hostile manner. But still, I think, we have been left clues as to how the nature and limits of the Prophetic ministry were being stated. Promises were being declared and expounded, as the Anonymous said, and Montanus was proclaiming the present and coming intervention of God. God (the Lord/the Spirit) had spoken. It was imperative that people should listen.

3.2 PROPHECY AND ECSTASY

3.2.1 Christian prophecy

The New Prophecy was just that – prophecy, the chief manifestation of prophetism in the post-apostolic age.[22] There was still prophecy in some congregations (Irenaeus *Adv. haer.* ii.49,3): visions, exorcism, foreknowledge and those who believed they could judge a prophetic gift (*HE* v.16,8). Some believed Montanus, others were critical. Without the continued existence of and affection for prophecy in some Christian circles the New Prophecy's rise and success is hard to explain.[23] Of course some prophetic Christians were feeling marginalised, even threatened, by the growing influence of clerical officialdom – as seen in the apocalyptic *Martyrdom and Ascension of Isaiah*, in the interpolation which is 3:13–4:22. There lovers of office were deplored, and also wicked elders and shepherds who 'make ineffective the prophecy of the prophets'. Prophets were already few in number.[24]

So what happened at Ardabau and Pepuza was probably out of the ordinary even in the experience of prophetically minded Christians of the day. Yet the *utterances* of the Three were not much at odds with what we think we know about Christian prophecy in the New Testament and beyond (see 4.3 for the women's oracles and visions) and what seemed bizarre to earlier commentators is now more locatable within the spectrum of Christian prophecy.[25]

3.2.2 Ecstasy

In Asia Minor it was the *form* of the prophecies and their associations with ecstasy which attracted attention. The Prophets were accused of ecstatic excesses, with Montanus carried away by the Spirit (πνευματοφορῆθηναί; cf. Hermas *Man.* xi.16), unforeseen possession and (spurious) ecstasy (παρέκστασις). Out of this came inspiration to speak (λαλεῖν) and to utter strange sounds (ξενοφωνεῖν). The Anonymous said all this was at odds with Christian tradition (*HE* v.16.7). And Priscilla and Maximilla were as bad, showing abnormal, frenzied speech (v.16,9). Such παρέκστασις and false prophecy (v.17,2; cf. the 'bastard' utterances, 'bastard' spirit in v. 16,8–9 and v.17,2) was not confined to the Three, for it was also true of Theodotus, an administrator in the Prophecy, who was said to have experienced heavenly ascents and died after one such experience (v.16,14). Foolish ecstatics, unaware of their own actions, abused themselves and others, related Epiphanius' anonymous early source (*Pan.* xlviii.5,8). It was to be argued, of course, that such things could be legitimised by reference to Scripture and were far from 'untraditional'.

Condemnation and defence of ecstasy loomed large in the propaganda. Miltiades wrote a treatise to counter claims that Christian prophets had spoken in ecstasy. He was dismissive of the Prophets' good feelings which followed ecstatic speech,[26] and he warned that voluntary ignorance (ἀμαθία) might lead to involuntary psychosis (μανία). The words of Maximilla on another occasion indicate that the question of a Prophet's sense of compulsion (against her will) was part of the debate (Epiphanius *Pan.* xlvi ii.13,1; see 4.4.2 below).

The key question was whether prophets should be in full possession of their intellect when prophesying. Hippolytus (in Rome and not at the heart of the ecstasy debate in Asia Minor) said they should use reason *to judge* their prophecies while in Asia others told of the earliest Christians prophesying in full possession of *their* senses (the New Prophets interpreted matters differently). In any case, Paul had established the criterion of behaviour having to be for the common good (1 Cor. 6:12; 7:35; 10:33; 12:7; *Pan.* xlviii.3,1–2; xlviii.8,1; cf. xlviii.2). The catholic side denied that there had been trances or altered states of consciousness for Amos, Isaiah, Ezekiel or even the Seer of the Apocalypse (*Pan.* xlviii.3.4–6; xlviii.10,1), and in their view Montanus did not speak like the men of the past (xlviii.4,2), despite Prophets' appeals to scriptural precedents (e.g. Gen. 2:21; cf. Tertullian on ecstasy *De anima* xi.4; xxi.2 or Psalm 115:2; *Pan.* xlviii.4,4–5; xlviii.6,1; 7,1 and 5).[27] While Justin and Athenagoras had allowed that the prophets of old *had* spoken in ecstasy, anti-Prophecy writers seem not to have agreed. It was clear wits, said Epiphanius, and not derangement, which characterised the true prophet (*Pan.* xlviii.7,8).[28]

Other writings by the Prophets' contemporaries have not survived, but later ones took up the theme. Didymus in *Frag. in Actus Apost.* x.10 said that the 'disciples of mad women' had simply failed to appreciate the meaning of 'ecstasy'. The Spirit-possessed prophet was *not* uncomprehending at the moment of prophesying. Of course Acts 10:10f. (Peter's vision), for example, did speak of ecstasy, he conceded (as the Montanists had pointed out: cf. Acts 11:5; 22:17), but that word might signify any number of things; from derangement so that the person did not understand what was said and done (this last did not apply to Peter or the prophets!), through wonderment to a sense of being led into spiritual things. Divine ecstasy was a matter of sobriety, Didymus (like Epiphanius) affirmed, not of mania (cf. *Frag. in Ep. ad Cor.* 2 v.12).[29]

In Asia Minor hostility to ecstasy was the main plank of opposition. From the outset the catholic side altered the rules of the game. No longer were *moral* criteria being used to judge prophets (though later Apollonius adduced lots of gossip about leaders in the Prophecy). Nor was faulty theology attacked. Instead the Anonymous and writers after him condemned the manner of prophesying and ecstasy as unacceptable loss of self-control. We are in the realms of parapsychology. Some of it depended on what you meant by ecstasy, of course, and the protagonists were choosing to mean different things by the same terminology.[30] Tertullian acknowledged that ecstasy and ἀμεντια were matters of dispute between the Montanists and the 'psychics' (*Adv. Marc.* iv.22,5).[31]

Not all Patristic writers damned ecstasy,[32] but quite probably the ecstatic prophetic state was unfamiliar to those who wrote against the first Prophets. Christian prophecy of all kinds was in decline and probably was not practised in many congregations.[33] Some anti-Prophecy writers may have called to mind pagan practices as they formulated their objections, though they were remarkably unexplicit if they really regarded the Prophecy as pseudo-Christian. They condemned unintelligible outbursts and disturbing behaviour but Aune gives an apposite warning when he writes that

The presence of abnormal behaviour of the type associated with trance and possession cannot be inferred from the root meanings of such terms as *mania*, *enthysiasmos*, *entheos*, *katochē* , or the like, where no explicit description of such behaviour accompanies these terms. (*Prophecy*, 21).

These were precisely the terms used of the Prophets (Eusebius *HE* v.16,7 and 17,2; Epiphanius *Pan.* xlviii.4,6; xlix.2 Quintillians). Yet we have no descriptions of the roarings, states of collapse, wild bodily movements etc., which commonly have been associated with religious frenzy both in the ancient world and in more modern times (*pace* Gregory of Nazianzus' reference to Montanist Bacchic ravings, *Orat.* xxii.12). Catholic critics were worried enough by a mode of speech which was odd and unintelligible and was evidently linked (they thought) with irrationality. Had the Prophets really appeared in, or on the edge of, Christian congregations after the manner of the Galli of the Great Mother, our sources, I think, would not have been slow to make this clear.

3.2.3 Was there glossolalia?

What of the unintelligible speech? The Prophets did speak intelligibly, at least at times. There were collections of their sayings (Eusebius *HE* v.16,17) and by Hippolytus' time there were 'many books' in circulation (*Refut. omn. haer.* viii.19). Yet the Anonymous wrote of ξενοφωνεῖν, προφητευοντα, προφητικῷ χαρίσματι(*HE* v.16,6–8), χαλεῖν ἐκφρόνως καὶ ἀκαίρως καὶ ἀλλοτριοτρόπως(*HE* v.16,9). Montanus (or the spirit, the Greek is problematical) could not be silenced and the Prophets were described as immoderate in speech (*HE* v.16,8 and 12).[34] Here we have language reminiscent of the Christian roots of ecstatic prophecy such as are clearly visible in

1 Corinthians 12–14. Even in Paul's day it had not been without its problems. So let us return to Paul.

Prophecy was one of the gifts of the spirit (1 Cor. 12:4) and it would remain in the Church, albeit in imperfect form, Paul said, until the eschaton (1 Cor. 13:9f.). But gradually the power of prophecy had been curtailed and Irenaeus knew there were those who would not mourn its passing. The Anonymous acknowledged Paul's positive view of prophecy, and he even used Paul's promise *against* the Prophets when no one new of the stature of Montanus, Priscilla or Maximilla arose (*HE* v.17,4; cf. Epiphanius *Pan.* xlviii.1).[35] Tertullian also indicated that Montanists shared the Pauline view of *charismata* (*Adv. Marc.* v.8), whereas Marcionites could produce no prophet who spoke by the Spirit of God in ecstasy, in rapture (ἀμεντια), so as to utter a psalm, a vision or a prayer. Furthermore, when Praxeas in Rome attacked the God-given *charismata* he was not showing that love which was the chief of them (1 Cor. 13:3; *Adv. Prax.* i; cf. Epiphanius *Pan.* xlviii.11,4). Epiphanius preserved a truth when he wrote that dispute about the gifts of the Spirit made schismatics of the Prophets (Epiphanius *Pan.* xlviii.12,1; cf. xlviii.1,4; xlviii.2,3).

Was glossolalia among the gifts? The first Christians experienced glossolalia, though R.H. Gundry has tried, unconvincingly I think, to argue that Paul was describing *xenolalia*, i.e. the ability to speak in known (but unknown to the speaker) languages, and was not writing of 'ecstatic utterance', as the New English Bible translated the phenomenon of 'speaking in tongues'. So according to Gundry it was *the absence of an interpreter* and not the ecstatic nature of the speech which made it unintelligible.[36] This view has not found acceptance. Nevertheless, in the case of the Prophets the exercise of the gift of tongues, i.e. *glossolalia*, probably without the accompanying interpreter required by the apostle (1 Cor. 12:8ff.; 14:13–19), would indeed explain the accusation of strange and unintelligible speech.

Writers assume that glossolalic or xenolalic speech was no longer a feature of Christian life by the second half of the second century, though we should not overlook Irenaeus *Adv. haer.* v.6,1; cf. ii.31,2f. and 32,4 (see too Chrysostom *Hom. in 1 Cor.* xxix; on 12:1–11). Probably it was rare, though in pagan and Gnostic circles there were similar phenomena. Lucian reported the nonsensical speech of Alexander of Abonuteichos and Irenaeus gave some examples from Gnosticism (*Adv. haer.* i.21,23). The fact is that unintelligible speech was often linked with prophecy in the ancient world and indeed some commentators on the 1 Corinthians phenomenon have assumed its pagan origin.[37]

T.W. Gillespie, for example, has attempted to show that in the Corinthian Christian community there was a pattern of intelligible prophecy followed by unintelligible speech (glossolalia), just like that which might be found in Graeco-Roman paganism.[38] We might also compare Origen's *Contra Celsum* vii.9, with its description of probably Christian prophets (from the 170s). Using self-commendation formulae such as 'I am God' or 'a son of God' or 'a divine spirit' and 'I have come', they told of the imminent destruction of the world and the coming of the Holy One with heavenly power. After telling of blessings and eternal fire they uttered unintelligible, frenzied, totally pointless words which hearers appropriated as they wished.[39]

This report is reminiscent of Paul's warnings (1 Cor. 14:8) on ecstatic speech and of the difficulties of deriving meaning without interpretation (1 Cor. 14:13–16; cf. too Irenaeus *Adv. haer.* iii.13).[40] Similarly the New Prophets' speech was strange and there was room for a variety of responses to it. Epiphanius' anonymous source claimed that their utterances were of an oblique character (λοξά) as well as being (in his opinion) crooked (σκαληνά) and perverted (*Pan.* xlviii.3,11). I believe that glossolalia figured among the earliest Prophets. As for the 'I' first-person form found in some Montanist oracles (cf. Origen's account above), there are parallels in paganism,[41] and it was misunderstood and misrepresented by Montanism's opponents. But the Apocalypse bears witness to it too. In this, as in glossolalia and in other respects, including eschatology, ethics, encouragement to be uncompromising and in use of the Scriptures, Montanism showed itself to be *Christian* prophecy, albeit one whose leaders sometimes offered hostages to fortune.[42]

3.2.4 Revivalism

What we are seeing is an upsurge of prophetic activity associated with hard times – there was the 'suffering' needing interpretation of which Maximilla spoke (see 1.3 on date), there was belief in God's promise that the Spirit's presence would be in the Church until the End. Pauline and Johannine writings informed this belief. The revival captured the imagination of many in Asia and by its intensity and seeming disorder scared the catholic leadership.

Yet the Prophets were perhaps not greatly removed from Paul. The apostle had associated prophecy with reason, yet allowed for an element of rapture and for speech of a supernatural kind while consciousness was in suspense. The latter, non-cognitive utterance or 'speaking in tongues' (1 Cor. 14:4–23), was an inferior gift but Paul possessed it in abundance. As Paul knew, it could be taken for madness. But a Prophet might point to Isaiah's promise that God would speak to his people in strange language (Isa. 28:11). For the Prophets this revival of glossolalia must have been proof of the Spirit's activity. Of course it could not go unchallenged.[43] They were going against the decline of Christian prophetic enthusiasm and the phenomena now manifesting themselves became the object of theological reflection for the first time.[44] In Asia they became the main point at issue.

In Rome, by contrast (2.2 above), one of the main questions was the relation of this Prophetic phenomenon to the promised Paraclete of John's Gospel. Roman debate on this matter brought greater clarification (and disagreeement) in the realm of pneumatology but in Asia Minor too, I think, the Prophets' roles had been understood in terms of the Paraclete promise.

3.2.5 *The Spirit of prophecy*

We do the Prophecy an injustice if we think of its 'Paraclete' revelations only in terms of obsession with rigorous discipline, fasting and the like.[45] Such things, in any case, have been overestimated and looked at without regard for catholic parallels.[46] The Paraclete of the Montanists which Tertullian knew was innovative in its teaching, truthful and revealing in its interpretation of Scripture and demanded wholehearted discipleship. For him at least it was a bringer of much-needed revelation to the Church and was not seen as

a fussy and old-fashioned martinet, ministering to the anxieties of small, puritanical groups who felt that they lived on the edge of a very slippery slope.[47]

Tertullian's knowledge had come from Rome as well as Asia, I think, but in Asia Minor in particular the in-breaking of prophetism (in this case of the New Prophecy) would have been associated with the Paraclete (2.2.4 above). That accorded with the emphases of John's (Asian) Gospel. Prophetism and Paraclete went hand in hand and, with prophecy in decline, the sudden surge of activity could not but be associated in some minds with the promised Paraclete. So the lack of discussion of the Paraclete in Asian (as distinct from Roman) anti-Prophetic sources should not be taken to mean that the two came to be associated only in Rome. Rather the Paraclete scarcely figures in Asian sources because the conjunction of Paraclete and prophetism was taken for granted. Debate centred instead on form, function and criteria for testing the prophecies, so as to discredit them.

M.E. Boring's 1978 study of 'The Influence of Christian Prophecy on the Johannine Portrayal of the Paraclete and Jesus'[48] is of particular interest. Behind the portrayal of these two figures of revelation, said Boring, was the Christian prophetism of John's congregation. The Paraclete, he suggested, is the Holy Spirit whose presence is indicative of the rebirth of prophecy manifested in 'pneumatic Christian speech charisma',[49] which include prophetic speech, the conviction of hearers, teaching, bearing witness etc. (John 16:3–16; cf. 1 Cor. 14:24f).[50] The Paraclete is not 'in' believers, in mystical fashion, but rather in being μεθ᾽ ὑμῶν—παρ ὑμῖν and ἐν ὑμῖν (1 Cor. 14:16f.) it is in the midst, one of a group, like Jesus present amongst his disciples (cf. 1 Cor. 14:25 on prophecy in the congregation).[51] The Johannine Paraclete teaches, reminds, acts as guide and declares what is to come (John 15:26; 16:13), interpreting for the present the Christ event and the community tradition. It expands, as well as repeats, that tradition. We should think, therefore, of a function accorded to 'an identifiable group' in the Johannine community, exercising the Spirit's gifts on the community's behalf.[52] The Paraclete is the only link between the exalted Christ and the Church – part of a 'revelatory chain of command' (as in John 14:16: Father–Son–Paraclete–community–world).[53] It is both the Spirit which inspires prophecy and the power at work manifested in the Christian prophets of John's own community – Spirit and prophet as 'one functioning entity'.

Nowhere in his article did Boring mention Montanism. Nevertheless, his portrayal of the relationship between prophetic activity and the Johannine Paraclete is suggestive. If the New Prophecy *was* a revival of a prophetism which had been known in Asia Minor Christianity and which had itself coloured the portrayal of the Johannine Paraclete, then we do not have to look far for explanation of why the work of the Three and the activity of the Paraclète should have become linked. In Rome such an association may well have been less obvious and debate ensued.

Montanus, Priscilla and Maximilla, then, were Prophets for the community and functioned as Paraclete figures. They taught, expounded and expanded the tradition (see below 3.9), declared things to come (see 3.3 on eschatology), convicted hearers of wrongdoing or compromise (3.5–3.6) and stressed the need to bear witness (i.e. to be a μάρτυς, 3.8). They *were* immoderate, in the content of their message as in its delivery. These were not the weighed words of measured bishops but challenging and disturbing words from prophets – disturbing and agitating the populace (Eusebius *HE* v.16,8), producing grief or doubt (using a derivative of ταράσσω: cf. Matt. 2:3; 14:26; John 12:27; 13:21; Acts 15:24; Gal. 1:7).[54] For the Three παρακαλεῖν[55] meant speaking 'with almighty power in the name of God'. It was proclaiming the word in the power of the Holy Spirit.[56] This was Christian prophetism. Maximilla could be seen to function as a mouthpiece of the Paraclete precisely because in her came 'word and spirit and power' (Eusebius *HE* v.16,17; cf. 1 Cor. 2:4; 1 Thess. 1.5 and see 4.3.2 below). To associate such work with the Paraclete must have seemed as much a commonplace of *Asian* Christian tradition as the teaching of the fulfilment of Joel's prophecy or Paul's teaching on spiritual gifts or the apocalyptic emphases of the prophetic Seer.

But this was not understood everywhere. It was left to the debaters in Rome and those they influenced to develop a doctrine about the Paraclete which proved after centuries to be far removed from the Asia Minor revival of prophetism (5.4 below). Indeed, as early as Tertullian it was necessary to explain to some the relation between teaching about an age of the Paraclete and the tradition of the Church. The work of the Paraclete was not associated just with Montanus, as Hippolytus well knew (*Refut. omn. haer.* viii.19), and it is unfortunate that in his description of the Prophecy's beginnings Eusebius' statement about 'Montanus the Paraclete' (*HE* v.14) has misled many into assuming a heretical identification between the two.[57] The New Prophecy was just that. It was prophecy and it considered itself Christian. 'We too must receive the spiritual gifts', the Prophets said (Epiphanius *Pan.* xlviii.1). But the catholic side identified it as *false* prophecy – one which had not passed the test and which was demonic and deceiving and wrongly characterised by ecstasy (*Pan.* xlviii.2–3; xlviii.10,11).

Faced with the refusal to recognise them, the Prophets maintained that what they had been doing had been done before – by Agabus and Silas, Philip's daughters, Ammia and Quadratus.[58] When challenged that the manner of prophesying was innovative, they responded that

that was not so. The catholic leadership simply kept maintaining that the Prophecy was *false* prophecy (the Anonymous in *HE* v.16,8; cf. especially Matt. 7:15–23 and also *Didachē* xi; *Acts of Thomas* lxxix). Maximilla's saying about being pursued like a wolf from the sheep is a response to just such an accusation. The catholic leadership had been taken by surprise, I think, not least because the Prophets quickly gained a following which was not deterred by their babbling glossolalia and noise (*HE* v.16,7–8; v.16,12). The Anonymous found the church of Ancyra rife with it, babbling and babbled about (*HE* v.16,4).

3.3 ESCHATOLOGY

Most writers assume that Montanism featured a lively expectation of an imminent Parousia, apocalyptic speculation and chiliasm. In fact there is less evidence about Montanist eschatology than one might expect. I shall begin with chiliasm before moving to other evidence of apocalyptic speculation (3.3.1–3.3.2) and then turning to realised eschatology and Parousia (3.3.3–3.3.5).

3.3.1 Chiliasm

Christian chiliasm or millennialism is belief that for 1000 years Christ and his elect will reign on earth in an interim period between second Parousia and final judgement.[59] Yet as Charles Hill's study *Regnum Caelorum* has shown, this neat, indeed simplistic, definition is belied by the variety of so-called millennialist views: from 4 Ezra and 2 Baruch (which sources were echoed and modified in Christian writings); through Papias, Cerinthus, Justin, Irenaeus and Tertullian to Commodianus and Lactantius. Alongside these, and sometimes encountered in the same writers, are no less orthodox alternative views as well as clear amillennialism.[60]

The consensus view has been that Montanists, too, were chiliasts. Harnack believed that chiliasm was 'one of the principal issues involved', while F.C. Baur spoke of Montanist chiliastic 'Schwärmerei' and apocalyptic other-worldliness which was opposed to a growing secularism.[61] Chiliasm was taken to be characteristic of Asia Minor,[62] and the *innovatory* element in Montanist eschatology, it was argued, was simply its expectation that fulfilment of apocalyptic promises would be achieved *soon* and that the New Jerusalem of Revelation 21 would descend *at Pepuza*. This was the 'highly original' feature of Montanist eschatology.[63]

Are such claims true? Charles Hill has raised some pertinent objections,[64] based on his work studying eschatological expectation. He challenged the belief that chiliasm was indeed the norm among Christians and suggested the excesses of the Prophecy were not to be blamed for stimulating the decline of millennialism in the Church.[65] Some scholars are now more cautious when writing of the Prophecy's alleged chiliasm, it is true;[66] but Hill has gone further and suggests not only that the 'marriage' of Montanism and millennialism was something humanly contrived but that the two ought to be divorced.

Montanism's earliest opponents did not accuse it of chiliastic enthusiasm. No extant oracle speaks explicitly of chiliasm. Jerome and Eusebius, later critics of Montanism, were respectively an anti-millenarian and a critic of the allegedly unintelligent chiliast Papias. Neither condemned Montanism on such a ground, though, as Jerome conceded towards the end of his life, belief in a New Jerusalem understood in material terms had belonged to many a martyr and good believer (*Comm. in Ier.* xix.10). All things considered, 'we hear curiously little of any apocalyptic element in the Montanist doctrine', Knox admitted.[67]

Notwithstanding this silence, scholars have assumed that chiliasm was so much the norm among Christians that no one criticising or describing the Prophecy would have thought it worth a mention. The promise made in the Christophany to Priscilla or Quintilla is often taken as proof of chiliastic teaching.[68] It was said that Jerusalem would descend, though Epiphanius did not say clearly that the descent was *at* Pepuza. The ὧδε of *Pan.* xlix.1 is unclear. The apparition may have indicated, on the one hand, that *here* (Pepuza) will Jerusalem descend from heaven. On the other hand it may be *thus*, i.e. that the Christ figure itself is representative of that descent (cf. too 4.3.3–4.3.4). In addition the present infinitive may indicate either 'comes down' or 'will come down' in this context.[69]

There was more to this than Epiphanius has told us, but the expectation reflects the teaching of Revelation 21 – a notoriously troublesome chapter, for it is hard to discern the relation of chapter 21 to other promises in the book and in any case most Christian chiliasts, looking back to the Revelation, wrote of a glorified millennial Jerusalem *rebuilt*, rather than descending.[70] So, said Hill, the usual interpretation of this Christophany would in fact suggest something *unusual*, and 'The saying does not really furnish us with any trustworthy evidence of chiliasm at all.'

The leading roles played by women (as in the case above) have also bolstered writers' assumptions that the Prophecy was a millenarian movement. Parallels may be adduced with many other such movements in and on the fringes of Christianity, but it seems to me unsound to presuppose a necessary connection and to assume that in the context of millenarian fervour *alone* did Christians envisage female leadership. I shall pass, then, to Tertullian and return to the case Hill makes.

The Montanist Tertullian (*Adv. Marc.* iii.24) wrote of the heavenly Jerusalem descending for the millennium,[71] an event prefigured in a vision seen in Judea. Such prefiguration had been promised in the New Prophecy. The future manifestation of the heavenly Jerusalem was certainly a widespread Christian expectation and Tertullian did not say that the Prophets had promised its imminent descent. In *De res. mort.* xxvi (cf. *Adv. Marc.* iii.24,1) he had warned against materialistic interpretations of the millennium; there he preferred to allegorise (cf. (i) Hippolytus *Comm. Dan.* iv.23; iv.10 and (ii) Eusebius' criticism of Papias). So on the basis of *Adv. Marc.* iii.24, Hill maintains that by associating the city with the millennium Tertullian was departing from the view of Irenaeus his mentor on such matters and was fusing Irenaeus' millennialism with 'Montanism's non millennial expectation of the eternal Jerusalem's descent to earth at some time in the near future.' Hence Tertullian was responsible for the 'marriage' of the two. Either the Montanist expectation of the descent of the heavenly Jerusalem *was* chiliastic (and based on a *misunderstanding* of Rev. 3:12; 21:2 and 10 and the whole chiliastic tradition, Hill says) or its a concern is not the beginning of an earthly millennium at all 'but rather the beginning of eternity, as in the book of Revelation'. If this latter interpretation applies, then Montanus' own receipt of the Paraclete revelation would be the beginning of that thousand years referred to in Revelation 20.

Is Tertullian being a 'rogue' Montanist in *Adv. Marc.*, espousing a chiliasm additional to 'mainstream' New Prophets' beliefs? Or might he be recording faithfully an account (of Jerusalem and the millennium) he has received which might suggest that the 'misunderstanding' of Revelation 21 was a reality among some Christians? The latter option seems just as plausible to me.

In Cappadocia an unnamed third-century ecstatic prophetess (probably Montanist, I shall argue in 4.4.1) declared that Jerusalem of Judea was her real home and she urged others to go there (Cyprian

Ep. lxxv).[72] The account may indicate that for Montanists, Tertullian included, *Judea* was indeed expected to be the place where God's promises would be made manifest, though the time of their consummation was not known. If this were so, what of the vision to Priscilla–Quintilla about Pepuza/Jerusalem?

3.3.2 *Montanism and the millennium*

Critics have puzzled over the fact that Tertullian seemingly knew nothing of the descent of Jerusalem at Pepuza (if that was what the revelation meant).[73] Perhaps it was absent from his collection of Montanist revelations. Perhaps he chose to ignore it. Possibly the vision has no authenticity, though the consensus of scholarship on Montanism continues to treat it as reliable. My own preferred explanation for his silence is different. The vision, I suggest, *post-dated* Tertullian's writings, because it was granted to Quintilla rather than to Priscilla. Quintilla, I shall suggest (4.3.3), did not belong to the first era of the Prophecy, though the Quintillianist branch of the Prophecy (probably a third-century development) traced from her the literalistic, prophetic interpretation of Revelation 21 as applied to the region of Pepuza.[74] It had not been part of the earliest Prophetic teaching and so was not part of Tertullian's thinking either.

Did Tertullian introduce an element alien to the Prophecy? Details of the Prophets' chiliasm are admittedly hard to come by; but given that both the Revelation and 4 Ezra were known in the Prophets' circle, then (the evidence of Tertullian's knowledge apart) familiarity with teaching about a millennium may be assumed. The relation of this to the *Jerusalem* visions is more problematic, however. Another North African source suggests Montanists valued Johannine material relating to the millennium – Augustine described Montanist loyalists pricking infants with needles (*Haer.* xxvi). If a child died following such an operation, he recorded, it was classed as a martyr. If it lived, it would be a priest of significance. The ritual was perhaps baptismal scarring or tattooing,[75] and related to the bearing of *names* or marks, so as to indicate the elect versus those who are loyal to the Beast (*Rev.* 3:12 (to Philadelphia); 13:1) 6, 16f.; 14:1, 9ff.; 16:2; 19:20; 20:4; 22:4). In the Apocalypse such marks figure on forehead and right hand[76] and Epiphanius, who mentions the same phenomenon, does tell us that (in the rites of the Tascodrougites (or perhaps Quintillians), Priscillians and Pepuzians) these were rites of 'mysteries of the name of Christ' (*Pan.* xlviii.14–15). Augustine has surely preserved a garbled version of a rite to be explained in terms of Revelation 20:4, where those who have stood fast, prepared even for *martyrdom*, will return to reign *as priests* with Christ *for one thousand years*.[77] But Jerusalem does not figure in these Patristic accounts.

Hippolytus, who defended the Apocalypse and the Fourth Gospel, wrote against the anti-Montanist Gaius.[78] We know something of his stance from material preserved by the later Dionysius bar Salibi in his commentary on the Revelation. This tells us that Gaius was hostile to the Apocalypse and dismissive of its plagues, locusts, establishment of a kingdom and binding of Satan *for one thousand years* (*Rev.* 8:8; 9:2f. and 21:2f.). Such things, I think, had appeared in the first Prophets' timetable of promised events before the End (see 1.3.7; 3.3.4). So Gaius went to some lengths to discredit the source, ascribing it to Cerinthus and associating it with sensual pleasures (Eusebius *HE* iii.28,1). Presumably his discussions with the early Prophets *had* included their expounding upon the millennium.

The New Prophecy, I feel certain, was part of that Christianity in which figured visions of heaven (3.2.1), ascent to encounter the Lord (Theodotus and the *Pass. Perp.* iv) and hope of millennial reign with the Redeemer. That much we have some evidence for. In such circles in time past (prior to the Prophecy proper) angelology would also have been important, but there is no evidence of this in our sources. The Apocalypse shows that veneration of angels had ceased to be acceptable (*Rev.* 19:10; 22:8f.).[79] When looked at dispassionately, the sources for the Prophecy/Montanism do not suggest an excess of apocalyptic fervour. Yet in that respect, as in others, its fanaticism has continued to be assumed.

3.3.3 Jerusalem of earth and heaven

It is safe at least to say that *Jerusalem* was of concern to the Prophets, even though we know tantalisingly little about their expectation of Jerusalem's descent or their perception of the relation of that descent to a millennial hope. Montanus gave the name 'Jerusalem' to the towns of Pepuza and Tymion,[80] and (see 3.4–3.7) the Prophets seemed to be trying to ensure in those places a purity of life and fervour of belief such as would characterise the Jerusalem of promise. There is nothing in the early sources to suggest that the name 'Jerusalem' was adopted because its descent was expected at the site(s) of Pepuza and Tymion. Eusebius, suspicious of chiliasts, offered no such comment.

In my view Revelation 3 (the letter to Philadelphia) is of as much significance for understanding the Prophets' relation to Jerusalem as is Revelation 21. In the 'Jerusalem' Prophetic communities (prefigured in Revelation 3) Christians were called on to 'hold fast' and not to deny the Name (Revelation 3:8 and 11). The name of God's city and of God himself would be written on them (3:12) and Christ had promised to 'come quickly'. Jerusalem in Revelation 3 was as much people as place.[81] Similarly it was the Prophetic *people* of Pepuza, Tymion and other such 'Jerusalem' communities, and their quality of discipleship, that mattered.

Does this point to an eschatology more realised than the norm for Christians? Powell thought so (disagreeing with Labriolle) and I agree. Jerusalem was the name *already* given to Pepuza and that led to the expectation of the descent there (and not vice versa).[82] Christ's message to Quintilla that 'this place is holy' was a reminiscence of Jacob's naming of Bethel in Genesis 28 (cf. Perpetua's vision of the ladder between heaven and earth in the *Passio*). It showed Pepuza/Tymion to be a kind of Montanist Bethel.[83] So the heavenly Jerusalem was present already 'to those whose eyes were opened', said Powell, and (assuming that the *apokalypsis* granted to Quintilla was that 'here [or "thus"] Jerusalem comes down from heaven')

we have an eschatology radically different from the apocalyptic futurism usually ascribed to the Montanists – an eschatology largely realised in a present spiritual experience.[84]

It is my belief, of course, that Quintilla received that particular vision in the *third* century – confirming and expanding upon an existing understanding of community experience and hope. The 'shift' from a primarily futuristic to a more realised eschatology may have occurred quite early in the Prophecy's history, though as time progressed (and promises were not immediately fulfilled) its advantages would have become apparent.

3.3.4 Parousia expectation

What of Christ's second coming and the associated signs? It is probable that the first Prophets had pointed to signs of the times and in the second century there was still a lively expectation of the return of Christ. The *Epistula Apostolorum* asked 'how long O Lord?' and answered that the Parousia would be in the second half of the century.[85] Even Ignatius of Antioch, seemingly more concerned about his personal eschaton than about that of Christians in general, declared (pre-111 CE) 'these are the last times' (*Eph.* xi,1). The occasional foolish Syrian bishop led out his congregation to the wilderness to encounter Christ (Hippolytus *Commentary on Daniel* iii.18), and one in Pontus convinced his people that soon Christ would come as judge. His flock abandoned its work and sold its goods (*Comm. Dan.* iii.19): he told them, 'if this Parousia does not occur as I have said, then no longer believe the Scripture but let each one do as he will'.[86] Judas, exegete of Daniel, ceased his reckonings at *c.* 202 CE (Eusebius *HE* vi.7) and Christians of the second and early third centuries still prayed for the Parousia to be delayed – a prayer which indicates that the imminence of the event could not be ruled out.[87] The Prophets lived in this atmosphere, familiar with the Gospels' and Revelation's promissory language of the Lord's 'coming'.[88]

Maximilla said that after her there would be no further prophet (or prophetess, according to some MSS, a reading Labriolle accepts). Instead there would be the End (συντέλεια *Pan.* xlviii.2,4; cf. Matt. 13:39–49; 24:3; Mark 13:4; Heb. 9:26). Her predictions of warfare and anarchy had not come true by the time the Anonymous wrote (*HE* v.16,18) but they suggest references to the signs preceding the End or the Lord's return, as found for example in Matthew 24:6 and its parallels, Mark 13:7 and especially Luke 21:9. Maximilla, it would seem, was doing some eschatological timetabling. Such things, after all, were commonplaces of apocalyptic speculation, as we see also in 4 Ezra 9:3f., or the Christian 6 Ezra, Asian in provenance (15:5, 11; 16:22,29). Speaking of 'the things to come' was the work of the Paraclete as described in John 16:13f. (see 3.2.5 above). This may indeed have promoted the identification of the Prophets' work with that of the Paraclete. In any case Maximilla's words provided a useful weapon for the catholics.

I suspect, too, that the Prophets provided vivid descriptions of future joys for some and the pains of hell for others. The suggestion is speculative but the *Apocalypse of Peter* abounds with such description and Germanus, eigth-century patriarch of Constantinople, writing to Antimus the deacon (*Ad Antimum* v), claimed not only that Montanists refused penance for post-baptismal sin and refused fellowship to digamists (cf. Tertullian, 3.5.4 below) but that they also believed in eight heavens in the age to come, fire-breathing dragons and lions. The unrighteous would suffer their fire and suspension by the flesh.

All this is reminiscent of the *Apocalypse of Peter* (vii; xi (Ethiopic);

xxii; xxiv (Greek Akhmim fragment)), with its suspensions, fire and
flesh-devouring beasts (viii (Ethiopic, not in Akhmim) *et passim*),
images of lions, reptiles and so on (xxxii (Ethiopic, not Akhmim)).
Montanists would surely have liked this *Apocalypse*, given its strong
condemnation of pre-marital unchastity (*Ap. Peter* xi (Ethiopic)) and
of adulterers (vii; cf. Akhmim fragment xxiv). For, according to
Montanists (so Germanus claimed), those born of fornication or
adultery would suffer judgement. Again we should compare the
Apocalypse of Peter in which (viii (Ethiopic) and xxvi (Akhmim)) those
who had been aborted and were the offspring of unmarried mothers
appeared weeping and punishing their parents at the pit of
excretions.[89]

The *Apocalypse of Peter* is a product of the second century; indebted
to 4 Ezra and 2 Peter; alluded to by Theophilus of Antioch in the
180s; known by Clement of Alexandria (who believed it was by the
apostle Peter: Eusebius *HE* vi.14,1) and dated *c.* 135 CE by Weinel
and Maurer. Its provenance may have been Egypt. Given the present
state of the evidence, we can do no more than speculate that such
ideas circulated among the first Prophets too; but I think it is
probable. The New Testament Apocalypse, which was certainly
known to them, concentrated on the triumph of the Lamb rather
than on the finer details of the fate of the damned, and Germanus is a
late source who may be reflecting only the tendencies of a later
Montanism. Yet, even so, his evidence would indicate that interest in
apocalyptic literature had not waned among them.

We are on firmer ground with the oracles of Maximilla which do
seem to point to eschatological timetabling. Maximilla described
herself as the interpreter of 'this suffering' (πόνος; Epiphanius *Pan.*
xlviii.13,1; Aland no. 15, see too 4.3.2 below). The word is rare in the
New Testament but it appears in Revelation 16:10f. and in
Revelation 21:4, where it tells of the abolition of suffering, come the
establishment of new heaven and new earth (cf., too, in eschatological
setting in LXX Isa. 66:7, and against Jerusalem in Jer. 4:15). Part of
Maximilla's role, as here described, would have been to expound the
relation between the suffering of the righteous and the intervention
of God to redeem them. These were matters closely associated in
Jewish and early Christian thought. For the 'promise' (ἐπαγγελία)
of this oracle may be compared the great 'promises' (*HE* v.16,9)
which the Spirit in the Prophecy made at the outset to those of its
own community. They induced an undue pride, the Anonymous
reported, and for Klawiter they concerned the eternal glory to be

shared (also citing Montanus' oracle in Epiphanius *Pan.* xlviii.10,3; Aland no. 6; cf. Matt. 13:40–3).[90]

3.3.5 *Findings*

So what can be said about eschatology and the New Prophecy? Belief in the Lord's return was alive and commonplace amongst second-century Christians; it was surely to be expected among the Prophets too, though our sources provide surprisingly little explicit evidence of it and not enough to claim that its Parousia hope was the *cause* of what has been seen as the Prophecy's legalism and its separatism.[91] Nor can it be shown that they thought the Parousia was *imminent*. The Prophets' oracles tell of a number of ways in which the loyalist might die (see 3.8 below), but they make no reference to the Parousia overtaking the faithful. We must be cautious in estimating the fervour of such a hope. Nor is there cause to alter this assessment if we look to Tertullian.

Tertullian pre-conversion and Tertullian the Montanist accepted the Lord's second coming as a 'given'. While *De spect.* xxix.3; xxx.1f. suggest that in his view the second coming of the Lord was not far off (cf. *De exhort. cast.* vi.1f.; ix.5; *De monog.* vii.4; xvi.4f.) only in *De paen.* i.3 is the impression given that it is imminent. As de Clercq noted, there is no acute yearning for the Lord's return in his work (*De orat.* v.4 apart, perhaps).[92] Tertullian is more concerned with the idea of judgement and with a quality of life which brings readiness for the End. He has little interest in eschatological timetables. The things of the eschaton were not imminent for him. Indeed, in *De anima* xxxiii.11; *De res. mort.* xxii.2; xxiv.7 and elsewhere he refers back to the familiar New Testament warnings found in Matthew 24:36, 1 Thessalonians 4–5 and 2 Thessalonians 2. What should be deduced from this? Either Tertullian's lack of concern was untypical of Montanists and he was ignoring the details of the end times *as Montanists analysed them* or else such timetables did not loom as large in the Montanist scheme as we have been led to believe.

I do not doubt that the Prophets were interested in 'the things to come' nor that they were certain Christ *would* return and that some time the Jerusalem of promise *would* appear. But, meanwhile, there was Christian life to be considered in their own 'Jerusalem' communities, in which a foretaste of God's promises could be known. There were mysteries to be revealed, encounters with the divine to be disclosed, teachings to be mediated to the Prophetic faithful, discipline to be ensured. This had been the work of the Prophets, the Three and their associates, and it could not cease entirely after their demise.

I believe that chronologically the Prophecy emerged and grew at a time conducive to speculation about the eschaton. Nevertheless we are ignorant of most of the details and without the evidence to say that here was a community in which eschatological fervour explains all. This was not something referred to by its earliest opponents. The fact is, there have been too many over-confident assessments, too much conflation of sources to provide neat summaries or an amalgam which strays from the facts or reconstructs them imaginatively. Take Cohn in *The Pursuit of the Millennium*:

The Montanists accordingly summoned all Christians to Phrygia, there to await the Second Coming, in fasting and prayer and bitter repentance.

Never are we told explicitly that the first Prophets expected an imminent return of Christ, and we are not told until Quintilla's vision that he, or the Jerusalem of promise, was expected at Pepuza. Moreover, it is not clear *either* that Montanus wanted a single, Pepuza-based assembly (Eusebius *HE* v.18,2) *or* that the purpose of the gatherings he inaugurated was to await the Parousia. On the contrary, Montanus and his associates seem to have been organising for more than a very short life for the groups, arranging salaries and collections. 'Oddly enough', Frend wrote in *Martyrdom and Persecution* (p. 292), 'for so eschatological a community, they seem to have had a full-time financial officer'. The oddity, I think, has lain in overemphasis of the Prophecy's eschatological fervour. As for their fasting, this too did not go much beyond what catholics did, as we shall see (3.4).

And what of G.L. Bray's description of preparation for the imminent descent of the Seer's New Jerusalem at Pepuza, 'scheduled for the year 177' and accompanied by the abandonment of families and belongings? This is surely wide of the mark.[93]

Powell's suggestion appeals to me:

We must ask, therefore, whether the New Prophecy, in its original form, did more than share general late second century beliefs concerning the eventual descent of the New Jerusalem at a parousia expected but not imminent, for which martyrdom provided the antecedent tribulation.[94]

At least it is difficult to move much beyond that, without straining the evidence. What was being promoted in the Jerusalem communities of Pepuza and Tymion was a *quality* of Christian discipleship which certainly involved some rigour beyond the catholic requirements and which asked for readiness to face suffering and martyrdom rather than to contemplate compromise with a hostile world. The communities' self-understanding had been influenced by the world-view of apocalyptic. Their beliefs and practices were fed by the pronouncements of the chief Prophets. The details of their expectation are hidden from us. When we try to reconstruct the New Prophecy of the first generations it is as well to acknowledge how little we know.

3.4 FASTING AND FEASTING IN THE PROPHECY

3.4.1 The prevailing interpretation

Second- and third-century catholic writers, Tertullian and the extant oracles of Montanus, Priscilla and Maximilla all commented on three things about the Prophecy: fasting, marriage versus sexual continence and the withholding of forgiveness. Hence it has been claimed that Prophetic communities were rigidly ascetic, legalistic as well as pneumatic, their rigour the product of apocalyptic–millenarian hope. As was the case with claims for rampant millenarianism, this impression is probably misleading. On the one hand Apollonius did blame (the now dead) Montanus for enacting fasts and for sanctioning the annulment of marriages. But on the other hand he wrote of a group in which 'gluttony' triumphed as offerings poured in and salaries were paid to those (including the unnamed 'prophetess') who propagated the teaching (*HE*; v.18,1–2,4,7,11). There was love of ornament, theft, revelry, the practice of usury and the acceptance of gifts, so he claimed, and there had even been a Prophet with painted eyes and dyed hair – more like something out of Phrygian paganism. Tertullian would have disapproved (cf. *De cult. fem.* v–vi; viii).

Even allowing for exaggeration and lies, such things do not speak of a community of avid ascetics, insistence on community of goods (as Bonwetsch suggested) or determined cleansing of the elect before the advent of the Day of the Lord, *pace* those who have taken Montanism to be the supreme example of ascetic practice twinned with eschatological fervour and prophetism.[95] My examination of various aspects of Prophetic discipline will begin with fasting.

3.4.2 Fasting in the Roman Prophecy

The evidence comes from a number of areas. Hippolytus in Rome told of Prophetic eating of 'cabbage', or perhaps radishes (ῥαφανοφαγία), writing with as much dismissiveness of such plants as the average small child. They practised dry fasting (xerophagy) and there were new fasts and festivals among them (*Refut. omn. haer.* viii.19; cf. x.25: cf. Tertullian *De jej.* i and xiii; *De monog.* xv), even fasts on the Lord's day and the Sabbath, he said, if a vision had required it (cf. *Comm. Dan.* iv.20). Priscilla and Maximilla had propagated the novelties (cf. Apollonius in Eusebius *HE* v.18,2).[96] Such things were not peculiarly *Roman* Prophets' practice.[97]

3.4.3 Tertullian and fasting

In *Africa* Tertullian tells us a great deal. He was well disposed to fasting and linked the Prophets' innovations with revelations to Montanus, Prisca and Maximilla (De jej. i). Like Prisca herself (*De exhort. cast.* x.5, Aland no. 11) Tertullian saw a relation between sexual abstinence, holiness and the receipt of visions, dreams and private revelations (cf. *De jej.* xii.1; *De anima* xlviii). Prisca's *purificantia* may have intended reference to fasting as well as sexuality (4.3.4 below) and in *De jej.* ix.1 Tertullian associated xerophagy with the receipt of secrets – Daniel too had eaten pulses!

Nevertheless, Tertullian saw the self-abasement and sobriety of fasting as ends in themselves rather than primarily means to visions. Sins decreased, he said, and the believer was prepared for the rigours of the prison and the final conflict (*De jej.* xii.1f.). Fast, 'lest perhaps tomorrow we die' (*De jej.* xvii.5f.). Fat Christians pleased the lion and the bear (*De jej.* xvii.9), but God was more pleased with the slender, who passed more readily through salvation's narrow gate. Being lighter, the slender Christian would rise faster! In *De jej.* xii.3 he defended his stance with characteristic vigour and probably exaggeration.

'Psychics' were averse to discipline, Tertullian maintained, seasoning his accusations with scurrilous rumour. There had been one catholic 'martyr', a stranger to 'discipline', who was so intoxicated, overfed and indebted to the visiting catholics' 'cookshop' mentality (cf. *De pudic.* xxii.1) that he was anaesthetised from the attentions of the torturer. Incoherent, he had died without actual apostasy.

Tertullian approved of the Paraclete's reforms on the discipline front, and we learn details only from him (*De virg. vel.* i.5; 8; *De res. mort.* xi; *De monog.* ii.1, 4; ii.1,10 (contrast ii.1,11); *De jej.* ii; xv; *De pudic.* i; *De exhort. cast.* vi.2). He insisted, nevertheless, that in essentials the Prophecy had brought no novelty.[98] Indeed, his accounts suggest that the Paraclete had not been particularly burdensome in its demands. There were two weeks of xerophagy prescribed, Sabbaths and the Lord's day excepted (*De jej.* xv), but gratification was *deferred* not forbidden *in toto*. Food, after all, was necessary for life (*De anima* xxxviii.3), Tertullian acknowledged, and in terms of some of the fasting the Prophets simply made *obligatory* what catholics themselves allowed as a matter of choice. In fact, said Tertullian, the discipline of the Prophecy was a *via media* between the self-gratification of the catholic 'psychics' and the wrong-headed (Gnostic or Encratite) despising of the gifts of God (cf. *De monog.* i.1; xv.1–3; Eusebius *HE* v.3,2–3 [martyrs of Lyons]). I shall return to Tertullian in due course, for further details of this discipline. The fact that our details *are* from him poses a problem, of course. Can we be sure that such fasting, xerophagy etc. had been associated with the original Asia Minor Prophecy?

3.4.4 Fasting in the Asia Minor Prophecy

We lack details of the xerophagies and other fasts among the *Asia Minor* Prophets but it is reasonable to assume that they did exist in some form, as Apollonius suggested. The first generations of Prophets were not extreme ascetics – one of the accusations against them had been of revelling with guests at table (συνεστιᾶται, Eusebius *HE* v.18,6). But the kinds of practices described by Tertullian and Hippolytus are not without parallel in the kinds of sources to which the Prophets liked to refer. A good example is 4 Ezra.

The author of 4 Ezra tells of the eating of vegetable food (and indeed 'flowers'), fasts of varying severity and lengths of time, abstention from meat and wine. This is not so much because of ascetic ideas about the need to purify the body as it is 'technical preparation for a vision experience'.[99] We might compare Daniel 10:2f. especially, for Daniel, too, in three weeks of mourning (as Ezra mourned) 'ate no delicacies, no meat or wine entered my mouth, nor did I anoint myself at all'. As a document 4 Ezra had undergone Christian revision in Asia, I think,[100] and we see that fasting is associated with apocalyptic revelation. The sight of the New Jerusalem came after Ezra had been told to *refrain* from fasting fully and instead to eat only vegetable food (as the Prophets did at times). So the New Prophets' concern about fasting fits an existing apocalyptic literary pattern.

In any case, most Christians knew that hunger was an aid to dreams. Fasting and revelation are linked (e.g., in *Didachē* viii.1;

Hermas *Visiones* ii.1; ii.1,2; ii.10,6–7 (linking humility, fasting and receipt of visions); v.1; *Similitudines* v.1,1; v.2; v.3) and most of Hermas' visions had come to him through prayer and fasting. Beyond Christianity Galen and his contemporaries knew of a positive relationship between sensitivity to the supernatural, on the one hand, and a dry diet or dry fasts, on the other. Even avoidance of the bath had its advantages: keeping water from the surface of the body brought a crisp lightness to the individual (Galen *In Hipp. praed.* i.5; cf. Tertullian *De jej.* i.4). The Greek world knew all about the benefits of fasting to would-be prophets and prophetesses as well as to visitors to shrines and oracles.[101] Christians were no less well informed. The Prophetic fasts and xerophagies were condemned, however. Obviously this was not because fasting was considered a bad thing *per se* in catholic circles. The problem was one of innovation.

3.4.5 *The accusations of innovation*

Montanism became fragmented and varied and its practice did change as time went on; this was due no doubt to local factors and perhaps to the visions and revelations in churches which would bring a new day of fast or some other modification. Yet at times and in some places Montanists seemed *less* rigorous than the Christians round about them, in terms of fasting at least.[102] At the outset it had been Prophetic *novelty* and increased rigour which was condemned. Once more we have to rely on Tertullian for the details.

We learn that the Prophets prolonged recognised 'stations'[103] by a few hours until the evening (cf. *De jej.* i.10; x.1f.; Philo on the fasts of the Therapeutae, *De vita cont.* i; iv) and that they had introduced the two weeks of xerophagy already mentioned, in which succulent foods, wine and juicy fruit were eschewed. They avoided the bath at such times (*De jej.* i.4; ii.1ff.; xv.2). Xerophagy seems to have been new to Tertullian's audience and unacceptable to Africa's catholic clergy (see especially *De jej.* ii and ix), for he had to appeal to some rather unconvincing precedents in Scripture to defend it. If Tertullian was being strictly honest about these innovations, they seem insufficient to merit either the catholics' ire or their accusations not just of pseudo-prophecy but of heresy (*De jej.* xi).[104] At first sight it is hard to see what the fuss was about. But of course 'revelation' from a group considered *pseudo*-prophetic would be suspect and the issue of fasts was one of a number which related to the wider question of the role of the Paraclete in continuing revelation. Also these new fasts were *obligatory*:

hence they would have called into question catholic clergy's discretion on imposition (cf. *De jej.* xiii). Nor would catholics have liked the reminder that their objections to the Prophecy were based, not on issues of wrong doctrine (wrong doctrine preceded wrong discipline, Tertullian thought, but the Prophets were innocent) but on reaction to a discipline stricter than their own (*De jej.* i.3).

3.5 FORNICATION, CELIBACY AND MARRIAGE

3.5.1 An intemperate temperance
Asia Minor, especially Phrygia, was a good place for a movement strict in its view of sexual continence. Let us begin with the Christian Socrates:

The race of the Phrygians appear to be more temperate than other races, for seldom do they swear. The Scythians and the Thracians are naturally of a very irritable disposition (and) those who inhabit the East are addicted to sensual pleasures. However, the Paphlagonians and the Phrygians are not given over to either of these vices, nor are the sports of the circus or theatrical exhibitions now wanted among them. It seems to me that for this cause these people gave assent readily to the epistles written by Novatus [Novatian]. Among them fornication is considered the grossest crime (*HE* iv.28).

Temperance was not a word used of the Asian Prophets. They were accused of extremism and hypocrisy. Montanus, it was said, allowed annulment of marriage (Eusebius *HE* v.18,2) – and Priscilla and Maximilla were the first women (among the Prophets) to desert their husbands (*HE* v.18,3).[105] We do not know whether their husbands had been Christians (1 Cor. 7:11, 13f.; cf. Hermas *Man.* iv.1,8). Then Priscilla (reported Apollonius with derision) was accorded the title 'virgin' (*HE* v.18,3). The same is not said of Maximilla. Perhaps she was, too, but her situation did not leave her open to accusation. Was Priscilla simply given a title of courtesy indicating dedicated celibacy whereas Maximilla was known to have had a 'spiritual marriage'? (cf. 1 Cor. 7:26ff.). Whatever the truth, it seems that the Prophecy could 'loose' and 'bind' (Matt. 16:19; 18:18) in respect of marriages.

There was no precedent in Paul's teaching in 1 Corinthians 7:27 and neither Tertullian nor Hippolytus wrote of such annulments. Tertullian would not have found the teaching congenial, for despite his reservations he supported the rightness of marriage. It was heretics who did not. Tertullian may have chosen to ignore it and perhaps the

separation of partners was countenanced more easily in Asia Minor
because of the history of Christianity there. Most probable of all, in
my opinion, is that Montanus' 'annulments' were not intended as an
edict for all and Priscilla and Maximilla (with special vocations) may
have been the only recipients.

We know that there *was* dedicated virginity among some Montanists
(Epiphanius' prophesying Quintillianist virgins being one example)
but also there were marriage and children. This was certainly so
among Prophets in Tertullian's Carthage, where the martyrs Perpetua
and Felicitas were mothers (4.5 below). Moreover, the later epigraphy
from Asia does not suggest that Montanist communities were made
up of celibates (5.13). If, as some posit, the first Prophets were living
in a state of heightened, almost frenzied, expectation of the End, there
is nothing in our sources to suggest that they responded to this by
recourse to unbending sexual or other asceticism. No more had Paul
(1 Cor. 7). I think it was not so: it was more a case of building and
preserving a right kind of 'Jerusalem' community – and the rule was
'horses for courses', within clear-cut boundaries of course. Again,
Paul had taken the same line. Celibacy may have been preferable but
marriage was to be honoured.

3.5.2 Catholic practice
How great an innovation was this? Again, the answer must be not
very. Some second-century Christians already maintained a life even
of married celibacy (Hermas *Man.* ii.2,3; ii.3,1; iv.1,1) or avoided
marriage as a superior option. Women of the apocryphal *Acts*
abandoned family life,[106] and the normally level-headed Justin
Martyr wrote without disdain of the Christian man in Alexandria
who tried, in spite of the laws, to find a sympathetic surgeon to
castrate him (*1 Apol.* xxix; *Dial.* xlviii.8). The 'Assyrian' Tatian,
formerly Justin's pupil (Eusebius *HE* iv.19,1), and much more of a
hard-liner in many respects, brought from Rome an Encratite
denunciation of marriage and all sexual relations (cf. Epiphanius *Pan.*
xlviii.1) and in Asia Minor Melito of Sardis was described as a eunuch
(Eusebius *HE* v.24,5). Hippolytus could write of eunuch priests in
Rome too, such as Hyacinthus (*Refut. omn. haer.* ix.12,10). 'Eunuchs
for the kingdom of heaven' were known to the author of Matthew's
Gospel (19:12) and there were men who lived wholly 'in the Spirit'
(*HE* v.24,5; iii. 21,3), just as did the daughter of Philip.

Dionysius of Corinth kept up an extensive correspondence with catholic churches in the 170s, much of it about encratism in orthodox congregations (Eusebius *HE* iv.23,6). He urged bishop Pinytos of Cnossus not to make compulsory a heavy burden (βαρύς cf. Matt. 11:30) where ἁγνεία was concerned (*HE* v.23, 7–8), and Pinytos responded with formal courtesy and the request that at some future time Dionysius would feed his congregation more solid food! Even remarriage after widowhood, so abhorrent to the Montanist Tertullian, was disliked by other Christians too (Athenagoras *Legatio* xxxiii; cf. 1 Cor. 7:39f.; 1 Tim. 2:3; Hermas *Man.* iv.4,1 and Clement Strom. iii.12.82.3).[107]

Thus, the danger of wrongly directed ascetic practice apart (i.e. the fear of Gnosticism and full-blown Encratism), there must have been many catholics in the decades of Montanism's rise who were not averse to the emphases on virginity, discipleship free of obligations to a spouse or refusal of remarriage (cf. too Rev. 14:1–4;[108] Matt. 22:30 and especially Luke 20: 35f.;[109] the prophetess Anna in Luke's Gospel and Tertullian's appeal to the example of Judith in *De monog.* xvii). Paul, of course, had wished that Christians, both unmarried and widows, might be as continent as he was himself (1 Cor. 7:1,7–8).

3.5.3 Women and the marriage market

The move in the direction of sexual continence was understandable, especially where women were concerned. It offered freedom from childbearing and its attendant dangers, and in any case there must have been a shortage of Christian men, as well as early widowhood among girls married young to men older than themselves. Mutual female support was necessary and sanctified celibacy followed.[110] In fact the oversight of Christian marriage must have been a minefield for church leaders.

Ignatius of Antioch had advocated some kind of episcopal control of marriages in Smyrna, while allowing continence to those who could embrace it in the right spirit (*Pol.* v). A century later in Rome Callistus was faced with what was probably the dilemma of an excess of well-born Christian women. Marriages to (albeit Christian) men of lower status would have created social and legal disadvantages. Sanctioned concubinage with a Christian partner might be an answer. Hippolytus disliked Callistus with a vengeance! Hot-headed alleged former slave who was Monarchian in doctrine (Hippolytus *Refut. omn. haer.* x.27,3f.), willing to tolerate former schismatics without penance and even thrice-married clergy, Callistus is readily dismissible as 'a sordid character with a suspect past' (albeit 'a skilled administrator' whose reputation may have suffered from 'salacious exaggeration').[111] The fact is, of course, that problems with penance and marriage were real in churches and solutions varied from community to community, though Callistus' liberal approach was untypical (*Refut. omn. haer.* ix.12.22f.; cf. Tertullian *De pud.* i).[112] Tertullian himself was well aware of women's failure to find 'suitable' partners. In his experience Christian women (mistakenly, of course) would opt for a (well-born) slave of the devil and would shun Christian men of low degree. There were few wealthy men to be found in the churches, he averred – those who were were married already! (II *Ad uxor.* viii). For Tertullian dedicated virginity was an answer surely preferable to exogamy. Indeed it was the ideal. But that did not imply condemnation of marriage (cf. I *Ad uxor.* ii–iii and II *Ad uxor.* vii.7ff.).

The Paraclete, said Tertullian, had preached a *single* marriage (cf. *De monog.* iii.1f.) and not abstention (ii.8,10). As in the case of fasting (3.4 above) and as with willingness to die for the Name (discussed in 3.8 below), the Prophets' teaching about sex and marriage suggests that the gap between them and catholic Christians was in many respects narrow. Tertullian, with an axe to grind on matters of discipline and hence good cause to portray the teaching of the Paraclete as demanding, offers us nothing which points to extremes of asceticism. Given the Prophecy's recognition of marriage, however, what is to be made of Tertullian's hearty dislike of *re*marriage (digamy)? Was this something he had taken from the Prophecy itself?

3.5.4 Digamy

If the original New Prophecy had outlawed remarriage then it came as music to Tertullian's ears and probably bolstered a distaste for remarriage which he had harboured for some time. Tertullian had trawled for Jewish scriptural, Christian and pagan precedents for arguing the rejection of remarriage and he used them in both pre-Montanist and Montanist writings (I *Ad uxor.* vi–vii; *De exhort. cast.* viii.1f; xiii.1f.; *De monog.* xvii):[113]

Marriage, as we have seen, was allowable in Tertullian's thinking but it was a second-best option nevertheless. Marriage dulled the spiritual faculties (*De exhort. cast.* x), a view implied even in *De monog.* iii.10, where Tertullian defended the 'comforter' Paraclete's teaching which allowed marriage. Of course marriage was instituted by God and could not be evil (cf. I *Ad uxor.* ii–iii) but the principal sanctity belonged to virgins (*De exhort. cast.* x; cf. I *Ad uxor.* i,viii; *De virg. vel.* x). To opt for marriage was to compromise with the flesh.

Remarriage (digamy) was uncompromisingly rejected, in accordance with a precept of the Holy Spirit (according to Tertullian's exegesis of I Cor. 7).[114] Digamy, after all, was not allowed to the clergy. Presbyters were chosen from among the laity. So to be in a state of (monogamous) preparation was incumbent on the laity. *Everyone*, in case of necessity, should be in a right state to perform sacramental acts (*De exhort. cast.* vii; cf. his observations in *De monog.* xii). Then I Corinthians 7 was ransacked for arguments in the debate on virginity, marriage and remarriage (cf. *De monog.* iii; xi;[115] I *Ad uxor.* v), and the hard-hitting Montanist *De monogamia* (later in date than *Ad uxor.* and *De exhort. cast.*) put matters succinctly against 'psychics' whose marriages outnumbered their fasts. Not even the unclean birds had entered the Ark with two females, Tertullian thundered (*De monog.* iv.5). Again he was preaching Montanism as a *via media*. 'Spiritual' (i.e. Montanist) Christians avoided the extremes of heretics who did away with marriages, on the one hand, and 'psychics', who accumulated them, on the other (*De monog.* i.1; cf. iv.1ff.). Not surprisingly the latter castigated the Paraclete's 'discipline' of monogamy as heresy (ii; xv), though we do not know that there was formal condemnation of Tertullian's views.[116]

Tertullian did not regard such teaching as novelty or a burden (cf. Eusebius *HE* v.23,7f.). Just as Christ's New Law had abrogated that divorce which had been a concession to hardness of heart, so now, at the appointed time, the Paraclete had abrogated second marriages (*De monog.* xiv). This was not innovation but *restitution* of monogamy (iv.1), given that Scripture was witness to its rightness (iv–vii citing some dubious examples). In any case the Paraclete was Comforter, so marriage was *allowed* and absolute continence was not demanded of all (iii. 10; xv). Where was the hardship in that?

Is all this just Tertullianism or does it represent the teachings of the earliest Asia Minor New Prophecy on remarriage? We cannot be certain and Tertullian cited no oracle in support.[117] Forbidding digamy may have seemed to him a logical corollary of the Prophecy's tending to celibacy as the preferred option, but I think the balance of probability lies with the New Prophecy having outlawed digamy from the start. Epiphanius' early anti-Montanist source contrasted (a) the measured catholic view of remarriage for a 'weak' laic (*Pan.*

xlviii.9,5–8) with (b) the Prophets' forbidding of digamy and rejection of those who fell to it. There is, too, a Carthaginian inscription (*CIL* viii. 25045) published by Seckel in 1921 and discussed by Bickel in 'Protogamia'. This has been thought to represent Montanists' (or Donatists') own decision-making, but its origins are uncertain (cf. too 5.1.5 below). Here digamists were to be avoided just as intercession for deceased digamists was forbidden. Germanus of Constantinople, writing to the deacon Antimus, recorded that digamists were refused fellowship by Montanists (*Ad Antimum* v). Praedestinatus (*Haer.* i.26) and Augustine (Haer. lxxxvi) appealed to Tertullian's view on the matter. Taking a stand against digamy seems to me to be in line with the Prophets' thinking. While not condoning extremes of asceticism, and while allowing marriage, they were more closely aligned with those Christians in Asia who looked to celibacy as the superior option. Hence remarriage would not be condoned. Paul had felt much the same (1 Cor. 7:40) and what had been his personal opinion had now metamorphosed. It was a ruling of the Paraclete.

3.6 FORGIVENESS

3.6.1 *Penance in Carthage*

I begin with Tertullian, who had much to say on this topic, before moving back to the Asian New Prophecy. Tertullian said that the 'new discipline' (*nova disciplina*) of the Paraclete was unforgiving of the post-baptismal sinner. The Church should tolerate no sinner in its midst who was fornicating or adulterous, idolatrous or guilty of shedding blood – and least of all among the clergy (cf. later Cyprian *Ep.* lxvii.4; lxix; *De unit. eccles.* vi; *De lapsis* xxxiv; Tertullian *De pudic.* xii; *Apol.* ii.6; *De bapt.* iv; *De spect.* iii; *De idol.* i). Some sins (looking to the condemnation in the Jewish Scriptures) were beyond the Church's pardon, the Montanist Tertullian argued: pardon was God's alone (cf. Mark 2:7; *De pudic.* xxi.2; i.7f.; xix) – citing idolatry, murder, apostasy, injustice, blasphemy and fornication (cf. *Adv. Marc.* iv.9 where false witness occurs). He had acknowledged that martyrdom assured such forgiveness for the guilty (*Apol.* l.16; *De bapt.* xvi.2 cf. *De scorp.* vi.9), for in such a case 'love covers the multitude of sins' (quoting 1 Peter 4:8), but even the cult of martyrs became disturbing to him.

The Montanist was a purist. No tares might grow among the wheat (cf. Hippolytus on Callistus *Refut. omn. haer.* ix.12,22f. and the pre-Montanist *De idol.* xxiv.24) and now there would be no appeal to the ark in which *all kinds* were held safe (cf. Cyprian *Ep.* lxix.7). Whereas in time past Tertullian *had* allowed a second plank after wreckage on the rock of post-baptismal temptation (cf. Jerome *Ep.* cxxx.9; Tertullian *De paen.* vii; xii; *Apol.* i.16), it was no longer so. He had once allowed a final, post-baptismal chance in respect of apostasy, fornication and idolatry (cf. *De paen.* viii; *Adv. Marc.* iv.9 and *De paen.* iv where pardon follows), but Tertullian had also feared that knowledge of such an 'indulgence of the Lord' (*De paen.* vii.11) might lead to laxity. Despite such fear he had continued to teach that *once only* penance was allowable (*De paen.* ix). The process of *exomologesis* was stringent and humiliating enough (*De paen.* ix–x; cf. *De pudic.* xiii).[118] Indeed it was probably little wonder that some would-be Christians postponed baptism (*De bapt.* xviii), indulged in a pre-baptismal surfeit of forbidden pleasure before the Christian discipline closed around them (cf. Basil of Caesarea *Hom.* xiii.89), or else afterwards kept their post-baptismal sins for God's hearing alone (*De paen.* vi).[119] Given *exomologesis*, Tertullian had been aligned with the less rigorous in Christendom, for not every Christian teacher had allowed the possibility of repentance of sin post-baptism (see Hermas *Vis.* ii.2; *Man.* iv.3; *Sim.* ix.19). Then Tertullian changed, as he said in the Montanist *De pudicitia*.

He had come to despise the way the wind of pardon was blowing;[120] and, in line with this thinking on post-baptismal sin, Hermas' work *The Shepherd* (never a favourite with Tertullian, *Orat.* xvi.1) became for him 'The Shepherd of the adulterers' (*De pudic.* xx), unfit to be counted as authoritative literature for Christians (*De pudic.* x.12). An edict of the catholic Church had remitted after repentance the sins of adultery and fornication (*De pudic.* i.6) – it seems that there was still a hard line against the mortal sins of murder and apostasy (*De pudic.* v.15; xxii.11). This was not good enough for Tertullian and his *societas sententiae* with the catholics on such matters had to end (*De pudic.* i.10–11,14; xxii). It would be easy to err with the majority, of course, but truth was upheld in the company of the few, he said. He would not apologise for his own improvement (!) (*De pudic.* i) nor for his disgust that those who fell in the heat of passion, rather than the horrors of the prison – those who had been tickled rather than tortured into their present fallen state – might be allowed to repent (*De pudic.* xxii).

Perhaps some of the African bishops were in sympathy with his position (cf. Cyprian *Ep.* lv) but the bishop labelled 'Pontifex Maximus' (*De pudic.* i) was not. Tertullian's stance was clear. The Paraclete's discipline demanded separation from adulterers, fornicators[121] and digamists too. The Christian writings he had used in the past were now reappraised accordingly. The letters to the seven churches in the Apocalypse, which advocated repentance, had been referring to errorists *and not to the already baptised*, he claimed. The prodigal son, the woman in Luke's Gospel whose coin was lost and the lost sheep, characters which in the pre-Montanist *De paen.* (viii) had signified God's acceptance of the repentant, now in the Montanist *De pudic.* (vii–viii) had not signified Christians at all – whatever the forced exegesis of the other side claimed. They were pagans sought by God! Tertullian argued with fervour and in detail,[122] categorising sins, with appeals to 1 John 5:16, Hebrews 6:4ff. and possibly 1 Samuel 2:25 (ii; iv; xx). His new position even involved a movement away from what he had previously taught about martyrs.

3.6.2 Martyrs and the right to 'loose'

In the church of Carthage (and elsewhere) catholics facing martyrdom had possessed the right to 'loose', i.e. to remit sins (cf. *Pass. Perp.* vii.1 and see 4.5 and 4.6 below). The ordinary Christian in Carthage looked to communion with such confessors and martyrs as a means to spiritual uplift (the Spirit entered prisons along with the confessors, Tertullian maintained, *Ad mart.* i.3), and they had power to grant peace (*Ad mart.* i.6; cf. Saturus' vision of the warring clergy in *Pass. Perp.* vii–vii and xiii). Through visiting them in prison and in commemorating their steadfastness after their deaths Christians built community solidarity.[123] Decades later Cyprian's power-struggle with African confessors from the Decian persecution shows African belief in their right to 'bind' and 'loose' was tenacious (*Ep.* lviii.1). But the Montanist Tertullian denied even to martyrs such power. The cult of martyrs was open to abuse, he suggested. Christians, the lapsed, fornicators and other gross sinners crept into prison cells to kiss the martyrs' bonds (cf. II *Ad uxor.* iv,1) or else to gain absolution (*De pudic.* xxii.1f.). This was easier than the humiliating rites of grovelling *exomologesis* but the darkness also afforded opportunity for further sin! In any case, it was God alone who determined what might be condoned. The merits of the true martyr availed for his or her own sin, of course, but there could be no forgiveness extended to others.

3.6.3 Forgiveness and the first Prophets

Was it the teaching of the first Prophets that occasioned Tertullian's change of mind? It is hard to say. There are some late references to Montanist refusal of penance: for example, writing to the rigorist Novatianist Sympronianus, Pacian of Barcelona told of 'Phrygian' condemnation of it (*Ad Symp.* i–ii). Jerome, too, blamed Montanists for exercising an unbending and unforgiving discipline ('rigidi autem sunt'), debarring Christians for many offences, he wrote (*Ep.* xli ad Marcellam iii). He also said they used the epistle to the Hebrews in their arguments against post-baptismal penitence (Heb. 6:4–6), and this reference to Hebrews is of interest. Hebrews looked to the Jerusalem of promise (Heb. 11:10,16; 12:22; 13:14 see 3.2 above); Hebrews reflected a church community in which *mutuality* was important, rather than human priestly power (10:24f.; 12:15f.). Hebrews was a 'prophetic' document and was surely known to the Asia Minor Prophets, as Jerome said (see 3.8 below).[124] His evidence is plausible in this respect. But, like Pacian after him, Jerome knew something of Tertullian, who had also referred to the Hebrews 6 passage in *De pudic.* xx.1–2 (and probably in ix too), believing Hebrews to be the work of Barnabas. Thus Jerome's evidence of itself takes us no way towards determining whether the *first* Prophets had been so rigorous.

Tertullian may be suspected of using the excuse of the Paraclete to impose a harsher discipline congenial to his own temperament. But in this case there *is* an extant oracle from a Prophet. We have to rely on Tertullian for it, of course, but then the paucity of such sayings surely suggests that he did not simply invent them at will. It is preserved in *De pudicitia* and it suggests (unattributed) that the first Prophets had eschewed the right to pronounce forgiveness.[125] The Church did indeed possess the right of pardon, it was said, but the 'I' of the oracle would not give it, lest those concerned should sin again (*De pudic.* xxi.7; Aland no. 7).

The Church's right to bind and loose had been stated in Matthew. 18. The oracle's reference to it speaks of a polity among the Prophets which accorded power to 'spiritual' Christians when 'gathered'. Tertullian's own response was that the Church did indeed have the right to pronounce forgiveness, but it had to be the church of the Spirit with the 'spiritual' individual exercising such power (cf. *De pudic.* xxi–xxii) – the Church was not a bevy of bishops.[126] Not only did the clergy concerned show no evidence of the requisite gifts, said

Tertullian, but in any case the Paraclete had spoken against loosing. We do not know the *Sitz im Leben* of the oracle or whether post-baptismal sin *of every kind* was not to be pardoned. (Possibly, for example, a period of intense persecution and the fate of the lapsed was in mind.) The oracle points, nevertheless, to a hardening of the teaching on forgiveness as of discipline generally in the earliest Prophecy.[127] It accords with what we see in the letter to Asia and Phrygia from the Christians of Lyons and Vienne (177 CE).

There the martyrs gladly 'loosed' those who had lapsed under pressure of persecution (*HE* v.2,5; cf. v.1,45; v.18,6),[128] whereas evidently some others (in the East?) would not and were also allowing *freed* confessors to retain the power of the keys and the title 'martyr' (*HE* v.2,2–4; cf. v.18,6–7). In Asia Melito of Sardis, contemporary of Apolinarius, had written a treatise on *The Key*, as well as others on prophecy and on the Apocalypse. This may point to debate in that region about binding and loosing. All things considered, it seems that the earliest church of the Prophecy and its confessors/martyrs possessed the power of the keys but that their tendency (in line with the Spirit's instructions?) was to bind.

But what of Tertullian's denial of the keys to a martyr (cf. *Ad mart.* i; *De Scorp.* x.8; *De paen.* ix.4).[129] Possibly Tertullian was not averse to using and ignoring the Prophecy as it best suited his polemical purposes (thereby creating great difficulties for the historian). Perhaps he interpreted the Prophecy's teaching that the Church should 'bind' so as to suggest that confessors/martyrs had no right to an opinion, lest it err on the side of generosity! While the document from the Gallic Christians may indicate that some martyrs elsewhere were not being forgiving, and while the oracle cited indicates that the church of the Prophets was prone to binding rather than loosing, this has to be weighed against something Apollonius said. He enquired in a barbed way whether the spurious Asian 'martyr' absolved his companion the avaricious Prophet or the latter brought forgiveness to the known criminal 'martyr' (*HE* v.18,6–7). This indicates that the power of the keys was known to be exercised among them, but it need not indicate that absolution was freely handed out. Apollonius may in fact have been commenting ironically on their reputation for rigour.[130] Tertullian, in his own rigorist way, may have been reflecting a tendency which *was* known to exist in the Asia Minor Prophecy, the setting for the Paraclete's utterances. The Prophecy did not forgive lightly, and that went for its martyrs as well.

The New Prophecy, therefore, tended towards greater rigour in all respects, but the degree of difference between itself and catholics should not be overstated. It is as well to remember that in the second half of the second century the Prophets were not alone in the kinds of concerns which led to that rigour.[131]

3.7 OBSERVATIONS ON MONTANIST DISCIPLINE

The apostles, said Tertullian, 'spiritual' men, had been 'pillars of discipline' (*De pudic.* xxi).[132] Now 'discipline' was the key to the significance of the New Prophecy; that was what the Paraclete brought fresh to the Church, together with a right understanding of the Scriptures. Tertullian found a consistency in what the Spirit revealed. The new did not stand at odds with the old, but rather it clarified what hitherto had been unclear. In any case, Tertullian asked, why should it be assumed that the devil added constantly to the store of thinking on iniquity but that God's work had (at worst) come to an end or was (at best) for now at a standstill? The Paraclete brought Christ's revelation to a mature Church, one come of age. What it could not have taken in at first was granted to it now, so that discipline might be perfected (cf. John 6:12f.; 14:26; 16:12ff.; *De virg. vel.* i; *De monog.* ii.4). Firmer rules of morality applied than in the time of its Gospel-age infancy (*De monog.* xiv.5). So the Paraclete gave direction for discipline ('disciplina dirigitur') and gave revelation about Scripture ('scripturae revelantur', see 3.9.3 below and cf. *Adv. Prax.* ii.1; xiii.5; *De monog.* ii–iii; xiv.3–6; *De jej.* xii.2). It reformed the intellect ('intellectus reformatur', see *De virg. vel.* i.4f.). Tertullian doubtless refined and developed the original Prophetic message in the light of his own preferences (which the Prophecy seemed to support). But he was probably not so far removed from the 'original' Prophecy as some have suspected.

The teaching of the Three and their successors had implications for the catholic 'psychics' and their understanding of the Church, whether they were in Africa, in Rome (where Hippolytus was implacably hostile to any notion of fresh revelation) or in the East. For it impinged upon the Church's teaching on forgiveness,[133] on marriage, on fasting and on the clergy's right to determine orthopraxis. The implications of the Prophecy had not been lost on the bishops of Phrygia, Asia and Galatia. It was not lost on those who challenged Tertullian's understanding of things in Carthage or on Hippolytus.

Authority was at stake, as was the interpretation of the Scriptures, as we shall see (3.9). The Prophets were claiming the moral and spiritual high ground.

With Robin Lane Fox I too believe that

The heart of Montanism had not lain in heresy or millennial teaching, let alone in militant apocalyptic. It lay in a faith that the Spirit could speak personally, bringing Christian 'discipline' up to the mark.[134]

Bringing 'up to the mark' involved greater toughness. If the Prophecy did not differ from catholic practice in essentials, if it did not put itself at odds with the spirit of the Scriptures (though there was room for disagreement about how they were to be interpreted, of course), then where was the problem? The problem was that the Spirit-Paraclete demanded the last word on all subjects.

I find no reason to assume (with Faggiotto and others)[135] that Phrygian Montanism, condemned by catholic bishops before the end of the second century, was wholly a different creation from the New Prophecy of the West. We must be cautious about assuming a high degree of apocalyptic frenzy or asceticism in the Asia Minor Prophecy, and cautious about asserting that the Western kind was so much gentler in its asceticism and prophetism as to be capable even of being received formally in Rome. Tertullian probably did not greatly distort the picture of the Prophecy. Its discipline *was* more demanding where it was innovatory. The extant oracles of the Prophets, the sources of Eusebius, Epiphanius and the Roman Hippolytus, suggest these things. But Tertullian told the story more clearly and probably with *some* embellishment.[136]

As Schneemelcher observed,

even the trouble taken by opponents to disparage the morality of the Montanists means that a part of Montanus' preaching did relate to ethical renewal and repentance.[137]

These concerns were original to the New Prophecy. It was bound to anger the catholics, and not just because of the claims to personal and superior revelation but because of the implication and later accusations about catholic laxity which new fasts, xerophagies and guidance on marriages and forgiveness implied. If the assumptions of the Prophecy about revelation prevailed, then catholic clergy no longer had the final word on matters of orthopraxis.

3.8 CONFESSION AND MARTYRDOM

3.8.1 Martyrs and Prophets

The most excellent Christians in the early Church were neither the virgins nor the visionaries. They were the Christians whom pagans put to death.[138]

Martyrdom was a second baptism. Like the first it effaced sin (cf. *Pass. Perp.* xviii.3) and Saturus in the *Passio Perpetuae* (4.5.1 below), 'baptised' in the blood of his confrontation with a leopard, heard 'Saluum lotum!' of the crowd – 'well washed!' – in ironic and cruel echo of post-bath greetings. Satan was defeated in martyrdom (Eusebius *HE* v.1,23 and 27; *M. Apoll.* xlvii; *M. Fruct.* vii.2; Hermas *Sim.* viii.3,6; Origen *Contra Celsum* viii.44; *Mart.* xlii).

The number of Christian martyrdoms should not be exaggerated (see Origen *Contra Celsum* iii.8), although Cyprian wrote of innumerable martyrs (*De mort.* xxvi). And few converts were made in response (Tertullian *Apol.* i and l; Justin *2 Apol* xii; *Dial.* cx; *Pass. Perp.* xvii.2–3; Hippolytus *Comm. Dan.* ii.38). Nevertheless, a great deal of scholarship has been devoted to sifting the sparse evidence for persecution of Christians.[139] Without doubt Christians did suffer as a result of local ill feeling, personal vendetta and the need for scapegoats in times of political unrest or natural disaster (Tertullian *Ad mart.*; *Ad Scap.*). Many proved unwilling to compromise, despite what was sometimes the best will of weary provincial officials, so that Christians and pseudo-Christians alike, rounded up and interrogated, sometimes did face an ignominious death. Melito of Sardis in his *Apology, c.* 175 CE was amazed at the mob, the informers and the attacks after 'new decrees' in Asia (Eusebius *HE* iv.13,8; iv.26,5f.) which led to Christian martyrdoms.[140]

In Christian ranks martyrs were honoured. Traditions of the apostolic age and beyond described them in heaven already, rather than awaiting a general resurrection.[141] Martyrs would judge (cf. Hippolytus *Comm. Dan.* ii.37,4; Dionysius of Alexandria in Eusebius *HE* vi.42,5) and the reviled would be vindicated (Matt. 10:32; Rev. 6:9; 18:24). 'Take careful note of what we look like', said Perpetua and Saturus in the *Pass. Perp.* (xvii.2 (cf. xviii.8)), 'so that you may recognise us on that day'.

Martyrdom brought the keys to paradise itself (Tertullian *De anima* lv.4f.) and readiness for it brought spiritual gifts and privi-

leges (*Ad mart.* iv). In confession and martyrdom, Cyprian said
some decades later, a woman triumphed over the disabilities of her
sex (*De lapsis* ii; cf. Augustine's *Sermons* cclxxx–cclxxxii). Origen
echoed the prevailing view that martyrs, like angels, apostles and
patriarchs, acted as intercessors (*Comm. in Cant.* iii; *Hom. in Lev.* iv.4;
Exh. Mart. xxx). All this must have fed some Christians' willingness
to embrace death. Marcus Aurelius probably had Christians in
mind when he complained of exhibitionistic abandonment to
death. *Parataxis*, he said, a spirit of resistance, was not the most
worthy reason for giving up one's soul (*Meditations* xi.3; xii.28).

Catholics distinguished between their own and *other* victims of
the hatred of Christianity, including Prophets, and there was a
'heads I win, tails you lose' colour to the arguments. The Prophecy
did have its martyrs, though the Anonymous felt obliged to respond to their claims of *many* martyrs (*HE* v.16,20f.). It was surely
to be expected in Asia – the martyrologist of Polycarp and the
Gallic Christians knew of Asian Christians who held martyrdom to
be an esteemed vocation.[142] But the Anonymous claimed that none
of the Prophets (its leading figures?) had been persecuted by Jews,
killed by evil people or crucified for the Name (*HE* v.16,12), which
suggests the New Prophets had been likening themselves to those
written of in Matthew 10:16–23, 32–41; 23:34ff.; 24: 28–36. In
counter-accusation the catholics were branded 'prophet-slayers',
like the scribes and Pharisees. Probably the Prophets recalled individual prophet-martyrs of the past who had also tried to recall an
erring people to true faith – perhaps Zacharias (referred to by the
martyrs of Gaul) was one example.[143]

The Anonymous was right, of course: so far as we know the
Three had not suffered greatly (except at the hands of hostile catholics) and none had died a martyr's death. No more did Tertullian, author of many a stirring plea to seek the martyr's crown. Indeed, Themiso was accused of having bought his escape from
prison (*HE* v.18,5, a practice condemned by Tertullian in *De fuga*
xii–xiii). This is not a picture which accords with writers' assumptions that the Prophets were unusually active in their pursuit of
martyrdom.[144]

For the New Prophets martyrdom was proof of the power of the
prophetic Spirit among them (Eusebius *HE* v.16,20 (Anonymous);
cf. v.18,5). The Anonymous did not deny that the Prophecy had
its martyrs, but the Marcionites could claim as much![145] The split

between New Prophets and catholic Christians was reality when he wrote, so that catholics facing imminent death in Apamea had been known to shun all contact with 'Phrygian so–called martyrs' – not because of the fanatical desire for death which is often assumed to be central to the Prophecy, but because of 'the spirit in Montanus and the women' (*HE* v.16,22). Perhaps in this instance released Prophet confessors had offered support to arrested catholics.[146] Equally probably they were also about to meet death. But the Anonymous was not going to give hostages to fortune by acknowledging the validity or the number of the Prophets' sacrifices.

3.8.2 Prophetic zeal for death

Writers have tended to assume that the first Prophets and the later Montanists rushed lemming-like towards martyrdom and promoted such actions in others. In fact our sources tell no such story.

Tabbernee has studied clearly 'orthodox' and *possibly* Montanist martyrs who may be said to have encouraged their fates and he finds that quite a number of the *orthodox* (i.e. the catholics) freely drew themselves to the attention of the persecutors, though the sources do not censure them. St Croix, in the classic 1963 study of Christian persecution, made similar observations about voluntary martyrdoms:

the part they played in the history of the persecutions was much more important than has yet been realized . . . [they were] by no means confined mainly to heretical or schismatic sects such as Montanists and Donatists.

So even if eagerness to embrace death *was* common among the Prophets (and such evidence is sparse),[147] such actions would really not have been different from those of some catholics of which we know. Klawiter argued otherwise, seeing fanaticism as a prime cause of the Prophecy being rejected, and Benko's opinion is more extreme still, equating Prophetic willingness to die with 'the self-mutilation and bloody castration' of Cybele's Phrygian priests, 'driven by frenzy'.

What the Galli did in their supreme sacrifice in order to be united with their goddess, the Montanists did through martyrdom. The abuse of their bodies, especially their sexual continence, was a bloodless castration (p. 158).

To such a writer 'Montanist' equals near-suicidal fanatic. For some the use of the very adjective 'Phrygian' in the early sources (particularly where criticism is implied) is taken as evidence of a Prophet/Montanist on the scene. It may be simply a geographical designation, of course, e.g. Alexander in *Mart. Lyons* (*HE* i.49f.),[148] though I would concede that Quintus *the Phrygian* of *Mart. Pol.* iv, on the other hand, may possibly have been of New Prophetic persuasion. Quintus (whose resolve failed), if he was not the product of a later anti-Montanist interpolator's imagination, may have been influenced by an upsurge of enthusiasm in his homeland,[149] though *Philadelphian* Christians were martyred at this time with no hint that their martyrdoms were anything other than of 'proper' *Gospel* type (1.2.4 and 1.3.6 above). Saturus (*Pass. Perp.* iv.5; cf. ii.1), however, was the first and only pre-Decian *voluntary* martyr whose associations with the New Prophecy we may assume fairly safely.[150] He had discouraged apostasy in others *Pass. Perp.*ix.3ff.; xxi.2ff.).[151]

3.8.3 *Seekers after death*

If we were to look determinedly and not too critically for other (possible) Montanists courting death, then we might appeal to the following instances:

(i) In *Ad Scap.* v.1 we have an instance of Asian mass voluntary martyrdom (*c.* 184–5 CE in the proconsulship of Arrius Antoninus). The governor had obligingly executed some zealots, though he thought that there were surely enough precipices and ropes around for their needs! Tertullian did not say that those concerned were Prophets.[152]

(ii) Around 160 CE, Agathonike was martyred in Pergamum (*Mart. Carpus* [A] xliv) and 'threw herself joyfully upon the stake'. There are variant forms of the Greek and Latin texts of these *Acta*, however, which make it less than certain that her death was due to fanatical volunteering at all.[153] In any case there is no cause to think she was of the Prophecy.

(iii) Tertullian argued to Scapula, the proconsular governor of North Africa, that condemnation pleased Christians more than acquittal (*Ad Scap.* i). They went forth to contend of their own accord, he said, and here, wrote Barnes, 'Tertullian represents every Christian in Carthage as being a Montanist.'[154] This too readily equates rigour with the Prophecy and ignores catholic proclivities too.

(iv) Eusebius in *HE* viii.11,1, referring to the time of Diocletian (cf. Lactantius *Inst. Div.* v.11), tells of a town *in Phrygia* in which all the inhabitants were confessed Christians who refused all approaches to commit idolatry. Hence their town (or congregation, following Lactantius) was burnt as they prayed and all perished. There were

Montanists in Phrygia in the late third, early fourth centuries, but Eusebius does not name the town. Refusal to apostasise was not the monopoly of Montanists of course.[155]

(v) Finally there is the *Life of St Theodotus of Ancyra* (Ankara) which *may* refer to events in Galatia involving Montanist Christians during the persecution of Maximinus Daia (312 CE). The *Life* refers to voluntary martyrdom. Gregoire and Orgels (in the 1951 issue of *Byzantinische Zeitschrift*) argued its Montanist associations, countering Delehaye's case in *Analecta Bollandiana* (1903) that the *Life* was mostly a fiction. This document tells of a Christian community, probably centred in Ancyra but with loyalists also in the village of Malos. Malos has been identified with the area of modern Kaleçik, north-east of Ankara.[156] These Christians revered martyrs (*Life* x–xii; xxxii–xxxvi) and had dedicated virgin women (some of them of considerable age) in their midst. The virgins were martyred too. This community believed that visions came to the living (to Theodotus) from the martyred dead, as also revelations of the holy cross and appearances of 'Fathers' and a saint (xiii–xix). Theodotus, a lay merchant (i–iii; xxvii), was also described as προστάτης ('patron/protector') of the Galileans (xxxi) and one who exercised oversight (iii). Despite being restrained and discouraged (xx), Theodotus refused to seek escape and gave himself up (xxi). After prison and torture he was martyred (xx–xxxi). Here was a man of καρτερεία ('resolve'), ἄσκησις ('spiritual discipline') and εὐσέβεια ('piety'). Archaeology has confirmed the existence of a cult of St Theodotus in the region. The account mentions a church dedicated to the Patriarchs. This is an otherwise unattested kind of dedication, which calls to mind, of course, Jerome's statement about the Montanist Patriarchate (*Ep.* xli.3).

This last parallel apart, there is nothing *distinctively* Montanist in the account. Mitchell notes, too, that the *Life* refers to other sectarian groups, notably the Apotactites, who laid claim to the loyalties of three of the martyred virgins (cf. Epiphanius *Pan.* xlvii and lxi; Basil *Ep.* cxcix. 47). These were rigorists of Encratite type who would not readmit the lapsed or sanction remarriage. It is unfortunate that a lacuna at this crucial point prevents us knowing what the author thought was really the women's allegiance. We may not rule out Montanist links with the *Life* but it is surely safer to say that it is the product of a rigorist and non-catholic community. In particular we should not assume (as does Mitchell) that voluntary martyrdom must indicate Montanists on the scene (citing Tertullian *De fuga* ix on

p. 102). In any case the community concerned was by no means uniformly courting martyrdom. While Theodotus refused to abjure Christianity, encouraged Victor on the same course and courted the governor's attention (iv–ix; xx–xxi; xxxi), by contrast friends tried to *restrain* Theodotus (xx), some Christians *fled* from the persecutors to the countryside (x–xii), while others ventured into the city *in disguise* (xx). Finally, at the time when the virgins were being put to death Theodotus was in hiding!

None of the sources cited above may be used with confidence to assert Montanist zeal for martyrdom (cf. 3.8.2–3.8.3). Tabbernee's warnings are apposite. The fact is that *catholics* sanctioned behaviour which was, or was little short of, voluntary martyrdom,[157] and the catholics' precursor in dying for the Name, Ignatius of Antioch (d. *c*.107–10 CE), has been described as a fanatic by more than one writer. I have argued elsewhere that Ignatius had actually given himself over to the authorities. Ignatius, described by John Henry Newman as providing the whole of the catholic system 'in outline' at least, so extolled the martyr's role, so longed to be 'ground as wheat', faced by fire, sword etc. that Edward Gibbon wrote of letters which 'breathe sentiments the most repugnant to the ordinary feelings of human nature'![158] There is nothing akin to this in our sources on Montanism.

3.8.4 Tertullian the zealot

Tertullian is much to blame for the accusations, of course. The assumptions about the Prophets and martyrdom stem from a reading of Tertullian's Montanism and his 'unrelenting rigorism in the face of the ultimate test of a Christian's religious sincerity'.[159] Tertullian could cite some examples of ill-use of Christians – e.g. proconsul Vigellius Saturninus (180–1 CE) who was associated with the deaths of the Scillitan martyrs (cf. *Ad Scap.* iii.4). Fear of the knock at the door and insecurity were probably pervasive.[160] Yet Africa was not exceptionally terrorised. No African bishop was martyred until Cyprian (258 CE), which may indicate a deliberately low profile among some Christians and a pragmatic approach to flight in times of oppression. Such things became inimical to Tertullian himself. Against such a background, and however rare actual martyrdom, Tertullian the natural hard-liner did not need contact with Montanism to assure him that witness unto death was the right action, or that Gnosticism was an insidious force which might deflect the faithful from their determination in that respect.

Tertullian said flight was not to be condoned, though earlier he had pronounced it preferable to apostasy (*De scorp.* i.11;[161] cf. the earlier *De pat.* xiii.6f.). The evangelists had been clear (Matt. 10:32,39; cf. *Ad Scap.* xii.1f.; xv.1ff.) – though admittedly Matthew 10:23 (cf. 23:34) was a problem, especially by the time Tertullian had rejected utterly the possibility of flight (cf. the Montanist *De fuga* vi.1; ix.1; *De cor. mil.* i.4f.). The change in his thinking coincided with his allegiance to the insights of the Paraclete but it was not a big step for Tertullian to have taken. His biblically based teaching on public confession and martyrdom is largely independent of his Montanist sympathies. The words of the Paraclete-inspired Prophet (we do not know which one) had simply confirmed Tertullian's own certainty. Nearly all of the Spirit's words exhorted to martyrdom, he contended. The Paraclete *denounced* those who fled (especially clergy) and those who practised bribery (*De fuga* ix.4; xi.3; xiv.3).

The key utterances are in *De fuga* ix.4 (Aland nos. 8 and 9) as follows:

(a) 'Publicaris?' inquit, 'bonum tibi est; qui enim non publicatur in hominibus, publicatur in domino. Ne confundaris: iustitia te producit in medium; quid confunderis laudem ferens? Potestas fit, cum conspiceris ab hominibus.'

(b) Nolite in lectulis nec in aborsibus et febribus mollibus optare exire, sed in martyriis, uti glorificetur, qui est passus pro vobis.

Public exposure is good, the Prophet had declared, the alternative being exposure 'in the Lord'. Such public exposure came of righteousness and it brought praise (were some Christians ashamed of their acquired criminal status?) and the power of opportunity ('potestas est'). On another occasion the Spirit had called on Christians to welcome death *by martyrdom*, rather than in bed, miscarriage or fever, to the glory of Him who had suffered for them. The latter saying appears again in *De anima* lv.5, which is post-203 in date as the martyred Perpetua's (*sic*) vision (actually that of Saturus) was mentioned in lv.4. There it is attributed to the Paraclete. Here the language of childbirth and of encouragement to public appearance suggests that *women*, in particular, were the original addressees.[162] Tertullian chose to argue (and perhaps it was so) that the witness of the New Prophecy was for the acceptance of martyrdom and that the Paraclete fulfilled the promise of accompanying and supporting accused Christians (Luke 12:11f. and John 14:17f.; 16:13). Martyrdom

was not to be avoided. Here, then, in the evidence of Tertullian, lies
the root of assumptions about the Prophets' zeal for martyrdom.

3.8.5 Findings on martyrdom

The New Prophecy encouraged readiness to embrace martyrdom
and it discouraged flight in persecution. It seems to me less certain
that it also advocated surrender of oneself to the authorities or that all
Prophets were longing for death. It is true, nevertheless, that the
Prophets tended towards rigour when pressed and apocalyptic
sources such as had fed their expectations and interpretations did
revere martyrs and spoke of a narrowness of the way. 'Only one can
walk up that path', declared the apocalyptist of 4 Ezra. 'If now that
city is given to a man for an inheritance, how will the heir receive his
inheritance unless he passes through the danger set before him?' (4
Ezra 7.8–9). In fact much of the language of the rigorous life and
sacrificial death was readily to hand in Christian circles and would
not have been peculiar to Montanists. The martyr, like the prophet,
was a pillar, granted that status by God's grace: 'I am making you this
day a fortified city, and as a pillar of iron', Jeremiah had recorded
(Jer. 1:17–18). The 'pillar' was one charismatically endowed so as to
endure and to support others. The Seer's prophetic promise to
Philadelphian Christians who would 'overcome' was that they would
be a pillar. Attalus of Pergamum, martyred in Gaul, was also a pillar
and a prophet (*HE* v.1,17),[163] and Kraft has associated such language
with a charismatic view of church order for which Asia provides
evidence.[164] I think that Ignatius of Antioch's letter to Philadelphia
(vi.1) preserves a dismissive play on the word 'pillar' in the
Revelation's letter to that same place. One did not have to be a
Montanist in Asia to take such apocalyptic and charismatic language
seriously, but for those weaned on apocalyptic sources and stories of
the martyrs it must have been a short step to a determined resistance
which was easily misunderstood.[165]

Yet some at least among the Prophecy's followers must have looked
to a more normal death and taken steps to avoid attention. Why else
would their Paraclete have counselled otherwise? We hear that some
Prophets suffered imprisonment and were then released, calling
themselves 'martyr' rather than confessor, and enjoying esteem.
Some catholics did, too, though the martyrs of Gaul wanted the title
preserved for a witness unto death (Eusebius *HE* v.2,3–4). Others (if
what is said of Themiso is true) did as some catholics did and bribed

their way out of prison. The prophetic Spirit willed, but some flesh was weak. Where Prophetic *practice* of confession and martyrdom was concerned one must doubt that it differed much from that of the catholics. The earliest writers (Apolinarius, the Anonymous and Apollonius) did not accuse them of courting death and, while Prophets boasted of martyrs when pressed about the validity of their teaching, that, as the Anonymous wrily observed, was a boast equally applicable to Marcionites.

The Paraclete's utterances on the matter were congenial to Tertullian, however, and thus they found their way into posterity, to be taken as the whole truth about Montanist practice. Later Fathers do not associate Montanism with ardent desire for the martyr's death in the way in which readers of Tertullian do as a matter of course.

3.9 THE CONTROVERSY ABOUT SCRIPTURE AND REVELATION

This section will concern three things:

(i)   some observations on the use of Christian and other writings by the Prophets and their followers
(ii) the debate about revelation and sacred writings
(iii) the significance of Montanism for the establishment of the canon.

3.9.1 The use of biblical tradition

(a) I begin with *the Gospels*: from Matthew's Gospel the Prophets' took the accusation that the catholics were 'prophet-slayers' and the promise that prophets would be sent (Matt. 23:34; Eusebius *HE* v.16,12). The catholic side appealed to warnings about *false* prophets, deceivers and the need for testing (Matt. 7:15 (Anonymous); 10:9 and 12:33 (Apollonius); John 5:43 (Epiphanius *Pan.* xlviii.11,3); 1 John 4:1 (*HE* v.16,8; v.18); cf. 1 Tim. 4:1; 3 in Epiphanius *Pan*, xlviii.2; xlviii.8, 10). Maximilla must have heard such warnings often, for one was echoed in her saying 'I am driven away like a wolf from the sheep' (4.1.2; 4.3.2 below).

We know little of how John's Gospel was used in the Asian debate. Epiphanius preserves appeal to John 5:43 and cf. *Pan.* xlviii.13,5//John 7:37 while xlviii.11,4 may be echoing John 1:16. Tertullian used the Fourth Gospel in arguing about the Trinity (citing the Paraclete in favour of his view, *Adv. Prax.* ii; viii) and about the Paraclete itself (cf. *De monog.* ii.2–4; *De jej.* x; *De virg. vel.* i.7–8 and 11; cf. Origen *Comm. in*

Matt. xv.30), then at a later stage we hear that Marcella, the Roman woman known to Jerome (*Ep.* xli), had received a collection of Johannine texts from a Montanist. Such New Testament 'proof-texting' had probably always been the norm in defence of the Prophecy and the Acts of the Apostles had fed the appeal to the prophets Agabus, Judas, Silas and the daughters of Philip (Acts 11:27f.; 15:32; 21:9f.; *HE* v.17,2f. see also 4.4.3(ii)below).[166]

(b) As for *the Apocalypse*, I think of the Seer's letter to Philadelphia as an important source for the self-understanding of Prophetic and like-minded Christians in Asia. Yet it is never cited as such in any writings. Revelation 3:7–13 offers support for the Prophecy's teaching on endurance and victory, on the return of the Lord and Christians' relation to the city of God (together with Rev. 21–2). Other passages of the Revelation fed Montanist belief and practice in other respects and consequently some anti-Montanists rejected the work altogether (see too 3.9.6 below). There are some reminiscences of its visions, e.g. in Maximilla's reference to 'suffering', with regard to the millennium and perhaps in Montanist 'naming' and 'marking' practices. At an early stage of the debate the command to 'add nothing' was quoted against the Prophets. This command is not peculiar to the Revelation, though the Prophets would probably have recognised it from that source. They were accused of so adding (*HE* v.16,3//Rev. 22:18f.).

(c) The Prophets appealed to *Jewish scriptural* precedents, especially when defending their ecstatic behaviour: LXX Genesis 2:21 (Adam's ecstasy);[167] Numbers 12:7; Isaiah 1:1; 6:1f., 8f.; Ezekiel 4:8–12; Daniel 2:1ff.; Psalm 115:2 and other passages (cf. Epiphanius *Pan.* xlviii.7 and Eusebius *HE* v.17,3). There were 'interpretative citations', as witness the use of Isaiah 63 (see 3.1.2 above), and Epiphanius, introducing his early source, conceded that the Prophets accepted all the writings of the old and new covenants (*Pan.* xlviii.1,3). Above all, however, *Paul* figures in the debates.

(d) *Paul* is a very significant source. There are strong echoes of Pauline teachings in Montanist sayings ascribed to Maximilla (4.3.2) and, when Themiso wrote his 'catholic epistle', the words of instruction were described as written in imitation of 'the apostle' (presumably Paul; Eusebius *HE* v.18,5).[168] Other writers were wary of publication (*HE* v.16,3 (Anonymous)[169] and cf. iv.23,12, of Dionysius of Corinth, whose scruples do not seem to have affected his output!). Both sides, catholic and Prophetic, were claiming the Pauline high ground. Abercius Marcellus encouraged the Anonymous in anti-Montanist activities and he was an ardent Paulinist. So Paul was cited and argued over on marriage, on prophecy, on the role of women in churches (3.2.2–3; 3.5.1–2; 4.4.3), both in the early stages of the Prophecy and over the centuries of Montanism's existence (e.g. Epiphanius *Pan.* xlviii.8,4–8; Tertullian *De monog.* xiv.3). Labriolle's 'Index Scripturaire' in *Les Sources* indicates a high incidence of appeal to Pauline passages – especially from 1 Corinthians and Romans – as against John's Gospel or Matthew's and far outweighing explicit appeal to the Revelation. Irenaeus, too, may have been hinting at a clash of Johannine–Pauline interests in the debates. For he warned about those (see 3.9.6) who made nothing of the promised Spirit (Joel 2:28f.//Acts 2:17f.) and who in rejecting John's Gospel and its Paraclete teaching were taking the prophetic gift from the Church (*Adv. haer.* iii.11,12; cf. *Dem.* xcix). Such a stance presupposed rejection of Paul too, for Paul had advocated prophecy.

In Rome Gaius set Paul against the (Cerinthian) Revelation (cf. Eusebius *HE* iii.28,2). The Apocalypse's plagues, he said, its fearsome angels and the binding of Satan for a thousand years contrasted with Paul's promise of unexpected intervention – 'like a thief in the night' – until which time unbelievers lived on in quiet safety (1 Thess. 5:2ff. but cf. too Rev. 3:3; 16:15). Paul's view was of course preferable. Significantly, perhaps, Gaius had named *thirteen* epistles as Pauline, not including Hebrews (Eusebius *HE* vi.20,3). The Prophets were probably great students of Hebrews, living as they did in the shadow of a great cloud of witnesses (Heb. 12:1).

Hebrews had taken a rigorous stance on post-baptismal repentance and apostasy (Heb. 6:4ff.; 10:26f.; 12:16f.; cf. Tertullian *De pudic.* xxi.1f; Jerome *Adv. Jov.* ii.3); it promised 'rest' (3:11,18; 4:1–11) and gave teaching on a city to come (11:16; 12:22; 13:14). It was much concerned with the new covenant dispensation (8:8–13; 12:23) and the 'promises' of better things (8:6; 10:23; cf. *HE* v.16,9). Nevertheless we may not assume (*pace* the silence of Gaius) that the Prophets took Hebrews to be the work of Paul (it was by Barnabas, according to Tertullian *De pudic.* xx). But Montanism's opponents in Rome may well have discerned in Hebrews those very elements which have led present-day scholars to label it a work of expository Christian prophecy.[170] Hence some may have fought shy of it. Hippolytus said Hebrews was not by Paul but he echoed its sentiments nevertheless.[171]

Centuries later the Egyptian *Dialexis* and Didymus provide many examples of later appeal and counter-appeal to Paul.[172] The Montanist in the *Dialexis* said Paul's teaching had persuaded people to acknowledge Montanus and the perfection come in the Paraclete. Montanus, no less than Paul the persecutor, had become a chosen vessel and Paul had shown there would be prophets after Christ. The Orthodox, on the other hand, argued from Paul's language that the Paraclete *had* been in the apostles (which Montanists allegedly denied) and that Paul had spoken only allegorically. Montanists, bemoaned Augustine (*Contra Faustum* xxxii.17), not only presumed to forbid what Paul had allowed but because of their teaching on the Paraclete-to-come they held that Paul had not taught the whole truth. Paul reappears time and time again in the sources and the stance against Montanus and his followers became, in the eyes of some, a vote *for* Pauline orthodoxy. Montanus, the Orthodox asserted in the *Dialexis*, 'is being done away with to this very day, but the teachings of St. Paul are growing in power'.[173] More than John or Matthew the figure of *Paul* stands between the protagonists throughout the centuries of these debates.

3.9.2 *Appeal to other sources*

The interpretation of Christian writings played a large part in the first controversies of the Prophecy. Epiphanius recorded the Prophecy's disagreeement with the divine Scriptures, as well as its mistaken theological assumptions (*Pan.* xlviii.13,6),[174] and while the Prophets appealed to the same writings as did the catholic side, the catholics felt the need to challenge the Prophets' use of them. Nevertheless Henning Paulsen has argued persuasively for the essential conservatism of the Prophetic position.

Their own publications apart, the sources name no presently non-canonical writings as part of the Prophets' 'canon' of valued texts. It seems clear to me that they did know sources such as 4 Ezra and its growing Christian accretions, probably the *Apocalypse of Peter* (perhaps known to Tertullian, known to Theophilus of Antioch and Clement of Alexandria, and cf. Muratorian fragment ll. 71–3) and *The Shepherd*. Such items were familiar and used in other Christian circles as well, of course – and so the Prophets were not accused of valuing what was already anathematised. The Christian canon was not yet fixed and the context of allusion to such writings suggests that they fed the Prophets'/Montanists' community self-understanding, rather than that they were appealed to in support of doctrine or figured in the best-known debates with the catholics. No anti-

Montanist writer specifically condemns these works, least of all because of some association with Prophetic propaganda, though Roman rejection of *The Shepherd* in the Muratorian fragment and hesitancy about the Petrine Apocalypse may have been fuelled by Prophetic liking for those sources.

We are told of 'innumerable books' in circulation for Prophetic use (Hippolytus *Adv. omn. haer.* viii.19; cf. Gaius in *HE* vi.20,3; Didymus *De Trin.* iii.41; cf. later Jerome *Ep.* xli ad Marcellam). Probably we should think of collections of the Prophets' sayings and manifestos such as Themiso's epistle, apocalyptic writings already mentioned and expositions of past and present prophecy. Montanists relied on a plurality of authorities, wrote Pacian of Barcelona later (*Ep.I ad Symp.* ii), though early anti-Montanists had suggested that they valued the writings other Christian writers valued too. We do not know whether or at what point they came to accord equal authority to writings outside of those we now regard as canonical, but book-burning became part of the action against them in the post-Constantine age (5.3).

3.9.3 Revelation and sacred writings

Early writers said that Prophetic Christians were orthodox in relation to Law, Prophets and Gospels (Hippolytus *Adv. omn. haer.* viii.19) and in relation to Paul (cf. Tertullian *De monog.* iv.1). Yet Prophets also claimed authority for revelations which post-dated 'apostolic' sources. Tertullian, of course, discoursed authoritatively on everything from the prescribed length of a virgin's veil and the corporeal form of the soul (4.4.2) to paradise and the heavenly Jerusalem, on the basis of other people's visions, though he used visions and Prophetic oracles as *secondary, supportive and subordinate* to teachings in Scripture and the *regula fidei* (as Robeck's thesis has shown, 'The Role and Function of Prophetic Gifts for the Church at Carthage', ch. 9). The work of the Paraclete, said Tertullian, *illumined and interpreted* Scripture (cf. 3.7).[175] Not everyone was convinced, however. For its part, Rome would acknowledge no additional revelation.

Questions were raised about whether *any* prophets might be recognised who post-dated the apostles and also, it would seem, about the use of Christian writings which could offer propaganda value to Montanists and others. Underlying issues of normativity of tradition and acceptability of interpretation were now turning into matters of narrow definition. The Roman Muratorian canon rejected Hermas'

work *The Shepherd* as an item of recent composition (ll. 78f. cf.
Tertullian *Orat.* xvi,1; *De pudic.* x.12). *The Shepherd* was edifying
literature but might be included 'neque inter Prophetas, completum
numero, neque inter apostolos'. The number of prophetic writings
was deemed complete.[176] The crisis of the Prophecy would have fed
such dispensationalist views. In Rome Hippolytus argued for study of
the Scriptures and not of human traditions and fables which led astray
the uneducated (*Adv. omn. haer.* viii.19; x.25; *Comm. Dan.* iv.19–20). It
was not that the Prophets were rejecting the normativity of 'scriptural'
sources (as Henning Paulsen has recognised), but rather that
Hippolytus was stressing the need for *exclusivity* in use of such texts (cf.
the dependent Ps.-Tertullian, *Adv. omn. haer.* vii). The Prophets loved
Scripture too. But not only were the catholics arguing for the use of
only certain writings but they were attempting to standardise
(*normieren*) the way they were understood and interpreted.

There was disagreement over the witness of Scripture on certain
issues. For example, spiritual gifts were expected to continue in the
churches (promised by Paul and in the Paraclete) and the Paraclete
would be a revealer. But if such things belonged only *to the apostolic age*,
then there was a *prima facie* case for the falsity of the Prophecy (*Pan.*
xlviii.2,1–3; 2,9 and 3,1) – unless the gifts were by nature different,
which remained to be proved (xlviii.8,1). This argument was familiar
to Origen (*Comm. in Matt. ser.* xxviii; *De princ.* ii.7,3). Then there was
the question of whether the language of the Paraclete passages
justified a claim of something greater than the apostles had known
(*Adv. omn. haer.* viii.19; cf. John 14:25; 16:12f.; cf. Ps.-Tertullian *Adv.
omn. haer.* vii). Was not the notion of a Paraclete revelation *additional* to
that from Christ too dangerous to go unchallenged (however much it
seemed defensible on the basis of the Fourth Gospel:[177] John 16:12f. cf.
Tertullian *De virg. vel.* i; *De monog.* ii–iii; *De fuga* xiv.3; *Adv. Prax.* i,
contrast Hippolytus *Adv. omn. haer.* viii.19; ix.25; Filastrius *Haer.* xlix;
Ps.-Tertullian *Adv. omn. haer.* vii; Theodoret *HE* iii.1)?

Probably first in Rome the catholic side began to close ranks on
such issues. In North Africa R[Pass.] was aware of what was now a
conservative catholic position and he deplored those Christians who
had taken to confining wonderful happenings to 'times and seasons'
in the past. Later, Jerome provided detailed advice to the Roman
Marcella about the use of scriptural passages and how to rout a
Montanist in debate.[178] Rome was particularly hostile to any
suggestion of new revelation,[179] but the fears were not peculiar to

Rome and we should not assume with Blanchetière that Tertullian was first to systematise the thought of the New Prophecy with regard to the Paraclete. It is just that he appears first in our sources as 'the real theoretician of the progressive revelation theory, ending with the age of the Paraclete'.[180]

3.9.4 The catholics' dilemma

These were troublesome issues for the catholics. Catholic thinkers had problems enough, with the challenge of Marcionism, of Encratism and Gnosticism, and the neighbours' anti-Christian feelings. They did not need 'own goals' against the Christian Church scored by people who in most respects seemed orthodox enough, if tough-minded and demanding. In their own ranks were able men who had been defending Christianity for decades: Melito, Apolinarius, Irenaeus, Justin Martyr and Dionysius of Corinth – producing works of apology, of exposition and letters of pastoral advice – 'literary personalities, each having his individual profile'.[181] Faced with the Prophetic Themiso, however, they found themselves deploring that publishing tendency in others and (like the Anonymous) were suddenly wary of publication, lest they be misunderstood as claiming authority. Yet the actual accusations against the Prophets seem oddly muted and misdirected if the catholics actually feared for the integrity of Christian literature.

Hippolytus was critical of reverence for Montanus and the women, of Prophetic writings and of novelties based on their teaching. Yet he came up with no stronger a specific accusation than that the Prophets had introduced additional fasts. Similarly, while Origen maintained that the significance of the Johannine Paraclete had been misunderstood (and consequently Christian churches had been thrown into confusion by the Prophets), his illustration concerned nothing more weighty than Montanist fasting and teaching about marriage (*De princ.* ii.7,3). So what was the conflict really about? The catholic side, I suggest, did suspect that there was jeopardy to the growing pre-eminence ('canonisation') of writings. These were the writings which increasingly were used to defend and describe the catholic view of order and authority. It must also have feared the possible triumph of a view of those texts which could resurrect an already part-buried history. In short, it feared a prophetic–apocalyptic tradition deemed now not to meet the needs of the Christian in the world as it was. This was a world into which the Church sought to fit more readily. So, for example, the arguments about prophetic succession were not only about the Prophets' insistence that prophecy and revelation were not things of the past, to be relegated historically to the pages of sacred writings – the arguments were also about authority (prophetic as well as apostolic) and who had the right to speak.

The options with regard to respect for Christian writings seemed clear-cut: either the Prophets *were* 'adding to' existing writings and to the content of 'the word of the new covenant of the Gospel' (*HE* v.16,3 (Anonymous)) or else, like the catholics, they drew their faith from the prophetic and apostolic Scriptures. In fact they were doing both. 'Tertullian's extant Montanist writings can yield only a bare half-dozen oracles of the New Prophecy'[182] – his arguments continued to be based on Scripture. On the other hand, the Prophecy meant that the reliability of sober, learned, male catholic leaders might be challenged on the basis of allegedly *new* insights, or of prophetic and other charismatic powers (cf. Tertullian at the close of *De pudic.* xxi) and even by women. Worst of all, the existence of such insights might then be defended by appeal to writings which the catholic side valued too – though viewed through quite different spectacles. 'We too must receive the spiritual gifts', the Prophets had declared (Epiphanius *Pan.* xlviii.1,4). Against the background of developing catholic ideas of authority and hierarchy such language must have carried overtones of dangerous democratisation.

The arguments about writings and about ongoing revelation could not be divorced from questions about the nature of the Church. Both sides had valued the same kinds of writings; both sides acknowledged the rightness of the two fold basis for Christianity's growth – i.e. apostolic and prophetic work (Eph. 2:20). But in the Prophetic–catholic clash we see 'apostolic' increasingly being set over against 'prophetic' and given greater weight by the catholic side. The Prophets made appeal to prophetic succession, the catholic side laid increasing weight on apostolic succession and writings of time past, thus invalidating any allegedly new insights. The Prophets looked to the merits and memory of apostolic *and* prophetic figures in Asia (*HE* iii.31,2–5), while we find Gaius pointing to the trophies of martyred apostles in Rome (*HE* ii.25,6f.). Themiso, daring to write a 'catholic' epistle, was accused of blaspheming the Lord, *the apostles* and the holy Church (*HE* v.18,5: (not a reference to Lord/apostle canonical divisions, I think). Looking back, Pacian of Barcelona noted that arguments about *apostles* and *prophets* and the name *catholic* were among many that Montanists had stirred up (*Ep. I ad Symp.* ii). Reliance on the insights of time past was safer, especially if the Church could keep a hold on the 'correct' interpretation of those insights. Present revelation was disturbing, brought problems of testing and challenged established authority.

3.9.5 *Montanism, new covenant and the Christian canon*

In the end Montanism added nothing new to the canon of New Testament Scripture, though on the other side attempts were made to rob the Church of writings such as the Fourth Gospel, the Revelation and perhaps the letter to the Hebrews, on the grounds that they gave aid and succour to the Prophetically inclined. That was not the stated explanation, of course. The Montanist crisis, claimed Campenhausen, called a halt 'to the uncontrolled growth of the New Testament'.[183] Moreover, that crisis was linked with the shift to an understanding of 'new covenant/testament' being enshrined in writings.[184] Was this so? It is true that the Anonymous' connection between καινή διαθήκη and a body of Christian writings (to which we should refrain from adding) is the first such association in Christian literature (cf. Maximilla's συνθήκη in *Pan.* xlviii.13,1 and the 'covenant of Christ' for which Irenaeus was a zealot, *HE* v.4,2). Yet in Montanus' day a closed canon did not yet exist. The fact that some decades later the Anonymous feared his writing might be treated with undue respect points in precisely that direction. When the Anonymous echoed the sentiments of Revelation 22:18f.,[185] he probably had in mind not so much the danger of adding *writings* as the danger certain Prophetic teachings and writings (including their interpretation of shared tradition) were posing to *the message* – the good news of the Christian dispensation (cf. his usage in Eusebius *HE* v.17,2).[186] Too much emphasis on *writings* may distort the truth about the debate.

W.C. van Unnik, Zahn, Harnack, Hoh and others doubted that Irenaeus had in mind primarily *a body of writings* when he too used the phrase καινή (and παλαία) διαθήκη. Irenaeus knew Christian writings which bore witness (a) to the plan of salvation and (b) to the works of the Spirit which were the mark of the new covenant age,[187] but *teachings* as much as books were matters of concern. What was Christian life to be like in the new covenant age? How and by whom were Christians to be taught about such matters and (yes) which writings best represented the truth about such things? Irenaeus was concerned about 'new covenant' matters but not primarily about books.

The New Prophecy was also closely in touch with the new covenant idea, of course. It told of the outpouring of the Spirit (Joel 2:28f.), its oracles speak of the reality of the promised renewal and the changed heart (Jer. 31:31ff.; Ezek. 34:26ff.), of the need for the holiness of God's people and of a relation to God which was no longer dependent on ethnicity (but was aware of Israel's rejection of the Christ, as were Paul and the Seer).[188] It was familiar with the sentiments of the epistle to the Hebrews and its 'Jerusalem' communities echoed hopes of the gathering of God's people.[189] The Prophets (cf. Irenaeus *Adv. haer.* iv.17,1ff.; 33,14) stood in a tradition which had to be at odds with Gnosticism, certain as they were of the action of the one God throughout history. 'New covenant' would not have been synonymous with a body of writings. Rather, for the New Prophets, the question of authoritative writings and authoritative interpretation thereof was inextricably related to, and dependent on, the question of the nature of the Church.

Writers should beware simplistic equations of the following kind:

The Prophets preached fresh revelation/wrote new books: catholic churches rejected additional revelation/drew lines of demarcation and so gave us the canon.[190]

We never hear that the Prophetic writings were described as a 'new Gospel'. We do not know for certain that such writings were ever cited as Scripture in Montanist circles or 'were combined as a third section with the old bible to form a new Montanist canon' (so Campenhausen, denying such a thing). This is not to say that the Prophecy had no bearing on catholic thinking about Scripture, but the truth was probably more complex.[191]

Paulsen posited three ways in which Montanism *was* significant for the formation of the New Testament canon: (i) it was impetus to catholics' evaluation and interpretation of material for ecclesiastical (*kirchlich*) standardisation (avoiding 'radical amputation' of past history, unlike the Alogi, see below); (ii) it caused catholics to acknowledge one sector of the tradition *within the written material* as valid and normative, with claims to exclusivity, and (iii) there was catholic standardisation of interpretation of that tradition (*Normativität, Exklusivität und festgelegter Interpretation*).[192] When decisions did come to be made about the authoritative nature of documents, the lines of demarcation thus being devised were of value, but they were not made quickly. Long after the rise of the Prophecy we find a text-by-text, collection-by-collection acknowledgement of Christian documents going on and the rejection or relegation of others,[193] including Christian apocalypses.[194] The Revelation of John survived, and that despite the worst efforts of some of its detractors.

3.9.6 The Alogi

Gaius,[195] catholic champion in *HE* ii.25, emerged later as a villain. Dionysius bar Salibi's twelfth-century *Commentary on the Apocalypse* preserved elements of Hippolytus' defence of John's Gospel, a defence needed because Gaius had assigned both the Gospel and the Apocalypse of John to Cerinthus (*Comm. Apoc.* i). Eusebius was remarkably silent about any such attack on the Fourth Gospel but he knew about the hostility to the Apocalypse (*HE* iii.28,1f.). Probably this hostility to things Johannine was an attempt to rob Prophetic Christians of ammunition in the ongoing debate, for they appealed to both sources for key aspects of their teaching. Gaius, we know, was at odds with the chiliasm of the Apocalypse and he expounded Revelation 20 in a non-eschatological fashion. Hippolytus, too, who preserved the details of the argument, was all for an eschatology dominated neither by fanatical interests nor hope of sensual pleasure. But he had no truck with refusal to acknowledge the truth claims of Scripture. The lost work *On the Gospel of John and the Apocalypse* probably clarified his views. Gaius, on the other hand, was approaching the texts with the sharp knife of reason, bringing into play unfavourable comparison with other well-known Christian material, Synoptic Gospels included. The sources did not agree one with another.[196]

The Apocalypse fared better in the West than it did through the centuries of debate on canon in the East. Anti-Prophetic feeling may well have had something to do with initial hostility to it and *pace* what we know of Gaius this is a pointer to the fact that the first opponents of the Apocalypse (and of John's Gospel too) were probably Asian rather than Roman.[197] Irenaeus and Epiphanius must be considered.

Irenaeus (*Adv. haer.* iii) told of some who wished to nullify the prophetic Spirit promised by God for the last times (Joel 2:28f.; Acts 2:17f.) and presumably they denied that prophecy would exist in the Church until the End. Hence they would have nothing to do with John's Gospel, which made promise of the Paraclete (John 14:16; *Adv. haer.* iii.11,9; cf. *Dem.* xcix on those who did not acknowledge *charismata*).[198] His description is in a troublesome passage which has been variously interpreted, even to mean that Irenaeus opposed New

Prophets who rejected the Gospel but the emendation proposed by
Labriolle (from 'qui pseudoprophetae quidem esse volunt' to 'qui
psudoprophetas esse nolunt') makes of those concerned opponents of
'false prophecy'. Their actions, regardless of whether their intentions
were good, would have served to drive prophecy itself from the Church.

Later, Epiphanius wrote of the enigmatic *Alogi* (*Alogoi*, *Pan.*
li.3–34), a neat word-play indicating both that they were unreasonable
and disbelievers in the Logos of which John wrote. They too rejected
Fourth Gospel as well as Apocalypse, ascribing them to Cerinthus,
and employing much the same arguments as Gaius (*Pan.* li.4,18,22).
Some interpretations of this source would allow us to date the Alogi in
the episcopate of Eleutherus (assuming his knowledge of the *Syntagma*
of Hippolytus) – thus aligning them chronologically with those
anti-Johannine types opposed by Irenaeus. But Epiphanius' chronology is, as usual, not straightforward and his 'Alogi' may well date
from several decades into the third century. Despite these uncertainties
of chronology many writers take it for granted that all of these sources
(Hippolytus on Gaius, Irenaeus and Epiphanius) refer to a single
phenomenon, the impetus for which was the success of the Prophecy –
though of course other groups used the Fourth Gospel in ways
anathema to some catholics, notably Gnostics post-Valentinus. If it
was a single phenomenon, where might such an anti-Johannine
group have emerged?

Gaius was associated with Rome. Irenaeus had lived in both Asia
and Gaul but he also had knowledge of the Roman situation.[199]
Epiphanius' source at this point (*Pan.* li) was not the same as that in
xlviii and, while it may possibly have been Roman we may not rule
out the option that it was Asian.[200] A case has been made for *Rome* as
the centre of 'Alogism' on the grounds of Rome's rejection of fresh
revelation and its opposition to the prophetic spirit (Heine and
Klawiter among others).[201] But this does not seem self-evident to me.

First, I think we are dealing with a *group* rather than an individual
(*pace* suggestions that 'Alogism' might be boiled down to the single
person of Gaius himself – Bludau (writing in 1925) was able to cite a
number of Germans who pondered that view – the rest being
Epiphanius' imaginative expansion).[202] Secondly, I assume, as do
most writers, that when Irenaeus wrote in *Adv. haer.* iii.11,9 he had
much the same phenomenon in mind as that which Epiphanius
labelled 'Alogi'.[203] Thirdly (and given what I have written about the
Paraclete in the *Asian* anti-Montanist debate, 2.1; 3.2) Irenaeus'

reference to the Paraclete need not indicate a *Roman* anti-Prophetic phenomenon,[204] even though Gaius at a later date *did* represent a Roman version of it. Like Praxeas emigrating from Asia and carrying Asian anti-Prophetic views to fuel his case in Rome, Gaius' adoption of the view of *Asian* extremists would have given him a special edge in the debate.[205] Anti-Prophetic arguments were widely disseminated by his time, with Serapion knowing Asian material and Tertullian writing against the claims of Apollonius. Labriolle's preference was for an orthodox *Asian* group which attacked sources essential for Prophetic pneumatology and eschatology.[206] I agree. Epiphanius' report about Thyatira was of interest in this respect.

Epiphanius reported an attack on the Apocalypse because it was not genuinely prophetic. It had been wrong, after all, in prophesying to a church in Thyatira, since that church's lapse into Montanism meant there had been no (true) church there at all! Epiphanius may be confused here and is gauche of syntax, Labriolle observed.[207] But Thyatira subsequently returned to orthodoxy, of course, and Epiphanius could compare the Prophetesses with the 'Jezebel' of Thyatira attacked by the Seer. This letter to Thyatira (Rev. 2:18–28) indicates tensions between Christians of more than one persuasion. Evidently such tensions continued, as Christians were capable of being swayed one way and another in Thyatira. Perhaps opposition to a prophetic–apocalyptic view of things was also long-lived in Thyatira, despite large numbers having succumbed to the Prophecy at one point in its Christian history. If one were looking for a place in which to posit the existence of tendencies (the Alogi) hostile to the Apocalypse and things Prophetic, then the region around Thyatira might be it. The Alogi were untypical of response, however, and fortunately their views did not triumph.

3.10 WHAT WAS THE NEW PROPHECY?

3.10.1 The scene

Henry Chadwick's inaugural lecture, The *Circle and the Ellipse*, told of tension between two models of authoritative self-definition in the early Church – the one centred on Jerusalem (the circle), the other, having moved outward (the ellipse), centred on Rome.[208] Despite effort and successes Rome never replaced Jerusalem as a focus for loyalty and never achieved unilateral sovereignty over the churches.[209]

Jerusalem still held sway in the minds of the Prophets, heirs as they
were to the Christianity of Papias and the daughters of Philip, and
that of Quadratus and Ammia in Philadelphia; heirs to those who
spoke of the Jerusalem of promise and who regarded prophecy and
miracle as ongoing realities (Eusebius *HE* iii.37,1; iii.39,8–12; iv.3,2),
protestants on the date of the celebration of Easter. These things did
not *necessarily* separate them from their catholic co-religionists – much
the same was true of Irenaeus, for example. But by the closing decades
of the second century this was not the norm in Asia Minor and seeds of
difficulty were inherent within it.

The Church was making gradual accommodation with the
authorities and with wider society. Some Christians were quite
comprehensively accommodating, as Tertullian complained. Rome,
as imperial power rather than as focus in the ellipse, was now to be
encouraged to toleration, not railed at as the great harlot. Rome was
the source of social progress, of wise leadership and safe travel, to be
rendered its due by a soberly led, hierarchically structured Church.
Ignatius had hoped for much the same decades before. Such unity
would be a bastion against docetic heresy, against 'giving occasion' to
the heathen and also against the destabilising effect of judaising
apocalyptic speculation and troublesome prophets. 'War in heaven'
may have interested some (Ignatius *Eph.* xiii.2 cf. Rev. 12:7; 13:7),
but Ignatius looked for congregational unity behind firm leaders,
which unity brought an end to all warfare. Enthusiasm, like asceticism,
where not subject to the cooling and moderating influence of the
episcopate, had to be the enemy of such order (*Eph.* v; *Trall.* iv–v;
vii–viii; *Smyrn.* viii; *Pol.* v).[210] Decades later the Prophecy proved to be
just the kind of thing Ignatius might have feared. It was firmly set in
an Asia Minor Christian tradition but was not so particular and
localised as to make it unportable. It has been described as a Jewish
Christian phenomenon.

3.10.2 *The Prophecy and Asia Minor Christianities*

'Jewish Christianity' is a notoriously troublesome designation. Jean
Daniélou was willing to encompass vast tracts of material under the
blanket of *judéo-christianisme*,[211] but problems of definition have made
writers more cautious in recent years. The Prophecy was not full of
converts from the fold of Judaism (though possibly it made such
converts from time to time). Rather it was allied with long-established
forms of Christianity which valued the insights of apocalyptic

literature and which refused to jettison (perhaps even were determinedly resurrecting) long-standing Christian practices which were
being gradually and quietly marginalised in the service of catholic
unity, order and orthopraxis. Many of these could trace their
ancestry to the original Jerusalem community. Prophecy itself (with
ecstatic prophecy including glossolalia), was among them.

The Prophets, I suggest, regarded themselves as Israel – a nation of
priests like Israel's own (Rev. 1:6; cf. 1 Peter 1:1; 2:5; James 1:1). John
the Evangelist had spoken of the vine and branches (John 15:1) and
John, the disciple beloved of the Lord, was said to have worn the
petalon, the gold plate which Jews associated with High Priesthood,
inscribed Ἁγίασμα κυρίου (LXX Exodus 28:36), ܩ‍ܘ‍ܕ‍ܫ‍ܐ‍.[212] Nevertheless, in the Johannine circle such identification with Israel would
have gone with rejection of 'the Jews' proper (cf. John 9:28), who
were no longer God's people (cf. Rev. 2:9; 3:9). The Prophets would
have felt the same. 5 Ezra belonged within the same circle of ideas as
had informed the Three and their followers and in that work, also, the
Jews were rejected and the nations inherited. *The Church*, now, was
Zion, new Jerusalem (5 Ezra 2:10; 2:40f; cf. Rev. 7:9 and Gal. 4:24;
Isa. 54:1). *Christians* (not ethnic Jews) were signed with the Name and
sealed (5 Ezra 2:16; 2:38 cf. Rev. 7:3–8; Ezek. 9:4) and *Christians* were
heirs of the covenant. The terms and promises of the new covenant
were being expounded within the Prophecy too, in the light of the
Spirit's activity.

Asia Minor brought contact between Christians and Jews and it
was home to a variety of Christianities.[213] The Prophecy was of a
similar mode to some and should be seen as reaction against others.
Asia Minor had been home to Pauline-type communities,[214] which
had reacted with Asian Judaism and paganism to give us the modified
outlook of the pastoral epistles and Polycarp.[215] Cerinthus emerged
some time early in the second century, representing a Jewish
Christian stance with Gnosticising overlay. The Seer's communities
were as opposed to alien gnosis as were the now-modified heirs of
Paul, their kind of Jewish Christianity preserved and developed
through the work of prophets and transmitters of oral traditions (cf.
those known to Papias in Hierapolis). A Qumran-influenced Paulinist
circle has also been posited, associated with the production of the
epistle to the Ephesians, and there must have been refugees from the
Fourth Evangelist's fragmented circle – more conservative than those
who defected to docetism (which the Johannine epistles indicate) and

perhaps ill at ease with some aspects of catholic congregational life. They all made use of Gospel writings but the relationship between them is much debated.[216]

There surely had been ecclesiological frictions and strained relations in the multifarious small churches of Asia Minor, and decades before the Prophecy blossomed. Had there been for some time, for example, Christians (formerly of the Fourth Evangelist's circle) nostalgic for Paraclete-led community life?[217] And when Ignatius castigated uncooperative congregants who acted apart from their bishops and without consent, should we think of a 'proto-Montanism'?[218] Was the Seer challenging distortions of Pauline teaching when he condemned neighbouring communities (and their leaders) for being less rigorous than was desirable?[219] In Thyatira, for example, meat sacrificed to idols was consumed without demur (cf. 1 Cor. 8) and 'fornication' (sexual laxity or idolatry) was in evidence, condoned by a female prophet cited as 'Jezebel' (Rev. 2:20). Thyatira took little account of the so-called 'Apostolic decree' (Acts 15: 23–7),[220] and the requirements which Christians of the Seer's circle honoured. In the triumph of Montanism in Thyatira (Epiphanius *Pan.* li.33) we may be seeing a swing towards the successors of that rigorous Christianity which had condemned the pragmatic 'Jezebel'.

What must have been a history of interaction, tension and rival claims between Christian groups in Asia found an echo again when, from *c.* 160 CE, the teachings of the Prophecy resurrected issues such as the relation of the Church to Israel and the interpretation of Paul and his teaching. Here was a conservative Christianity practised by Gentiles but conscious of the heritage of Christianity's Palestinian beginnings. It was in that sense Jewish Christian, but we should not look to Ebionism, as one nineteenth-century critic posited. Phrygian paganism, in my view, played no demonstrable part in the Prophecy's rise, but a Christianity strongly influenced by the Johannine traditions of Fourth Gospel and Apocalypse and by the teachings of Paul on spiritual gifts explains adequately what we see in the early Prophecy.

Nevertheless, J. Massingberd Ford (a commentator on the Revelation too)[221] has argued that the Jewish Christianity of Montanism should be more precisely located. In 'Was Montanism a Jewish-Christian Heresy?' (1966) Ford reminded us that both in the area of its origin and in North Africa there were substantial populations of Jews.[222] Asia Minor Judaism was of sectarian type, she suggested, and Christian converts from it imported its dietary practices and visionary and angelological interests (citing Paul's problems with Christians in Colossae). In matters of detail the Prophecy might be linked with three branches of sectarian Judaism: the Qumran sectarians, the Therapeutae and the Karaites.

From Qumran and elsewhere came explanation for Montanist use of a solar calendar in relation to Easter/Passover reckoning (Sozomen *HE* vii.12,18; Pseudo-Chrysostom *Ep.* vii (*PG* lix. 747); cf. the Gospel of John[223] and Eusebius *HE* v.24,3ff.). If Sozomen and Pseudo-Chrysostom were correct (and the latter seemed bewildered by the practice) then Montanists of a later period were probably conserving practices from the time of their origins (see 5.1).

The Therapeutae allowed women 'a part in the religious community' (though not as priestesses) and they prolonged fasts beyond the ninth hour (cf. Philo *De vita cont.* i and iv)[224] as well as valuing visions and oracles (Philo *De vita cont.* ii.11f.; iii.25). As for the Prophets eating radishes (Hippolytus *Refut. omn. haer.* viii.19), this, Ford suggested, was related to Jewish Passover practice (pointing to the Mishnah – hardly sectarian Judaism).[225]

Hippolytus in fact associates *rhaphanophagy* with *xerophagy* in this passage, linking both with new fasts and feasts instituted by Priscilla and Maximilla – not with Passover observance in particular or judaising in general. Moreover, *rhaphanophagy* may equally refer to eating of cabbage or similar greenery.[226] As for xerophagy, attested by Tertullian and Hippolytus, this, Ford suggested, was linked with vows of abstinence from moist food and wine as found in Mishnah *Nedarim* and *Nazir*.[227]

Parallels do exist in such Jewish texts, there is no denying it. They can be found in others which I cite too. But the kind Ford cites are often very generalised and do not provide exact parallels with Prophetic practice.[228] Though she is not postulating *direct* Jewish influence on the Prophecy but is claiming that 'the rather heterodox Jewish background of Asia Minor, especially of Phrygia' provided material and practices for adoption, still the claim is too great. The Prophecy, I suggest, was a product of an existing brand of *Christianity* which itself had been moulded in association with, and opposition to, Judaism of more than one kind. The Prophecy was indeed Jewish Christian. But to try to shed light on its significant characteristics by appeal primarily to the *Jewish* rather than the *Christian* is a mistake, I think.[229]

3.10.3 Why was the Prophecy condemned?

In many respects there was little to separate the Prophets from their catholic co-religionists. Differences were mostly differences of degree. Theological orthodoxy was not at stake and both sides appealed to the same Christian writings. There was the matter of *exposition* of those Christian writings, of course, but the threat was not that an enlarged or parallel 'canon' of writings was being created (for no such canon had been finalised). Nevertheless, the Prophets claimed direct authority of the Spirit (which clarified the meaning of Scripture) and that might prove at odds with the teaching authority of the catholic clergy. Novelties of discipline challenged catholic orthopraxis and robbed catholic teachers of the initiative in such matters. They were in danger of losing the moral high ground to Prophetic Christians at least as rigorous in discipline as themselves and in some respects more so. *Authority* was at stake.

A potentially successful Prophecy could not be allowed to flourish, and in Asia Minor objections to ecstasy, to inappropriate behaviour and the personal failings of the Three (in the absence of anything weightier) provided grounds for condemnation. By the time of serious debate in Rome and Africa things had moved on. The Prophecy, through Proclus, Tertullian and doubtless others of whom we do not know, was now having to define and defend itself more comprehensively. It had to explain its place in God's *heilsgeschichtliche* scheme, the relation of its revelations to received tradition and the significance of its insights for the existing catholic churches.

The Prophecy was proclaiming the in-breaking of a new order, bypassing established authority by direct revelation and putting to the forefront something which had been relegated to the margins. I do not think it began as an act of revolt against catholic clergy (however much individual prophetic Christians might have resented the decline of prophetic ministry.[230] Catholic leaders may have perceived a dangerous laicisation and democratisation but not even Tertullian denounced clericalisation *per se* or sought to divorce charismatic empowerment from Christian office. No, this was not just a case of envy of bishops. The Prophets intended *to prophesy*, in the context of troubled times and to a Church which could not but benefit, they thought, from inspired interpretation of its present experience and the declaration of God's promises for it (Epiphanius *Pan.* xlviii.13,1). To suggest it was revolt is to think of the Prophets as having been radically estranged from that Church. I find no cause to assume that they were, any more than Papias had been, or Quadratrus, though catholic clergy of their aquaintance (like Ignatius half a century earlier) must have found such Christians unsettling at times.

If the Prophets did hope to invoke the Spirit and preach hope and renewal with no greater repercussions than enlivened and encouraged Christian communities, then that was a naïve expectation! Estrangement from catholic clergy was inevitable, especially when the Prophecy started to achieve some success and its leaders refused to be silenced in the face of clergy objections.[231] The door had not been slammed on prophecy, although J.L. Ash suggested that episcopal seizure of 'prophetic' control had tried to render the charisma powerless in the hands of others.[232] There is *some* truth in this,[233] but the gifts of the Spirit were not completely absent from congregations (clergy powers apart) and the attractiveness of the Prophecy indicates that we should not overestimate the wholeheartenes of episcopal moves in that direction. But prophecy had come to be seen as a troublesome bedfellow and prophecy itself was one of the bones of contention. The Prophets were driven out, or perhaps seceded, our sources suggest both things. The reason, said Epiphanius (*Pan.* xlviii.12,1), was 'because of spiritual gifts'.

I conclude that all followed from the fact of that dangerous entity *prophecy*, and this one of a special kind: inapposite, 'untraditional' and incorporating innovatory discipline. Here was no sober didacticism and no *gravitas* of male catholic leadership. Here were 'wild and barbarous' people (Epiphanius *Pan.* xlviii.12,3), defending the message on the basis of cherished scriptural sources. I do not agree with Klawiter that the Prophets' enthusiasm for voluntary martyrdom was the key point at issue between them and the catholic Christians. Such enthusiasm has been exaggerated. Nor was the compulsion to prophesy a conscious revolt against a Church which had become not just 'unspiritual' but institutionalised and worldly (as Protestant scholarship has sometimes asserted). It is too simple to posit a planned uprising of the uncompromising *pneumatiki* against the *psychichi*, though a 'spiritual'–'psychic' line of demarcation was certainly drawn later. Of course, any prophet worth salt might point to a loss of first love (Rev. 2:4 to Ephesus), might warn of a tendency to compromise (in such accusations lies the background to the debate about martyrs, *HE* v.16,12; 20f.). A degree of catholic caution and pragmatism was understandable – there had been sufficient threats to Christianity from without the Church and on its sidelines. But it is

hard to argue that catholic churches had been concerned only with
matters of pragmatism to ensure survival or with maintaining order
and uniformity of practice within the ever-widening fold. Neither
Polycarp, the martyred catholic and prophetic bishop (*M. Pol.* xvi.2),
nor Irenaeus, irenic bishop and man of the Spirit, may be dismissed
simply as bureaucrats of a worldly and institutionalised catholic
Church.[234] No more were those catholics who died gladly for 'the
Name'. It is hard to say what the initial motivation was. We know
only what happened *as a result* of the Prophets' activity. The 'psychic'
epithet followed on rejection.

Once the Prophecy had been rejected, then its polemic grew
harsher against the catholic 'psychics' and 'catholicism' itself. A
number of later sources say that Montanists argued over the
significance of the term 'catholic'; and perhaps the term 'Phrygian'
heresy was more than simple geographical description and was
designed to rob it of any hint of catholicity. Positions became
entrenched and they were hostile. Later generations of Montanists
'upped the stakes' and explained and defended their stance and their
leaders in ways the catholics were able to challenge theologically (see
5.2–3). The latter may deliberately have driven them into that
corner. I am suggesting, however, that such Prophetic hostility to the
catholic Church and alienation from it was a *product* of rejection and of
consequent soured relations. It was not the cause of them.

In time isolation did breed an inward-looking peculiarity in the
fragmented Prophecy/Montanism. Ultimately (although by that
time it was already a shadow of its former self) it was condemned as
heresy and was wiped out (5.3).

Might the Prophecy have lived in and with the catholic congregations, as quite possibly it did for a time in North Africa? Might even
the allegedly ambitious Montanus, the peripatetic Priscilla, and
Maximilla with her sense of vocation to prophesy have been
accommodated within the far-from-uniform congregations of Asia
Minor? Might their loyalists have survived in mainstream churches
further afield – an irritant to those who favoured minimising the
hardships of Christian existence? Might Prophetic Christians have
been grit for the creation of an ecclesiastical pearl in which the gifts of
the Spirit and God's prophetically revealed demands for each
generation were publicly tested and the Spirit was acknowledged as
poured out on prophesying young men and handmaidens alike? It is
hard to see how.

Robert Eno recognised 'an unhappy constant' accompanying the ongoing development of Church structures. It was conflict.

Since they have spread to become a multitude they are divided and rent asunder . . . and condemn one another.[235]

By Julian the Apostate's time it seemed sufficient to leave Christians to damage themselves by the level of internal dissension.[236] As for the Prophecy, its separation from the Church had not been inevitable, Eno thought, for 'charismatic movements usually settle down rather quickly'.[237] There was, however, 'a fundamental type of conflict' with a hierarchically controlled Church which opted for maintaining order and continuity at the expense of spontaneity and the effervescence of the Spirit. In my view the catholic side recognised realistically that this phenomenon could not be accommodated comfortably without serious disruption to the order it cherished and even to its own Christian self-understanding. Where prophecy is in the cauldron a potent mixture must result.

The Prophecy emerged too late. The catholic hierarchy was already capable of communicating with like-minded Christians over a wide area and by the closing decades of the second century it was well versed in the art of assembling support for its position. With the coming of the Prophecy it recognised the existence of uncomfortable questions. Who or what determined the Church's discipline? Who had the last word on what was genuine prophecy? Where did authoritative exposition of Christian writings lie? Who spoke in God's name to the present troubled generation? Here in its sphere of influence was a non-conforming and potentially popular presence which constituted, if not a calculated threat, then an inevitable challenge. It chose not to meet it, but rather to take steps to rid itself of it.

3.10.4 A discomforting presence

It is not for historians to address the question which Soyres posed and which I quoted at the start of this study, namely, was the Spirit which Montanus preached and for which Perpetua died the Spirit of God, or was it the father of lies? Plenty of writers have stated their positions on the matter and they have given few hostages to fortune by being gracious to the Prophets. The question of devilish possession versus possession by the Spirit is not one I choose to address. But I do think the Prophets would not have been comfortable people to know. I

have come more and more to believe them as I read their claims, at
least to believe that *they* believed they were on the Lord's side and
were not self-seeking charlatans. Maximilla said as much. She was a
partisan, she claimed, in a righteous cause (see 4.3.2) and the
Prophets, if they too were enemies of Gnosticism, might have been
allies with the catholics on that front at least.

As for the Prophets' words – a number of the oracles of Priscilla and
Maximilla remain to be considered in chapter four. I will say at this
stage that I have also come to see in the much-maligned utterances of
the Three (or what survives of them) not the worthless mouthings of
egomaniacs – for they have often been portrayed that way – but
occasional glimpses of what was once a rich heritage of prophecy and
biblical exposition. It is now hard for us to envisage this, for it is
almost entirely lost to us, just as it is hard for a late twentieth-century
Briton to capture the soul of an Asian Christian charismatic in the
time of Marcus Aurelius.

I regret that despite having the evidence of the extant oracles, the
Passio Perpetuae and the Montanist writings of Tertullian, so *little* from
the Prophets' side has survived. Conversely, so much of what one
suspects is vituperative slander of them *has survived*. As a result there is
much that we do not know of the New Prophecy of the second and
early third centuries and many of the assumptions usually made
about it are at least questionable. The Prophets themselves pronounced with great certainty, but we must acknowledge a degree of
agnosticism.

CHAPTER 4

Montanism and women

4.1 THE FIRST WOMEN PROPHETS

4.1.1 'If Montanus had triumped . . .'

If Montanus had triumphed, Christian doctrine would have been developed not under the superintendence of the Christian teachers most esteemed for wisdom, but of wild and excitable women.

The quotation from Salmon's study of Montanus in the late nineteenth-century *Dictionary of Christian Biography* speaks volumes. It presupposes the primacy of Montanus; a particular susceptibility of women to wild excitement together with their incapacity for insight on matters of doctrine and also the triumphalism of women in any religious group unwise enough to give them space. It is a good example of its kind.

Our sources provide many references to women as well as utterances and records *from the women themselves*. Montanism is unusually rich in that respect, though still there are difficulties in recovering the women's history. For, as Virginia Burrus has observed about ancient heretical movements, the heresiological sources are written 'from the point of view of self-identified orthodoxy' and they are written by men, 'who utilize the figure of the heretical female as a vehicle for the negative expression of their own orthodox male self-identity'.[1]

Women of the earliest Prophecy were not heretical (Burrus' analysis concerned fourth-century women) but sources for much of later Montanism confirm the picture she paints – namely we have the reverse, negative image of the good orthodox woman which the catholics were helping to create and to contain. The female heretic was 'the threatening image of a community with uncontrolled boundaries' – allegedly sexually adventurous, verbally and theologically untrammelled, divorced from her rightful (private) sphere.[2] There are hints of this even in the earliest sources on the New Prophecy.

Two significant prophesying women were mentioned at the outset: Priscilla (Prisca/Priscilla, the latter form a diminutive, were the same person) and Maximilla. Even the names Montanus and Maximilla sounded fierce and barbaric to Epiphanius' source (*Pan.* xlviii.12,3). The enigmatic Quintilla appears first in Epiphanius (*Pan.* xlix,2; cf. li,33) and I shall argue that Quintilla (who was *not* Priscilla or Maximilla under another name),[3] post-dated them in her activity. John of Ephesus has seemed to refer to a revered Montanist woman called Carata but this is a misunderstanding. We know nothing of such a woman.[4] I shall come to other unnamed prophetesses and leaders (perhaps Montanist) when epigraphy is discussed (4.4 and 5.1).

Prophecy was a legitimate ministry for appropriately gifted women, as Paul had allowed, and in Asia Minor in particular there was already public religious activity of continent, visionary, autonomous Christian women, as well as men. If the passage in Galen's work was not an interpolation, it was well known that some Christians exercised restraint from intercourse all their lives, as well as showing contempt for death, and in the 170s Athenagoras was telling of aged Christian virgins and eunuchs being brought closer to God (*Leg. pro Christ.* xxxiii). We need only turn to the apocryphal *Acts* to find such continent women who in Asia Minor and elsewhere had courted the disfavour of their families and society, had left husbands and looked to the examples of the apostles.

Blessed are the continent for to them will God speak. . .
Blessed are they who have wives as if they had them not, for they shall
   inherit God . . .
Blessed are the bodies of virgins, for they shall be well-pleasing to God

read the *Beatitudes* of Paul in *The Acts of Paul and Thecla*, in which Phrygian Iconium is one of the places where such women might be found. Female confessors baptised (*Acts of Paul and Thecla* xxxiv) and there were female prophets such as Myrta in Corinth (*Acts of Paul*). There are even some coincidences of names with the Prophecy – a Maximilla in the *Acts of Andrew* xxx and an Ammia (cf. Eusebius *HE* v.17,2–4) in the *Acts of Paul and Thecla*. The *Acts* were not Montanist, however, and the Prophecy was free of the docetism which infected some of the *Acts*. But in such sources we can see a conflict between the authority of Rome and Christian values, a conflict which had echoes of the apocalyptic tradition to which Montanism looked, and more marked still is the tension between local *Asian* values, on the one hand, and the women's lifestyle on the other.

So before ever the Prophecy emerged catholic bishops must already have encountered feisty Christian women who chose sexual asceticism. There were still also the quieter 'virgins who are called widows' in the churches, of course (Ignatius *Smyrn.* xiii).

As for the female prophets in and around the churches, our sources are quiet about them, except for an occasional flash of light such as Papias' musings about the daughters of Philip. We should have known nothing of Ammia of Philadelphia, for example, foremother of Priscilla and Maximilla and honoured by the catholic side too, had not Eusebius' zeal to preserve the catholic opposition to Montanism caused him to include her name (*HE* v.17,3–4).[5] We are largely ignorant of the foremothers of Priscilla and Maximilla.

4.1.2 Accusations and exorcisms

Hippolytus recorded that chronologically Montanus had appeared before the women (*Refut. omn. haer.* viii.19,1; cf. x.25,1) and in Asia Minor the Eusebian Anonymous (*HE* v.16,7 and 9; cf. v.14,1) had implied that Montanus was *first* to be deceived by 'the Adversary'. This chronology came to be assumed so that later, for example, the Orthodox in the *Dialexis* condemned Priscilla and Maximilla as false prophets primarily because they had followed their 'guide' Montanus. He was seen as the instigator of, and the dominant partner in, the Prophecy. Like Helena to Simon Magus (Irenaeus *Adv. haer.* i.23,2; Justin *1 Apol.* xxvi,3), like Philoumene to Apelles (Eusebius *HE* v.13,2; Tertullian *De praescr. haer.* vi,6; xxx,6), like Marcellina to Carpocrates (Irenaeus *Adv. haer.* i. x. 25,6) and so on 'Montanus' women' were dependants, appendages of the male heresiarch.[6] Jerome wrote that these 'noble and rich women' were used to seduce communities by money, before then polluting them with heresy (*Ep.* cxxxiii.4 ad Ctesiphon; cf. Irenaeus on the Gnostic Marcus, *Adv. haer.* i.13,1–4), though far from being rich patronesses the early evidence points to their being simply prophets who were accused subsequently of accepting gifts of money and sumptuous clothing (*HE* v.18,4). Montanus was taken to be the diabolical and the *leading* figure.

New Testament writers and later apologists liked to picture male heretics as considerable womanisers and seducers,[7] but then 'the afternoons were long in a Gnostic's company', as Robin Lane Fox observed.[8] Yet Jerome, following Didymus, said that Montanus was a castrated male – a nugget of information seemingly, and oddly, unknown either to the earliest writers or to later Asian commentators. In any case, neither his sexual liasons with Prophetesses nor the women's revels with men ranked high in the list of accusations – unless we count Cyril of Jerusalem in *Catechesis* xvi,[9] or Isidore of Pelusium (*Ep.* i.24,2f.) on his alleged infanticide and adultery. Such accusations were untypical and late, though as we shall see there *was* an ongoing process of denigrating and demonising the Three.

The opposite was probably the truth. The 'annulment of marriages' and the adoption of the title 'virgin' were surely marks of a genuine desire for sexual continence among the New Prophets. We may safely disregard an accusation such as that from Timothy of Constantinople in the seventh century that Montanus 'procured' two harlots.[10]

One Prophetess taught that *purity* (like fasting, cf. Tertullian *De anima* xlviii.4) was more conducive to the work of the Spirit, to harmony, visions and auditions. This included celibacy but was probably not synonymous with that alone. Tertullian's *De exhort. cast.* x makes the point (Aland no. 11),[11] probably eching the Prophets' own experience.[12] Similarly, said the Prophetess, it was the *holy* minister who knew how to minister righteousness. This was part of the 'gospel' she preached, said Tertullian (echoing the covenant people ideas of Lev. 11:44f.; 19:2; 20:7f.; (LXX) Ps. 17:26f.). Parsimony of the flesh was investment in the Spirit![13] The first Prophets may well have demanded celibate leaders. This was not a group of libertines.

The celibate Priscilla and Maximilla were greatly honoured leaders. Their oracles were written down, circulated and accorded high status, to the chagrin of the opposition (see 3.9). And theirs was not the only female witness to be preserved. Perpetua's prison diary, which was incorporated into the *Passio Perpetuae*, is the earliest extant writing by a Christian woman (see 4.5). The preserved utterances of Priscilla and Maximilla offer (the 'Magnificat' apart) the first certain instances of Christian women's words being recorded and accorded (by some at least) divinely inspired status, but such a 'first' could not go unchallenged. Hippolytus deplored the Prophecy's 'countless books' (*Refut. omn. haer.* viii.19), singling out the two Prophetesses for attention.

In order to re-establish that ordered Church and universe which dissent as well as heresy threatened, the catholic side systematically blackened the Prophets' reputations, especially those of Priscilla and Maximilla. By the fourth century Cyril of Jerusalem felt obliged to interrupt some catechesis in which the Prophets were to be mentioned, so as to offer only hints of their misdeeds. This was out of respect for the women present (*Cat.* xvi, 1.8; cf. Ambrosiaster, *II Ep. ad Thess.* 5). First there had been the accusations about accumulation of personal wealth, abandonment of wifely duties and Priscilla's wrongful receipt of the title 'virgin'. More damning still were rumours that Maximilla, like Montanus, had died by suicide (like Judas Iscariot, *HE* v.16,13 [Apolinarius]) and that Theodotus, who had suffered a 'bad trip' on one of his heavenly ascents, had died as a result of his disorientation. Yet all such things considered, the *early* anti-Montanist writers had been relatively muted in their criticisms of the women. Rightly Anne Jensen noted that even the dismissive use of (wretched/weak/silly) 'women' (*Weiber*) was rare in early sources,[14] for women were often characterised as 'silly' and easy prey for seducing heretics (cf. too Epiphanius *Pan.* lxxviii.23,4; xlix.2,1–5; 1 Peter 3:7; cf. Origen *Contra Celsum* iii.55; Tertullian *De cult. fem.* i.1; cf. Jerome *Ep.* cxxxiii.4 ad Ctesiphon; Minucius Felix *Oct.* v.4; viii.4; Clement of Alexandria *Paed.* iii.4,28f.; Jerome *Ep.* liii; Sulpicius Severus *Hist. Sacra* ii.46; Sozomen *HE* vii.10,4).

The women were not heretical. There were no accusations of false teaching about the person of Christ or the Trinity (cf. Tertullian *De jej.* i; Hippolytus *Refut. omn. haer.* viii.19; x.25; Epiphanius *Pan.* xlviii.1,4). Instead it was a *mode* of prophesying and a Christian lifestyle which was being debated – orthopraxis and the catholic Church's right to determine its nature. Inappropriate prophesying, xerophagies and cabbage-eating, altered times of fasts, marriage and sexual abnegation – these things were linked with what was said of the women – or, as Tertullian put it immoderately in later defence, it was about the guts and genitals of the 'psychics' (*De jej.* i). Priscilla and Maximilla were in the vanguard, of course. The Spirit/Paraclete spoke in them as in Montanus (so Apollonius in *HE* v.18,2), bringing this new discipline (Hippolytus *Refut. omn. haer.* viii.19; x.25; cf. Tertullian *De jej.* x; xii; Origen *De princ.* ii.7,3; *De monog.* i.3–6; ii.1–4), so they were condemned in the literature of the catholics accordingly.

Exorcism of *the women* came quite quickly and seems to have continued as an aspect of the catholic Church's response. In later centuries Montanists had to undergo rebaptism for entry into the fold of orthodoxy, and as part of preparation there might be exorcism. At the outset, however, and like Montanus,[15] these intransigent women had been designated 'mad' (cf. later criticism of 'disciples of delirious women', Didymus *Frag. in Act. Apost.* x.10),[16] victims of the devil, of a 'spirit of deception' and 'bastard spirits' (v.16,7f.; v.16,13f.). 'Holy bishops' had been sent to test them (v.16,16f.; cf. v.18,13). Zoticus (probably of Cumane, not Otrous (*HE* v.16,5; v.16,16f.)) tried unsuccessfully to confute the Spirit in Maximilla (*HE* v.18,12f). Sotas of Anchialus' attempt on Priscilla had similarly been thwarted (*HE* v.19,3). Here was war: male against female; prophet against prophet; cleric ('eminent men and bishops' *HE* v.16,17) against laywoman. Nowhere are we told that Theodotus or Miltiades, Proclus or Aeschines, Alexander, Themiso or Montanus were exorcised.

As well as exorcising, catholic Christians congregated to condemn the Prophecy, probably providing the background for Maximilla's memorable utterance as preserved by Asterius Urbanus (Aland no. 16):

I am driven away like a wolf from the sheep. I am not a wolf, I am word and spirit and power.

Either the Spirit was here denying that it was the spirit of error or else Maximilla was distinguishing between herself (the alleged 'wolf', cf. Matt. 7:15; John 10:12; Acts 20:29; cf. *Did.* xvi.3; Ignatius *Phld.* ii.2; Justin *1 Apol.* xvi.13; *Dial.* xxxv.3; lxxxi.2) and the Spirit she knew. In any case she was speaking of that same work of God of which Paul had written in 1 Corinthians 2:4 (cf. too 1 Thess. 1:5 and the partial parallel in John 6:63), though many writers have failed see the close integration of Paul's words with her own. As Dennis Groh has observed, 'scholars . . . do not expect a charismatic prophet to quote scripture'.[17]

The Seer's prophecy had been saturated with the Old Testament; the Teacher of Righteousness at Qumran had determined meaning under inspiration so as to do more than reflect on words but to discern in them 'oracles which form a living unity with his own message';[18] Maximilla's prophesying was not dissimilar but, whereas the weakness of Paul (described in 1 Cor. 2 and 129) had served to manifest more clearly the power of God, Maximilla was a woman. Here was a weakness which, with her alleged wildness and her ecstasy, was an insurmountable barrier. Troublesome women should be seen off. They should be exorcised.

Exorcism was well established in Christianity and widely used.[19] Pagans remarked on it, and the official exorcist appears still in the third century.[20] Tertullian (*Apol.* xxiii.4 *et passim*; *De cormil.* xi.3; *De idol.* xi.7, cf. *De orat.* xxix) thought exorcism was a gift any Christian (man) might use (cf. too Minucius Felix *Oct.* xxvii; Origen *Contra Celsum* vii.67; Cyprian *Ad Donat.* v), though as a Montanist he had taken to arguing that abstention from sex aided the exorcising process (*De exhort. cast. x.1*). The (probably third-century) Syriac Pseudo-Clementine *De virg.* i.12 told of male Christian virgins who used the rite of exorcism as an excuse to call on their female counterparts and Athanasius regarded the sign of the cross as particularly effective. Indeed, so characteristic of Christians did such things become that Julian the Apostate spoke dismissively of the quintessence of Christians' theology: it was signing the cross on their foreheads and hissing at demons (*Ep.* xix to a priest). Exorcism, then, seems to have been commonplace in Christian circles. It was associated with healing, of course (as in the New Testament), and with pre-baptismal preparation (cf. Hippolytus *Trad. Ap.* xx.7; Cyril of Jerusalem *Procrat.* ix; *Cat.* xvi.19; Augustine *De pecc. mer. et remis.* i.34).

The female Prophets probably *were* thought to be infected with the sickness of evil spirits, perhaps akin to the infection of paganism itself (such had been the condition of a woman exorcised by Tertullian, *De spect.* xxvi,1f.). But we have to wait for Didymus and Jerome for clear accusations of paganism.[21] *Ecstatic* prophecy was a factor against them, of course (*HE* v.16,7; Epiphanius *Pan.* xlviii. 2 and 10f.). Tertullian (who himself had always perceived demons everywhere: *Apol.* xxiii; *De spect.* viii) found himself at odds with the catholics on this matter – for such prophecy was either divinely or demonically inspired and the catholics were certain which! The very presence of states of ecstasy helped to decide the catholic leaders *for* exorcism.

We see that lines of demarcation were being drawn between Christians and the sex of some of the protagonists would have marked them out as deviants. Exorcism here should be seen not least as an attempt at social control. It failed and the Prophecy was not immediately stemmed. Nevertheless, news of such acts would have spread and illustrated to the catholic faithful their leaders' certainty that a demonic subversion was in the midst.

These were not the last instances of exorcism of Montanist women. In Firmilian's time (4.4.1) there was even an instance of success. I know of no cases of the exorcism of Montanist men but then catholics may well have seen failure to re-establish an acceptable female norm as a prospect too awful to contemplate. Demonisation got worse as the centuries of Montanism progressed and the existence of female Montanist presbyters and bishops did not help (4.6; 5.1). In later writings Priscilla, Maximilla and Quintilla became 'Jezebel' of the Apocalypse (Rev. 2:18–21; Epiphanius *Pan.* li.33). With Montanus, the women and their subsequent followers (Priscillianists, Quintillianists) were accused of vile blood-procuring 'mystery' rites and the abuse of infants. We find this first in Praedestinatus on Tertullian's lost *De ecstasi* (*Haer.* i.26) and then in source after source of the fourth century and later (Cyril *Cat.* xvi.8; cf. Epiphanius *Pan.* xlviii.14f.; Filastrius *Div. haer. lib.* xlix; Jerome *Ep.* xli ad Marcellam; Augustine *De haer.* xxvi–xxvii). Of course Montanists denied mixing blood with meal for their rites (Timothy of Constantinople *De iis qui ad ecclesiam accedunt*), but they were not regarded as a reliable source! In the *Chronicle* of Michael the Syrian it would be recorded that Montanists had killed Christians. It was the devil himself, wrote Epiphanius, who spewed out teaching from such women (*Pan.* lxxix.1).[22] The women Prophets had fallen a long way from the initial accusations of instituting new fasts, encouraging the eating of cabbage and adopting the title 'virgin'.

Church history accorded to Montanus the dubious privilege of being the arch-villain in all this. Could it be that the history was wrong? Priscilla and Maximilla figured as large in the sources on Montanism as did the eponymous Montanus himself and, given that the acknowledged leadership of women is a rare phenomenon in the early Christian centuries (indeed in the history of the Church over two millennia), this fact is remarkable and deserves consideration. Can it be, then, that 'Montanism' was a serious misnomer and that our sources' interest in *women* in the Prophecy was not misplaced? Did the interest stem from a recognition (unspoken in our sources) that Montanus had not been the moving force in it at all but the women? The idea has been mooted recently and before continuing it needs to be aired.

4.2 PRISCILLIANISM OR MONTANISM: WHO FOUNDED AND LED THE NEW PROPHECY?

4.2.1 The misnomer of 'Montanism'

'Montanist' and 'Priscillianist' are fourth-century designations (Epiphanius *Pan.* xlix.1 and xlviii.14), suggestive of reverence for both the people concerned. Yet some early sources show a remarkable vagueness about Montanus himself, with language such as 'they say . . . 'or' . . . it is said to be . . .' (*HE* v.16,7), and we should compare Origen, who in the commentary on 1 Corinthians fragmentarily preserved through Catenae (lxxiv on 14:36) argued strongly against the activities of Montanist prophetesses *without showing interest in Montanus at all* (see 4.4.2(iii)). So were the women the significant figures of the Prophecy's beginnings? If so, then even Knox's acknowledgement of the women's importance would be wide of the mark: 'We may even guess that they somewhat overshadowed the author of their inspiration.'[23] Was Montanus never such an 'author' at all? Anne Jensen has posed the question in her book *Gottes selbstbewusste Töchter*,[24] and her argument runs as follows:

It was *a posteriori* assumptions in the Church which created the term 'Montanism', for catholicism thought in terms of heresies with a nameable and male head.[25] Eusebius (*HE* v.14,1) wrote of those who boasted of Montanus as the Paraclete and of the women as his prophetesses but now only polemicists 'of the lowest intellectual level' believe that Eusebius actually *identified* the Paraclete and Montanus, Jensen concedes. Nevertheless, writers have failed to appreciate that for Eusebius 'Paraclete' meant, literally, 'advocate'. So Montanus was a supporter or helper, the advocate of Priscilla and Maximilla and not their Paraclete or inspiration at all, and they were not his spiritual dependants. Indeed, the early witnesses show that the main prophetic activity was by the women, it was they who were refuted and exorcised.[26] The earliest extant oracles are from them. Montanus was the chief *organiser*, along with the likes of Theodotus (who was ἐπίτροπος) and Alcibiades (*HE* v.3,4). In *HE* v.16,4, for example, it is not the sect of Montanus but 'the sect of Miltiades' which is mentioned. Of course such organisational ability was a charism, Jensen concedes, but it was not one of the chief ones (cf. 1 Cor. 12:28). So, given the evidence of the respect shown for Priscilla and Maximilla and with due exercise of the hermeneutics of suspicion, Jensen surmises that Prisca/Priscilla must stand 'in der erste Stelle',

though we should not think of a 'head'.[27] Priscilla was the most
significant Prophet in a movement in which both sexes might have
determining roles.

4.2.2 A reply

My verdict on Jensen's thesis has to be 'unproven'. We *should* be
critical of scholars' assumptions, not least when they concern female
dependence or 'intuitive' suitability for something like Montanism.[28]
But it is one thing to argue for an egalitarian ecclesiastical format,
which perhaps had things in common with Paul's vision and in which
those with the most significant *charismata* (notably prophecy) held
sway. It is another to suggest that such a model brought prominence
to *the women* and that Montanus was less than a major prophetic figure.

Montanus *was* an organiser. He made possible assemblies at
Pepuza; he appointed collectors of money; he organised the payment
of salaries. Organisation was indeed among the minor gifts. *But he was
also a prophet* and not just a prophet, he was (according to *HE* v.18,2) a
διδάσκαλος. He *taught* the annulment of marriages (*HE* v.18,2) and
fasting. The *charismata* of teaching and prophecy were the *primary* ones
in Paul's scheme, along with that of apostleship (1 Cor. 12:28; cf. Acts
13:1). Montanus is not to be demoted in terms of charisma.
Furthermore, the Anonymous linked his activities with a lust for
leadership (*HE* v.16,7 φιλοπρωτείας). His claim (v.16,9) that Montanus
subsequently 'raised up' women prophets (the women were probably
prophets already) does accord with that view. Nor is there anything
to indicate that other Prophets, male or female, were free from
organisational tasks (see 4.6.4) and that this was particularly
Montanus' sphere. Above all, I suggest, there is not the evidence to
show that Montanus' role in relation to the women was that of
advocacy of *their gifts*.

Apollonius refuted the teaching and its *leaders* (using ἀρχηγός),
criticising their lifestyles (*HE* v.18,1–11) – Montanus, Priscilla and
Maximilla, Themiso and Alexander. I agree that we should recognise
a number of significant figures (not omitting Theodotus *HE* v.16,14).
But Apollonius was writing in the early third century and there are
problems of chronology involved. We should not necessarily assume
that all of these people were in leadership at the same time. As for the
fact that attributed prophetic *logia* in our earliest sources belong to
Priscilla and Maximilla [29](those explicitly from Montanus coming
from fourth century sources),[30] this is true. We should note Epiphanius,

says Jensen, and the fact that the Montanus utterances *defend* what was happening, especially in relation to ecstatic prophecy. This shows that Montanus was an *advocate*. But Epiphanius, though writing in the fourth century, was in fact utilising an earlier source at this point. Moreover there are unattributed *logia* preserved by Tertullian which may belong to Montanus (e.g. *De pudic.* xxi.7; *De fuga* ix.4). In any case some of the sayings of the female Prophets were no less concerned with defending the Prophecy, its nature and content, than were those of Montanus (Epiphanius *Pan.* xlviii.12,4 and 13,1; Eusebius *HE* v.16,17). In these respects I am unconvinced by Jensen's case.

A more telling item is that of prophetic succession in Eusebius *HE* v.17,3f. The succession seems to run from early prophets of the new covenant (Agabus, Judas and Silas and the daughters of Philip) through Ammia and Quadratus to the Montanist women who succeeded them – with no Montanus![31] He does appear immediately, however, in the challenge by the Anonymous to show who it was who succeeded in prophecy. We may not deduce from this passage, I think, that Priscilla and Maximilla (*HE* v.17,4) were inheritors in the succession, whereas Montanus was not.

According to early sources what was recognisably *the Prophecy* appeared first within the circle associated with Montanus. He, Alcibiades and Theodotus, all of the same 'party', were described as having first spread fervour about it (*HE* v.3,4 cf. v.14,1; v.16,7 and 9). This is a matter of chronology and need not imply the women's spiritual dependence upon Montanus. We find the Three in close association in Tertullian (*De jej.* i; *Adv. Prax.* i; cf. *De jej.* xii), as well as in Eusebius *HE* iv.27, Hippolytus *Refut. omn. haer.* x.25 and much later in the epistle of the Synod of Carthage (*PL* x.661). Tertullian, who honoured the Prophecy, was not concerned about the details of Prophetic leadership and certainly never suggested the women were dependants. Some later sources which did *were* guilty of precisely that kind of uncritical polemic which Jensen described.[32] The Three were equally revered in Prophetic circles: at the same time I find nothing to establish a case against the idea that the 'founding fathers' of 'Montanism', in terms of its first appearance, may have been precisely that – *men*.

We should not lay so much store by the Eusebius passage when looking for the source of the alleged 'misunderstanding'. Eusebius may have been less then even-handed in his presentation of things (*HE* v.14), but the association of the Paraclete with the Prophecy itself (meaning the Spirit which, working through them, led into all truth and convicted hearers) was early (cf. Proclus in Rome (*HE* ii.25,6; iii.31,4); Filastrius (*Div. haer. lib.* xlix)). Hippolytus wrote of the Paraclete coming in Priscilla and Maximilla (*Refut. omn. haer.* viii.19), albeit presenting Montanus as a prophet before (or over) them.[33] Tertullian[34] certainly knew of the age of Montanus, Prisca and Maximilla as the age of the Paraclete.[35] So by the third century some catholics were clearly associating the Paraclete with manifestations through Montanus and the women.[36] Was Eusebius unaware of, or hostile to, such understanding, so that he employed 'paraclete' in the sense of advocate? (Cf. his usage and the word-play in *HE* v.1,10 on a martyr with the 'paraclete' and the spirit of Zachariah.)[37] I do not think so.

There are anomalies, of course. Priscilla *was* a leading figure and in the decade of the 230s CE, for example, Firmilian omitted all reference to Maximilla in correspondence with Cyprian, telling of the Spirit which spoke *through Montanus and Priscilla* (*Ep.* lxxv.7). Another Asian writer, Basil the Great, reported that *Montanus and Priscilla* (again no mention of Maximilla) had appropriated the name Paraclete (*Ep.* clxxxviii). According to Epiphanius the Quintillianists looked to Priscilla and Quintilla as their great prophetic sources (*Pan.* xlix.2; cf. li.33). So Priscilla sometimes figures to the abandonment of Montanus, but then our sources refer to the Three (and Quintilla) in a variety of combinations. I do not think it is safe to infer much from this.

I think Jensen is right to argue against the dependence of the women on Montanus and right to stress their equal significance with him. Yet it seems to me to be as difficult to establish the priority of the women as it is wrong simply to assume the priority of the man. It is hazardous to posit anyone as *the* most important figure, as Jensen acknowledges. The early sources do pay great attention to the women, but, given the perceived danger from women, they would, wouldn't they? It was surely no more advantageous for the Anonymous to claim, as he did, that Montanus was the first to manifest the Prophecy than it would have been to blame the heinous ravings on women. He was probably telling the truth.

Nevertheless, Montanus was perhaps not the most prolific Prophet of the Three, though he is not to be relegated to the role of administrator and public relations specialist. *Montanism*, inadequate as it is as a denomination, should probably remain. In any case, *Priscillianism* is spoken for already.

4.3 THE ORACLES AND VISIONS OF PRISCILLA, MAXIMILLA AND QUINTILLA

4.3.1. Priscilla

Prisca's saying on continence, holiness and visions has already been mentioned (Tertullian *De exhort. cast.* x).[38] Another of her sayings should also be noted. This is in Tertullian's *De res. mort.* xi and there we see not only an interest in sexual continence but also that like Ignatius of Antioch (*Pol.* v.2) Prisca would not have such a thing divorced from 'honour of the flesh of the Lord'.

They are carnal (*carnes*) yet they hate the flesh.

The saying's *Sitz im Leben* was anti-docetic, I think.[39] The unusual plural *carnes*, if it is to be paralleled with the language of Revelation 17:16; 19:18,21 (as Froehlich suggested in his study of Gnostic language) may also speak of people likenable to the Whore and the forces of the Beast. They do not bear the mark of God. The oracle matches Tertullian's emphasis in *De res. mort.* lxiii. He cites Joel 2:28f.//Acts 2:17f. as proof of the checking of false teaching and proof of faith reanimated in resurrection of the flesh. Opposition to docetism/Gnosticism, fasting and refusal to spurn martyrdom would have been just the kind of teaching which attracted Tertullian to the Prophecy (cf. *Adv. Marc.* iii.8–11; *De carne Christi passim*). The Spirit now clarified teachings enshrined in documents which were *pristina instrumenta*; heretics had no right to the Scriptures (*De praescr. haer.* xiv.14; xvi.1f.; xix.2f.)[40] and the New Prophecy had come to refute all heresy, shedding light on inspired writings so as to dispel the subtleties of heretical interpretation and explain the mystery (cf. *De res. mort.* lxiii).[41] Prisca's saying, which may be about the carnality of those who who deny the Lord's flesh and the resurrection of the body, would have been just one salvo in the battle.

She may also have been behind the oracle in *De fuga* ix.4 (Aland no. 8), about public exposure and dying in martyrdom rather than in abortions (cf. *De anima* v.5), which may have been directed primarily to female sympathisers.[42]

4.3.2 Maximilla

We owe to Maximilla the statements already discussed on prophecy and 'the end' (συντέλεια) *Pan.* xlviii.2,4; cf. Matt. 13:39f.; 24:3; Heb. 9:26),[43] and on being driven away (Eusebius *HE* v.16,17). Another saying (Epiphanius *Pan.* xlviii.12,4, Aland No. 14[44]) indicates that Maximilla was disclaiming personal authority and pointing to the source:

Do not hear me but hear Christ,

she declared. It seems that Maximilla more than the others was forced to defend her own prophetic status. Perhaps she was considered to be the most troublesome, perhaps she survived longest, or ministered longest of the Three. A third self-justificatory saying appears in Epiphanius *Pan.* xlviii.13,1 (Aland no. 15) and it is a crucial one for the self-understanding of the Prophecy, I think.

Maximilla said she was compelled (ἠναγκασμένον), whether willing or not, to come to know God's γνῶσις. The Lord had *sent* her so that with regard to the present suffering (πόνου) and covenant (συνθήκης) and promise (ἐπαγγελίας) she might be *a partisan, a revealer and interpreter*. Epiphanius also said that the God-compelled Maximilla (ἠναγκασμένον) compelled her hearers, whether or not they too were *willing* (*Pan.* xlvii.13,7).[45] What are we to make of this?

Paul used the verb (ἀναγκάζω) and related forms in 1 Corinthians 7:26; 2 Corinthians 6:4; 12:10. In the last of these, as in 1 Corinthians 2:4 which had an echo in her 'wolf' saying', Paul's *weakness* and *the power* of God are described. The closest parallel with the oracle is in 1 Corinthians 9: 16ff., where Paul says he preaches the gospel by compulsion, with a trust laid upon him and with no credit to himself whether he preaches willingly or unwillingly. Maximilla, thoroughly familiar with Pauline and other writings about prophetic leadership, may have chosen to present (or indeed may have felt inwardly) parallels between Paul's situation and her own. The Prophets were laying claim to the Pauline 'high ground' again, as the catholics claimed the legacy of the apostle (see 3.9.1).

This oracle is rich in biblical prophetic–apocalyptic associations and it accords well with my conclusion in chapter three that the Prophecy *was* looking to the Parousia of the Lord and was millenarian in outlook.[46] It is also poetic in structure, with easily remembered triads and alliteration:

(i) The ἐπαγγελία recalls the Lucan account of Jesus' pre-ascension words to his disciples in Luke 24:49 (cf. Acts 1:4). They waited for the coming of that power from on high which the Prophets also looked to as the first manifestation of the Spirit to the Church, and the relation of Paraclete promises to the *initial* coming of the Spirit at Pentecost was a matter of debate between Prophets and catholics.[47] In 2 Peter 3:13 and 3:4 (cf. 1:4), also, the word *promise* relates to a new heaven and earth, to the coming again of the Lord and (in 1:4) to partaking of divine nature, having *knowledge* of God and Jesus (1:2). Such knowledge (both γνῶσις and ἐπίγνωσις are used) should be cultivated (1:6,8).

Elsewhere ἐπαγγελία relates mostly to promise of an eschatological kind, with emphasis on the necessity for righteousness and ethical renewal (*1 Clement* xxvi.1; xxvii.1; xxxiv.7; xxxv.1–4; *2 Clement* v.5; x.3f.; xi.6f.; xv.4; Hermas *Vis.* i.3,4; ii.2,6; iii.2,1; *Sim.* i.7). Both ideas may be in mind, i.e. the interpretation concerned both the promised Spirit of God (a reality in Maximilla's own day) and the promise of things to come which was especially applicable to those who responded to the Spirit in righteousness, patience and faith (cf. *HE* v.16,9; Heb. 6:12f.; 8:6 *passim*.)[48]

(ii) The συνθήκη is probably that which the Seer envisaged when he described the God–Christian community relationship in covenantal terms; such as in Revelation 21:3 when the New Jerusalem descends and God tabernacles with humankind; and when the one that 'overcomes' shall inherit all things (Rev. 21:7).[49] The language of the Revelation itself looks to Leviticus and Jeremiah, Zechariah and Ezekiel and, like the Seer, who wove Scripture to be one with his new insights, Maximilla transmitted for her own generation those revelations and secrets which made sense of present suffering, of the marginalisation of Christians and of God's apparent tardiness in intervening. The covenant *was* the Christ–community relationship, the Christian dispensation as the Prophets thought it should be known.

(iii) Maximilla and the Spirit which spoke through her had been 'sent' (ἀπέστειλέ, see (i) above) for this task. The verb is also reminiscent of the seven spirits 'sent forth' into the earth in Revelation 5:6; of the sending forth of prophets and of the messenger of the covenant (LXX Isa. 6:8; 48:16; Jer. 1:7; 7:25; (cf. 23:21) *et passim*; Ezek. 2:3; Mal. 3:1; Matt. 10:16; 23:34 and cf. Paul in 1 Cor. 1:17). It is not the verb form found in the Johannine Paraclete passages, where πέμπω is used (John 14:26; 16:5; 7; cf. Rev. 1:11; 11:10) but John uses it of the sending of Christ himself (3:17; 5:36; 6:57; 7:29; 8:42; 17:8; 20:21 (contrast 4:34; 5:23; 7:28; 8:26; 13:20); 1 John 4:14).

(iv) Maximilla's role, then, was that of interpreter (ἑρμηνευτής)[50] of covenant and promise, and again we may look to Tertullian *De res. mort.* lxiii for possible clarification. Mutilation and misinterpretation

166   *Montanism*

of Scripture, compounded by the addition of apocryphal tales, had led to aberrant Christology, he said, and a faltering of faith. The Spirit/Paraclete, now poured out on handmaidens and servants (citing Joel 2:28f., as we saw in 4.4.1 above), had clarified the meaning of Scripture, explaining the mystery and countering heresies. (Cf. too the language of 2 Peter 1:16, 19–20; 2:1.) Maximilla was of the same school of thought – a 'partisan' on what the Prophets took to be God's side. I take Maximilla's words to imply that the γνῶσις of God which she had to understand was at odds with another and abhorrent γνῶσις, which distorted the God–Christian covenantal relationship – not least because its teaching on the person of Christ would have rendered the sealing of the new covenant in blood impossible ('denying the Lord that bought them', as 2 Peter 2:1 put it). It would have made of suffering, and of Christian doctrine (διδασκαλία) in general, something unacceptable.[51]

Epiphanius, of course, seized upon the word γνῶσις and used it as a stick with which to beat Maximilla. But I think the Prophecy was not heretical and the *Sitz im Leben* of Maximilla's oracle may well have been *opposition* to heresy.[52]

(v) *Suffering* is the last element to be considered. The need for interpretation of suffering points to a time of persecution, warfare and plague. The word (πόνος) occurs only in the Revelation in the New Testament (16:10f.) and in Revelation 21:4 we have a description of the end of all suffering, when the new heaven and earth appear and the new Jerusalem will be reality. The covenantal relationship will be experienced directly, with God in the midst (23:1–3). It looks as though Maximilla (and presumably other leaders of the Prophecy) saw the Prophets' role as clarifying and preaching what the nature of the Christian covenant community should and would be, and this against the background of suffering (cf. *1 Clement* v.4 of the sufferings of Peter). Her partisanship was of a kind of Christianity (cf. Paul in Acts 24:5; 28:22) which was steeped in the study of the promises of Scripture and alive with apocalyptic hope. The term μηνυτής, 'one who discloses something hitherto not known', speaks of the same thing.[53]

Here we catch a glimpse of a New Prophecy which saw itself in the vanguard of renewal in the Church. Through its interpreting of the promises and the writings of the new covenant, it was the safeguarder of their integrity. The threats to them were not just half-heartedness in the face of secularisation, growing institutionalisation or persecution.

There was a threat, too, from those who would distort their meaning and dehumanise the Lord of the Church.[54] Maximilla was probably the best-known figure in the movement for a time.[55] If the Anonymous is reliable (*HE* v.16,19),[56] she was dead by *c.* 179–80 CE.

4.3.3. *Quintilla*

It was at Pepuza that Quintilla or Priscilla (Epiphanius *Pan.* xlix.1) encountered Christ in female form.[57] Filastrius and others knew of Pepuza as that place where Montanus, Priscilla and Maximilla had spent their 'useless' (prophetic) lives (*Div. Haer. lib.* xlix) and it was *Pepuzites* which became an epithet for some believers of Montanist persuasion.[58] Quintilla came to be associated with it, too. She does not appear in our earliest sources, unless she is the Prophet referred to by Apollonius in *HE* v.18,6,[59] and if we place her quite a number of decades *after* the rise of the Prophecy, then certain problems of chronology and of Montanist eschatology are eased (see the discussion of millenarianism in 3.3.10). Quintillians, named after her, were listed in association with other Montanist groups (Augustine *Haer.* xxvii; Epiphanius *Pan.* xlix.1,14–15; 23 li.33,8; lxxix.1,7).[60] Praedestinatus wrote of two churches in Pepuza, one dedicated to Priscilla, the other to Quintilla. It seems that the *Pepuzites*, who continued to function at the geographical hub of the early Prophecy, felt themselves a cut above the Cataphrygians in general (Praedestinatus *Haer.* i.27).

4.3.4 *Quintilla: a later Prophet*

To make the case for Quintilla being a later Prophet *Pan.* xlix.1 must be considered, viz. the Christophany at Pepuza. Most modern commentators regard the account as authentic,[61] and its significance will be considered in due course. Christ came while the Prophetess was asleep, coming in the form of a woman and in a bright robe and putting wisdom into her. The place was revealed to be a holy place and there (or 'thus', perhaps) Jerusalem would descend. I have argued[62] that the vision was determinative for Montanist (or at least Quintillianist)[63] understanding of the end time; but who (Priscilla or Quintilla?) received this vision and when? I believe it was Quintilla and at a time when the Three were dead. Here are some reasons for that view:

(a) Tertullian knew of no such Prophetic expectation about Jerusalem and so it must have post-dated his writing;

(b) Priscilla disappeared from record relatively early in the Prophecy's life. It would be surprising if such a justification for calling Pepuza 'Jerusalem' had been given to her and that no early anti-Montanist (e.g. Apollonius) mentioned it;

(c) The Anonymous said that since the death of Maximilla no Prophet of stature had emerged (Eusebius *HE* v.17,4) and Epiphanius' source claimed that the Phrygian heretics had had no Prophet after Maximilla (*Pan.* xlviii.2.1–2). Epiphanius wrote later of Quintillians, which must have been a subsequent phenomenon. I assume, then, that decades passed before a significant successor appeared;

(d) As Powell observed in 'Tertullianists', there is point in giving weight to revelations which came to a later Prophetess by attributing them to a founder (hence Epiphanius' uncertainty about which Prophet saw the appearance; some believers, I assume, were attributing it to Priscilla) but no merit in claiming the reverse;[64] and

(e) (also an observation from Powell) the *form* of the material, which contains no direct 'I' utterance but is in *oratio obliqua*, distinguishes it from many of the extant utterances of the Three.[65]

The balance of probability is surely in favour of Quintilla and the Quintillianists being *later manifestations* within Montanism. The date of Epiphanius' source on them must provide a *terminus ante quem* but that date is not easy to determine.[66] I do not favour Bonwetsch's suggestion that Firmilian's unnamed prophetess (dating from *c.* 235 CE see Cyprian *Ep.* lxxv.10) was Quintilla herself, though Aland too thought it possible. Nevertheless, it may well have been in a situation such as that described by Firmilian, viz. of intensified persecution and of natural disaster, that at some point Quintilla rose to prominence, to become eponymous founder of the group which continued to remember the appearance of Christ to her. We do not hear of books in her name or of collections of her utterances but loyalists continued to visit the sanctuary at Pepuza for rites of initiation (*Pan.* xlix.1) and the Quintillianists were literalistic in interpretation of the Revelation.[67]

What of Quintilla's experience? Commentators have been scathing, with appeals to Freudian-type insights in some cases. Some have seen it as clear indication of the heresy of the Montanists and/or the lunacy of its leaders. Yet the apparition is not incomprehensible. Christ in female form, it is reported (for the words are not her own), appears to Quintilla in the room in Pepuza where she is sleeping. Christ, in bright robe, imparts (using ἐνέβαλεν) wisdom into Quintilla,[68] revealing the (presumably hitherto unknown) relation of the promised Jerusalem to Pepuza. Schepelern's suggestion of a sacred marriage scene falls down not least because both the figures in this scene are female,[69] but let us begin with the Apocalypse.

Revelation 12 describes the woman clothed with the sun who is the Church, just as it also tells of Jerusalem as the Church, the adorned Bride (Rev. 3:12; 19:8), the wife of the Lamb. The Bride appears in that fine white linen which is the attire of angels (15:6) and the righteousness of the saints.[70] Such images were not new. 4 Ezra, in the field Ardat/Ardab, told of the transformation of a mourning woman into one with shining face and a countenance flashing like lightning. Then the heavenly Zion was revealed (4 Ezra 9; 10:25ff.).[71] Hermas, too, envisioned the Church as female (*Vis.* ii.4,1, and in his field encountered her, *Vis.* ii.1,1–4). *2 Clement* contains a section (xiv) as intriguing as it is opaque,[72] dealing with the 'spiritual' Church 'manifest in the flesh of Christ'. Here was a pre-existent Church. She was made spiritual as was Jesus himself, who was made manifest in the last days so that he might save.[73] To offend the Church (the flesh), then, was to forfeit the Spirit: 'Guard the flesh that you may receive the Spirit' (*2 Clement* xiv.3). Here was a sentiment with which Prisca would surely have concurred. Like Powell, I think that what we have in the appearance of Christ to Quintilla is the manifestation of the Church above, even now coming down in the Spirit.[74] It is more likely still if we interpret the ὧδε of Epiphanius *Pan.* xlix.1 as 'thus' (rather than 'here') Jerusalem descends. Nor do writings such as 4 Ezra, *The Shepherd* and the Apocalypse exhaust possible parallels with and influences on this Christophany scene. The theme of wisdom is clearly important. The female Christ imparted wisdom to Quintilla and Wisdom was itself female.[75] Moreover, in the Apocalypse the word 'wisdom' (an attribute of God and of the Lamb in 5:12; 7:12) occurs prior to the revelation of a hitherto hidden meaning (e.g. Rev. 13:18 and the number of the Beast; 17:9 and the significance of the scarlet beast). In like manner Quintilla's receipt of wisdom is followed by a revelation to her (ἀπεκάλυψέ) of the descent of Jerusalem. God granted the spirit of wisdom (πνεῦμα σοφίας) and revelation (καὶ ἀποκαλύψεως), wrote Paul (Eph. 1:17f.), so as to enlighten believers about the saints' glorious inheritance.

Quintilla was re-expressing a commonplace of expectation in circles familiar with sapiential and apocalyptic ideas: Wisdom, precreated, would be granted to the righteous at the eschaton. It was necessary for the receipt of eschatological secrets (1 Enoch 5:8; 9:10; cf. 48:1; 4 Ezra 5:21; 14:40; 13:54; also 8:4, 12,52) and so Wisdom came to Quintilla and allowed her to have such knowledge, as did Enoch and Ezra before her. There is not the suggestion, however, that Wisdom had been hidden as part of the Woes, as in 4 Ezra 5:9, for example (cf. 5:38; 8:4).

The limited originality in this scene (and in oracles and dreams of other Montanists) lies in the charismatic exegesis of texts which is applied and in the prophetic subsuming of bits of Scripture and tradition to the experience and insight of the Prophet. Thereby something fresh was created.[76]

4.3.5 A remaining source

There is another important Montanist source, which comes from early third-century North Africa. This is the *Passio Perpetuae*. It is a source rich in dreams, visions and the insights of women. It will be examined in 4.5, since women martyrs must be looked at as a special category in this study, not least because of theories about the relation of confession and martyrdom to the clericalisation of Montanist women. Clericalisation will figure in 4.6. What follows is an outline of what else we know of Montanist women after the death of the Three, some colourful, others 'the Montanist in the street'.

4.4 ONGOING FEMALE PROPHECY AND WITNESS

4.4.1 Women Prophets in the East

Despite the claims in *HE* v.17,4 and *Pan.* xlviii.2,1–4, we do know that the phenomenon of prophecy continued in Montanism. In North Africa, at least, it continued in catholic circles too,[77] and Cyprian told even of catholic *children* who had visions and auditions from the Holy Spirit (*Ep.* xvi.4). There were prophesying 'disciples of Maximilla' and Epiphanius told of white-clad prophesying virgins among the Quintillians.[78] Women held the title of 'prophetess', but whether among the Quintillians or Cataphrygians he was unsure. It was all one to him (*Pan.* xlix.1). There were others too.

(i) In Cappadocia Firmilian's prophetess claimed to be possessed by the Holy Spirit. She performed wonders in a state of ecstasy and walked even in snow barefoot with no ill effect (was this asceticism or a prophetic 'sign' related perhaps to mourning customs cf. 2 Sam. 15:30; Isa. 20:2f.; Ezek. 24:17,23; Mic. 1:8). She also promised to make the earth tremble – perhaps a prophetic 'word of the Lord' in 'I' form, echoing, e.g. Psalm 60:2f. or proclaiming the Day of the Lord as in Joel 2:1f. (esp. 2:10; cf. Amos 8:7–10). This was a time of frequent earthquakes in Cappadocia and Pontus (Cyprian *Ep.* lxxv.10) and a time of persecution. She had appeared suddenly and gained followers, giving the impression, so Firmilian claimed, that she belonged in Jerusalem and was returning there. The reference to *Judea* may possibly be a gloss on his part and perhaps we should understand 'Jerusalem' in its sense of ideal community.[79] She may well have been a Montanist, taking the opportunity afforded by persecution and disaster in a neighbouring province to spread the word and to point to the signs of the consummation of all things.[80]

Firmilian claimed that she succumbed to exorcism, but not before she had seduced into illicit relations the presbyter Rusticus (or perhaps just a rural presbyter) and an unnamed deacon (this fact was conveniently 'discovered' later). A good exorcist was amply supported by a bevy of brave and encouraging male co-religionists and the familiar descriptive pattern emerges: here was *a woman*, autonomous, false in her prophecy, demonic in her possession and sexually a threat to Christian men. Just possibly this was the enigmatic Quintilla, drumming up that following which she eventually achieved. But that seems unlikely unless (a) the 'Jerusalem' of her preaching was far away from Judea and was that which had been revealed to her by the wisdom-bearing Christ or (b) she was in her salad days, before the time of her most famous revelation.

(ii) Secondly, we know of Nanas. Her home territory was Cotiaeon in Phrygia, metropolis of the Tembris valley, now modern Kütahya.[81] Nanas was no consecrated virgin but married, for it was her husband who recorded her gifts on her gravestone, telling of her displays of speaking in tongues, of angelic visitations to her, of her powerful offerings of prayer. Was she too a Montanist?[82] Probably, I think. Unlike some of the other women described in this chapter Nanas was not vilified. She was buried amongst friends, in an environment where women of her kind gained respect, where a 'spiritual' woman might be remembered as such in an inscription on her grave.

(iii) Such a woman might even bear a name like that of Montanus. We find this in another inscription from the region of Dorylaeum (modern Eskisehir):

λουπικῖνος Μουντάνῃ συνβίῳ χρειστιανῇ καὶ πνευματικῇ μνήμης.[83]

Loupikinos remembered his wife, a 'spiritual Christian', and the π + π decoration completes the picture – here was an address πνευματικὸς/πνευματικῇ a spiritual Christian to/for other spiritual Christians.[84]

(iv) The theme of *seven virgins* which appears in Epiphanius *Pan.* xlix.2 occurs also in an account which purports to tell of the martyrdoms of seven named virgins, probably during the persecution of Maximinus Daia in 312 CE. The source, the *Life of St Theodotus of Ancyra*, has been referred to in 3.8.3(v) and, though it may not be claimed for certain as Montanist, it speaks of visions and apparitions, martyrdom, a disciplined lifestyle and a veneration of martyrs and *patriarchs* (cf. Jerome *Ep.* xli.3). The Christian virgins in it numbered seven but they were not said to be prophets, as in Epiphanius' account. The women were accused as Christians and forced naked into carts to be part of a procession during a pagan rite. They refused to sacrifice and were martyred by drowning – weighed down by stones in the lake not far from Ancyra where the idolatrous images were being immersed. The martyrs' bodies, recovered at great risk by other Christians, were then interred near the chapel of the patriarchs (*Life* xiii–xix). They were not young women. Tecusa, the spiritual mother of Theodotus himself, was in her seventies (xiii). With Alexandreia, Phaiene, Claudia, Euphrasia, Matrona and Ioulitta she had been spared the rape intended, but they were unwillingly associated with what was probably the rite of the *lavatio*, on the closing day of the Cybele-Attis festival in spring.[85]

If these people were indeed of Montanist persuasion (and I am unconvinced) then the source shows Montanism's continued recourse to visions, refusal to compromise belief and the honouring of consecrated virgins.[86]

4.4.2 *Women Prophets, Carthage and the evidence of Origen*

(i) I turn now to the evidence of Tertullian. He respected and quoted Prisca and Maximilla. He respected female prophecy and criticised Marcionites not least because they had no great female speaker who looked into the secret things of the heart and foretold what was to come (*Adv. Marc.* v.8,2). Such gifts existed in his own Christian ranks, and in the Montanist *De anima* ix.4 Tertullian left us a picture of what one such prophetess did.

She received gifts of revelation while in a state of ecstasy, visions and auditions of God and of angels (cf. Nanas). Like prophets described in 1 Corinthians she could see into hearts and also provided healing remedies. The services in church helped,[87] for revelations came during psalms and readings, sermons and prayers. On an occasion when the soul was being discussed she received a vision of its corporeal form. Conveniently this bolstered Tertullian's own view, for our author was not averse to citing visions, whether in defence of teaching on the soul, martyrs in heaven, the length of a virgin's veil or Jerusalem of the millennium. I take her to be part of the Montanist *ecclesiola in ecclesia* in Carthage. Notably, however, she did not prophesy *publicly*. To judge from what Tertullian says, she did not interrupt or address the congregation at all but rather she spoke with those (a self-selecting Prophetic group?) who stayed behind after the service. She then communicated her insights and her words were recorded carefully, so that a process of testing might follow.[88]

This was indeed, as Knox remarked, a 'tame enough specimen' of the female prophetic type.[89] Tertullian approved tacitly of this woman's reticence. Silence and 'the priesthood of chastity' (*sacerdotes pudicitiae*) belonged to women, he had argued (*De cult. fem.* ii.12,1; ii.13; *De virg. vel.* ix), so did the possibility of prophecy, of course (*Adv. Marc.* v.8,11 cf. 1 Cor. 11:5), but modesty was a must. Was this Tertullian's peculiar version of the Prophecy's teaching on the female Prophetic role? Or did most 'spiritual' women function in this relatively low-key way? It seems unlikely that all Montanist female prophecy was so modestly conducted – Firmilian's prophetess was not so reticent and, as we shall see, later writers had to stress *against* Montanist women the importance of *private* ministry. Perhaps Tertullian knew little about the 'unprivate' mode of prophecy of Prisca and Maximilla – or chose to overlook it. The Anonymous, after all, had stated clearly that they had prophesied. It is not impossible that Tertullian may have thought that the only women granted freedom to prophesy, in tandem with the right to *public* activity, were Prisca and Maximilla.

He also tells of a woman who had the unnerving sensation of being clapped on the neck by an angel while in church (*De virg. vel.* xvii). She too, I assume, was of the Prophetic faction and, if Tertullian was at all representative of it, that faction was arguing strongly for the veiling of virgins in church. This veiling should be comprehensive, not just a token (*De orat.* xxi–xxii; *De cor. mil.* iv.2ff.; *De virg. vel.* i.1ff.), for it was the bidding of the Paraclete (*De virg. vel.* i), despite its being contrary to the usual practice in the church of Carthage (cf. ii–iii).[90] The angel served not just as a warning to the unconvinced but also indicated the precise length of the veil required! We are not told in this instance how the message was conveyed to those present.

(ii) Origen's evidence demands longer consideration, for here we see some bases of complaint emerging. Origen wrote about Montanist prophetesses in commenting on 1 Corinthians (*Catenae* in Sancti Pauli Epistolas ad Corinthios (on 1 Cor. 14:36)). This evidence probably relates to the early decades of the third century, after the demise of the Three, a period in the history of the Prophecy about which we know little. But he writes in the past tense. Some women were 'disciples of women', products of Priscilla and Maximilla rather than Christ and evidently they had presented arguments in support of their public activity. Origen set about refuting them.

It was not the *fact* or the *mode* of their prophesying which concerned him, but rather that their activity was unacceptably *public*. His arguments presuppose that the women concerned were prophesying in church settings and were addressing gatherings: 'you would not find that Deborah addressed the people as Jeremiah and Isaiah did', he maintained, and he appealed to the well-worn 1 Timothy 2:12 and Titus 2:3–4 as well as to 1 Corinthians 14:34f. for support. The women looked to the precedent of Philip's daughters (Acts 21,9; cf. Origen *Comm. in Matt.* xxviii; Eusebius *HE* iii.21,2–4; xxvii.1) but *they* had never prophesied in an assembly, Origen retorted (a point Eusebius never raised).[91] Paul had certainly let a woman prophesy in church, of course, but Origen thought otherwise. *Public* prophecy was the point at issue,[92] and it could not be defended by appeal to Deborah, Huldah and Miriam (in the Hebrew Scriptures) or Anna in the Gospel of Luke. *None* of these women had ever addressed the people (other than perhaps a group of other women, who did not count in this context): they had never spoken 'in church' (appealing to 1 Cor. 14:35 again).

In any case, Montanist prophecy was questionable. 'When you say', Origen challenged, 'that your prophetesses have prophesied, then show the signs of prophecy among them' (cf. 2 Corinthians 12:12). With 1 Corinthians 14 as its starting-point, Origen's language shows that Paul's teachings on prophecy and a woman's place were being debated. Only from Epiphanius, however, (*Pan.* xlix.2,1–5) and in the *Dialexis* do we discover the use of that most egalitarian of Pauline passages, viz. Galatians 3:28. This told that 'in Christ' there was no distinction between Jew or Greek, free or slave person, male or female. It was used by the Montanists to defend women among their clergy. Origen did not mention it, but some of Origen's arguments (e.g. about Philip's daughters) are reminiscent of what we have seen in Asian anti-Montanist sources and his words on the significance accorded to Priscilla and Maximilla remind us of Hippolytus in *Refut. omn. haer.* viii.19,1f.; cf. x.25,1f. Phrygians (and women), he said, had been captivated by *women* (cf. Didymus *Frag. in Act. Apost.* x.10, 'disciples of delirious women').[93] Irrespective of whether their speech was of the saintliest kind, females should not speak, for the sayings 'come from the mouth of a woman'. It was a sentiment with which, at another time, Tertullian had concurred.[94]

Montanist women, it would seem, were insufficiently reticent for the catholics' liking. Epiphanius went further in itemising objections to women's public role, deploring the Montanists' reverence for Eve[95] and the clericalisation of females (Pan xlix.2–3). So too Didymus (*De Trin.* xli.3) and his source the *Dialexis* deplored their writing of books and anathematised the collection of the oracles of Priscilla and Maximilla. Women might prophesy, said the Orthodox – Scripture offered precedents, viz. Deborah, Philip's daughters, Miriam and the mother of the Lord (cf. Epiphanius *Pan.* lxxix). But such women had not exceeded the bounds of modesty and private consultation. They had not 'dishonoured the head' (1 Cor. 11:3–5) by prophesying with head uncovered or by writing books. Even Mary had refrained from writing and was 'veiled' by virtue of the male evangelist recording the words for her (*De Trin.* iii.41,3).[96] Both John Chrysostom (*In illud* 'Salutate Priscillam et Aquillam' i) and Jerome (*Ep. ad Rom.* xvi) maintained that Priscilla, the instructor of Apollos (Acts 18:24f.) had instructed *in private*.[97] It is clear, then, that it was the mythology of Priscilla and Maximilla and the freedom of public (including church) activity accorded to Montanist women which upset the catholic side after the demise of the Three, more than the fact or form of prophesying itself.

4.4.3 Findings on continuing prophecy
So prophecy and receipt of revelations had not ceased with their demise. Ecstasy had not ceased and the ideal of a Christian 'Jerusalem' community continued. But, separated from the catholics, the successors

of the New Prophets devised their own church structures (see 5.1), within which women had a more significant place than their catholic sisters enjoyed (4.6). Maybe Tertullianists, like the remarkable and puzzling Tertullian, were less liberal where the female sex was concerned.

The ideal of Montanist Christian womanhood embraced the *public* sphere as well as the private spheres and in ways anathema to the catholics. The *Passio Perpetuae* will illustrate this further. A suitably charismatic woman was called upon to respond to the Spirit's leadings in the congregation and even (like Priscilla and Maximilla or the prophetess known to Firmilian) to be an itinerant evangelist and prophet. She might flout society's conventions in the cause of total discipleship – leaving her husband. The Montanist woman was called on to accept willingly *public* declaration of her faith in times of trial. There was to be no shunning of the public gaze out of modesty or appeal to domestic and female obligations. Catholic women were known to take such a stance, of course – not least Blandina – but if the extant oracles preserve the truth, the Montanists were anxious that *women*, no less than men, should be *wholly* disciples: disciplined and fervent, continent and Spirit-filled, uncompromising and *seen*. They did not fear to defend their stance, debating Scripture and appealing to revelations. There is nothing to suggest that they relied on men to be their advocates.

Virginia Burrus catalogued the determined relegation of women to the private sphere in catholic writings which were *not* concerned with Montanism (see 4.1.1). The present section has shown that the pattern is consistent, too, in those writings which *did* deal with it.[98]

4.5 IDEAL WOMAN, IDEAL MARTYR

The *Passio Perpetuae* is unmarred by the excesses which mark some later martyrologies and it provided the model on which a number of later accounts were based. It preserves the earliest extant writing by a Christian woman, viz. the prison diary of Vibia Perpetua, and the finished work is the product of a Montanist redactor (R^{Pass}) who used the personal diary of Vibia Perpetua to show that the graces of martyrdom and of visions were not confined to the past (*Pass. Perp.* i).[99] The martyrdoms of Perpetua, Felicitas, Saturus and the others probably occurred on 7 March 202–3 CE.[100]

4.5.1 Montanist martyrs?

The balance of probability rests with Perpetua and the others being among the first-fruits of the Prophecy in Africa. R^{Pass} must have recognised in them fellow-travellers at least. They were part of a circle which was clearly sympathetic to strains which we now take to be characteristic of Montanism: visions, ecstasy, reference to the promise of Joel 2:28f. (the work of the Redactor)[101] and the taking of curds/cheese (Latin *caseo*) are among the many parallels. The last is reminiscent of Epiphanius' reference to the practices of the 'bread and cheesers' (τυρός 'cheese'), the possibly Montanist-associated Artotyrites of Asia Minor (*Pan.* xlix,2; cf. Augustine *Haer.* xxviii) who used cheese as part of the greater oblation (the fruit of the flock as well as of the earth). But we should not lay too much store by this late parallel. Such consumption (Augustine described Perpetua's receipt of *buccella lactis*, 'a mouthful of milk') was found in Carthage in Tertullian's time,[102] and surely would not have been confined to Montanists 5 (cf. too the milk and honey of *Epistle of Barnabas* vi.16f.; Hippolytus on Alexandria and cf. 2 Enoch 8:1–8 (A); 8:1–3 and 5ff. (B)).[103] In the *Passio* Perpetua takes it as part of a dream sequence in which the milking of the ewe by the shepherd (the Lord) is subject to typical dream time-compression. Hence curds/cheese rather than milk is offered.[104] 'Amen' heightens the sense of a eucharistic setting for the act.

4.5.2 Martyrdom and ecstasy

The visions of Perpetua and Saturus are heavy with reminiscences of Christian baptism, symbols and liturgical practices, full of interaction between rites of initiation and the expectation of martyrdom. Martyrdom becomes the fulfilment of baptism and baptism is the meaning of martyrdom.[105] In early Christianity confessors (incarcerated for the Name) expected to enjoy direct contact with the divine realm through visions and dreams (iv; x; xi–xii). There would be power of intercession and in *Pass. Perp.* we see even release for the suffering dead (vii–viii),[106] plus the answer to their own prayers (cf. *Pass.Perp.* xiv,3–5 on the premature birth-giving of Felicitas). Christ and his Spirit were with the potential martyr from the time of having to speak for the faith to the end itself.[107] We see all of this in this document of encouragement to Christians in a time of stress.

Ecstasy, significant in the debates about the Prophecy in Asia Minor, figures in the *Passio* too. Perpetua herself experienced ecstasy as she faced the crowd and the beasts ('adeo in spiritu et in extasi fuerat': xx, 8) and she and her companions (like the R^{Pass}) were well versed in apocalyptic expectation.[108] None of these things makes the martyrs unequivocally Montanist. The document is intensely *Christian*, but then the Prophecy was little different from much of the Christianity of its age. It was all a matter of emphasis and of degree. It is all such things *combined with* (a) the Montanist Tertullian's knowledge of the events and the visions and (b) the confident, indeed assertive, use which R^{Pass} made of them to further enthusiastic Christianity, which make me suspect strongly that these martyrs had been of the Prophecy.

Probably R^{Pass} was writing no later than *c.* 207 CE, the time which many have assumed to be that of Tertullian's conversion to the Prophecy.[109] If the martyrs were first-fruits of the Prophecy, then it must have reached Carthage or Thuburbo (if some of the martyrs were Thuburbitan) by 203 CE at the latest.[110] If thereafter it was not separate from African catholicism but was integrated with it,[111] then we would not expect catholic complaints at the work of R^{Pass} and catholics and Prophets alike could lay claim to Perpetua's memory. At a later date Augustine lauded Perpetua, as had Tertullian,[112] and the catholics dedicated a basilica to her.[113] It was not new for the *two* sides, catholic and Prophetic, to claim a female prophet as a foremother. The same thing had happened with Ammia.

4.5.3 *Vibia Perpetua*

The *Passio Perpetuae* preserves a distinctly *female* account of suffering and the triumph of certainty. Tertullian told prospective martyrs to travel 'in spirit' from their cells (for the pain of the chain was not felt when the mind was in heaven, *Ad mart.* ii) and Vibia Perpetua did just that. What do we know of her? She was not even baptised when the story starts (cf. ii.5). She was a young nursing mother of good family (ii.1) who had fallen victim to the edict of Septimius Severus (*c.* 200 CE). This bore in particular on recent and potential converts to Christianity and Judaism.[114] She was an exemplary figure, as much as Saturus the teacher of the Christians (who was later 'to give himself up of his own accord' iv, 5): one of the reconcilers of clergy in the dream sequence (which indicates, too, that Perpetua spoke Greek); one who supported and encouraged others in the face of death (xx,6 and 10); a woman who in dream and in reality took on the male role (*Pass. Perp.* x,7), as a gladiator for Christ. Of all the *charismata* which a Christian might wish for after baptism the Holy Spirit brought to

Perpetua 'bodily endurance' (*Pass. Perp.* iii.5).[115] Let us consider her 'maleness', for writers have made much of it.

4.5.4 Perpetua, female and male

In the account of her dream recorded in her prison journal Perpetua was set as a male athlete against a vicious-looking Egyptian. He represented the devil, the adversary, who utilised the ill will of pagan society and of bewildered family, so as to oppose Christians.[116] Satan was the ultimate adversary in the context of martyrdom.[117] Now the baptised Perpetua 'became male' as she was stripped for the dream contest and like Israel she overcame 'Egypt'. This 'becoming male', I would argue, was more an instance of how *both* sexes transcended expectation and stereotype in the act of martyrdom than it was of Gnostic thought proper. Rosemary Rader has argued in like manner,[118] while Robeck and Frend, among others, have drawn attention to the language of *Logia* 23 and 112 of the *Gospel of Thomas*. Frend (followed by Pettersen) has suggested that the detail may be 'Pythagorean'. Yet the language of athleticism is common in such contexts,[119] as also is the reversal of gender-based experiences. On the one hand, *men* in martyrologies are portrayed as bringing themselves and others to birth (e.g. Alexander in *HE* v.1, 49 and Ignatius *Romans* vi.1). On the other, the *women*, mothers though they are to the 'children' they influence (cf. Blandina), become athletes for Christ. Their 'male' actions counter the crowd's response to the beauty and vulnerability of their bodies.

In the *Passio* the emphasis is different from some of the examples which Kerstin Aspegren discussed in her study of *The Male Woman: a Feminine Ideal in the Early Church*. Unlike the motive in some apocryphal sources, for example, and in non-Christian philosophical literature, Perpetua's 'becoming male' causes her to lose none of her female qualities. The narrative is not particularly concerned with sexuality – neither Perpetua's marriage nor Felicitas' birth-giving are matters for comment and the fathers of their children are not named in the account. Instead, filled with the Spirit, Perpetua both embraces and transcends all human nature, becoming a symbol of the universal Christian, depicting male and female roles, as Francine Cardman has indicated:

when the prophetic spirit breathes where it will there is no sexual preference. She is called bride, mother, sister, daughter and lady; but also leader, warrior, victor and fighter. She is at times gentle, womanly, kind, motherly, tender; at other times strong, fierce, daring, courageous.

Of course there *is* contradiction of 'nature' and of natural assumptions, for example those of the Greco-Roman family and about the maternal role. And here, as in other *Acts* of martyrdom, the women's (Perpetua's and Felicitas') actions are described and circumscribed in the light of their being *female*. As Francine Cardman has noted, men and women are portrayed differently in *Acts of Martyrdom*, most strikingly so in those two narratives, the *Passio Perpetua* and the *M. Pionius*, which probably drew on material direct from the protagonists.[120] Men continued to be recognised as persons of note in the world (citing Justin the teacher, Pionius' influential friend who tried to dissuade him on account of his 'character'). Women, on the other hand, when their lot was deplored, were regarded as notable for their youth, beauty and responsibilities to their offspring. Notable examples are Agathonike in the *Acts of Carpus* (cf. Eusebius *HE* iv.15,48), Perpetua herself and Crispina in the Diocletianic *Martyrdom of Crispina* iii. There was sexual threat and innuendo in accounts of women's martyrdoms, such as do not occur with the men: 'The chastity of the women, much praised by the authors of the acts, is a point of extreme vulnerability before their persecutors.' Accused of being less than chaste, threatened with prostitution or even delivered naked to a brothel, women in the *Acts of Martyrdom* were vulnerable in a way men were not.[121] As Tertullian observed, condemnation of a Christian woman to the pimp rather than the lion was tacit acknowledgement of the importance of chastity to Christians (*Apol.* l).

So in the *Passio Perpetuae* Perpetua and Felicitas were delivered naked into the arena, the latter dripping milk after her recent parturition. Even the crowd was shocked (*Pass. Perp.* xx). A heifer was chosen as the beast of torture, in a macabre attempt 'to match their sex' (xx). Yet such things apart, the *Passio Perpetuae et Felicitas* avoids that sexual innuendo which is discernible elsewhere. Rather like Blandina in Gaul, who hung 'in the shape of a cross' and appeared to her fellow confessors 'in the form of their sister him who was crucified for them' (*HE* v.1,41), Perpetua and Felicitas were a potent reminder of the Lord himself. Their acts were among those things which, for R[Pass], we had 'heard and have touched with our hands' and which now were to be declared (*Pass. Perp.* i,6; 1 John 1:1, 3). Through such things came fellowship with the Lord. Perpetua became, as Alvyn

Pettersen has observed, 'an *alter christus*',[122] her womanliness transcended.

4.5.5 In the public sphere

Perpetua emerges as a determined spokeswoman for justice and integrity. Her statements stand in contrast to Cardman's (correct) observations that in the *Acts* generally the women's exchanges with their interlocutors were shorter then men's, reflecting 'an assumption about the propriety of public speech'.[123] Perpetua was unsubmissive. She confronted directly and with a touch of sarcasm the military tribune who was mistreating the prisoners. She demanded:

Why can you not even allow us to refresh ourselves properly? For we are the most distinguished of the condemned prisoners, seeing that we belong to the emperor; we are to fight on his very birthday.[124]

With Saturus she spoke steadfastly to the curious mob, offering it words of judgement, mocking its curiosity (xvii.1).[125] She resisted successfully all attempts to dress her for the ordeal in the style of a priestess of Ceres (xviii.4) and, as W.H.C. Frend observed in his study of Blandina and Perpetua (p. 172), the language and ideas of these confessors were those 'reflected in Tertullian's panorama of the Day of Judgement' (*De spect.* xxx). Her public stance is 'unfeminine' but other and more basic reversals of natural and unnatural are here too.

4.5.6 Felicitas

In texts such as this women's normal experiences are contradicted and the natural becomes a hindrance to 'the supernatural birthing process'. I shall begin with Felicitas, who was probably Perpetua's slave (though caution is required in interpreting the term *conserva*, *Pass. Perp.* ii, which may indicate only a fellow Christian).[126] Perhaps Felicitas and another arrested catechumen, Revocatus her 'brother', were married. If so, it is a further measure of the gyno-centric character of much of this martyrology that the father of Felicitas' child (a man who figures again in *Pass. Perp.* xviii) plays so peripheral a part in the account. Felicitas is a plebeian. Revocatus was her only relative apart from what was her *real* family now, i.e. her fellow prisoners, and Felicitas was pregnant. She gave birth prematurely to a girl, so that her journey to death with her fellow confessors might not be barred (xv). Pregnant women might not suffer the penalty. Felicitas was glad of safe delivery, that now she could fight the beasts, going from one blood bath to another, from the midwife to the gladiator, ready to wash after childbirth in a second baptism (xviii,3).

In time and place this birth was 'unnatural' (though the pain involved was natural enough). Her calm response to the prospect of orphaning her child was 'unnatural' too and, for Augustine, Felicitas in her birth-giving was both like Eve and like the mother of the Lord (*Serm.* cclxxxi.3).

At this point we have a momentary glimpse into the lives of other Montanist women in times of stress. We see a woman, an unnamed 'sister', who was not called upon to die but who took Felicitas' premature girl child to raise as her own. The infant and her foster-mother were part of a family which was bound not by blood but by the Spirit. 'Natural' loyalty was transcended by loyalty to the group 'in Christ'. Felicitas' natural family may indeed have been dead, or long separated from her by the exigencies of slavery or even estranged from their Christian daughter by virtue of her Christianity. We do not know and such things did not concern the R^{Pass}. Felicitas does not even express concern for her child, only relief that she would not be separated from her co-confessors in their birthing through martyrdom. *They* were her family now. Her unnamed 'sister', foster-mother to Felicitas' orphaned child, had a different burden to bear.

In like vein *Perpetua's experiences* countered the assumed rules of motherhood. The lactating Perpetua came to terms with losing her infant son, not yet fully weaned, and he was finally lost to her non-Christian family. After the separation she reported that her breasts caused her no discomfort. Here too is contradiction and transcendence of traditional female experience.

4.5.7 *The visionary Perpetua*

But Perpetua was also a visionary of greater things. She saw a ladder between heaven and earth, with a serpent at its foot, these things preserving echoes both of Jacob in Genesis 28 and of elements in 4 Ezra.[127] The 4 Ezra description of Israel's way – the steep and narrow way to the place of promise, with fire and water near at hand, and of 'level ground' and a 'field' (which was of course Ardab)[128] was paralleled by Perpetua's narrow ladder. This, with its threatening instruments for the unwary, was the means by which the 'garden' was reached. Perpetua *expected* to receive such visions and expected that in her (and in the others) the cause of God would triumph against their enemies.

4.5.8 Ideal of Christian womanhood

Perpetua, then, was mother and Christ-bearer, lover of justice, visionary, counsellor, confessor and intermediary on behalf of the afflicted. Perpetua the New Prophet represented for R[Pass] an ideal not just of martyrdom but of Christian womanhood and discipleship. 'In Christ' there was neither male nor female (Gal. 3:28). In Christ there was neither slave nor free person.[129] If Felicitas was indeed the slave of Perpetua, then we see hand in hand, side by side, the mistress and the slave, together in the amphitheatre (*Pass. Perp.* xx,6). None of the impediments which the world associated with women's bodies was significant in this, their wholehearted discipleship of Christ. The Montanist redactor would have left for us a graphic exposition of Galatians 3:28, long before we learn from Epiphanius that Montanists (Quintillians) appealed to that passage in defence of their ecclesiology.[130]

So, just as the apocryphal *Acts* presented women in roles which challenged the social and religious norms, so in the *Acts of Martyrdom* women were defying the conventions of patriarchal family life and of female submissiveness. Tertullian acknowledged that Christian women could not avoid public gaze – they attended church services, stayed out all night for the Easter vigil, walked the streets on errands of mercy, participated in nocturnal gatherings and entered prisons to meet with confessors (II *Ad uxor.* iv). The Paraclete had not advocated a conventional, stay-at-home death for those most likely to die in birth-giving. And Perpetua did not shrink from her most public appearance. Instead the 22 year-old (ii,2), formerly a mistress (*domina*) in the world,[131] but now the wife of Christ ('matrona Christi', xviii,2; cf. *HE* v.1,35), calmly outstared the onlookers in the amphitheatre. She had defied her interrogators and denied obedience to her distraught father (ii; v–vi; ix). Frend somewhat dismissively calls her a spoilt and wilful only daughter, attracted to Christianity in frustration at her lot. But to the Redactor and his circle, at least, she was much more. Perpetua trod on the head of the serpent (iv.4; iv.7; xviii.7).[132] We could see her as proof of the maxim of Ignatius that Christianity shows itself great when the world hates it (*Romans* iii.3) and an example of what Tertullian and the first Prophets had in mind (*De fuga* ix.4) when they demanded a totality of response to Christ.[133]

4.5.9 *The Montanist message to women*

In the work *Ad martyras* Tertullian left us a balanced presentation of male and female heroic role models. Those who looked to the things of the Spirit had endured the most brutal tortures and deaths, he wrote, even desired them for fame's sake (iv.2–3). Holy *women* were called on to be worthy of their sex! Public exposure and the call to withstand the gaze of the throng was the call of righteousness – not to be the cause of confusion nor to be avoided at all costs. Death through domestic sufferings was not the natural calling of Christian women.[134] Not surprisingly, then, Tertullian paid tribute to Perpetua. She had behaved as any future role model should. In Augustine's day (*De natura et origine animae* i.10,12) the *Passio* was read in churches and by some it was regarded as Scripture.

What message may be derived from this? Montanism treated women as spiritual equals. In the age of the Paraclete, with the Spirit poured upon them, Christian women, no less than Christian men, might radically challenge the world's (and the Church's) assumptions. Of course, catholic men and women were no less faithful unto death. Nor did the anti-Montanist catholics preach private activity for women when the Prophecy began. They did not denigrate Ammia or Philip's daughters, even by suggesting that they had operated only in some form of Christian *purdah* – although they must have thought that Maximilla and Priscilla went too far. North African Christianity (the New Prophecy apart) may have been of a distinctive and relatively egalitarian kind anyway.[135] Yet having acknowledged these things I think there is cause to think that such expectations *were* more alive amongst the New Prophets and their successors than they had been amongst their catholic opponents. Belief in a Christian order which dissolved barriers of sex *was* stronger in Montanism. The women within it functioned in ways which appeared outrageous to the catholics and this seems to have become no less marked as time passed and the triumph of the catholic position was assured. Perpetua is ideal martyr as she is ideal woman, prepared to make the ultimate sacrifice even as she is mother and wife, well-born lady, mistress, visionary, ecstatic, confrontational lover of justice and counsellor. The Montanist vision and interpretation of Christ's intention was different from that of the developing catholic churches. Had that not been so, then the phenomenon of female clericalisation would not have emerged.

4.6 THE CLERICALISATION OF THE WOMEN

4.6.1 Female deacons and prophesying virgins

Our sources on this refer to a variety of Montanist groups. Epiphanius said the Quintillianists ordained women as clergy (*Pan.* xlix.2,1–5) and appealed in support (a) to Miriam and Philip's daughters as prophesying precedents and (b) to Galatians 3:28. Since in Christ was 'neither male nor female', then equally men and women might be presbyters and bishops. Ambrosiaster reported (*Comm. in Ep. 1 ad Tim.* iii,8–11) that Cataphrygian ordination of female deacons was linked to the juxtaposition of 'deacons' and women in 1 Timothy. Quintillianists, on the other hand, respected Eve as the first person to have tasted of the tree of knowledge and hence women were granted episcopal and other office (Epiphanius *Pan.* xlix.2–3). The claim allows Epiphanius to counter with both Genesis 3:16 and 1 Timothy 2:14. Perhaps their defence of Eve arose in the context of increased denigration of Eve, and also (by association) of womankind in the fourth century and later (see 5.2.3). Evidently, if the writers are telling the truth, a number of different arguments might be adduced when Montanists were challenged about their egalitarianism.

Augustine (*De haer.* xxvii; lxxxvi) wrote of the pre-eminence of women amongst the Pepuzians and their sacerdotal status. He seems to imply that Quintilla/Priscilla's vision of Christ in female form had had something to do with this status but he tells us little. Later John of Damascus, who knew the works of earlier writers (*Haer.* lxxxvii), wrote of clergy women among the Pepuzites/Quintillians. There is no doubt that Montanists had women clergy. The epigraphy (5.1.2; 5.1.4) as well as anti-Montanist writers show this.

Prophecy had become clericalised and institutionalised and women with the title of 'prophetess' still existed (Epiphanius *Pan.* xlix.1). Among the Quintillians, he reported, seven white-clad, lamp-bearing, prophesying virgins functioned 'many times' in congregational worship. Such gatherings were enthusiastic and emotional, full of the language of repentance (*Pan.* xlix.2). All such wrong-headedness was likenable to Bacchic frenzy in his view (xlix.3).

Klawiter suggested that Easter lament over the crucified Christ was the setting for this rite, but Epiphanius' reference to 'many times', to repentance and to the sins of humankind suggests a wider application, I think.

The seven probably owe something to the promises of the Revelation and some writers find a parallel in the five lamp-bearing wise virgins of Matthew 25:1ff., who await the coming of the bridegroom.[136] The Revelation abounds with *sevens* – with candlesticks and stars and 'angel' intermediaries (1:12f.,20; cf. 1:16; 3:1). In Revelation 2:1 Christ holds seven stars and walks in the midst of the lampstands. In Revelation 4:5ff. the seven fiery lamps before the throne are spirits of God. The combination of wearing white and carrying light suggests these virgins were intended as figures bringing revelation. We should compare Hermas' vision of the woman who is the Church (*Vis.* ii.1,2), ἐν ἱματισμῷ λαμπροτάτῳ; the 'bright clothing', ἐν ἐσθῆτι λαμπρᾷ, of Acts 10:30 (also Acts 1:10; Mark 16:5; Matt. 17:2; 28:3) and the λίνον καθαρὸν λαμπρὸν of the angels in Revelation 15:6. White is the colour worn by those in heaven (Rev. 4:4; 7:9,13; 15:6 (angels); 19:8 (the wife of the Lamb); 19:14). It represents the righteousness of the saints (19:8) and churches are castigated for the defilement of their garments or praised for their worthiness to wear white (3:4f.; 3:18). The background to the women's actions lies in biblical, prophetic–apocalyptic sources, I think, and not in pagan rites.

It is Jerome who tells us that whereas among catholics the bishops held first place, the followers of Montanus gave that honour to the patriarchs of Pepuza. Beneath these were the *koinōnoi*, and *episkopoi* were reckoned only third in the hierarchy (see 5.1 below and cf. *Cod. Just.* i.5.20,3), a fact which Jerome took to be a calculatedly insulting application of the principle that 'the first shall be last' (*Ep.* xli.3 ad Marcellam). Inscriptions verify this picture. We know of two male Montanist bishops by the names of Diogas and Artemidorus and with the former there is also a woman mentioned, Ammion. She is described as a female presbyter.[137] The epitaph is in the Museum of Uşak (ancient Traianopolis) and belongs to that group which has been designated Montanist *not* because of the much-debated *christianos* or *pneumatikos* language (see 5.1.2–3) but rather because of clerical titles in it.

4.6.2. Infecting the catholic fold

Clericalisation of women was not the catholic way, of course, and evidently it caused unease. It might spread its influence! Some sources and commentators have blamed the example of Montanism for the errors of uppity *catholic* women. The canons of the so-called Council of Laodicea are of interest (probably a post-Nicene fourth-century summary of Phrygian catholic thinking), since the eleventh forbade the appointment of *presbytidēs* (female presidents or women of seniority) in churches and canon 44 forbade women any access to the altar.[138]

The significance of *presbytis* is much debated. As with every (biblical and extra-biblical) instance of a title of authority accorded to a woman, some commentators have struggled hard to derive from it everything other than its most immediate meaning. Daniélou (in his study of *The Ministry of Women in the Early Church*, London 1961), for example, opted for 'widow(s)' when *presbytis/presbytidēs* occurred in early sources. Yet given the area from which the canons emerged, it may be that the high profile of some catholic women around Laodicea had come about simply because certain churches had failed (or had not tried) to abolish freedoms which some Christian women in Asia had long enjoyed.

Yet an alternative for some writers is to blame Montanism:

we can easily assume that women were appointed as presbyters in a number of churches influenced by Montanism . . . by way of imitation, or with the intention of keeping the more active women within the orthodox church – for if they had found no use for their activism within the orthodox churches those women may well have been drawn away by the Montanist preachers.[139]

Afanasiev, an Orthodox writer, assumes far too easily and with the most cursory discussion that 'The Montanist roots of "female presidents" appear to be unquestionable.'[140] Only due to the influence of some aberrant group, it would seem, could orthodox women have had positions of prominence, and here also is a cool acknowledgement that 'orthodox' churches would have provided no outlet for women's skills and energies and would try to curb whatever freedoms local circumstance had granted. Yet what the canon actually indicates is that there *were presbytidēs* in catholic churches in the region of Laodicea. It does not tell us how long that had been so or how untypical was the phenomenon. In many congregations such female officialdom would surely have been abhorrent. But there is a great deal we do not know about others and in Asia in particular. By this time Montanism was long condemned in catholic Asia. There is no cause to blame it for happenings in catholic circles.

The second example is the sixth-century *Epistula Lovocato et Catiherno presbyteris*, from three Gallic bishops. This directly likens female participation in catholic rites to the reappearance of the *horrenda secta* of Montanism. It complains at length of women associates (*socias*) acting as *conhospitae* at contemporary eucharistic celebration (ll. 20–5 of the text) – a novelty and *superstitio* in catholic Gaul, it claimed. The passage shows that by this time Montanist women were sufficiently demonised in the Church's mythology to be cited as an aberrant parallel to what happened in some catholic churches. The writers were ignorant of real Montanism, however, and of the Pepuzites (cf. Epiphanius *Pan.* xlix.2,3 on Pepuzite female clergy), for they echoed 'fathers of the East' (*patres orientales*) who referred to the errorists as *Pepodites*. This probable corruption of *Pepuzites* was then assumed to derive from an eponymous Pepodius! Nevertheless, J. Friedrich posited that the 'associates' being described were *cenones* (cf. *caenonus/cenonus/cenonas* in texts of Jerome's letter to Marcella), a rank given only *to women* in Montanism, as successors of Priscilla and Maximilla. The masculine form *koinōnoi* which we hear of was a misunderstanding, for the Montanist *patriarchs* succeeded Montanus. The theory that *koinōnos* was in fact a female title, misunderstood and mistranslated (see 5.1.5), does not convince. Nevertheless this garbled sixth-century account of catholic doings may indeed preserve an echo of the fact that the rank was open to Montanist women (as well as men).[141]

4.6.3. Clerical orders

Montanist women seem to have been notorious for the roles they played. They had had a high profile as prophets from the outset and women were expected not to shun the public sphere in witness to their faith. The kind of Montanist women against which Origen was arguing (*Catenae* on 1 Cor. 14:36) evidently functioned in churches (4.4.2(ii) above) – a fact of which he disapproved, though the visionaries and prophets known to Tertullian in his Montanist phase had been more unassuming (Tertullian moved scarcely at all beyond his pre-Montanist conservatism where women were concerned). The women may also and always have performed functions other than that of prophesying. Though the functionaries we know of – Montanus the organiser, Theodotus the procurator (a translation Tabbernee rejects) – were male, this may not be the whole picture.

Most threatening was female participation in rites of baptism and of eucharist. Firmilian's prophetess sanctified the bread, made eucharist and baptised.[142] In her case there was no deviation from the familiar liturgy (but contrast Tertullian *De virg. vel.* ix; *De cult. fem.* ii.3).[143] The *Didachē*, we should remember, said prophets celebrated eucharist and were not to be constrained liturgically when doing it

(*Did.* x.7). Perhaps (and prophetically) she had chosen to use the usual rite. Perhaps *c.* 235 CE catholic and Montanist eucharistic rites, in the environs of Cappadocia at least, were the same. Just possibly she was no Montanist, which tells us that some Christian women in the East did carry out sacerdotal–sacramental functions, as the apocryphal *Acts* also seemed to suggest. If she were not, it is improbable that a Montanist woman would have been accorded less freedom.

The Prophecy was not rampantly egalitarian, its order not wholly new. Clericalisation would have come naturally to the Prophecy/ Montanism, which had been *of* the churches until driven out. It was neither anarchistic nor inherently anti-clerical. It continued the use of catholic clerical titles and it added others. At first it offered parallels with Paul's picture of the Corinthians (among them there had been prophets, teachers, helpers and administrators etc., 1 Cor. 12:27 ff.), which looks unlike the clear-cut Ignation threefold hierarchical ideal for the churches (*Trall.* iii, 1), but the contrast may be deceptive. They *retained* titles known in catholic circles, so presumably those who had held those titles in Christian congregations *had* figured in the Prophets' understanding of the Church.

There were, of course, *prophetic* Christians, versed in the language favoured among confessors and 'prophetic' types elsewhere, who referred to the *koinōnos*, 'companion', and *stylos*, 'pillar' (see 3.8.5), in mutual praise or in titular fashion. Some of this language was to harden later into Montanist clerical titles while catholics moved along other paths.

The Prophecy had never been intentionally anti-clergy *per se*, any more than had the intransigent prophetic types in Ignatius' day.[144] It was the experience of rejection which brought recriminations and hard language, not least from the layman Tertullian.[145] But that is a different matter. Nor was the Montanist *Passio Perpetuae* anti-clerical, though one incident has been interpreted that way.

In Saturus' vision he and Perpetua heard an appeal by a bishop and presbyter who were at odds (xiii). Confessors, including female confessors, were powerful figures but Perpetua and Saturus were surprised at the clerics' approach. The scene may well indicate inter-clergy disagreement about the Prophecy in Carthage ('open dissensions', Barnes wrote), and indicate too that the Prophecy was *part* of the church there. The vision does not suggest that Perpetua's circle was anti-clerical.[146]

Montanus had been no prophetic but power-seeking *presbyter*,
seeking to wrest position from clergy of common type (cf. Eusebius
HE v.16,7). The catholics would have said so clearly.[147] Montanus,
like Tertullian after him, had been a layman. It was a product of
catholic rejection of the Prophecy, I think, that issues hardened into
'spiritual' versus 'psychic', clergy versus lay, the 'bevies of bishops'
versus the prophetic individuals[148] and (often) men versus women.
Catholic leaders (or those we hear of) proved unwilling to recognise
the Spirit in the Prophets or to guide their flocks to the kind of renewal
and preparation the Prophets looked for. Once forced to separation
from the Church, women and men of the Prophecy found themselves
the only functionaries. They were the prophets, the priests, the
administrators and more – clericalised by default. As the catholic
clerical pattern changed, Montanism became an anachronism in
some respects,[149] retaining elements which the catholics were to leave
behind. One thing which survived the transition was belief in the
Spirit's capacity to empower female as well as male. Therein, I think,
is the foundation of Montanism's clericalisation of women. Not
everyone agrees with this view, however, and what follows is
consideration of an alternative emphasis.

4.6.4 *From confessor to cleric?*

Klawiter traces the ministerial or priestly status of Montanist
women to their role as confessors/martyrs.[150] The case rests on that
power and authority of the keys – i.e. the authority to 'bind' and
'loose' – believed to be invested in martyrs-in-waiting. This allowed
them to forgive even the lapsed, a power which traditionally was in
the hands of a presbyter/bishop. In catholic Rome a released (male)
confessor might be given the status of presbyter (cf. Hippolytus
Trad. Ap. x.1; *Ref. omn. haer.* ix.12,1–13), so this was one way to
achieve ministerial rank. Klawiter assumes a parallel with Montanist
women. Why?

(i) The *Letter of the Churches of Lyons and Vienne* knew that released
(perhaps New Prophecy) confessors were a problem elsewhere; there
was more binding than loosing going on (Eusebius *HE* v.2,5–6) and
the title *martys* (it is implied) was accorded to those who had not
suffered *unto death* (Eusebius *HE* v.2,2–3). Seemingly Irenaeus
wanted to undercut the authority of released confessors along with
the power of binding and loosing intrinsic to such status.[151] Tertullian
did indicate that the Spirit of the New Prophecy *was* more stringent

(*De pudic.* xxi.7; cf. xxii see above 3.5.1; 3.5.4; 3.6). Klawiter concludes, then, that confessor/martyr status was an important source of authority among the New Prophets.

(ii) Such Prophetic 'martyrs' were clericalised, he says. Alexander, a released confessor, 'exercised the power to bind and loose' and Themiso, another 'martyr', tried to establish his authority through the composition of a catholic epistle (Eusebius *HE* v.18,5–10 (Apollonius)).

(iii) Perpetua's suffering in Carthage, especially her visions of her dead brother Dinocrates, show that the imprisoned confessor possessed the priestly power of the keys – 'although the language of binding and loosing is not employed'. So, in parallel with Roman practice (where men were concerned), confession, imprisonment and martyrdom explain the ministerial status of Prophetic women in Asia Minor and their rights to the power of the keys.

I am unconvinced. Certainly Christians believed passionately in the power of confessors. Tertullian was scathing – dark prisons seethed with adulterers, the lapsed and other sinners seeking spiritual favours and in the case of some women, he hinted, being pressed into favours in return (*De pudic.* xxii; II *Ad uxor.* iv,1; *Ad mart.* i.6; *De paen.* ix.4; *De scorp.* x.8). The crisis in Carthage later, in the time of Cyprian (*c.* 250 CE), is witness to the importance of the confessor in Christian thought at this time (*Ep.* xxi; xxii; xxvii; xxxiv). And Klawiter is right about feelings in Gaul, I think. But he is claiming more, explaining the freedom accorded to *women* in particular, and the case does not stand up.

4.6.5. A reply

A number of things are not clear. Did only female confessors rise to clergy rank or was it that, once the precedent had been set, women of quite other virtues (as the Montanists saw them) might be so elevated? Confession, he says, was 'one road' to the power of the keys, yet we are not told what *other* roads there might have been, and for women in particular. Klawiter assures us that the polity of female presbyters and bishops 'does indeed go back to the origins of Montanism in Asia Minor'. Epiphanius had hearsay knowledge of Montanism there. But Epiphanius makes no explicit claim that the polity described derived from the teaching and practice of the first Prophets and he certainly did not associate it with the rank of martyr. Klawiter has to acknowledge that the sources say nothing about the status of released female confessors in Asia Minor. Thus far, then, the claim seems overstated.

To return to the relevant text from Apollonius (Eusebius *HE* v.18,6–7) concerning Themiso:[152] it is asked sarcastically whether the Prophet absolves (χαρίζεται cf. *HE* v.1,45) the martyr (of robbery) or the martyr absolves the Prophet (of avarice). The language implies that possession by the Spirit of *prophecy* also conveyed the right of 'the keys' for a Prophet. By concentrating on Peter and the keys in Matthew 16:18f. writers tend to overlook the wider *congregational* role in Matthew 18:15–20. The Church had the power to forgive sin. So the Paraclete also declared (according to Tertullian, see 3.6.3 above). But the Spirit speaking through the Prophet chose to 'bind' rather than loose. In *HE* v.18,6–7 prophet, no less than confessor, supposedly had rights of absolution and in the instances of female Montanist clergy we know of (in inscriptions and, e.g., Firmilian's prophetess) there is nothing to suggest that the women had been confessors.

Klawiter writes of women's ministerial status and their priestly power. The former (referred to on pp. 251, 254, 260) applied certainly to Priscilla and Maximilla, the only women of whom we have some knowledge among the first Prophets, but Klawiter shows little interest in Priscilla and Maximilla. This need not be synonymous with 'priestly' power, of course, or 'priestly office' (a term used on pp. 256f., 259f.) as catholics would have understood them, though in the case of Priscilla and Maximilla one could assume that the 'binding' Spirit operated through them as well as Montanus (Tertullian *De pudic* xxi.7). The Church had power to forgive sins but the Paraclete (via the Prophet) chose not to do so. The power, which rested within the Church, was here associated not with confession, but rather with the activity of the Paraclete in prophecy. Our sources never once describe Priscilla or Maximilla (or Montanus) as confessor-martyrs (see too *HE* v.16,12). So Klawiter's emphasis on confession is misplaced, I think, and does not accord, either, with what Tertullian tells us of leadership.

With the maturing of the Prophecy, 'rank and title', office and appeal to authority which was not based clearly on charismatic endowment were deplored (not that everyone in the Prophecy was free of wrong motivation!) and a degree of laicisation should be presupposed.[153] As a Montanist Tertullian had not moved very far in this respect from his position when a (critical) catholic.[154] He had always held to the priesthood of all Christians, in a general sense (cf.

Rev. 1:6; 5:10; 1 Peter 2:5, 9; Romans 12:1), though sacerdotal functions were restricted and also given only to men.[155] He never denied the authority of clergy (*De cor. mil.* iii.3) but the Montanist Tertullian did became critical of bishops who forgave sins which he now regarded as non-remissible (*De pudic.* xviii.18) and he thought contemptible bishops who showed no evidence of the spiritual gift of prophecy (*De pudic.* xxi.5–6). The right of forgiveness of sins, he argued, was granted to the church of the Spirit, and to the 'spiritual' apostle or prophet within it (*De pudic.* xxi).

He looked now for a heightened role for the laity, citing Revelation 1:6 (cf. *De exhort. cast.* vii.3: 'ubi tres, ecclesia est, licet laici'), and even sacerdotal functions might be envisaged for laymen. Tertullian cited Matthew 18:16ff. in support, which he interpreted differently from in his pre-Montanist days (contrast *De bapt.* vi and the Montanist *De fuga* xiv.1, and both interpretations in *De pudic.* xxi.10 and 16f.).[156] To use an *a minore ad maius* argument, if the individualistic but essentially conservative Tertullian, working at least at one remove from the Prophecy, was led to embrace a vision of the Church more egalitarian and Spirit-directed than hitherto, *how much more* must that vision have prevailed amongst the New Prophets of Asia Minor? So why should it have been confession alone, or primarily, which fitted women in such a church for 'ministerial' or 'priestly' status?

A writer's understanding of the *why* of Montanist women's clericalisation must be conditioned by his or her view of the Montanist vision of the Church. Klawiter, too, considered what the Montanist and catholic visions of the Church might have been. In the Lyons and Vienne document we have the catholic one – the Church as the Virgin Mother who bore the crucified Christ to the world through the crucified forms of female (Blandina) and male martyrs. The 'ideal' of the New Prophecy was 'not dissimilar', he maintained.[157] It was of the virgin woman who saw Christ in female or in male shape 'and who, as a woman, represents Christ to the world.' The one is inclusive, the other is not so, in that as it stands it lays a probably distorting emphasis on *female* adherents of Montanism and on Christ as female. Men as well as women lived lives of Montanist continence and we have just one (Quintillian) vision suggesting that in Montanist circles Christ might be experienced and described in female form. There was more to the Prophecy/Montanism than being able to envisage Christ in female form and allowing public Christian ministry to women. These things, I think, were *products* of a view of the

Church and of Christ's relation to it. They were not its totality. I shall
return to this point below, but not before noting what I think is
another weakness in Klawiter's case.

Klawiter's analysis supposes that confession was the *sine qua non* for
a woman's achievement of high status in Montanism. Thus it also
assumes that Montanists challenged opposition with unholy zeal. In
his Ph.D. thesis he presented zeal for martyrdom as the *cause* of the
catholic rejection of the Prophecy: 'it took a position on martyrdom
which the church deemed to be suicidal, irrational and destructive to
the life of the church.'[158] Like Tabbernee (see 3.8) I do not share that
view.[159] In any case severe persecution of Christians was not the norm
throughout all the areas and centuries of Montanism's history.
Assuming that it was *not* the case that all Montanists were ardently
seeking the chain and the dungeon, then (following Klawiter's thesis)
would not the granting of 'priestly authority' to Montanist women
and being 'permitted to rise to ministerial status' have been something
rare, if dependent on release from prison? In the fourth century our
sources seem to present it as the norm. But Klawiter gives no
indication of when or how a transition to other causes of female
'promotion' would have been made.

I have much more sympathy with Klawiter's earlier explanation in
his thesis on 'The New Prophecy'.[160] There he wrote that the right to
possess the rank of clergy might be explained by evolutionary change
within the movement but was rooted in the high status which women
had possessed as Prophetesses. The environment of Asia Minor would
have been a factor too, with clerical status reflecting offices of high
civic and religious rank for women there. Were he also to say that the
Prophets regarded their view of the sexes as in accord with the
promised Christian order and the leadings of the Spirit (as they
understood them), then I would agree more heartily still. For his view
of women liberated from subordinate femaleness only through
experience of participating in Christ's sufferings is too narrow a view:
he maintained,

The vision of a new creation which resulted from the experience of suffering
in Christ was strong enough to live beyond the circumstance of persecution
which had occasioned it,[161]

Montanist women, he concluded, were not resubjugated after such an
experience, as catholic ones were. Yet it is hard to envisage that it was
women's strength of vision which achieved such a feat! A woman's

vision of a new Christian order could bear fruit (in terms of her own public ministry) *only* in a setting in which that order was taken for granted and acted upon. That is, had not the New Prophets had such a vision already, I doubt that a female confessor's experience of prison would have been sufficient to challenge male domination (which is precisely what Klawiter is admitting in terms of catholic experience, of course). I am bewildered, therefore, by the final observation in Klawiter's article:

Perhaps there is an important lesson here for the Christian feminists of our own time.

4.6.6. A suggestion

My own view is different. The public, ministerial, sometimes priestly activity of Montanist women was the product of the New Prophets' and Montanists' belief in the in-breaking of a Spirit-guided, covenantally promised, Christian order. It accounted, too, for the public, ministerial and priestly roles of Montanist men. It went without saying that (in their eyes) that order was at the same time more 'original' (in terms of the will of the Christ) and more egalitarian than that which the catholics had embraced.

The New Prophets appealed to sources which envisaged such a new order – John's Gospel, which looked to the Paraclete as the source of 'all truth'; apocalyptic writings which were radically critical of their own age of compromise; Galatians 3:28; Joel 2:28f. (cf. Acts 2:16–21) – the rallying-cry of Pentecost preaching, according to Luke. For the first Prophets and subsequent generations Joel's prophecy was fulfilled not just in the events of Pentecost (as some catholic opponents claimed) but in the ecclesia of their own day (see, e.g., R[Pass] in *Pass. Perp.* i.3f.). In error the catholic Church (they argued) had become obsessed with the past and had failed to acknowledge the significance of events in its midst. *Now* were the extraordinary gifts promised for the end time ('in ultima saeculi spatia decretam') and, as Joel had promised, *women*, no less than men, were recipients and proclaimers of that Spirit.[162] Neither Joel nor the apostle Peter (in Acts) had hedged about that promise with statements on 'private' activity for women, and there was no text which demanded the incarceration of a woman before she might act as a minister to her co-religionists or declare the will of God to them. The 'truth' into which the promised Paraclete would lead (as the Prophets saw it) was surely not constrained so as to fit into catholic modes of male priestly activity and lay (and female) inactivity. Hence to assume that a New Prophet or later Montanist woman could become 'priestly' by virtue of having suffered as a confessor is probably right. But to say (if that was what Klawiter was doing) that it had been *a* or *the* key factor in women's clericalisation is probably to miss the point.

4.7 COMMENT ON MONTANISM AND WOMEN

To study what we know of women in Montanism is to study Montanism as a whole. The sources which relate to them (oracles, treatises, inscriptions, martyrologies and catholic works of many kinds) are also the sources which give us our other information about Montanism. In some of these sources it is Montanist men who seem almost an appendage, but the impression is probably a wrong one. We should not assume *either* that Montanism attracted more women than men throughout its history (though that has been a damning observation levelled with regularity against many Christian sects) *or* that women enjoyed greater authority than the men within it. There is no evidence that this was the case, and the limited inscriptional evidence suggests otherwise. Montanist women were deemed worthy of comment and castigation *because* they were women – potentially threateningly liberated role models for vacillating or disaffected catholic females – as well as being women at odds with right doctrine. In any case these two things could not be separated.

Given the pattern of change and decay in religions it seems reasonable to assume that Nanas was not like Maximilla nor even like Maximilla's less exalted and charismatic female contemporaries in the earliest days of the Prophecy. Theodotus of Ancyra, given to visions and fervent in his love of the martyred faithful though he was, was no Montanus. The fervour which others saw as hot-headedness or worse in the early Prophecy cooled. Office order and ritual became formalised. As time went on and the political climate changed, so too did the persecutors – from imperial representatives and the hostile mob to fellow-Christian imperial representatives. Yet later Montanists did not lack fervour. The Spirit for which Perpetua died was claimed as part of the experience of 'spiritual' Christians, some of whom (like Perpetua and Saturus before them) gave their lives. Similarly the memory of Montanus himself might be preserved, centuries after his death, in the names of faithful 'spiritual' women.

Quintilla's experience, and references to Joel 2:28ff. and Galatians 3:28 apart, there is little beyond the *fact* of Montanist women's public religious activity to tell us that here was a movement unusual in its response to the female (see also 5.2.3). It is enough. We do not know in what directions the women of some of the apocryphal *Acts* communities were scattered and we may only surmise the existence and demise of other (non-heretical) groups in which women and men participated in relatively egalitarian ways. With Montanism we *know* that the initial vision was not lost entirely. The fact that women could enjoy clerical status tells us this. Nevertheless we may draw few conclusions.

As for relations of equality between the sexes *within* Montanist communities, we know nothing. Perhaps it was only 'in the spirituals' and not 'in the temporals' (as seventeenth-century writers put it) that the female was the equal of the male. Certainly women like Perpetua (probably not in an endogamous marriage) and the barefoot, probably celibate, wandering prophetess known to Firmilian went their own ways, determinedly defying the expectations of society and of men. But they were surely not Montanists of the common kind. We hear nothing of it if many a married Montanist woman *within* her community struggled against family commitments, economic powerlessness and assumptions in her own home about her 'rightful place' while she longed to respond to a call of the Spirit to prophesy, to teach or otherwise to minister. The Montanist family may have been thoroughly hierarchical and patriarchal. It may be that Nanas and her sisters communed with angels but did not expect to be top dogs in their particular corners of the world. As the evidence stands, we have no way of knowing.

In any case we should not look on these women as self-consciously 'feminist'. We do not know that they were analysing and seeking to redress the wrongs done to womankind – though some at least among them chose to think of themselves as 'daughters of Eve' in a way very different from the catholic one. Montanist women, like the men in their circle, were self-consciously *Christian*. Given their understanding of present and promised liberation in the covenant of Christ, and of the Spirit having been poured out on male and female alike, they could do no other.

CHAPTER 5

The fate of Montanism

5.1 LATER MONTANISM: ECCLESIOLOGY AND EPIGRAPHY

The Three died. Themiso (of the 'catholic epistle') and Miltiades were then among the leading figures. Perhaps it was the latter's writings which were rejected in ll. 81–2 of the Roman Muratorian Fragment (cf. Eusebius *HE* v.16,3), for the Prophecy was known to its creator (see 3.9.3 above). We know little about the Prophets' churches, however, and there is near silence from Montanists themselves (though we learn a lot about catholic action against them, see 5.2 and 5.3 below). There is the account of the supposed Montanist of the *Dialexis* and some evidence from epigraphy, but mostly we are reliant on writers such as Epiphanius, Augustine and Jerome, none of whom had cause to present a balanced picture or desire to understand the finer points of Montanist teaching. As for 'the simple faithful' in the churches, they probably knew little about their more exotic neighbours and cared less. To the world 'the Montanist in the street' must have seemed like any other Christian, except of course that we know some of them lived exciting lives of the Spirit and communed with angels (Nanas).

Toleration (if it had ever existed) did not last. The age of Constantine and his successors brought emphasis on uniformity of worship and so Montanist peculiarities would have become obvious. Their celebration of Easter according to an alien calendar, for example, would have marked them out and might even have had them prosecuted. *Loyal* citizens of the state would be properly assembled (after catholic fashion) on the (proper) Easter Day (so the measure of Gratian, Valentinian II and Theodosius I, 382 CE). As more time passed, uniformity of belief and not just conventionality in worship was required (*Cod. Just.* i.5.18.4), so that Montanism was bound to suffer (5.2–3).

What do we know of them? Like the catholics they had churches and *martyria* (canons 9 and 34 of the Council of Laodicea; Procopius *Hist. Arc.* xi.16). They had common meals and what were unkindly labelled 'drinking parties' and they welcomed visitors – even supposedly apostate Montanists who were compromising by feigning allegiance to the True Church. *Cod. Just.* i.5.20.5 sought to stop such gatherings and such access. Catholics did not want the risk of Montanists convincing the simple-minded.

Montanists might be rich or they might be poor, though some of the later legislation wrought against heretics must have ensured that some people moved from one state to the other – ruined. Procopius, disillusioned with Justinian, suggested that legislation against heretics was not unrelated to greed! We know that Montanists had once bought and sold property, dealt in slaves and engaged in trade – even in the precincts of catholic places of worship, until legislation weighed ever more heavily against them and such things were stopped (e.g. *Cod. Just.* i.5.20.4 and 6). Some had received poor-relief (in Constantinople at least), until officials – on pain of being fined – were instructed not to provide it (*Cod. Just.* i.5.20.7–8). Not for the only time there is the clue that local officials, and probably Montanists' neighbours too, were not so zealous to destroy them as were the legislators. They did not really care if their merchant neighbour were a Montanist, or if a pillar of the local property-owning classes celebrated Easter on a different day. And in the second and third centuries, in the average Phrygian village or Roman enclave of Christian Asiatics, they were surely less concerned still. When pressure came at that time it came from those who despised Christianity, and they did not distinguish between Montanist and catholic.

We know little of Montanist church life but we know that Montanism was not uniform. I shall start with that fact.

5.1.1 Montanist diversity

There were groups not named after a Prophet or place (e.g. Priscillianists, Quintillianists, Pepuzites), namely the 'bread and cheesers' (the Artotyrites, cf. Jerome *Comm. in Ep. ad Gal. ii.3 PL* xxvi. 382) and the 'nose-peggers' (Tascodrougites – possibly the same as the Passalorynchites, cf. Jerome). The former took bread and cheese as part of the offering, fruit of the flock as well as of the ground, like the 'first men', added Augustine and Praedestinatus (presumably Cain and Abel: Augustine *De haer.* lxxxvi; Praedestinatus *Haer.* i.28; cf. Gen. 4:4). The phenomenon, like that of 'nose-pegging' was known in Eastern Montanism and writers also point to the use of cheese in Perpetua's (African) visionary experience of receiving curds (4.5.1). There is nothing to suggest that the vision was the origin of the practice.

There is some vagueness with respect to the Artotyrites. Subsequent writers noted only that Epiphanius joined them with the Pepuzians (Augustine *De haer.* xxviii) and Quintillians (*Pan.* xlix. 1–2) but they seem to know little about them: 'contra quos nullus dignatus est nec loqui', observed Praedestinatus – no one had bothered to polemicise against the Artotyrites.

As for the 'nose-peggers', I have taken seriously Epiphanius' (typically opaque and hostile) description of rituals in which there was (a) pricking with needles (scarring or tattooing as a rite of initiation) and (b) hand-over-the-face gestures. 'Nose-pegging', I assume, was a hostile description of such a gesture. I have posited (in this study and in an article forthcoming in *Vigiliae Christianae* in 1995) that these things may have been associated with rites conducted in a setting where the threats and promises of apocalyptic sources were rehearsed.[1]

In *Pan.* xlviii.14 Epiphanius linked the 'nose-peggers' with the Cataphrygians. These were known to exist in Phrygia, Cilicia, Cappadocia and Galatia but were present in numbers in Constantinople in particular. Possibly they belonged with the Quintillians, Epiphanius was unsure. But in any case the tattooing was to do with 'mysteries of the Name of Christ'[2] and the ritual gesture had to do with sorrow: the 'peg' (πάσσαλος, but known as τασκός in these circles), which was in fact a finger, was laid on the nose or at the nostril (ῥύγχος here known as δροῦγγος) during prayer. Hence the name Tascodrougites (probably one and the same as the Passalorhynchites referred to elsewhere). This was a gesture of pretended piety or of sorrow, said Epiphanius, and he was unimpressed. Such hints of practice in Montanist churches only tantalise. We have no details,[3] and Tabbernee ('Opposition' 447–51) refused to accept their association with Montanism at all.

Much of the evidence about Montanist church life is flawed in that it comes from opponents of Montanism. They concentrated only on those things which were colourful (lamp-bearing, prophesying virgins), at odds with orthodox doctrine (female clergy), bizarre ('nose-pegging') or suspicious (rites involving infants). We should not assume that every (or any) later Montanist eucharist was replete with blood from tattooing (Montanists denied such things: Timothy of Constantinople *De iis qui ad ecclesiam accedunt PG* lxxxvi.20) or that every Montanist was initiated at Pepuza (cf. Epiphanius on some Quintillian rites *Pan.* xlviii.14; xlix.1). Nor were all Montanist rites in secret (*Pan.* xlix.3). We should contrast Filastrius of Brescia on this, who tells us also in passing that Montanists baptised the dead. Were these babies who had died pre-baptism? Or perhaps this was vicarious baptism for 'fellow-travellers' or those whose fear of post-baptismal sin had caused them to wait (too long!) for the rite. Filastrius used the word *publice* of the celebration of their mysteries (*Div. haer. lib.* xlix, Heine, *Oracles* 138) and *Cod. Theod.* i.5.20.5 suggests the same public access. But there were probably rites in private houses as well as in larger places of assembly (especially where groups were small) so that these would have heightened suspicion of 'secret' activity.

The *Vita Constantini* iii.64 (letter of Constantine to the heretics) names Cataphrygians among those who did have private (house-based) as well as public places of assembly. Meetings in both were forbidden (iii.65). Evidently Montanism was not a rigidly closed sect. But so far as we know Montanist churches enjoyed no formal contact with catholic ones, though there was contact between Montanist congregations themselves. The following evidence makes this clear.

At Easter (Passover) a share in the (allegedly polluted) paschal offering was distributed from the mother church (or churches) of Pepuza (Filastrius *Div. haer. lib.* xlix) to 'pernicious accomplices' elsewhere ('perniciosis et falsis satellitibus'). Presumably the 'Pepuzites', guardians of the shrine of the Three, took responsibility for that distribution. The Montanist Patriarchate was associated with Pepuza (Jerome *Ep.* xli ad Marcellam) and Pepuza was still 'Jerusalem' (Augustine *De haer.* xxvii). Indeed, from what evidence may be gleaned Pepuza sounds like a Montanist Mecca, with pilgrimages to the shrine of the Three (a late Syriac source says that the sick came there for healing, see 5.3.3). We do not know how great were the numbers, of course, how widespread was a determination to visit Pepuza or whether such visitation was required in Montanist circles. In distributing this paschal offering Pepuza was doing for Montanists what Rome had done for its own in earlier times. But while Rome had deplored the nonconformity of Asian Quartodeciman

Easter practice, the Pepuzites and other Montanist (Phrygian)
loyalists had remained distinctive where the celebration of Easter was
concerned (Sozomen *HE* vii.18,12–14; cf. too Pseudo-Chrysostom
Serm. vii (*PG* lix. 747)). If there had been no mention of this in the
earliest anti-Montanist sources we should not be surprised. In Asia,
Quartodeciman practice might almost be taken for granted. It was
scarcely heresy. It was not until the time of Victor, in any case, that
Rome adopted an uncompromising line towards those who reckoned
Easter differently. Montanists, naturally, never fell into line and
stayed determinedly distinctive.

Eschewing a lunar calendar for a solar one and reckoning $365\frac{1}{4}$
days per annum, they pin-pointed the crucial fourteenth day of the
month (for Passover) and would celebrate Passover and Easter events
on that day *if it were a Sunday* (the Lord's day), otherwise Easter would
be on the Sunday following. No wonder, then, that in the late fourth
century Pacian of Barcelona aligned the Montanists with other
fermenters of schism about festival dates ('quam multiplices contro-
versias excitarunt de paschali die'), among them Blastus, Quartodeciman in sympathy, discredited in Rome and in receipt of Irenaeus'
letter *On schism* (Eusebius *HE* v.15; v.20,1). Blastus was a Montanist
fellow-traveller, Pacian seems to suggest (*Ep. I ad. Symp.* 1–2).
Eusebius, too, aligned the errors of the Prophets with those of Blastus
and Florinus in Rome (v.15; v.20,1).

The Montanists were staying true to a Johannine tradition, though
one writer has posited a link between Quartodeciman and Montanist
Easter practice with Montanism's added dependence on the tradition
of Messiah's birth in Revelation 12 and his expected return. Frend is
sympathetic to this picture of Montanists-in-waiting for the advent of
the millennium, using Johannine writings as the basis of their liturgy
and teachings and involved in 'a prolonged wake in the expectation of
the Bridegroom and the descent of the New Jerusalem at Pepuza'
(Rev. 21; *Pan.* xlix.1).[4]

Epiphanius determinedly lumped together all manner of sectarian
groups: Quintillians also called Pepuzians; Artotyrites; Priscillians
and Cataphrygians (which he did not treat as the generic name, *Pan.*
xlviii.1). We do not know whether nor to what extent Priscillianists
were like Quintillians, nor if either were like Tascodrougites (cf. *Pan.*
xlviii.14). Even when we have some details of Montanist practice we
cannot be certain they were applicable *to all the groups concerned*. If
'spiritual Christians' described in some epigraphy are rightly to be

labelled 'Montanists' (see 5.1.2), for example, then were they simply that, or more specifically Priscillianists or Tascodrougites? We do not know that loyalists in *all* the groups looked to the Montanist patriarchate as a source of authority or that all had strayed into trinitarian error in ways described in 5.2 and so on.

Of course there are a few things we *can* say on the basis of the evidence of later sources (much of it touched on in earlier chapters). Rigorism and eschatological hope continued to be features of Montanist life, as was shown in chapter three and in discussion of women in chapter four. Later anti-Montanist writers and some items of epigraphy show that Montanists continued to honour the Three and that there was refusal of penance, non-acceptance of digamists, distinctive fasting practice and an unusually high status accorded to women in their ranks. A few other details emerge too. In the *Dialexis* the Montanist defended the rightness of female prophecy and prayer and referred to veiling (Heine, *Oracles* 126). The debate presupposes that in the circle which produced the *Dialexis* Montanist prophesying women *were* veiled. Tertullian would have approved. Prophecy remained a reality too, among some Montanists at least, as witness the seven Prophetesses leading congregational worship in the depcription by Epiphanius (*Pan.* xlix.2). They called for repentance and reduced hearers to tears. Here was a reminder of that potent force of female prophecy which linked believers with the founding foremothers. Finally the 'pneumatic/psychic' distinction between Montanists and others also seems to have survived. Certainly Tertullian's usage was remembered: 'nos catholicas psychicos titulat', observed Praedestinatus (*Haer.* i.86). We may have evidence of it in some of the epigraphy also. Montanists, of course, were the 'spiritual' ones.

5.1.2 'Spiritual Christians'

The epithet 'spiritual Christian' seems to be a mark of Montanism in some of the epigraphy. Supposedly Montanist epigraphy (not all of it with the 'spiritual Christian' designation) has been much discussed and it is now accessible through the work of Gibson and Tabbernee in particular. In this study I shall consider it only briefly: (a) in relation to 'spiritual' Christians; and (b) in 5.1.3–4 when looking at open profession and Montanism.

(i) Frankios, χριστιανὸς πνευματικός, was commemorated in the probably fourth century Italian inscription discussed by Ferrua,[5] the

double epithet (πνευματικός καὶ χριστιανὸς) being found, too, on (ii)
the Roman memorial for Alexander the physician, but not on (iii) the
inscription about Ablabes, where no reference to 'Christian' appears
(see 5.3.1). (iv) The inscription noted in 4.4.1 (iii), from the region of
Phrygian Dorylaeum, contains both. This was a dedication by
Loupikinos for his wife Mountane (using the χρειστιανῇ form)[6]
including Π + Π (i.e. 'spiritual' as well as 'Christian' people):

Π + Π Λουπικῖνος Μουντάνῃ συμβίῳ χρειστιανῇ καὶ πνευματικῇ μνήμης χάριν

In this instance the likeness of the woman's name to that of Montanus
makes it very likely that the deceased was a Montanist,[7] a surer sign
than the *pneumatikos* language alone, which was employed by other
groups too and which is absent, in any case, from even (v), the
dedication to the Montanist *protodiakonos* whose name was inscribed
on a marble slab with basin, allegedly brought from Uçküyü:
+ Μοντάνου πρωτοδιακόνου + . 'A deacon called Montanus at this
period and in this place can only have been a Montanist', Calder
observed. This find was shown to him in the village of Bekilli, in the
region where Pepuza is probably to be sited. In the same area Calder
believed he had been shown the *cathedra* of a fourth- or fifth-century
Montanist church.[8] We should not assume that every *pneumatikos* was
a Montanist nor that someone not so designated was not. It seems
clear, nevertheless, that the designation 'spiritual (Christian)'
continued to be used in Montanist circles.

5.1.3 Were later Montanists confrontational?

Tabbernee has retained his scepticism about Montanist confron-
tationalism. He doubts that from the beginning Montanism was
markedly more confrontational and desirous of martyrdom than
contemporary catholicism and he is critical of the way some epigraphy
(the 'Christians for Christians' epitaphs) has been used in support of
such thinking. I shall return to Tabbernee below, after first looking at
the history of scholars' treatment of the 'Christians for Christians'
epitaphs, which have been taken as evidence of a Montanist enclave
in northern Phrygia and of Montanist aggressive open profession of
Christianity.

The material comes from the upper Tembris valley, the Altintaş
plain in the province of Kütahya (ancient Cotiaeon). Tombstones of
this upper Tembris valley and from Phrygia generally are a rich
source for determining lifestyle in the third century and later, for

understanding language (Greek with a variety of local peculiarities in both spoken and written forms) and for understanding religion too.[9] There was a lively crop of pagans and Christians in this region and many of the names on the stones are common names we know already from the history of Montanism in Phrygia: Ammia and Nana(s) (derivatives of 'mother'), Kordatos (Quadratus) and Zotikos. The distinctive 'Christians for Christians' stones sometimes conspicuously displayed a cross.

The single word 'Christian(s)' is almost commonplace, appearing on monuments from all parts of Phrygia and also in neighbouring provinces. (Gibson dated many of these to the third century.) The 'Christians for Christians' group is a special category among such 'phanero-Christian' material, however. Calder ('Philadelphia and Montanism') republished and discussed fifteen 'phanero-Christian' Phrygian monuments of which eleven were of the upper Tembris valley 'Christians for Christians' type, and more have been published since. Calder took them to be third-century and Montanist and assumed that epitaphs of the 'concealed' type (i.e. not making open profession of Christianity) showed Montanism 'had failed to gain a hold' in a region ('The New Jerusalem of the Montanists', p. 422). The assumption was that fanaticism (including public proclamation of one's Christianity) and rigorism were marks of Montanism.

In fact the 'Christians for Christians' items tell us that these were not excessively rigorous Christians. They did not reject marriage, for example – there were endogamous marriages, as the following illustrates:

Aurelios Theodoros and Patrikis and Prokla and Euktemon, *Christians, for* Aurelia Domna, their mother-in-law, *a Christian*. Aurelios Euktemon and Ammias for their child Onesime, a Christian [emphasis mine].[10]

So Calder's view of the material was questionable.

Elsa Gibson did a major study of this 'Christians for Christians' phenomenon, set within wider consideration of confession stelai and arranged so as not to prejudice the reader's judgement about the provenance of the Tembris valley type. The formula (which varies and is not always simply χριστιανοὶ χριστιανοῖς) *was* pre-Constantinian, Gibson thought, and found roughly parallel with use of the so-called 'Eumeneian formula'.[11] It was peculiar to the fertile upper Tembris valley, harsh in Winter ('the snow was rushing down horizontally', she recorded of a February visit). But was it Montanist?

She was cautious and her caution set her at odds with writers of several generations past.

Ramsay took to be Montanist such open-profession epitaphs as were then known.[12] Anderson did, too, though Labriolle was unconvinced.[13] Calder in 'Philadelphia and Montanism' and in later publication of epitaphs in 'Leaves from an Anatolian Notebook' vigorously made the case for Montanism in the Tembris valley and at first Gregoire, the publisher of the Loupikinos epitaph from nearby Dorylaeum, was convinced. Subsequently, however, (and to Calder's disgust) Gregoire changed his mind and declared the inscriptions to be catholic. Cecchelli was convinced too, suggesting even that such sectarian use of the title 'Christians' meant that catholics had to call themselves just that – catholics. Leclerq and Haspels were part of the growing consensus.

W.H.C. Frend was also convinced and remains to be persuaded otherwise. But, like Labriolle, Ferrua was not; nor was Schepelern. He advocated that the *pneumatikos* dedication, 'spiritual Christians to spiritual Christians' (as in Π + Π in the Dorylaeum case), *should indeed* be regarded as Montanist but perhaps this was in deliberate and particularistic contrast to the 'Christians for Christians' type and not simply a matter of variation on a theme. Ferrua, on the other hand, was dismissive of attempts to corner Montanism in a backwater (the Tembris valley), taking refuge there from catholic attention (so Calder), since it is known to have continued in Phrygia generally (see 5.2 and 5.3). In any case, Ferrua observed, northern Phrygia also produced Christian inscriptions which did *not* make great display of Christianity – so it could not have been a peculiarly Montanist enclave.[14] No more was it entirely a backwater. Part of the area belonged to an extensive imperial estate.[15]

Gibson then entered the debate, drawing attention to epitaphs now in Uşak. These were Christian, bearing crosses or a communion paten above a table, and one of them was clearly Montanist by virtue of reference to a female presbyter (cf. Epiphanius *Pan.* xlix.2). Yet these were 'not defiant' and they did not contain the word 'Christian' at all![16] Moreover, in other, post-Constantinian Montanist epitaphs (recognisable from their references to distinctively Montanist clergy such as Paulinos the *koinōnos*) neither 'Christian' nor 'spiritual' appeared. So were quite the wrong conclusions being drawn?

Southern Phrygia in the third century was a place where Christians and Jews did not try to conceal their allegiances. Epitaphs showed

names and formulae which gave them away, though they did not
make an issue of religion.[17] And Gibson posited a similarly tolerant
situation in the upper Tembris valley, where even the same masons
were employed by allegedly 'provocative' and unprovocative (but
non-secretive) Christians–and not by them alone. This did not speak
of a situation of tension and the need for Montanists to retreat to the
outback. Calder had noted the same thing in 'Philadelphia and
Montanism' (pp. 316, 349) – 'a good feeling and accommodation
between the Christians and their pagan neighbours', with Christians
holding municipal office 'and then entering into relations with the
Roman government and the Roman state religion'. There had been
little persecution in third-century Phrygia. Montanists (unless we see
them as uncompromising fanatics, incapable of normal social
intercourse) would also have enjoyed a relatively quiet life, if the
picture were correct, and the stones of Phrygia, Gibson concluded,
told of Christian people (not just the writers of 'Christians for
Christians' epitaphs) who were bold in description of their religion as
of their wealth, expansive in decoration and culturally and artistically
at one with their neighbours.

Methodologically one should not argue on the basis of later
developments in a region, though Gibson conceded that from the
fourth century onwards there was Novatianism there and determined
resistance to the impositions of Julian the Apostate; Phrygia was the
seat of heresies of many kinds and four orthodox bishops were
murdered in succession.[18] Montanists may indeed have found a home
in the Tembris valley at some time but Gibson thought Calder was
wrong about the 'Christians for Christians' epitaphs being Montanist.
The evidence was inconclusive. This had not been Gibson's view
some years before. She had changed her mind and reactions were
mixed.

Frend thought her conclusion over-cautious. In 'Montanism:
Research and Problems' he deplored Gibson's 'reductionist thesis'
and the hypercritical denial of Montanism's 'remains on stone'. But
Strobel, too, fought shy of saying that these must be wholly Montanist
creations.[19] Tabbernee brought a fresh twist to the debate, first in
'Opposition' and now in his published work.

The relevance of this material largely depends on its date. From
Ramsay to Strobel its third-century date has been assumed, based for
the most part on interpretation of *one* dated 'Christians for Christians'
example (no. 22 in Gibson), the relevant section of which is itself

dependent on restoration to achieve an assumed date of 248–9 CE
(333 Sullan era). But, says Tabbernee, this date is *earlier* than other
dated examples where the single word 'Christian' is used of the
deceased (with no such identification of those who made the
dedication), whereas one would expect the most open profession
('Christians for Christians') to be later. Tabbernee posits that a
different reading and restoration would make the epitaph fourth-
century (348–9 CE–433 Sullan era), and so put the question in quite a
different light. Similarly Frederick Norris in reviewing Gibson's work
in *Church History* (no. 49, 1980) regretted that she had not paid more
attention to the different readings Anderson, Buckler, Calder and
others had obtained from this example.[20]

Tabbernee took note of instances of peculiar grammar on these
stones (more than one hand has been at work in some Phrygian
epitaphs, and reuse of stones too). He suggested that the plural form
'Christians' would have been a later addition when in a context which
does not accord grammatically with the content of the message
(which may imply the singular, for example). It would date from a
time when 'Christians for Christians' was a formulaic cliché and the
crucial no. 22 would fit into that category. It had better be dated in
348–9 CE, while others would be later still.

This would mean that the epitaphs were no longer remarkable.
Open profession of Christianity would not have been provocative
post-Constantine and so no link with Montanism on grounds of
daring open profession would be necessary. The inscriptions would be
products of an orthodox community. The finding also got rid of any
need for appeal to Montanism's alleged provocative excesses.

Frend finds this revised date and orthodox setting 'unlikely'. His
call for more fieldwork and excavation of suspected Montanist sites
continues to fall on stony ground.[21] For myself, I have never been
convinced that the 'Christians for Christians' epitaphs were Montanist.
Nor have I believed that (even if they were) they added much to our
knowledge of later Montanism, beyond the fact that it existed in rural
Phrygia, had married adherents and did not fear to declare its
allegiances. Such things we knew already from other sources and they
are no less true of other Christians in Phrygia. More interesting is
scholars' agreement that relations between pagans and Christians
must have been good in third-century Phrygia. It was possible to
acknowledge in epitaphs that the deceased, at least, had been a
Christian, without incurring action against a family,[22] and we need

not think that Montanists would have fared worse. Phrygian Christians displayed on epitaphs the signs of their trade, their wealth, their culture and their standing in the towns where they lived. Their religion seems to have been little of a barrier.[23]

This does of course help to explain Montanism's continued existence into the era of Constantine and then into the following centuries, despite edicts and anti-heretical manoeuvrings (5.2; 5.3). Montanists survived because local feeling against them was not strong (albeit they would have suffered when attacks on Christians generally *did* flare and, when pressured to oppose them, their neighbours would have done so). Their peculiarities (of Easter observance, of women in public religious roles and so on) would have been known to Christians round about and deplored strongly by some. But probably they were little more than a matter for curiosity and ritual disapproval to others. Catholics before the age of Constantine must have known that (cultural accretions apart, common to all in a region) they shared more in common in the religious sphere with a Montanist *pneumatikos* than with the pagan next door. Coexistence with pagans would not be aided by internecine Christian strife. When a Christian State did become determined to cleanse itself of alien, heretical influences, then Montanism was of course on the list. Nevertheless, it was not easy to kill, as we shall see. This must say as much about orthodox Christians' lack of illwill (or indifference) towards it as it does of the determination of Montanists themselves.[24]

5.1.4 Epigraphy and Montanist clergy
We do not know at what date Montanism adopted the peculiarities of its clerical system. Montanus had made some provision. He had provided for Prophetic teaching to continue and for Pepuza to remain significant: it was to be a place of assembly for the faithful. A fiscal exactment of sorts was made from associated congregations by means of collectors appointed for the task (Eusebius *HE* v.18,2 (Apollonius)) and presumably the funds would support teachers and others. Apart from known leaders such as Themiso and Miltiades, Theodotus (who did not long survive, *HE* v.16,14 (Anonymous)) and then Proclus, Tabbernee surmises that local (catholic) clergy who were converts to the Prophecy provided institutional leadership.[25] But there is no evidence for this. Chronology is vague with regard to this transitional period. We do not know the nature of the succession.[26]

By Jerome's (late fourth-century) day, of course, Montanist clergy were well established and he wrote to Marcella (*Ep.* xli.3) about the peculiarities of Montanist fasting and their relegation of bishops to third place, contrary to catholic practice. He was implying that Montanists had abandoned interest in apostolic succession.

First in the Montanist hierarchy were the patriarchs of Pepuza, he said, then the distinctively Montanist *cenonos* (*caenonus*/*cenonas* in different MSS), probably a latinisation of the *koinōnous* as in *Cod. Just.* This was not something known only in Rome, for we have evidence of the *koinōnoi* and even patriarchs from other sources and in other settings.

As for the bishops, Sozomen tells us that Montanists had bishops not just in towns but in rural areas – 'villages' (*HE* vii.19,2), though such a situation was not unique to Montanists. Village bishops may well have been a continuation of much earlier Montanist practice, stemming, indeed, from a time before the catholic Church had abandoned such a pattern. For Montanism was in fact conservative, Vokes suggested, holding fast to an institution which developing catholicism altered as it favoured συνοίκησις. Montanism was merely anachronistic. The bishops must have been more numerous than the *koinōnoi* and patriarchs. The *cathedra* of just such a local bishop may have been discovered – in the region of Bekilli, perhaps quite close to Pepuza, as I mentioned earlier (see 5.1.2).

In Montanism, of course, a *woman* might function as presbyter or bishop.[27] Possibly they functioned in other ranks too, such as that of deacon, for there *were* deacons (cf. Ambrosiaster on 1 Tim. 3:2 and the *Cod. Just.* i.5.20.3), as there might be an archdeacon, *prōtodiakonos* (cf. 5.1.2). Deacons, presumably, were among the 'other clergy' of which we hear without details. We hear that the Quintillians had female presbyters and other female clergy (Epiphanius *Pan.* xlix.2,3) and an inscription mentioning a *presbytera* has been cited already.

5.1.5 The senior clergy
It is the *patriarchs* and *koinōnoi* who have been most discussed. To begin with the former, it seems reasonable to assume that there was always a patriarch in the mother community at Pepuza, but sources from other places also tell of patriarchs and possibly these were Montanist. Patriarchs were not wanted in Constantinople in particular, nor were any other Montanist clergy for that matter according to *Cod. Just.* i.5.20.3–though it may be that that was a prophylactic measure in the

edict concerned and that one would not normally have expected to find one there. It may also have been Montanist patriarchs who were in mind when the Council of Laodicea (canon 8) decreed that even the greatest in the Montanist clerical hierarchy had to be rebaptised.[28] The church of the patriarchs mentioned in the *Life* of Theodotus (see 3.8.3) is suggestive of Montanist associations, but the provenance of that document is unclear.[29] In such cases, as in Jerome, the word is in the plural and this does perhaps indicate that a patriarchate was not peculiar to Pepuza. Jerome, who tells us about the Montanist hierarchy and its patriarchs, had been in Ancyra in the preceding decade. So the probability of the office existing in Galatia at least, as well as Pepuza, is increased.

It is as well to remember that this was a title not confined to Montanist circles. It was known in Jewish ones as well, for describing heads of community. It is in the light of that fact that a Carthaginian inscription which referred to patriarchs, and which Seckel took to be Montanist, has now come to be regarded by some as Jewish.[30] So it is unsafe to argue that the Montanist office is clearly attested for North Africa too.[31] The only other epigraphy relates to Hierapolis and the fifth century (*CIG* iv. 8769). The waters are muddied further by the fact that catholics also adopted the title (albeit officially only in later centuries). Gregory of Nazianzus honoured Basil of Caesarea in that way (*Orat.* xliii.37; cf. xlii.33). It may be, then, that the Montanist 'patriarch' title owed a debt to Judaism filtered through Asian Jewish Christianity. It would be yet another example of that debt.[32]

I tend to think of them as akin to archbishops, but until further evidence emerges there can be no certainty. Montanist clerical egalitarianism probably never extended to the patriarchate, for we have no hint of it and such authority accorded to a woman would surely have had a Jerome, an Epiphanius or some other rushing pen to paper in an apoplectic rage.

There is better epigraphical evidence for the *koinōnoi* but still it is hard to determine how they functioned and the source of the title itself. (i) Praÿlios, a *koinōnos* described also as ἅγιος, is known from a dated (514–5 CE on Tabbernee's reckoning) inscription from some ten miles north of Philadelphia. His was a regional appointment, for it was ὁ κατὰ τόπον, and Tabbernee has argued that a 'regional bishop' is intended.[33] (ii) In Phrygia itself, from the area of Sebaste south-east of Temenothyrai, we have the inscription for the 85 year-old Paulinos, *koinōnos* and *mystēs*. The latter title was used in catholic

circles by the end of the fifth century to denote 'metropolitan'. This
epitaph has been cited already (3.8 n. 157), for it makes mention of a
'martyr', Trophinus (Trophimos).

There is at present neither epigraphy nor other literature unquestionably showing women in the rank of *koinōnos*, though Friedrich
argued in 1895 that the witness of Jerome to the *cenones* was paralleled
by the *socias*, women 'associates' referred to in the (probably
sixth-century) *Epistula Lovocato* (see 4.6.2). These were to be found at
the altar. *Cenones*, he maintained, indicated a peculiarly *female* office.
Here were the successors of the women Prophets and the male term
koinōnos was a misunderstanding. Friedrich believed that Jerome and
the *Epistula* were roughly contemporaneous, and of course Friedrich
was writing before most of the work on the epigraphy. His views
about the exclusively female character of this office have been
rejected,[34] but, although the *Epistula* is a source showing confusion, it
is not impossible that garbled knowledge of *female* Montanist *koinōnoi*
underlies some of its statements.

The significance of the term is also unclear. It has been suggested
the at the term *koinōnos* was equivalent to the Jewish communities' *ḥbr*
'*yr* (חבר עיר) which is attested in Rabbinic sources (with Tabbernee I
am uneasy about positing so *direct* a dependence on Judaism). Then it
was thought to point to financial officers/collectors (Eusebius *HE*
v.18,2), such as Montanus had appointed from the first. Paul in
Philippians 4:15 had spoken of a κοινωνία of giving and receiving
(suggestive of a two-way receipt of gifts from apostle and believers:
guidance and authoritative teaching one way, money the other) and
the word was used in relation to the collection in Romans 15:26 and 2
Corinthians 8:4. I think, nevertheless, that 'financial officer' is too
narrow a definition of *koinōnos*. It is hard to see why such people would
have been honoured as clergy (and above bishops) if it meant that
alone – unless Montanism were exceedingly geared towards financial
prosperity.[35]

Perhaps the *koinōnos* was someone whose role suggested (whatever
the administrative reality) the special 'fellowship' stressed in Montanist
teaching. This needs further discussion.

Koinōnos indicates partnership, fellowship, one in association or
communion with.[36] I look above all to the New Testament sources
and to the teaching of Montanism on the Spirit to determine why it
should have used such a word of an office. But with what is this
association/fellowship? A number of possible answers come to mind:

(a) That here we have spiritual descendants of the first 'associates' of the Three – guardians of an 'apostolic' (and prophetic) tradition of sorts which concerned the special teaching of Montanism. The Prophecy, it should be remembered, while rooted firmly in Christian soil, claimed to bring new insights to the Christian fold. The veracity of these insights and the orthopraxis associated with them would have needed to be explained and guarded, appealing to a tradition which was traceable back to the first generation eyewitnesses. Those with the title of bishop had such guardianship in the catholic fold but 'bishops' were relegated downwards in Montanism, as Jerome observed. The significance attached to the *companions* of the prophet Muhammad in Islam also comes to mind.

(b) The 'companionship' was perhaps that of a shared (with Christ) experience of suffering or witness. Those who see Montanists as much concerned with public witness and ever ready to embrace martyrdom like this option, and Frend and Klawiter are among those who see the 'companions' in this way (cf. Rev. 1:9). But presumably (as Tabbernee observes of Klawiter in this respect) this explains only the *original* adoption of the title, i.e. at first it would have been granted to confessors (Montanist 'martyrs') only,[37] just as the word was used of Polycarp, who became such a *koinōnos* of Christ through his martyrdom (*M. Pol.* vi.2; xvii.3). Like 'pillar', discussed elsewhere, it is possible that *koinōnos* was already just such a title among certain kinds of Christians in Asia Minor. But if this were its origin, when did the use of the title become routinised and lose its real significance? The three inscriptions about *koinōnoi* do not suggest that confession/ martyrdom had played a role in their achieving such rank.[38]

(c) I envisage the Prophets/Montanists as people who scoured sacred writings for inspiration, support and ammunition, amassing *florilegia* of quotations on their own behalf. So is the title the product of an amalgam of biblical references which fitted their concerns? For example, 1 Peter 5:1 is rich in language which would have spoken to their needs. There 'Peter' exhorts (παρακαλῶ) elders, as a witness (μάρτυς) of the sufferings of Christ and as one who also partakes (κοινωνός) in the glory which will be revealed (ἀποκαλύπτεσθαι). There he associates himself, his experience and expectations with those of the church elders. *koinōnos* was not obviously associated with an office in this case but rather we should probably assume that such concerns (for witness, for example) and future expectations were thought to be characteristic of all right-thinking Christians in that

congregation. Paul too was συγκοινωνός in the gospel with his readers
(1 Cor. 9:23 and cf. 2 Cor. 1:5f.). The teacher enjoyed a communality
of hope and experience with the led, as he (or she) also enjoyed
fellowship with the Lord.

Other New Testament passages relate the experience of fellowship
to the Spirit, and Tabbernee has chosen to emphasise pneumatology,
seeing the term as meaning 'companions of the Spirit'. The most
obvious biblical background is provided by 2 Corinthians 13:13 and
Philippians 2:1, the first being the Pauline benediction which includes
the words 'the fellowship (κοινωνία) of the Holy Spirit', the second
speaking of comfort (παράκλησις) in Christ and the fellowship of the
Spirit. I think he is right–the key to this term is in New Testament
usage. Pauline language and ideas were valued by Montanists, and
the idea of being one with the Spirit (as Montanists taught about it)
and one with Christ through faith (1 Cor. 1:9) also contrasts neatly
with being associates (κοινωνοί) of prophet-slayers (Matt. 23:30; cf.
Eusebius *HE* v.16,12). These were people expected to promote and
manifest that κοινωνία which should be a mark of Montanist life and
the language is reminiscent of 1 John 1:3,6f., speaking not just of
fellowship *with Christ* and *between Christians* but of the declaring (1:1) of
things seen and heard and touched. So there was a teaching and
exhortatory role associated with the *koinōnos*, I suggest, as well as
oversight (for the *koinōnos* was above the Montanist bishop).

So were these *koinōnoi* particularly endowed with *charismata*?
Perhaps so in the early days (if *koinōnoi* existed then), but we do not
know at what point or to what extent *charismata* also became
routinized. We have no idea on what grounds a *koinōnos* would have
been appointed in (say) the fourth or fifth century. Perhaps it was a
matter of appointing to office those judged to accord most closely with
all the resonances of *koinōnia/koinōnos*, so as to guard the communities'
insights about such things. Who knows? The truth is that we are
working in the dark and need much more literary evidence and
epigraphy before pronouncing on Montanist clergy.

5.2 MONTANISM AND THE HERESIES

Montanism had time and opportunity to change its form. Time and
opportunity to become a heresy. It did. But still the commentator
must tread with care. Its opponents, who have left us our evidence,
were operating in a climate in which 'heresy' was a recurring cry, and

they were eager for examples. Many of their claims about Montanism's unacceptable characteristics were based on the copying and reiteration of earlier writers', either adding nothing new or compounding existing half-truths and errors. Quite wrongly one may get the impression that Montanism was a live issue at the times and in the places represented by the writers concerned, whereas in fact the gadabout Epiphanius probably never encountered a Montanist in Cyprus, his home base, Pacian of Barcelona almost certainly never met one and we should not assume their presence in Illyricum in the fourth century because bishop Ulfilla, apostle of the Goths, countered similar heresies (including African Donatism(!) – so Auxentius in *Epistola de Fide, Vita et Obitu Ulfilae*).

The fact is that scarcely any of the anti-Montanists who wrote after the age of Constantine would actually have known such a creature, apart from an occasional bishop (e.g. Innocent I in Rome) or front-line opponents such as John of Ephesus and Jerome perhaps. From the third century onwards the opposition was increasingly of an academic kind – condemnation from a distance, with the repetition of what were becoming stereotyped descriptions. Montanism entered the annals of heresies and so was cited in lists of abhorrent teachings, regardless of the writer's ignorance of its true nature.

Evidence for later Montanism in the East is more extensive and relatively less questionable than in the West. It was declared heretical in both areas but, except in of Rome, Tabbernee found nothing convincing to show Montanism was alive in the West (Spain and Africa included) at the end of the fourth century ('Opposition', p. 402). He is probably right. In the East Arcadius and Theodosius II made Montanists' lives very difficult, though some continued to survive. The history of Montanism after the mid fourth century is largely the history of attempts to wipe it out as a heresy.

Yet the original Prophecy had been orthodox. Its innovations, based on revelations, had not concerned matters central to salvation but rather the day-to-day disciplined living of the Christian life. The beginnings of Montanist suspect theology were found in Rome. While Tertullian was formulating a searing attack on Praxeas (the anti-Montanist and the crucifier of the Father) there were Prophetic types in Rome (seemingly unknown to Tertullian) whose views on Father and Son were not orthodox. In Hippolytus and Pseudo-Tertullian we have the first references to the disputes about the Trinity which became associated with Montanism.

5.2.1 Montanism and the Trinity

Hippolytus wrote of Monarchian error among some of the Prophets.
This was common enough at the time. But others (the majority?)
among the Prophets confessed God as Father and creator of all and
Christ 'in accordance with the gospel', he said (*Refut. omn. haer.*
viii.12). We do not know what occasioned the 'shift'. Asian catholics
had condemned the Prophecy at an early stage (Eusebius *HE*
v.16,10), but not for heresy. Serapion said the Prophecy was detested
(*HE* v.19,2f.) but there is no hint that trinitarian theology was at issue
(nor in *HE* v.16,6; Epiphanius *Pan.* xlviii.1,4). In Africa Montanists
and catholics had coexisted without formal schism or excommunication and Tertullian himself was impeccably opposed to erosion of a
right understanding of the Godhead (though scholars do not agree in
describing his own view on the matter). The trouble seems to have
started in Rome.

Looking back, later writers accused Montanists of controversy and
separation from the catholic Church (Filastrius *Haer.* xlix; cf. Origen
In Ep. ad Titum, *PG* xiv.1306) and some linked schism with hints of
wrong doctrine. In the mid third century Firmilian was saying that
Montanists 'separated' from the true Church ('si se ab ecclesia dei
sciderant . . .') and self-evidently their doctrine must have been
heretical, their baptism invalid. Some present at the gathering in
Iconium here described were not so sure. Some Christians 'received'
the New Prophets and believed that they *did* recognise the Father and
the Son (Cyprian *Ep.* lxxv. 7 and 19). But Firmilian was undeterred.
Heretics generally, he maintained, tended to disagree on 'minor'
matters but they were united in having a wrong view of the creator.
Cataphrygians were in a different category: by the very nature of
their view of prophecy, he reasoned, they did not have the Holy
Spirit. So they could not lay claim to the Father or the Son. They had
to be (re)baptised. The same question was discussed in a gathering in
Synnada *c.* 258 CE. The baptism of Montanists became a recurring
theme in our sources. It is hard to tell whether at this stage of
Montanism's development very many of its adherents had strayed
from the kind of orthodoxy Tertullian had promoted:

God brought forth the Word, as the Paraclete also teaches, as the root brings
forth a tree and a spring a river and the sun a ray,

he wrote, almost as if citing an oracle and in wholly orthodox manner
(*Adv. Prax.* viii).

Many writers acknowledge Tertullian's important contribution to the formulation of orthodox trinitarian doctrine and also his debt to Montanism in moving away from binitarian thought.[39] Tertullian believed, of course, that the *regula fidei* he espoused (including teaching about the Trinity) was affirmed and clarified through the instruction of the Paraclete (*Adv. Prax.* ii.1f.; viii.5; ix.1).[40] He was not to be blamed for any Montanist wrong-headedness (as the catholics saw it) on this matter. But evidently there were fears about the Prophets' understanding of the Spirit and some catholics knew some Montanists who were Monarchian in tendency. Inevitably (whether justifiably or not) all Prophets became tarred with the brush of doctrinal error.

Yet any connection 'between Montanism and the various brands of monarchianism was only accidental', David Wright suggested.[41] 'There was no inherent affinity between the two . . . the New Prophecy was fanatical rather than heretical'.[42] And Pelikan was equally cautious. Modalism, he allowed, would have lent itself to the Prophecy's explanation of salvation history:

From what we know of modalism – and it is less than some historians of dogma seem to know – it could be well calculated to articulate the Montanist emphasis upon the new prophecy within the framework of a doctrine of the Trinity . . . [when] piety has devoted much attention to the issue of the successive dispensations of God, as Montanism did, modalism has provided it with the kind of trinitarianism it needed.[43]

God the Father manifested in the people of Israel and its prophets would have preceded the manifestation of God as Son in Jesus Christ and his prophetic work, to be followed by God manifested as Holy Spirit and Paraclete in the New Prophecy. Thus, Pelikan thought, the reports of Hippolytus and Pseudo-Tertullian were credible enough.

Nevertheless, everyone in the Prophecy did not think that way (was Modalism/Monarchianism one outcome for some of having to define and defend the Prophecy more thoroughly?).[44] And so 'it would be a mistake to gather from these reports that Montanism necessarily implied modalism'. By the fourth century, however, the accusation was all-pervasive. Pacian of Barcelona (*Ep.I ad Sympronianum*, ii) averred that Montanism brought argument about everything – Paraclete (cf. Origen *De princ.* ii.7,3), the apostles, Passover and the name 'catholic'. But, above all, it was Monarchian/ Sabellian heresy that was abhorrent. In the age of Constantine such

an accusation was serious. In the legislation of Constantine and his
successors, heretics would be enemies of the (Christian) State (see 5.3).

Montanism was not condemned at Nicaea (Jerome *Ep.* lxxxiv.4),
though it did get a mention (Socrates *HE* i.13.7 cf. Sozomen *HE*
ii.18). Yet at other points in the fourth century it was clearly regarded
as heretical. Canon 8 of the Council of Laodicea spoke of rebaptising
even the highest in Montanism. Unlike with Novatianists or
Quartodecimans (canon 7) or schismatics of other kinds it was not
enough to reinstruct and then anoint them to bring them back into
the fold (cf. Eusebius *Vita Const.* iii.66). They were heretics. In 381 the
Council of Constantinople condemned Montanism on the grounds of
Monarchianism (according to some MSS of the dubious canon 7) and
again rebaptism was a necessity. In Rome Jerome was similarly
condemnatory when writing to Marcella at about the same time,
naming Sabellianism as Montanists' primary fault (*Ep.* xli ad
Marcellam iii) – the making of Father, Son and Spirit into one
person. Didymus of Alexandria portrayed the Montanists as stupid
(*De Trin.* ii.15 and iii.18) but there is also a hint that a determined
refusal to jeopardise monotheism (as they saw it) lay behind the
Montanists' stance (cf. too *De Trin.* iii.23 and 38). Still catholics could
not admit Montanist baptism (*De Trin.* iii.41). Tabbernee put the
matter succinctly in 'Opposition' (p. 399): 'Montanists were treated
like pagans.' To become Christians, they had to be baptised.

Didymus preserved an 'oracle' of Montanus as evidence against
him:

I am the Father and the Son and the Paraclete (Aland no.2; cf. Cyril of
Jerusalem *Cat.* xvi.8 and Epiphanius *Pan.* xlviii.2).[45]

For the Montanist in the *Dialexis*, 'Montanus the saint' had possessed
the perfection of the Holy Spirit, i.e. the Paraclete, the Spirit of truth.
For the Orthodox, however, he had been identifying himself with
Father, Son and Paraclete.[46] An extended debate on the Trinity and
tritheism followed:

Is there not one God?

asked the Montanist in the *Dialexis*.

Do you not admit the clear distinction of the three hypostases?

demanded the Orthodox, asserting that

if the Son teaches that the Father is one, and the Paraclete the Holy Spirit
another, it must be believed.

But, objected the Montanist,

if there is one, and another, and another, there are three Gods.

There is no doubt that Montanus the saint, the prophet and the passive recipient of the Spirit's action *did* become much more in the eyes of some later Montanists. Basil of Caesarea (Ep. clxxxviii.1) accused Montanists of the unforgivable sin (Matt. 12:31) of blasphemy against the (humanised) Holy Spirit, compounded by the use of a trinitarian baptismal formula of Father, Son *and Montanus or Priscilla*. This amazing claim might be dismissed as a calumny were it not for the existence of an interesting inscription in the *Corpus Inscriptionum Latinarum*.

This inscription was found in 1875 at Khenschala, ancient Mascula in Numidia. It was inscribed on a rectangular marble slab which carried the A Ω symbols and a Constantinian monogram. It reads as follows:

FLABIUS ABUS DOMESTICUS I(N) NOMINE PATRIS ET FILII (ET) DO(MI)NI MUNTANI QUOD PROMISIT COMPLEUIT.[47]

Flavius had provided the inscription (undated) in the name of the Father, the Son and the lord Muntanus, to mark the fulfilment of a promise. The inscription suggests there had been more than a hint of truth in the fourth-century claims. Some Montanists probably *were* baptising in the name of their eponymous ancestor. With Labriolle, Monceaux, Pelikan and others I accept that the inscription is indeed Montanist and that at this late stage *some* Montanists at least were far removed from the Great Church.[48] One wonders what Tertullian's reaction would have been.

5.2.2 Montanism, Novatianism, Donatism

Novatianism (in the third century) and Donatism (in the fourth) were rigorous forms of Christianity, products of periods of persecution (Decian and Diocletianic), schismatic and unforgiving of the lapsed. They were to be found in places where Montanism also found a hold – both were in Africa (this being Donatism's place of origin), in Rome (where Novatianism originated), as well as in Phrygia and surrounding provinces. In Egypt, also, rigorist followers of Meletius, bishop of Lycopolis in Upper Egypt, organised a church of their own in response to events in the persecutions of Diocletian and Maximin.

Original Novatianism and Donatism were not heretical. The

Novatian bishop Acesius was at one with the orthodox at Nicaea so far as Arianism was concerned and Constantine himself allegedly failed to find doctrinal error in a Novatianist. Novatian, formerly a presbyter in the Roman church, died a martyr's death under Valerian in 257–8 CE,[49] and, as for Donatism, roundly attacked by Optatus and Augustine,[50] the Numidian schismatic bishops and others who consecrated Majorinus as a rival to bishop Caecilian of Carthage (311 CE) did so because they questioned the validity of the latter's consecration. The consecrator of Caecilian (Felix of Aptunga) had been accused of being a *traditor* during the persecution, i.e. he had surrendered the Scriptures. Donatus, who lent his name to the schism, succeeded Majorinus as rival.

There is a geographical overlap between Montanist/Novatianist/ Donatist communities. Harnack saw this and Frend took up the theme in his study of *The Donatist Church*. Montanist churches had bishops with sees in villages as well as towns and this was true of Novatianists also. Novatianist councils were held *in villages* in the fourth century and as late as the early sixth (in Pazos in 368 CE and Myloukome in 515 CE)[51] and Frend wrote of a tradition of continuous dissent from the Catholic religion in some places, with a prophetic church succeeded by a Montanist one, then by a Novatianist 'where native linguistic and cultural traditions were most vigorous' (*The Donatist Church*, p. 59). A brand of village, dissenting, non-catholic religion was heir of old national religions and Donatism, Montanism, Novatianism and 'certain aspects' of Coptic Monophysitism belonged to a common stream of Christian thought, both in terms of economic background and belief. In Synnada in Phrygia and at Carthage in 256 CE councils were looking for the rebaptism of heretics,[52] and in the late third century Montanism and Novatianism appeared vigorous precisely where native cults suffered decline – these being 'extreme and fanatical movements akin to African Donatism'.[53] Tertullian himself was best understood as 'the forerunner and father of Donatism'.[54] Frend's case is perhaps overenthusiastically made, yet it seems reasonable to surmise that in Rome and in the towns and villages of North Africa there would have been some Montanists who merged into the ranks of Novatianists and Donatists as their own fortunes declined.

In Augustine's day (so Praedestinatus), the Tertullianists converted *en masse* to the catholic side, thanks to Augustine's eloquence and logic. Their basilica was transferred to the catholics.[55] Perhaps so. I wonder, nevertheless, whether some of Montanism's faithful remnant had allied themselves not with congregations of catholic bishops in the mainstream but rather with the successors of Majorinus and Donatus. It would do them no good in the long run, of course, for it was not only Montanism which was destroyed.

5.2.3 Eve and Mary

The last word on Montanism and the heresies concerns the female and the feminine. The Christophany (in female form) to Quintilla is not an instance of heretical teaching, since the figure of Wisdom provides the explanation, I think. However, Epiphanius, who recounted that appearance, also told of the Quintillian belief that Eve was wise, the first to eat of the tree of knowledge (*Pan.* xlix.2.2). This is a claim reminiscent of some Gnostic sources, of course (cf. *Pan.* xxvi.2,6 and 3,1),[56] and it is not impossible that by the fourth century the Quintillian branch of Montanism, at least, had lent an ear to elements of Gnostic teaching where women were concerned. Eve's act would have been seen as emancipatory rather than as destructive and she might even be the foremother of the wise, prophetic, knowledge-filled women whose activities were presupposed in the oracles and visions of Maximilla and Quintilla.

One calls to mind, also, the frescos of the tomb of the Aurelii on the Viale Manzoni in Rome, dating probably from the first half of the third century. Along with a scene of Christ's entry into a city and pictures of Paradise for the blessed, there were Christian adaptations of scenes from pagan mythology and a serpent in Eden *who was more instructor than tempter*. The identity of the worshippers in this place is disputed. Certainly they were Christians of sorts and Cecchelli thought they might have been Montanists. But more probably they were Gnostics.[57] We should certainly not think that the early Prophecy had been tainted with Gnosticism (the claim of the *Libellus Synodicus* iii that Maximilla taught her disciples about the 870 aeons is not to be treated with respect). But as the centuries passed, some Gnostic ideas may have gained a hold in corners of Montanism.

Eve, Mary and salvation were topics much debated by the time of Epiphanius, of course. In his claim about the Quintillians and Eve he may simply have been reflecting one salvo in an ongoing battle between Montanists and catholics on aspects of Christian teaching. For it was in the fourth century that the Adam/Christ, Eve/Church parallelism was being further worked out (Methodius, *Symp.* or

Conviv. virg. iii.8; Ambrose, *Expos. Evang. Luc.* ii.7; Zeno of Verona, *Tractatus* i; xiii.10). Epiphanius himself took up the theme of Eve the death-bringer and Mary the life-bringer and otherwise furthered the cause of Mariology. It was in the *Panarion* that he castigated both Quintillians and the women of the Collyridian sect who offered bread (in priestly fashion) to Mary.[58] So were challenging assertions being made about the person of Eve? Was this a response to catholics' determinedly contrasting Eve, on the one hand (viewed negatively), and their Church (the mother of believers), on the other (the positive antitype)? In catholic churches the ministries of women were carefully circumscribed.

A later source is the sixth- or possibly seventh-century Barhad-beshabba, native of Beth Arbaye.[59] From him we learn that Montanists had four fasts annually of forty days (this should make us suspicious of his witness) and that they corrupted holy writings. Furthermore they allegedly taught that Mary was divine and that she had given birth to God's son after an archonite had had intercourse with her. These were not original claims. Bishop Maruta of Maipherqat (d. pre-420 CE) had recorded the same tales probably in the late fourth century, commenting also on the Montanists' (Marianists') indecorous speech. They had falsified Scriptures in the service of their own dogma, he claimed (Syriac).[60]

To judge from Epiphanius and these Syriac sources some Montanists had been rewriting salvation history. In the latter case, Mary, a female, played the divine role in Jesus' birth. In the former, Eve's role was radically reappraised.[61] Even allowing that the reports are reliable (and Tabbernee was dismissive in 'Opposition' p. 516) we have no way of knowing whether the teachings were, in Montanist terms, local aberrations rather than the norm. These are isolated and untypical reports and there are certainly no grounds for asserting, as Stephen Benko does, that 'This movement [Montanism] carried into Christian thinking a dependence upon the inexhaustible power of the feminine aspect of God'.[62]

The New Prophecy had first found itself squeezed into schism and as matters deteriorated it offered hostility for hostility. Increasingly isolated from the catholic mainstream but having still to defend itself from time to time, speculative theology may have come to the fore. In its early stage many of what would be Christianity's major doctrines were not yet formulated. Then the Prophecy in Rome became embroiled in debates about Father, Son and Spirit which wove into the formulation of those doctrines. When the dust had settled more than a century later, Montanists were on the wrong side. Probably we should believe the consensus view of our sources from the fourth century onwards that *by that time* the Montanist understanding of Father, Son and Spirit was not that of the orthodox, though caution is needed, given that 'Montanism' had split and diversified. Isolated, splintered into groups designated by the name of a prophetess (Quintillianists, Priscillianists), by their geographical base (Pepuzites, Cataphrygians) or by some perceived peculiarity of practice (Tascod-rougites, Artotyrites), Montanists must have seemed at best eccentrics, even to those neighbours who, for a long time, seem to have left them in peace. In some places, no doubt, teachings thoroughly alien to the catholic tradition had filtered into the original, orthodox Prophecy. Victims too of vile rumour, it was inevitable that, when legislation bit, Montanists would suffer the fate of other heretics. And so they did.

5.3 THE DESTRUCTION OF MONTANISM

5.3.1 Decline in the West and in the East

Though Montanism in its many forms took a long time to die, we do not know of any *single* event which made it extinct. We gain glimpses of its decline over centuries, coupled with a tenacious clinging to life, and this was not just in rural areas, though certainly it survived longest in Pyrygia and surrounding provinces. In towns and villages alike, until Montanists were driven into the catholic fold or were subsumed into the ranks of Novatianists, Donatists etc., they continued to exist. In what numbers we do not know. Just as it has been a recurring theme in earlier chapters of this study that 'we need more evidence', so it is with regard to the details of Montanism's end.

It was the Christianising of the empire which destroyed Montanism. Sozomen from Constantinople (an exact contemporary of the lay historian Socrates), looking back, wrote about 440 CE that heretics had all but disappeared as the edict of Constantine had closed their churches and forbidden meetings (*HE* ii,32,2, διὰ τοῦτον δὲ νόμον τούτων τῶν αἱρέσεων οἶμαι τὴν πολλὴν ἀφανισθῆναι μνήμην; cf. too Eusebius, *Vita Const.* iii.64 and 65). As a claim it was more ideal than reality. Novatians, well organised and well led as they were, eventually got more favourable treatment and, though Montanists ('Phrygians', as Sozomen called them, 'Cataphrygians' in Eusebius' *Vita Const.*)

would certainly have suffered under the regime of Constantine and his successors, still Montanists were numerous in Phrygia in the fifth century (Sozomen *HE* vii.19,2; cf. too *Cod. Theod.* xvi.5,34; Augustine *Haer.* xxvi on Cataphrygians). Half a century or so previously Filastrius of Brescia was describing distribution of the paschal communion from Pepuza (*De haer.* xlix). Montanism was far from dead. But it did not survive as long in other places.

In the mid fourth century Optatus of Numidian Milev claimed there were no Montanists in Africa (*De schism. Donat.* i.9,1), though he was more than familiar with Donatists! A century later Theodoret said there were no Montanists in Egypt or Libya (*Haer.* iii,1). Yet it is possible (but not certain) that Didymus the Blind, head of the catechetical school at Alexandria in the late fourth century, did know of Montanists there, and was not simply rehashing his sources (cf. Isidore of Pelusium *Epist. lib. quinque* I.242). Nor should we forget fifth-century Praedestinatus (i.86), who claimed (contrary to Optatus' evidence) that there had been Tertullianists in Africa to the time of Augustine (bishop from 395 CE), when at last they rejoined the catholics. Labriolle treated seriously this claim of an African presence in Augustine's day: 'La secte était encore vivante de son temps en Afrique', he wrote (*Les Sources*, cx), assuming his 'connaissance générale du Montanisme'. But Aland was less convinced.

Aland has been sceptical about the reliability of much of the evidence for Montanism's survival in the West.[63] Some of Augustine's statements might be taken to imply that it was no longer in Africa, though Montanism was still a reality in Phrygia (*Haer.* xxvi; cf. *Serm.* cclii; *Ep.* cxviii, 12), and the mixed nature of the evidence must show, at most, that Montanists must have been few in number and low in profile in Africa by the fourth century.

What of Spain? Bardy once stated that Montanism had never penetrated there and yet Pacian of Barcelona seemed to write of Montanist congregations in urban settings (*Ep. I ad Symp.* i.1 and 3) and of Cataphrygians/Phrygians who were diverse and had instigated many controversies (i,2). In fact he was citing a hypothetical example and (like Aland) I too think that the references to Cataphrygians are just grist to Pacian's polemic against Sympronianus. We should not assume Montanism's presence in Spain.[64] Priscillian of Avila gave no indication that he knew of Montanists there (*Tract.* i.27) and we should not read much into the fact that Gregory the Great, around 600 CE, was penning an epistle to Spanish bishops in which he mentioned the perversity of Cataphrygian pneumatology and challenged the validity of their baptism (*Ep.* xi.52). Montanism by this time was a useful paradigm when citing patterns of error, even in areas where it was long dead or had never been.

Rome is a different matter. We know much more. Praedestinatus recounted a tale of considerable African Tertullianist influence there *c.* 388 CE, prior to the triumph of 'the pious emperor Theodosius'. It concerned an African woman called Octaviana, married to a friend of the praetorian prefect Arbogast the Frank, he who supported the usurping emperor. According to Praedestinatus, a Montanist (Tertullianist) priest favoured by Octaviana was allowed to establish a *collegium* outside the city walls. The story (if there is any truth in it)[65] indicates a degree of accommodation with 'the world' and of influence with high-born women that we might not otherwise have expected of Montanists, and it would not have been long afterwards that surviving Tertullianists *in Africa* allegedly surrendered themselves to the arms of the catholic Church, succumbing to the rhetoric of Augustine. Had some African Montanists sensed the way the wind was blowing and sought patronage elsewhere? The *Roman* Tertullianist enclave, so Ferrua suggests (see n. 67 below), belonged in a spot outside the *porta Aurelia*. There is inscriptional evidence associated with that area and orientals and others were to be found there.

If such openness had ever really existed in Rome it soon came to an end. As early as 398 CE Honorius the Western emperor was promulgating laws against Montanists, Manichaeans and Priscillianists (*Cod. Theod.* xvi.5.4) and ordering books to be burnt. Progress was rather too slow for his liking, however, for Curtius, praetorian prefect in the capital, was reminded of the need to enforce edicts to the full (*Cod. Theod.* xvi.5.43). It is clear from our sources that local officials often felt no great desire to do so. However, the Albanian bishop of Rome, Innocent I (402–17), supposedly exiled quite a number of the Cataphrygians to a monastry. *Liber Pontificalis* i reads 'multos Cataphrygas invenit, quos exilio monasterii religavit'.[66] We are not told where they were sent.

Is it really feasible that there had been Montanist communities in Rome for centuries after Gaius debated with Proclus? The answer is yes. In the eighteenth century M.A. Boldetti published an interesting inscription which may point to just such a presence there. It reads as follows:

ΕΝΝΦΑΔΕ ΚΑΤΑΚΕΙΤΑΙ ΑΒΛΑΒΗΣ ΓΑΛΑΤΗΣ ΧΩΡΙΟΥ ΜΟΥΛΙΚΟ [Υ
Υ]ΙΟΣ ΦΩΤΙΝΟΥ ΖΗΣΑΣ ΕΤΗ ΤΡΙΑΚΟΝΤΑ ΠΝΕΥΜΑΤΙΚΟΣ. . .

Ablabés (for Ablabios?), son of Fotinos, was a πνευματικός, a
'spiritual' person (as distinct, perhaps, from one of the psychics). He
was from Galatia and a dove and an olive branch were inscribed on
the piece. On another probably fourth-century Roman inscription
Alexander the physician appeared, as a Christian and a πνευματικός,[67]
and if these inscriptions are indeed Montanist (and it is the
πνευματικός language which has led to the belief that they are), then
they break a silence about Montanism in Rome which stretches from
Hippolytus' *Refutation* to perhaps the end of the fourth century – i.e. a
century-and-a-half or more. Then came proscription. We hear
nothing of Montanists in Rome after the early fifth century. Honorius
in he West was more determined than Theodosius in the East (*Cod.
Theod.* xvi.5.48). The edict of Honorius in the *Codex Theodosianus*
relating to February of 407 CE, and mentioning Phrygians and
Priscillianists more than once is both the first and last instance of
Montanists being named in such a context.[68]

In the East they continued to be named. The source, book xvi of the
Codex Theodosianus, gives us 'a virtual synopsis of the religious and
legal *intentions* of the emperors from Constantine down through
Theodosius II'.[69] For the first time in such a Roman work it is spelt
out which religious beliefs and practices were acceptable and which
proscribed, indeed what right religion was to be. There was a
consequent 'narrowing' of the legal definition of a Christian –
although at the time of its publication in 438 there was as yet no
legislation *to enforce* conversion to the true faith. That would come, of
couse, and the Montanists, no less than pagans and Jews, would be
caught by it. The edicts impinged on Montanists of the fifth century,
though they did not destroy them totally.

Montanists had survived in Phrygia and in neighbouring provinces
too.[70] Epiphanius' *Panarion* (xlviii.14) confirms this, citing Quintillians,
Tascodrougites *et al*, and it mentions sectarians in Cilicia, Cappadocia,
Galatia and especially Constantinople (cf. *Pan.* xlviii.15 and see
Gregory Nazianzus *Orat.* xxii.12). Some non-Montanists found
themselves exiled to heretical territory – such as Paulinus of Trier,
banished to Phrygia (Augustine *De haer.* xxvi–xxviii); to 'the den of
Montanus and Maximilla' (cf., too Jerome, *Comm. in Ep. ad Gal.* ii.11).
Similarly, Hilary, opponent of emperor Constantius (353–61; *Contra*

Const. eccles. ii.32, written *c.* 360), had been surrounded by Montanists while he too was in exile, where for the first time, despite his close association with the religio–political wranglings of his age, Hilary actually *read* the much-disputed Nicene formula (*De Synod.* xci (*PL* x.545)). As legislation came more heavily to bear, even Montanists in the backwoods of the eastern provinces must have become increasingly ill at ease.

As late as John of Damascus' day, Montanists were being mentioned in relation to Pepuza (*Haer.* xlix), though there must have been little of Montanist Pepuza left and it is hard to take seriously such late evidence. But so long as Pepuza had survived in Montanist minds as a focal point that would explain their presence there and in neighbouring provinces too. Phrygian and *Galatian* settings recur in the inscriptional evidence, but it is hard to believe that the numbers of Montanists would have been very great. In the 420s and 430s Theodoret of Cyrrhus, north of Antioch (d. 466), was claiming that Pontus Poalemoniacus, Armenia, Cappadocia, Lycaonia, Pisidia, Pamphyla, Lycia and Caria knew no Montanism, Novatianism nor the Quartodeciman error ((*Ep.* lxxxi; civ and cxiii; *Haer. fab. comp.* iii.6). Of course it was not the case that their teachings had never penetrated such places at all. Both Epiphanius and Basil of Caesarea suggest the association of Montanism with Cappadocia, the latter discussing Pepuzites' baptism with Amphilocus of Iconium (*Ep.* clxxxviii,1).

5.3.2 Action against Montanists

It shows a remarkable tenacity that Montanism should have held out even in the part of the world where it had had its beginnings. It must have rubbed along with the neighbours despite alleged peculiarities of practice,[71] and probably it benefited from officials' unwillingness to enforce legislation. Some evidence suggests, however, that when the chips were down, and ordinary religious and social life was being made impossible, Montanists preferred death to dishonour. Apostasy (as they saw it) had never been countenanced.[72]

Life had become harder for such heretics (which Montanists now were) since the reign of Constantine. The story was one of proscription and banishment, book-burning and heresy-hunting, confiscation of churches by the catholics, capital offences and legal impediments. The death-knell probably sounded between 527 and 531 CE. Justinian promulgated laws against heretics and the *enforced* conversion of pagans was made explicitly legal (*Cod. Just.* i.11.100; cf. *Cod. Theod.* xvi.1.2; for 380 CE; xvi.10,23f. for 423 CE). This set a seal on earlier moves to encourage and promote such conversion, whether from paganism to Christianity or from its fringes to the true catholic religion and proper trinitarianism.[73] There was now a determined cleansing. The *Cod. Just.* i.5.20.2,3–7 speaks of fines of ten pounds of gold being imposed on governors who did not carry out its demands (cf. i.5.20.8 and *Cod. Theod.* xvi.5.40.8) and this is revealing. In the past Montanists, like other groups, sometimes survived unmolested because of such official apathy. Even at this late stage we read of at least one instance of bribery by Montanists of the East, so as to stave off the worst actions of catholic clergy. When pressure *was* exerted, Montanists had sometimes been able to stave off banishment and financial ruin. But that was not what the legislators had intended, of course, and the Code of Justinian (*c.* 530 CE) proscribed Montanism with all its might.

Its adherents were required to repent of their error (cf. Procopius *Hist. Arc.* xi.15 and 21).[74] Montanists in Anatolia (Constantinople gets a special mention) were forbidden to assemble, baptise, share common meals, be in receipt of welfare or buy slaves. Even the power of making a will was denied them. Twenty years later (*c.* 550), John of Ephesus, implementing such decrees, had his shock-troop catechist monistics converting pagans from their shrines – sometimes at least with 'geniality and forbearance' according to my colleague Frank Trombley.[75] For Montanists there was the burning of their churches and the disinterment of the remains of the Prophets.[76] The sixth century was not a comfortable one for the remaining Montanists.

This spate of legislation and action was a death sentence but it was the end of quite a long process. Such proscription was not new to Montanists. The *Codex Theodosianus*, its sixteenth book devoted to the many difficulties in Christianising an empire, had already legislated at some length against Montanists and other heretics. As early as 379 CE, under Gratian, Valentinian and Theodosius, there had come the uncompromising statement that 'All heresies are forbidden by both divine and, imperial laws and they shall cease forever' (*Cod. Theod.* xvi.5.5), and heresy was politicised. It had come to be seen as treason, as failure to be at one with the welfare of the State. And while loyalists of the true catholic religion (and clergy in particular) enjoyed privileges, including imperial exemption from certain taxation, from some forms of onerous public service, the extending of favours to their wives and children, privileges in relation to church estates and more (*Cod. Theod.* xvi),[77] matters were different for the Montanists. They had had to get used to the expulsion of clerics from municipalities and cities (see too *Cod. Theod.* xvi.5,34; xvi.5,47–8), perpetual banishment of those who assembled, even death for those who organised assemblies in rural areas and for those in city or countryside who allowed their buildings to be used. To deprive heretics of leadership there were penalties for creating Montanist clergy. Montanist books were burnt, with threat of execution for anyone found hiding such books. It seems minor in comparison that heretics were also banned from government and imperial service by virtue of edicts of 395 and 408 CE (*Cod. Theod.* xvi.5.25 and 42).

The likes of Montanists were now anathematised, their lives made miserable by restrictions and their freedom of livelihood curtailed. The property of heretics might be confiscated and awarded to the *Christian* next of kin. Wills made by Montanists might be invalidated and legal impediments were raised against commercial activity. A Montanist slave who fled an owner (and found true religion) incurred no guilt (xvi.5.40). The various edicts, of 410, 415, 423 and 428 CE (*Cod. Theod.* xvi.5,48 and 57ff.; xvi.5,65 and xvi.10,24), 'sind ohne westliche Parallele', Aland observed.[78] Montanism was more readily quashed in the West than in the East, as the legislation against it shows.

Eusebius' *Vita Const.* gives us some idea of what followed when such laws were promulgated (iii.66). The secret assemblies of 'the heterodox' were stopped, he wrote, their leaders driven out. Some of their followers slipped sideways into catholic congregations, hiding their true allegiances. Perhaps some Montanists were among them – but later the *Cod. Just.* i.5,20,5 was trying to ensure there was no opportunity for slipping back. The burning of churches and relics came later, with greater insistence on abandonment of the Montanist religion, and then inevitably Pepuza itself was the subject of invasion.

Montanist Pepuza was invaded in the sixth century. It may have suffered invasion before, but we do not know of it. On this occasion the crusade of John of Ephesus took its toll.

Michael the Syrian's twelfth-century account indicates that there had been harassment of Montanists in Pepuza before the crusade of John, but not long before. Under Justin the local bishop had colluded with the Montanists for financial gain and on that occasion the threatened Montanist relics had been saved by being switched for other bones. But there was no such salvation the second time. To the great distress of the Montanists at Pepuza the shrine of the first Prophets was desecrated and the bones destroyed. Justinian's envoys laid waste. But Montanism was not something to die without drama. According to the 'secret history' of Procopius (official historian to Justinian but with his own axe to grind), far from repenting of their error, Montanists were known to escape the attentions of the Christian brethren by locking themselves in their churches and burning themselves to death.[79] Was this another mark of the fanatical, suicidal tendencies which so many scholars have insisted were always part of the Prophecy/Montanism? More probably it is evidence of the depth of a community's despair. Tabbernee may be right – we should think of Justinian as the last imperial opponent of Montanism, whose legislation ended it (some stragglers apart perhaps), and yet there is the odd account relating to the year 721–2, from the time of Leo III.[80]

In the year 721–2, so the *Chronicle* (*Chronographia*) of Theophanes recalls for the year 6214 (*PG* cviii, 809), the emperor Leo III, the Isaurian, ordered that Jews and Montanists should be forcibly baptised.[81] Theophanes claimed, however, that rather than submit to such treatment the Montanists had gathered together at a time predetermined and burned themselves to death (shades of Procopius and Justinian's time). The passage in the *Chronicle* is of interest because it refers to the Montanists consulting their oracles before the fateful decision.[82] The significance of this is unclear and perhaps the language is deliberately defamatory, but they may have been consulting authoritative Montanist literature or appealing (if such persons still functioned among them) to prophetic individuals. Leo, wrote E.J. Martin, had a 'policy of a simplification of religion.[83]

Montanists were proscribed because they were heretics (5.2). Lists of heresies down the centuries attested to rejection of Cataphrygians, Priscillianists, Pepuzites, Montanists and the like. Scharf has surmised, nevertheless, that Justinian had regarded them as a potential *political* threat. Why? Because their view of the Paraclete was implicitly messianic, concerning as it did the promise to bring 'signs of the last things', and because they claimed a communal independence which seemed threatening. It was, indeed, a reputation for messianism and dissidence combined, Scharf suggested, which caused Jewish groups centuries later (under Leo III) to be linked with Montanists in texts. Hence 'it may be no accident that the two occasions when Justinian ordered their destruction both coincide with his decrees, followed by a military expedition, against the Samaritans'.[84]

This account from the time of Leo III takes Montanism into the eighth century (as perhaps does the reference in John of Damascus). Tabbernee dismisses the account ('Opposition', p. 538), not least because he does not countenance that the Prophecy was 'Jewish Christian'. There are many problems with the texts Scharf was discussing, as he acknowledged, and in none of the other literature considered in this study had there been an explicitly political dimension to the rejection of the Prophecy/later Montanism (except in so far as Christianity, as state religion, was to be purified of heresy). It is hard to envisage that what must have been small, relatively isolated and much-legislated-against enclaves would be perceived as threatening hotbeds of messianic fervour and Scharf's case remains unproven, I think. The source, in any case, should probably be regarded with caution. So too should the even later account of the routing of heretics by bishop Nicephorus of Constantinople, d. *c.* 829 CE, in Ignatius of Constantinople, *Life* of Nicephorus, iv.26.

Mass suicides apart, have we any Montanist reply to all of this? The answer is no. 'Montanus is being done away with to this day', claimed the Orthodox in the *Dialexis*, while the teachings of Paul, fought over by both sides in the debate, grew in authority. There had triumphed, as the Church saw it, true apostolic tradition, right trinitarian doctrine and a oneness of Church and State which Montanism's apocalyptically minded forebears could surely not have envisaged. Montanus, Priscilla, Maximilla and their like were indeed 'done away with'.

5.3.3 An end

Yet as this chapter has shown there is no definable 'end' to the phenomenon of Montanism; no one event or piece of legislation which can be said to have snuffed it out. Death was a lingering affair. Indeed, some have said that the spirit of Montanism survived in many a troublesome sect and in many a dissident claiming inspiration, and throughout Christian history. One event must have had serious repercussions in Montanist circles, however. It must have borne on all those types of Montanism which still traced their roots to the religion of the Three and which still remembered Pepuza as a sacred spot. That was the destruction of their great shrine in that town, with the desecration of the resting-place of Montanus, Priscilla and Maximilla. We are reliant on the *Chronicle* of Michael the Syrian for the following account (which Tabbernee disbelieves).[85] This study will end with it.

In response to an edict of the emperor, Justinian I, John of Ephesus went to Pepuza and burned the Montanists' place of assembly. Sounds of Montanist lamentation filled the air as the great shrine was forced open, its lead seals and iron coverings removed. The Montanists, still with the End in mind, cried out: 'Now the world is overturned and will perish.'

Without sympathy Michael's account said that in the past the sick had come to that place to seek healing and relief from the effects of evil spirits. For him this was evidence of Montanist bribery, to ensure a good reputation. Now there would be no more of such things. Montanist books were searched out and burned. The building (evidently not destroyed) was taken from them and eventually it would become a catholic church. The great shrine forced open, the remains of the Three were exposed. We do not know when the Three had been laid to rest in that place but more than three centuries after their deaths the Prophets were now disturbed. Their remains were not incorrupt. 'The Spirit?' chided the catholics, 'a spirit has no flesh and bones!' Before burning the bones of Montanus, Priscilla and Maximilla the catholic invaders made much of that corrupt state. The Montanists made bitter mourning in Pepuza. The Three had lain long in their resting-place, with plates of gold upon their mouths.[86]

Notes

I BEGINNINGS

1 H. de Soyres, *Montanism and the Primitive Church*, Cambridge 1878 (condensed reprint 1965), 131f. On Soyres see N. Bonwetsch, *Die Geschichte des Montanismus*, Erlangen 1881, 13ff.; R. Knox, *Enthusiasm*, 40ff.

2 Named leading individuals of the first to third generations included Montanus, Priscilla and Maximilla, Theodotus, Miltiades (Eusebius *HE* v.16,3 and not to be confused with the anti-Montanist Miltiades of *HE* v.17,1 and v.28,4), Aeschines, Themiso, Alexander and Proclus. Asterius Urbanus (*HE* v.16,17) collected sayings of the Prophets.

3 John Wesley, in T. Jackson (ed.), *Sermons on Several Occasions ii*, London 1825, 209 on the Church: 'A few worshipped him in spirit and in truth . . . they were prevented from being so extensively useful . . . Nay, I have doubted whether that Arch-heretic Montanus, was not one of the holiest men in the second Century'.

4 J.S. Whale, 'Montanus', *Exp. T.* 45 (1934), 497.

5 Cf. Theophanes in the *Chronographia* year 6120/722 CE).

6 *Cod. Theod.* xvi.5,34-48, 57ff., 65 and x.24. Cf. Didymus *De Trin.* iii.41; Sozomen *HE* viii.18; Theodoret *Haer. fab. comp.* iii.2; *Cod. Just.* i.5, 18ff.

7 Klawiter, 'The New Prophecy', 64ff. Aland 'new' was an addition to discredit it. See too Tertullian *Adv. Marc.* iii.24; iv.22; *De jej.* i; *Adv. Prax.* xxx; *De pudic.* xxi; *De res. mort.* lxiii; *De monog.* xiv; *Clement Strom.* iv.13,93.1; Firmilian to Cyprian, Ep. lxxv.19.

8 Tertullian's evidence is treated with caution throughout.

9 'Robust idiosyncrasy'; P. Brown, *The Body and Society*, 76. The quotation is Soyres, *Montanism*, 4f. See Labriolle, *Les Sources*, ix-xiii on why Montanist sources did not survive.

10 W.C. van Unnik, 'Ἡ καινὴ διαθήκη', 227.

11 Frend, 'Montanism: Research and Problems', 532, 534; 'Montanismus' in G. Müller (ed.), *Theologische Realenzyklopädie*, Berlin–New York 1993. I saw this pre-translation and publication, thanks to Professor Frend.

12 On Bonwetsch, Baronius and others see Faggiotto, *Diaspora*, 7ff.

13 Bonwetsch, *Montanismus*, 1–15. On earlier writers see Labriolle, *La Crise*, and cf. W. Cunningham, *The Churches of Asia*, London 1880, 3–11 (on

Baur, Neander, Baronius etc.); Soyres, *Montanism*, 4–24; Tabbernee, 'Opposition', 3–9; G.B. Maino, 'Il Montanismo e le tendenze separatiste' (Hilgenfeld, Dobschütz, Bonwetsch *et al.*). Blanchetière discusses others.

14 Klawiter, 'The New Prophecy', 2–24.
15 Whale, 'Montanus', 497; E. Renan, *Marc-Aurèle et la fin du monde antique* (see vol. vii of *Histoire des origines du Christianisme*), Paris 1891, 207–48 esp. 209. Montanism was 'une exagération . . . Mais comme toutes les exagérations, il laissa des traces profondes' (242, cf. H.E.W. Turner, *Pattern*, 125ff.).
16 See H. Gregoire in *Byzantion* 6 (1931), 426ff; *Les Persécutions*, 107f.; cf. Labriolle, *La Crise*, 495ff.
17 F.C. Baur, 'Das Wesen des Montanismus', Tübingen Theologisches Jahrbuch 1851, 538–94; *Das Christentum in die christliche Kirche der 3 ersten Jahrhunderte* 1853, 213–41; J. Réville, 'Tertullien . . .' in *Revue des deux Mondes* 1 November 1864, 166–99; contrast E. Renan, 'Les crises du catholicisme naissant. . .' *Rev. des deux Mondes* 15 February 1881, 793ff.
18 See Klawiter, 'The New Prophecy', 37f.
19 Labriolle, *La Crise*, 134ff, 566ff. *et passim*. Cf. too R.A. Knox, *Enthusiasm*, 25–49; Campenhausen, *Ecclesiastical Authority*, 181f., 187.
20 W.M. Ramsay, *The Church in the Roman Empire*, 434ff.
21 W. Schepelern, *Montanismus*, 129, 159-62. See 89ff., 192 for earlier writers on its pagan associations.
22 G. Freeman, 'Pagan Cults', 297–316; B.W. Goree Jr, 'Cultural Bases', Cf. too A.T. Kraabel's Harvard Th.D. dissertation 'Judaism in Western Asia Minor under the Roman Empire', 1968, 149ff.
23 S.E. Johnson, 'Asia Minor and Early Christianity', 138.
24 Whale, 'Montanus', 497.
25 Harnack, *Encyclopaedia Britannica*[11], Cambridge 1911, 757f.
26 Cf. too his *Das Mönchthum, seine Ideal und seine Geschichte*, Giessen 1881. On Harnack see Turner, *Pattern*, 126f.
27 Ritschl, *Die Entstehung der altkatholischen Kirche*[2], Bonn 1857.
28 Klawiter, 'The New Prophecy', 36.
29 R. Knox, *Enthusiasm*, 25, who referred to its 'barbaric cradling'. 'Montanism for us means Tertullian . . . an individual genius' who 'lapsed into heresy' (45f.).
30 E. Gibbon, *History of the Decline and Fall of the Roman Empire* ii (Everyman Library), London 1910 (original 1787), 9f.
31 Frend, *Saints and Sinners in the Early Church*, London 1985, 57, 72.
32 N. Cohn, *The Pursuit of the Millennium*, Harmondsworth 1970.
33 E. Huber, *Women and the Authority of Inspiration: the Reexamination of Two Prophetic Movements*, New York and London, 1985.
34 Whale, ibid.. Cf. Renan, *Marc-Aurèle*, 209 (Irvingites, Latter Day Saints); Harnack 'Montanism', *Encyclopaedia Britannica*[11], Cambridge 1911, 757 (Irvingites, Quakers); Goree, 'Cultural Bases', 133 n. 171 (Seventh Day Adventists).

35 On Nayler's messianic entry into Bristol in October 1656: Trevett, 'The women around James Nayler . . .' *Religion* 20 (1990), 249–73.

36 See e.g. R.M. Grant, 'Early Christian Geography', *Vig. Christ.* 46 (1992), 105–11; W.M. Ramsay, *The Historical Geography of Asia Minor*, London 1890; I.W. Macpherson, 'New Evidence for the Historical Geography of Galatia', Ph.D. thesis, Cambridge 1957. On Acts 16:6 see C.J. Hemer in *JTS* 27 (1976), 122ff.; *JTS* 28 (1977), 99ff; Labriolle, *La Crise*, 3ff.; K. Belke, *Phrygien und Pisidien*, Tabula Imperii Byzantini vii, Österreichische Akademie der Wissenschaften, Vienna, 1990 (inscriptions, maps, bibliographical indexes).

37 W.M. Ramsay, *The Church in the Roman Empire*, chs. 1 and 6; *Cities and Bishoprics of Phrygia*, Oxford 1895, 1897. For Ramsay's numerous publications on the region see W.H. Buckler and W.M. Calder (eds.), *Anatolian Studies*. Good sources are Magie, *Roman Rule* and A.H.M. Jones, *Cities*; G.E. Bean, *Turkey Beyond the Meander*, London 1980, 153f.; and cf. discussions of provinces in *CAH* and E. Dabrowa, *L'Asie Mineure sous les Flaviens* (Polska Akademia Nauk – Prace Kom. Fil. Klas. 18), Warsaw–Gdansk 1980. On the geography of Christianisation see Harnack, *The Mission and Expansion of Christianity in the First Three Centuries*[2], ii, London 1908, 182–260; H. Kraft, 'Gemeindeverbänden', 224–34; S. Mitchell, *Anatolia* (2 vols. – i *The Celts* and ii *The Rise of the Church*).

38 W.H.C. Frend, 'Early Christianity and Society', 58. On clashes of missionary 'schools' see Ramsay in *'The Expositor'* 3rd series, viii, 1888, 241–67, 401–27; and W.M. Calder, 'Philadelphia and Montanism', 320f. See too J.G.C. Anderson, 'Paganism and Christianity', 193–201; Calder in *'Anatolian Studies'*; Labriolle, *'La Crise'*, 7ff.; Goree, 'Cultural Bases', 63ff.

39 Eusebius *HE* v.18,2 (Apollonius); cf. Cyril of Jerusalem Cat. xvi.8. κώμη: *HE* v.16,7 (Anonymous); Theodoret *Haer. fab. comp.* iii.2.

40 Cf. Josephus *Ant.* xii.3; Acts 16:2; Ramsay, 'The Jews in the Graeco-Asiatic cities', *The Expositor* 6th series, v, 1902, 19–32; *Cities and Bishoprics*, i/2, 667ff.; Frend, *Rise*, 180ff. Major sources include J. Juster, *Les Juifs dans l'Empire Romain*, 2 vols., Paris 1914; A.T. Kraabel, 'Judaism in Western Asia Minor under the Roman Empire'; P.R. Trebilco, *Jewish Communities in Asia Minor*, Cambridge 1991, and the literature there. Christians had continued contacts with things Jewish: cf. Rev. 2:9; 3:9; Ignatius *Magn.* and *Phld.*; *M. Pol.* viii.1; xii.2; xiii.1; xvii.2f.; Apolinarius *Against the Jews* (Eusebius *HE* iv.27,1); Melito's Easter homily and Council of Laodicea Canons 16, 29, 37 and 38.

41 Klawiter, 'The New Prophecy', 74ff. See F.R. Trombley on Christianity and the tenacity of paganism, in *HTR* 78 (1985), 327–52, and *Hellenic Religion*, ii, 75. The quotations are from these sources.

42 W.M. Calder, 'Some Monuments', 352f.; A. Petrie, 'Epitaphs in Phrygian Greek', *Studies in the History and Art of the Eastern Roman Provinces*, Aberdeen University Studies xx, 1906, 119–34; K. Holl, 'Das Fortleben',

240–54; contrast Labriolle, *La Crise*, 7. Evidence for Phrygian language disappears post fourth century: S. Vryonis, *The Decline of Medieval Hellenism in Asia Minor*, Berkeley–Los Angeles 1971, 45ff.

43 Klawiter, 'The New Prophecy', 70ff.

44 W.M. Calder, 'The New Jerusalem', 421–5. Cf. Ramsay on Radet in *Cities and Bishoprics* ii, 573 and 'Pepuza' in *Dictionary of Greek and Roman Geography*[2], London 1872 (ruins near Besh-Shehr and Kalinkefi in the south of Uşak).

45 Tabbernee ('Revelation 21') cites Gibson's unpublished study 'Pepuza'. The Dazkiri plain, gateway for central Anatolia from Hierapolis / Laodicea, is too far east. Critics of the Three were probably nearby.

46 Ramsay, 'Phrygian Orthodox', 27–32. See also *Cities and Bishoprics* i, 243f.; ii, 573, 787 on a site beside Kara-Halilli and Deli Heuderli; Klawiter, 'The New Prophecy', 80ff.

47 Strobel, *Das heilige Land*, 1–34; Calder, 'The New Jerusalem', 422ff.

48 The other division was Salutaris, which included Hierapolis and Synnada. C. Roueché, in *JRS* 17 (1981), 103–20, on later reforms.

49 A.H.M. Jones, *Cities*, 73: Pepuza was the town Anastasius (d. 518) destroyed and replaced by Anastasiopolis. Ramsay followed Radet: the later Justinianopolis corresponded to the site of Hierocles' Pepuza; *Cities and Bishoprics* ii, 573f.; 'Phrygian Orthodox', 15.

50 Cf. E. Renan, *Marc-Aurèle*, 210 n. 4: 'Les petites localités n'étaient pas loin d'Ouschak'. Ramsay, 'Trois villes phrygiennes . . .', *Bulletin de Correspondence Hellénique*, vi, 503f. and partial change of mind in 'Phrygian Orthodox'. On Ramsay see Selwyn, *Prophets*, 32ff.

51 Kraft, 'Altkirchliche Prophetie', 260f. Cf. Tabbernee, 'Revelation 21', 53. In Rev. 21:10 (cf. 17:3f.) the Seer went 'in the spirit' to a high mountain to see the New Jerusalem. We need not assume its descent on one.

52 Ramsay, *Cities and Bishoprics* ii, 573; cf. *The Expositor* 6th series, viii, 1903, 58. I have not seen Markschies in *JAC* 37 (1994), 7–28.

53 Ramsay, *Cities and Bishoprics* ii, 573f. and n. 6. See too i, 199f.; ii, 346. Elsa Gibson in *Christians* is dismissive (125).

54 Calder, 'Philadelphia and Montanism', map, 311, 324. On this region see also L. Robert on Acmoneia in *Hellenica* 10 (1955), 249–53 and A.A.R. Sheppard in *Anatolian Studies* 29 (1979), 160–80.

55 C.H.E. Haspels, *The Highlands of Phrygia*, Princeton 1971.

56 Labriolle, 'Ardabau', *Dictionnaire d'Histoire et de Geographie Ecclésiastique* iii, Paris 1924, 1596.

57 Knox, *Enthusiasm*, 27f.

58 Strobel, *Das heilige Land*, 38ff.

59 Strobel, *ibid*. Against Ramsay on Dionysopolis = Ortaköy see 41, 45 and also 84f. While Atyochorion/Ortaköy are similar in sound (38, 45), such combinations 'sind doch wohl voller Unsicherheiten. . .'

60 T. Drew-Bear, 'Local cults in Graeco-Roman Phrygia', *Greek, Roman,*

Byzantine Studies 17 (1976), 261.

61 Strobel, *Das heilige Land*, 41.

62 The variant *Ardaban* appears in fifth-century Theodoret of Cyrrhus (Labriolle, *Les Sources*, 211 n. 172). Cf. F. Justi, *Iranisches Namenbuch*, Marburg 1895 (Hildesheim 1963), 21, 31ff. (Artabanos, Artabourios etc.); *CIG* iii, 3960b and *MAMA* vi, 176. On the text of 4 Ezra see M.E. Stone, *4 Ezra* (Hermeneia Commentary Series), London 1981, 304f.

63 On geography and history of Asia Minor: C.J. Hemer, *The Letters to the Seven Churches of Asia in their Local Setting* (JSNTSS 11), Sheffield 1986, 286–90; Trombley, *Hellenic Religion* ii, 74ff. Cf. W.M. Calder and G.E. Bean, *A Classical Map of Asia Minor*, Suppl. *Anatolian Studies* 7, 1957.

64 E. Preuschen, 'Ardaf IV Esra 9,26', 265. On Ardab as Zion cf. too R.M. Grant, *Augustus to Constantine*, New York and London 1970, 159.

65 On Philadelphia, 'new name', 'going out' etc. see Hemer, *The Letters*, 153–77 and cf. too R.H. Gundry, 'People as Place'; P. Carrington, *The Early Christian Church* ii, London and Cambridge 1957, 143ff.; C. Deutsch, 'Transformation of Symbols', 106–26.

66 Eusebius *HE* ii.39,11f. See too B.E. Daley, *Hope*, 17f.

67 Frend, 'Early Christianity and Society', 61.

68 Chapters 1f. = 5 Ezra, 15 = 6 Ezra, or alternatively they are 2 Esdras and 5 Esdras in later Latin MSS. 4 Ezra was probably in Aramaic or Hebrew. There were Greek and later Latin, Armenian, Syriac and Ethiopic versions. See A.F.J. Klijn, *Der lateinische Text der Apokalypse des Esra* (TU 131), Berlin 1983; B.M. Metzger, 'The Fourth Book of Ezra', in J.H. Charlesworth (ed.), *The Old Testament Pseudepigrapha*, London 1983, 517ff.; P.R. Davies, 'Daniel in the Lion's Den', in L. Alexander (ed.) *Images of Empire* (JSOTSS 122) Sheffield 1991, 160–78; A. Thompson, *Responsibility for Evil in the Theodicy of IV Ezra*, Missoula MT, 1977 (83ff. on the work's name); T.W. Willett, *Eschatology in the Theodicies of 2 Baruch and 4 Ezra*, Sheffield 1989; G.W.E. Nickelsburg, *Jewish Literature Between the Bible and the Mishnah*, London 1981, 287–94. For further literature see Stone, *4 Ezra* and 'On reading an Apocalypse' in J.J. Collins, J.H. Charlesworth (eds.), *Mysteries and Revelations* (JSPSS 9), Sheffield 1991, 65–78. On 5 and 6 Ezra see H. Duensing in E. Hennecke and W. Schneemelcher (eds.), *NT Apocrypha* ii, 689ff.; R.A. Kraft, in *HTR* 79 (1986), 159–69 and in *Aufstieg und Niedergang der römischen Welt* II.19.i, Berlin 1969, 119–36.

69 C. Hill, *Regnum Coelorum*, 43f. notes differences too.

70 The Revelation and 4 Ezra are probably products of similar circumstances. Cf. Rev. 6:6–8 and 4 Ezra 9:22. See too R. Bauckham, in L. Alexander (ed.), *Images of Empire*, 47–90 (cf. too 2 Baruch 36:8; 39:5); K. Wengst, *Pax Romana and the Peace of Jesus Christ*, London 1987, 118f. and contrast Stone, *4 Ezra*, 300.

71 A.L. Thompson, Responsibility, 235ff.; Hill, *Regnum Caelorum*, 43f.

72 Epiphanius *Pan.* xlix.1. See 4.4.3–4.

73 See 3.3.
74 See 1.3.5–1.3.7.
75 Armenian, Latin and Syriac read 'the bride shall appear, even the city appearing'. See Stone, *4 Ezra*, 190–223, especially 202ff. 4 Ezra speaks of water and fire on either side of the approach; cf. the geography of revelation in Hermas *Vis.* i.1,3.
76 Cf. Thompson, *Responsibility*, 223–8 on Zion, mother in 10:7; Stone, *4 Ezra*, 326.
77 The field and flowers, fasting and eating only plants are recurring motifs in 4 Ezra. See Stone, *4 Ezra*, 28, 35, 92ff.; 95, 302f.
78 Latin, Armenian have Ardab; Ardap in the Syriac with Latin variants (including Ardas, Ardad, Araat, Adar). See Klawiter ('The New Prophecy', 79), following Preuschen: 'a veiled reference to the original centre of Montanism'. Kraft posits the ancient *Araba* (wilderness/wasteland) ideal, both (i) in 4 Ezra ('the uninhabited desert' parallels 'Ezra's field where there is no human building': 9:24; 9:29; Stone, *4 Ezra*, 309) and (ii) among the Prophets ('Die altkirchliche Prophetie', 260f.). Cf. Frend, *Rise*, 254 and G. Schöllgen, "Tempus in collecto est", 76f.
79 On Montanists and apocalyptic sources see index of subjects.
80 Strobel, *Das heilige Land*, 46 n. 137.
81 Knox, *Enthusiasm*, 28f.
82 Labriolle, *La Crise*, 569ff.; Barnes, 'Chronology', 403–8; Williams, 'Origins'. Compare and contrast T. Zahn, *Forschungen zur Geschichte des neutestamentlichen Kanons* i Erlangen and Leipzig 1893, 3–57; Bonwetsch, *Montanismus*, 141ff.
83 Frend, 'Chronology'; 'Montanism: Research and Problems'; *Rise*, 195, 253, 265 n. 128. Most scholars seem to me to favour the Eusebian date but Barnes ('Chronology', 404) thinks harmonisation is most common.
84 See Barnes, 'Legislation Against the Christians', JRS 58 (1968), 41 n. 108; *Harvard Studies* 74 (1970), 314; 'Chronology', 403f. On conflicting dates for the Gallic martyrdoms see Grant, 'Martyrs of Gaul', 129–35.
85 Freeman-Grenville, 'Date', 8f. rejects Labriolle's solution, for it does not accord with Eusebian language in other instances.
86 *HE* iv.27 suggests Apolinarius wrote within the Prophets' lifetimes. He and Miltiades were probably the first to oppose them in writing.
87 Labriolle, *La Crise*, 570. His interpretation of the passage is suspect, as Freeman-Grenville illustrates: 'Date', 8f.
88 See Harnack; *Dic Zeit des Ignatius und die Chronologie der Antiochenischen Bischöfe* i, Leipzig 1878, 365; Ramsay, *Cities and Bishoprics*, 710.
89 Freeman-Grenville, 'Date'; Lawlor, 'Montanism', in Hastings (ed.), *Encyclopaedia of Religion and Ethics* viii, Edinburgh 1915, 828; R.B. Eno, 'Montanism', in J.A. Komonchak et al. (eds.), *The New Dictionary of Theology*, Dublin 1987, 676; K. Aland, 'Montanism' in M. Eliade (ed.), *The Encyclopaedia of Religion*, New York and London 1987, 81.

90 MSS of *Pan.* xlviii.2 concur. Suggested emendations align the date either with that in *Pan.* xlviii.1 or else with the date of Maximilla's death (implied in *Pan.* xlvii.2). The latter is done by reading 190 instead of 290 years (to the year 185, so Völter). For the former, Scaliger's emendation (so too Zahn) took the 290 years as an error for 219, to give 156–7 CE See Labriolle, *La Crise*, 574; Freeman-Grenville, 'Date', 10f.

91 The following proposed *c.* 140–1 CE as the date for Montanus: Tillemont (1694), Walch (1862) and Hefele (*A History of the Councils of the Church* i, Edinburgh 1871, 29). Selwyn, Soyres and Baratier also opted for early dates. Some cited the *Didachē* or *The Shepherd* as Montanist or anti-Montanist works.

92 See K. Holl, *Epiphanius Werke* ii, Leipzig 1922, 307 (conjecturally adding other words to the text); Calder, 'Philadelphia and Montanism', 38, 46; and cf. Blanchetière (citing Prigent), 'Le Montanisme originel', 130 n. 44; Freeman-Grenville, 'Date', 11f. for other proposed emendations. Evidence based on conjectural emendation is problematic.

93 Freeman-Grenville, 'Date', 13. On Abercius Marcellus see D. Bundy, '*The Life of Abercius*: its significance for Early Syriac Christianity', *The Second Century* 7 (1989–90), 163–76. Ramsay discovered the burial inscription in 1883: 'Early Christian Movements in Phrygia', *The Expositor* 3rd series ix, 253–66; contrast E. Dinkler, 'Älteste christliche Denkmäler', *Signum Crucis* (Ges. Auf.) 1967, 159f. It was plagiarised in the inscription of Alexander, *c.* 215 CE. See Aland, 'Bemerkungen', 110; Kühnert, 'Anonymus', identifying the Anonymous with Polycrates.

94 On the peace being under Commodus see Labriolle, *La Crise*, 580f.; Harnack, *Chronologie i.* 365; Ramsay, *Cities and Bishoprics*, 710.

95 With no evidence we may not assume that she was president of the elect for a long period. Contrast Harnack, *Chronologie* i 365.

96 On 172–80 CE as too short a time: Neander, Bonwetsch and Hilgenfeld (*Die Ketzergeschichte des Urchristentums* Leipzig 1884, 561–76), cf. Labriolle, *La Crise*, 587; Freeman-Grenville; Fischer; Maino; Goree, 'Cultural Bases', 88. Frend vacillates between 168–9 and 172: see *Rise*, 253, 265 n. 128; 'Chronology', 505f., 'Montanism: Research and Problems', 535.

97 Barnes, 'Chronology', 406–9, with a conjectural list of proconsulates. The years 168–9 and 171–2 remain unfilled (with a number of other uncertainties within it) and dates in the 170s CE are available. Contrast A. Degrassi, *Fasti Consolari del Impero Romano*, Rome 1952, 44. On other proconsulates in our sources see Freeman-Grenville, 'Date', 12 n.8.

98 Harnack, *Chronologie* i, 370ff.: Maximilla died in 179, the Anonymous wrote in 193. *Mission and Expansion*[2] ii, 75 dated the start in the 160s.

99 Wright assumes this in 'Montanists Condemned', 15. Quasten, *Patrology ii, Utrect–Antwerp* 1950, 318, and Barnes 'Chronology', 406, accept the date 213.

100 Fischer, 'Synoden' 247 (cf. also 249). Salmon in *DCB* iii, 937.

Bonwetsch, Zahn, Harnack, Daniélou and Knox also offer harmonisations.

101 Eusebius' *Chronicon* contradicts *HE* and Irenaeus by dating Tatian's fall in 173. The *Acts of Martyrdom* of Justin have him die between 162 and 167, in the prefecture of Rusticus. The *Chronicon Paschale* offers the year 165.

102 See Salmon in *DCB* iii, 936.

103 Strobel, *Das heilige Land*, 21ff.; Labriolle, *Les Sources*, 238; S. Gero, 'Montanus and Montanism', 520f. See also 5.3. Chabot thinks Michael the Syrian had Quadratus in mind. I thank Dr John Watt for his examination of Syriac Thesaurus listings. Compare and contrast Fischer, 'Synoden', 246; Kraft, 'Gemeindeverbänden', 235; Tabbernee, 'Trophies'; and on p. Oxyrhynchus I.5 see Harnack, 'Über zwei von Grenfell und Hunt entdeckte und publicirte altchristliche Fragmente', *SBA* 17 (1898), 516ff.; Paulsen, 'Papyrus Oxyrhynchus I.5', 443–53.

104 If the Anonymous was not writing until the 190s, then the deaths of Montanus and Theodotus could refer to the 180s only if (a) we assume Hippolytus was wrong about Montanus dying first or (b) if Maximilla's statement about the prophetic succession need not indicate that she was the only surviving Prophet. Oddly no sect was named after Maximilla.

105 Contrast A. Birley, *Marcus Aurelius*, London 1966, 328, and with doubts Barnes, 'Chronology', 407f.)

106 See n. 86 above.

107 Trevett, 'Apocalypse', 313–38. See also 'Anti-Episcopal Activity' (1983); 'The Other Letters' (1989) and *Ignatius* (1992), ch.5. On Ignatius surrendering to the authorities see Trevett, 'Ignatius "To the Romans" and 1 Clement liv–lvi', *Vig. Christ.* 43 (1989), 35–2.

108 A. d'Alès, 'La doctrine de l'Esprit en Saint Irenée', *RScR* 14 (1924), 497–538; H.J. Jaschke, *Der heilige Geist im Bekenntnis der Kirche. Eine Studie zur Pneumatologie des Irenäus . . .*, Münster 1976; A. Méhat, 'Saint Irenée et les charismes', in E. Livingstone (ed.), *Studia Patristica* vii/2, Oxford 1982, 719–24; Robeck, 'Irenaeus and "Prophetic Gifts"', in P. Elbert (ed.), Essays on Apostolic Themes: Studies in Honor of Howard M. Erven, Peabody, MA, 1985, 104–14; J. Reiling, *Hermas and Christian Prophecy: A Study of the Eleventh Mandate*, Leiden 1973; Aune, *Prophecy* 290ff. cf. Justin *Dial.* lxxxii.

109 Campenhausen, *Ecclesiastical Authority*, ch. 8; Ash, 'Ecstatic prophecy'.

110 See 3.2 and also 4.1.

111 Fischer, 'Synoden', 249, dates catholics' actions (*HE* v.16,10) pre-175 CE, questioning the word 'synod' and suggesting believers ('Christians' in congregations) rather than bishops came together to test and drive out the Prophecy (cf. 1 Cor. 12:10).

112 On Maximilla's 'wolf' saying see 4.3.4 .

113 Aland, 'Kleinasiatische Theologie', 109–16 see also Kraft, 'Altkirchliche Prophetie'.

114 J.M. Ford, 'Proto Montanism', 338.
115 J.M. Ford, 'Was Montanism a Jewish-Christian Heresy?', 145.
116 I did not consider this issue in 'Apocalypse, Ignatius, Montanism'.
117 See H. Sedgewick, *Marcus Aurelius*, New Haven 1921, 166; W.H. McNeill, *Plagues and Peoples*, Harmondsworth 1979, 113ff.; J.F. Gilliam, 'The Plague under Marcus Aurelius', *Amer. J. of Philology* 82 (1961), 225–51; J. Walsh, 'Refutation of the Charges . . . against Galen', *Annals of Medical History* 3 (1931), 195–208. Cf. too E. Renan, *Marc-Aurèle*, 162–248, on 165–72 CE. Dionysius bar Salibi (using Hippolytus) wrote that Gaius (anti-Montanist) contested the Revelation's teaching on *plagues*.
118 Frend, *Martyrdom* 239f., 261 n. 17, on the possibly spurious rescript of the emperor (Antoninus Pius or Marcus) mentioning 'recent earth-quakes'; Laodicea, Hierapolis and Dionysopolis suffered in 152 CE. Cf. CIG 3165; M. Rostovtzeff, *Social and Economic History of the Roman Empire* i, Oxford 1926, 348ff., 373; A.E.R. Boak, *Manpower Shortage and the Fall of the Roman Empire in the West*, Ann Arbor 1955, 15–21.
119 Justin and Athenagoras wrote apologetic works under Marcus. See Schoedel in *HTR* 82 (1989), 55–78; Grant, *Greek Apologists of the Second Century*, London 1988, chs. 9–12. On Melito's 'new decrees': Gregoire and Orgels, *Persécutions*, 174f.; G.E.M. de St Croix, 'Why were the Early Christians Persecuted?', *Past and Present* 26 (1963), 15ff. also *JTS* 18 (1967), 219; M. Sordi, 'I nuovi decreti di Marco Aurelio contro i Cristiani', *Studi Romani* 9 (1961), 365 contrast Barnes in *JRS* 58 (1968), 34f., 37f. Q. Lollius Urbicus, *praefectus urbi* who ordered executions according to Justin (Eusebius *HE* iv. 17,8f.; *Apol.* ii.2), was dead by the year 160. The martyrdoms must have preceded Marcus' time. See Barnes, *Eusebius and Constantine*, Cambridge MA, and London 1981, 141, 354 n. 137.
120 Fischer ('Synoden', 263) saw the Prophecy as hostile to the world and the State. Cf. J. Speigl, *Der römische Staat und die Christen*, Amsterdam 1970, 170f., 201. Unlike Sordi I do not see Montanism as an important factor in *arousing* persecution through public fears about 'state security' (*The Christians*, 72f.; 176f. 195). I think neither Celsus nor Marcus Aurelius in the *Meditations* attributed to Christians 'characteristics which were exclusively Montanist'.
121 Barnes, *Eusebius*, 131. The impression is given that it was 'Antoninus Verus' (Lucius Verus) who allowed the Gallic martyrdoms. See Barnes, *Eusebius*, 137f. for discussion.
122 On Eusebius' method, synchronisation and errors see Barnes, *Eusebius*, 141f.
123 Barnes, *JTS* 18 (1967), 433f., and 19 (1968), 529ff. M. Sordi, 'Nuovi decreti', 365ff. notes grouping of martyrdoms in the years 163–7 and 176–8.
124 W.H. Buckler, 'Labour disputes in the Province of Asia', *Anatolian*

Studies, 27–50 (bakers' strike and labour troubles in Pergamum) and 30–3. Cf. Rostovtzeff, *Social and Economic History*, 621 n. 45.

125 Frend, *Rise*, 175; cf. *Martyrdom*, 187, 284f.

126 Fox, *Pagans and Christians*, 65: 'Should the Antonine "age of anxiety" be rephrased as an "age of anger"', rooted in the social order and its division between master and slave?' For Maino, 'Il Montanismo' (120), Montanism was heresy 'eminentemente politica', arising in a setting of Asian anti-Roman feeling, persecution, war and natural disaster.

2. THE NEW PROPHECY TO HIPPOLYTUS AND TERTULLIAN

1 Labriolle, Les Sources, nos. 49–50, 52–7, pp. 50ff.; R. Heine, *Oracles*, 95ff. On Alexandrian Cataphrygianism see Faggiotto, *Diaspora*, 21–38.

2 See 3.7.2–3.7.4. The year 155–6 was for a long time the most favoured by scholars (see Barnes in *JTS* 18 and 19 [1967 and 1968] and B. Dehandschutter in his 1979 University of Leuven PhD dissertation). On anti-Montanist redaction of *M. Pol.* cf. Campenhausen, *Bearbeitungen und Interpolationen des Polykarpmartyriums*, Heidelberg 1957, 5–48; H. Conzelmann, *Bemerkungen zum Martyrium Polykarps*, Göttingen 1978.

3 A date *c*. 167–8 CE now seems more widely favoured. See too H. Kraft, 'Die Lyoner Märtyrer', 253ff.; H. Gregoire, 'La véritable date du Martyre de S. Polycarpe (23 février 177) et le "Corpus Polycarpianum"', *An. Boll.* 69 (1951), 1–38 (a much-criticised conclusion); Frend, 'Chronology'; L.W. Barnard, 'In defence of Pseudo-Pionius' Account of Polycarp's Martyrdom', *Studies in Church History and Patristics*, Thessaloniki 1978, 192–204; Dehandschutter, *ANRW* II.27.1.

4 Christian Smyrna would soon have known about the Prophecy. See Labriolle, *Les Sources*, xxxiff; Buschmann, 1995.

5 On the Anonymous: Labriolle, *Les Sources* xx–xxix; Faggiotto, *L'Eresia*, 20–41; Tabbernee, 'Opposition', 12ff. Like Lightfoot, Selwyn, Faggiotto, Aland and H. Grotz (*Die Hauptkirche des Ostens*, Rome 1964, 134) identified him with Apolinarius. He was Polycrates of Ephesus according to W. Kühnert and Campenhausen (*Formation*, 23) and, for a few, Asterius Urbanus. On Apollonius see Labriolle, *Les Sources*, xxviiiff. and on Alcibiades/Miltiades, *La Crise*, 31ff.; Faggiotto, *L'Eresia*, 27–35.

6 R.A. Lipsius, *Zur Quellenkritik des Epiphanius*, Vienna 1865 (delineating *Pan.* xlviii.2–13 as the special sources); H.G. Voigt, *Eine verschollene Urkunde des antimontanistischen Kampfes. Die Berichte des Epiphanius über die Kataphryger und Quintillianer*, Leipzig 1891 (*Pan.* xlviii. 1–13, the conclusion which most critics follow).

7 Heine, 'The Role of the Gospel of John', thinks it originated in Phrygia. There is a likeness between the Montanist material and exegesis in Epiphanius' source and that employed by Tertullian in *De anima, Adv. Marc.* and elsewhere. See Voigt in *Verschollene Urkunde*, 35ff.; 95, 213f., 225 *et passim*; Labriolle, *Les Sources*, liii–lxiv; Groh, 'Utterance', 80ff.

Tertullian was not the originator of the source (*pace* Voigt), for *De ecstasi* did not have a Greek original (Jerome *De vir. ill.* xl see Barnes, *Tertullian*, 253f).

8 Labriolle, *La Crise*, 162f. and, on Themiso, 28, 580ff.

9 Labriolle, *La Crise*, 25ff.

10 W. Bauer, *Orthodoxy* 132ff. A. Ehrhardt in *HTR* 55 (1962),106ff., shared the disgust.

11 The *Didachē* has occasionally been labelled Montanist. Hilgenfeld and Streeter wondered about Montanist influence and see especially F.E. Vokes, *The Riddle of the Didachē*, London 1938, 142ff. 209.

12 Turner, *Pattern*, 179. See Labriolle, *La Crise*, 27ff., rightly dismissing T. Barns' thesis about 2 Peter: 'The Catholic Epistles of Themison', *The Expositor* 6th series viii, 1903.

13 Tabbernee, 'Regional Bishops', 250; not Frend, 'Town and Countryside in Early Christianity', *Studies in Church History* 16 (1979), 36.

14 Labriolle, *La Crise* 145ff.

15 Cf. Harnack, *Die Zeit des Ignatius und die Chronologie der Antiochenischen Bischöfe* i, Leipzig 1878, 211ff.; Labriolle, *La Crise*, 152–5.

16 So too H. Achelis, *Das Christentum in den ersten drei Jahrhunderten* ii, Leipzig 1912, 45; Frend, 'Montanism: A Movement', 27. Contrast Labriolle, *La Crise*, 153 n. 5; Fischer, 'Synoden', 254 (and see 256f.).

17 See Labriolle, *Les Sources*, cxxxv and *La Crise*, 30 n. 5. C.J. Hefele, *A History of the Councils of the Church* i, Edinburgh 1871, cites these but contrast Labriolle, Fischer, 'Synoden', 250–4 and the literature there. The *Libellus* does not mention Priscilla.

18 We cannot say the Prophecy had influenced such actions (see 3.3.4) but they are evidence of an atmosphere conducive to its spread.

19 Faggiotto distinguished between an original, orthodox but apocalyptic movement and the later developments (*L'Eresia*, 133ff.; *Diaspora*), questioning the Asian provenance of Apollonius' work. See *L'Eresia*, 7 cf. 81ff., esp. 90. Polycrates' letters show how widespread was asceticism. On letter-writing between Christians see H. Koester in *HTR* 84 (1991), 353–72. It was probably important in action against the Prophecy.

20 K. Aland, 'Montanism/Montanus', in M. Eliade (ed.), *The Encyclopaedia of Religion*, New York–London 1987, 81.

21 Yes, but also Labriolle (*La Crise*, 146): *clergy* resistance was not unified and there was 'complicity and connivance' in some parts of Asia.

22 *The Expositor* 3rd series, ix, 146.

23 Exp. T 45 (1934), 499.

24 Trevett, *Ignatius*, 131-8.

25 On the Prophecy in Rome see Klawiter, 'The New Prophecy', 191–243; Heine, *Oracles* 53–9, 89ff.; J.P. Meier and R.E. Brown, *Antioch and Rome*, London 1982; J.S. Jeffers, *Conflict at Rome: Social Order and Hierarchy in Early Christianity*, Minneapolis 1991 (contrasting the Clementine and Hermas wings of the Church); the works of G. La Piana; A. Ferrua; A.

Faggiotto, *Diaspora*, 39–51; C. Cecchelli, *Monumenti eretici*, 208ff.

26 Cf. W. Bauer, *Orthodoxy*, 207. Dionysius bar Salibi credits Hippolytus with having written *Capitula adv. Caium* against Gaius. Epiphanius (*Pan.* li) associates Gaius with the Alogi (see 3.9). It is not certain that Gaius *was* of the Alogi though he probably did share the reservations of some in Rome about Johannine writings (after all, Gnostics, Montanists, Quartodecimans and others appealed to them). See J. Rendel Harris, 'Presbyter Gaius and the Fourth Gospel' in *Hermas in Arcadia and Other Essays*, Cambridge 1896, 43–59; J. Gwynn, 'Hippolytus and his "Heads against Caius"', *Hermathena* 6 (1888), 397–418; E. Prinzivalli, 'Gaio e gli Alogi', *SSR* 5 (1981), 53–68; Fragments of the *Capitula adv. Caium* in I. Sedlacek, *Dionysius bar Salibi. In Apocalypsim, Actus et Epistulas* (CSCO 53.60; S.18–20), Paris 1909–10. I have not seen the Yale Ph.D. dissertation by J.D. Smith, 'Gaius and the Controversy over the Johannine Literature', 1979. Cf. Tabbernee, 'Trophies'.

27 H. Chadwick, *The Circle and the Ellipse: Rival Concepts of Authority in the Early Church*, Oxford 1959, 11. See too Maino, 'Il Montanismo', 120ff.

28 So too Klawiter, 'The New Prophecy', 196ff. See Labriolle, *La Crise*, 257–75 on interpreting *Adv. Prax.* i. On Montanism and the Quartodeciman controversy see Piana, 'The Roman Church', 215–22. The Roman bishops are dated as follows: Anicetus 155–66 CE; Soter 166–74; Eleutherus 174–89; Victor 189–99; Zephyrinus 199–217.

29 'Praxeas' (i.5) appears otherwise only in Pseudo- Tertullian (*Adv. omn. haer.* viii.4); perhaps a pseudonym – 'busybody' (Barnes, *Tertullian*, 78, or perhaps 'mischief-maker'). Praxeas has been identified with Callistus and Epigonus the Noetian, among others (Hippolytus *Refut. omn. haer.* ix.7,1; x.27,1–3). See Barnes, *Tertullian*, 78f., 229; Labriolle in *BALAC* i (1911) 228ff.; R. Cantalamessa, 'Prassea e l'eresia monarchiana', *Scuola Catholica* 90 (1962), 28–50. Usually dated *c.* 213 CE, for some *Adv. Prax.* may be post-Callistus.

30 See J. Pelikan, 'Montanism and its Trinitarian Significance'.

31 For Eleutherus as the bishop see Harnack, *Chronologie* i, 375f., Schwegler, Ritschl, Réville and Bonwetsch. It seemed to such writers improbable that Victor would have acknowledged the Prophecy when the Anonymous, Abercius Marcellus, Apolinarius etc. had been against it. Cf. too H. Kraft, 'Die Lyoner Märtyrer', 257ff. Piana, Hilgenfeld, Zahn, Voigt, Monceaux, Preuschen, Faggiotto and Tabbernee think Victor was the bishop concerned. Heine and Labriolle opt for Zephyrinus.

32 Eusebius HE v.1,9f.; v.1, 49; v.3,2f. Since Eusebius did not quote all the letter, Soyres concluded that a Montanist document was involved (contrast Frend, *Martyrdom*, 16f. and Salmon in *DCB*). Contrast Monceaux (*Histoire Littéraire*, 404).

33 Bishop Anicetus was a Syrian and distributed Eucharist to those whose celebration differed. Under Victor the Roman Quartodecimans under Blastus (Eusebius *HE* v.15; v.20,1) were forced into schism.

34 G. Salmon, 'Montanus', *DCB* iii, 937f. Salmon argues against any followers of the Prophecy *in Rome* before Zephyrinus' time (940) and that he was the initially sympathetic bishop. Compare and contrast Labriolle, *Les Sources*, 43f.; Klawiter, 'The New Prophecy', 198 and Faggiotto, *Diaspora*, 39f.

35 On Hippolytus see the sometimes contentious work of P. Nautin, *Hippolyte et Josipe: Contribution a l'histoire de la litterature chrétienne du troisieme siècle*, Paris 1947; *Le dossier d'Hippolyte et de Meliton*, Paris 1953; G. Dix, *The Treatise on the Apostolic Tradition of St Hippolytus of Rome* rev. edn, London 1991. See too 3.3 n. 86 and Cerrato, 'Hippolytus'.

36 Piana, 'The Roman Church', 207 and 'Foreign groups in Rome. . .', *HTR* 20 (1927), 183–403.

37 G. Strecker, Appendix 1 in Bauer, *Orthodoxy*, 279. Since P. Nautin's work in the 1940s some scholars identify two 'blocks' of material in the 'Hippolytus' corpus, one Asiatic in origin. *Contra Noetum* is sometimes listed with the Asian material.

38 Tertullian's anti-Monarchianism in *Adv. Prax.* suggests soundness of doctrine while a Montanist. See Barnes, *Tertullian*, 142.

39 J. Pelikan, 'Montanism and its Trinitarian Significance', 103.

40 See 5.2–5.3 on other developments.

41 See J.E. Stamm, 'Charismatic Theology in the *Apostolic Tradition* of Hippolytus', in G.F. Hawthorne (ed.), *Current Issues in Biblical and Patristic Interpretation* (Studies for M.C. Tenney), Grand Rapids 1975, 267–76.

42 In 1551 a large fragment of a marble statue (of an allegorical feminine figure, it has been suggested) was discovered in Rome in the locality of the catacomb of St Hippolytus the martyr. A chair figures in the work and on the rear right-hand side of the chair there is a list of Christian writings. It includes *A Defence of the Gospel and the Apocalypse*.

43 R. Heine, 'The Role of the Gospel of John'; 'The Gospel of John and the Montanist Debate'. Heine's work in *Oracles* presents separately Asian, Roman and African sources.

44 Heine, 'The Role of the Gospel of John', 97.

45 Heine citing A. Harnack, *History of Dogma* ii, New York 1961, 100; H. de Soyres, *Montanism and the Primitive Church*, Cambridge 1878 (condensed reprint 1965), 58; Aland, 'Bemerkungen', 132.

46 Heine, 'The Role of the Gospel of John' 3. See Faggiotto, *Diaspora*, 13f., 67–86.

47 Heine, 'The Role of the Gospel of John', 10.

48 D.E. Groh, 'Utterance and Exegesis', 82. R.A. Lipsius thought the Eusebian Anonymous was Epiphanius' source, *Zur Quellenkritik*, 225f.; Vokes suggested it was the *Syntagma* ('The Use of Scripture', 318). See too Labriolle, *Les Sources*, lviiiff. and Faggiotto, *Diaspora*, 13f., 67ff.

49 R.E. Brown 'The Paraclete in the Fourth Gospel', *NTS* 13 (1966–7), 113–32; D. Moody-Smith, 'Johannine Christianity: Some Reflections on

its Character and Delineation', *NTS* 21 (1974–5), 222–48; M.E. Boring, 'The Influence of Christian Prophecy on the Johannine Portrayal of the Paraclete and Jesus', *NTS* 25 (1978–9), 113–23; David Hill, *Prophecy*, 146ff.

50 Heine, 'The Role of the Gospel of John', 15.
51 Cf. Filastrius *Div. Haer. lib.* xlix.
52 See Klawiter, 'The New Prophecy', 64ff. Like Klawiter I think its 'newness' was linked to being prophecy of new covenant time. Cf. 1.1 n.7.
53 T.D. Barnes, *Tertullian*, 195 and in 'Tertullian the Antiquarian', 4.
54 See scholars' views in U. Neymeyr, *Die christlichen Lehrer*, 107ff. and Barnes, *Tertullian*, 11f., 117 (esp. *De exh. cast.* vii.3; *De monog.* xii.2).
55 Klawiter, 'The New Prophecy', 244.
56 Klawiter, 'The New Prophecy', 248 n. 2; 'pugnacious personality', 280.
57 B. Nisters, *Tertullian. Seine Persönlichkeit und sein Schicksal*, Münster 1950, 114.
58 Quotation from G.L. Bray, *Holiness*, who argued that Tertullian defended the Prophecy but did not propagate it and never left the Great Church. While right about the second, Bray is surely wrong about the first. Monceaux, *Histoire*, 399f., 414 saw Tertullian as ever a catholic.
59 See Labriolle, *History and Literature*, 62.
60 H.J. Lawlor, 'The Heresy of the Phrygians', 486.
61 See also 4.5 nn. 99–101 and n. 64 below.
62 G. Claesson, *Index Tertullianeus* (Études Augustiniennes), 3 vols., Paris 1974–5 (a word index); 'Chronica Tertullianea' annually from 1975 in R. Braun, J.-C. Fredouille and P. Petitmengin (eds.), *REAug*. For critical editions of individual works pre 1954 see 'Bibliographica Selecta' in *Corpus Christianorum series Latina* I, xii–xiv, Turnhout 1953 and up to 1976 'Index Bibliographicus' in R. Braun *Deus Christianorum*, Paris 1962, 596ff., 725f. R.D. Sider, 'Approaches to Tertullian', *The Second Century* 2 (1982), 228–60.
63 Tertullian *Ad Scap.* iii.4. See Barnes, *Tertullian*, 60 on the 'slander and innuendo' of the *Metamorphoses* of Apuleius of Numidian Madauros. Martyrs from Madauros are sometimes thought to predate the Scillitani. Barnes, *Tertullian*, Appendix C, 262ff.
64 If Carthage had more than 100,000 inhabitants, then perhaps 1 per cent of those were Christians. Cf. Schöllgen, *Ecclesia Sordida*, 54f., 268. Other sources on African Christianity: Frend, *The Donatist Church*, Oxford 1952; J-L. Maier, *Le Dossier du Donatisme* (2 vols., TU 134 and 135), Berlin 1987, 1989; V. Saxer, *Morts, Martyrs, Reliques*; A.J. Church, *Carthage or the Empire of Africa* (original 1886), New York reprint 1971; L.R. Holme, *The Extinction of the Christian Churches in North Africa*, New York 1898; J.P. Brisson, *Autonomisme et Christianisme dans l'Afrique Romaine*, Paris 1958.
65 Frend, 'Heresy and Schism as Social and National Movements', in D. Baker (ed.), *Schism, Heresy and Religious Protest*, Cambridge 1972, 39f. Its Judaism too, he suggests, was 'of strict and legalistic type' (see too n. 68)

and in Carthage Christianity had an exclusive and harsh outlook (Tertullian *Apol.* xxxix.1; *De spect.* ii).

66 Frend, 'The North African Cult of Martyrs', *Archaeology and History in the Study of Early Christianity*, London 1988, XI, 154.

67 Discussed in Robeck, *Prophecy in Carthage*.

68 C. Aziza, *Tertullien et le Judaisme*, Paris 1977 for Tertullian's close association with Jewish life and rabbinic thought. Cf. J.M. Ford, 'St Paul the Philogamist', *NTS* 11 (1965), 326–48 and work by Frend in *JTS* 21 (1970); *Studia Patristica* x (1970); Mélanges for M. Simon, *Paganisme, Judaisme, Christianisme*, Paris 1978. Not so Barnes, *Tertullian*, 92.

69 Barnes, *Tertullian.*, 57ff.

70 Barnes, *Tertullian*, 58, 10.

71 *Tertullian*, 59. There is no evidence for this.

72 Contrast J.G. Davies, 'Tertullian, *DE RESURRECTIONE*', 90ff.

73 See W. Telfer, 'Origins', 514ff.

74 On criteria for knowing Tertullian's Montanist writings see Barnes 'Tertullian's *Scorpiace*'; *Tertullian*, 55 *et passim*. Also R. Braun, *Deus Christianorum*, 563–77; J.-C. Fredouille, *Tertullien et la conversion*, 487f.

75 Barnes, 'Tertullian the Antiquarian', 13: 'full of Graecisms . . . archaic words . . . compressed almost beyond the bounds of intelligibility . . . the most difficult work ever written in Latin'. It probably dates to a time close to his conversion to Christianity, so J. Klein, *Tertullian: Christliche Bewusstsein und sittliche Forderungen*, Hildesheim 1975 reprint, 252–68. Contrast J.-C. Fredouille, *Tertullian*, 470ff.

76 On *De carne Christi* predating *Adv. Marc.* see R. Braun, 'Chronologica Tertullianea: le "De carne Christ" et le "De Idololatria"', *AFL Nice* 21 (1974), 271–281; J.-P. Mahé, 'Le traite perdu de Tertullien *Adversus Apolleiacos* et la chronologie de sa triade anti-gnostique', *REAug* 16 (1970), 3–24 and *Tertullien: La Chair du Christ* (SC 216/217), Paris 1975.

77 Barnes, 'Tertullian's *Scorpiace*', 114f.; *Tertullian* 30–55 on chronology of the writings.

78 See Robeck, 'Prophetic Gifts', 28f; *Prophecy*, 4f. Contrast U. Neymeyr, *Die christlichen Lehrer* (n.3) 106f.

79 Cyprian, though indebted to him, does not name Tertullian. In any case Cyprian would not have respected a schismatic and generally he does not name, quote or refer directly to writers.

80 Powell sees no evidence for separation in the *Pass. Perp.* either. On Tertullian as sectarian and disillusioned catholic see A. Quacquarelli, 'La cultura indigena di Tertulliano e i Tertullianisti de Cartagine', *Vet. Chr.* 15 (1978), 207–21.

81 Monceaux, *Histoire*, 404

82 D. Powell, 'Tertullianists', 34. *De monog.* ii.1f. is an even clearer case, Powell suggests.

83 Labriolle, *History*, 64; *La Crise*, 461ff.

84 Powell, 'Tertullianists'. *Adv. Prax.* i.7 acknowledges differences about the Paraclete.
85 See *De pudic.* i.10.
86 J. Moignt, *Théologie trinitaire de Tertullien* i, Paris 1966, 57ff. See Powell, 38f., on non-refusal of catholic Eucharist, acknowledgement of bishops and Tertullian's ambiguity as proof of lack of formal schism.
87 Cf. Praedestinatus in 5.3.2; See Barnes, *Tertullian*, Appendix, 258f. Augustine's treatment of Tertullianistae as a sub-sect has allowed Tertullian to be seen as a man in constant rebellion and isolated, Barnes notes: 'the Tertullianistae need have no place in a study of Tertullian'.
88 Powell, 'Tertullianists', 40 quoting Schepelern, *Montanismus*, 25. Tertullian, he notes, acknowledged the Holy Spirit as a plenary gift to the apostles (*De pudic.* xii.1) but presented the Paraclete as introducing nothing new (*De monog.* iii.1) and with a disciplinary and restitutionary role (*De virg. vel.* i.4; *De monog.* iv.1).
89 '. . . his Montanism came from Montanus, from Phrygia' (Powell, 49).
90 *Continued* contact with the Prophecy of the East need not be assumed.
91 'The Heresy of the Phrygians', 485f.
92 I agree, though Tertullian flavoured the Prophecy he described.

3. THE TEACHINGS OF THE NEW PROPHECY

1 Klawiter, 'The New Prophecy', 129ff, 141. Cf. Dodds, *Pagan and Christian*, 62f. for a Jungian assessment of Peregrinus.
2 Fox, *Pagans and Christians*, 241–61. Cf. too Frend (on Peregrinus Proteus), *Rise*, 176; S. Benko, *Pagan Rome and the Early Christians*, Bloomington IN 1984, 103–39 (on Alexander).
3 Klawiter, 'The New Prophecy', 154 n. 1.
4 Aune, *Prophecy*, 313. Contrast Goree, 'Cultural Bases', 92 and W.C. Klein in 'The Church and its Prophets', *ATR* 44 (1962), 12.
5 Heine, *Oracles*, x–xi.
6 *PG* lxxxvi.20.
7 Text in G. Ficker, *ZKG* 1905, 445ff.; Heine, *Oracles* 113, 115, 117, 123.
8 Aland ('Bemerkungen', 143–8) categorises oracles as authentic (sixteen in number), doubtful and as remnants of what may have been an oracle. The oracle numbers in this study follow Aland, who cross-refers to Labriolle, Bonwetsch and Hilgenfeld (*Die Ketzergeschichte des Urchristentums*, Leipzig 1884). The Hennecke–Schneemelcher (eds.) *NT Apocrypha* ii, 686f. lists 15, omitting no. 2 of Aland's 'genuine'. Cf. Labriolle, *La Crise*, 34f. The following synoptic table of oracle *numbering* (without category) is taken from K. Froehlich, 'Montanism and Gnosis', *Orientalia Christiana Analecta* 195 (1973), 96. I have added Heine's section references.

Table 1 *Synoptic table of oracle numbering*

Aland	Hilgenfeld	Labriolle	Bonwetsch	Heine
1	–	3	–	3
2	1	3	5	103
3	4	1	3	1
4	5	2	4	2
5	2	5	1	3
6	3	4	2	4
7	18	9	18	70
8	19	6	15	46
9	19	7	16	38
10	7	16	7	49
11	8	15	8	37
12	9	17	9	11
13	3	11	13	6
14	10	13	10	7
15	11	14	11	8
16	12	12	12	5
17	6	10	6	17
18	–	18	21	18
19	–	19	–	19
20	15	8	19	65
21	17	–	–	38
22	–	–	–	43
23	21	–	–	39
24	cf.14	–	cf.14	23
25	20	–	17	47

9 See D. Aune, *Prophecy* , 70ff., 313ff., 324.

10 Trevett, *Ignatius*, 134ff.; Aune, *Prophecy*, 3 29; Paulsen, 'Bedeutung', 29ff.

11 Heine, *Oracles*, 3 and cf. 'The Gospel of John and the Montanist Debate', 95ff. Epiphanius found this saying at odds with John 5:43 (*Pan.* xlviii.11,1–4; K. Holl, (ed). *Epiphanius*, 235). Intertestamental literature was rich in speculation about angelic figures and representatives of God. *11QMelch* has the figure of Michael (Melchizedek), prince of light and Michael in turn, as the Spirit of truth, has connections with the Paraclete. See M. Hengel, *The Son of God. The Origin of Christology and the History of Jewish Hellenistic Religion*, London and Philadelphia 1975, 43ff.; *The Johannine Question*, London 1989, 111f.

12 On Christian prophecy and 'charismatic exegesis' see E. Cothenet, 'Les prophètes chrétiens comme exégetes charismatiques de l'Ecriture', in J. Panagopoulos (ed.), *Prophetic Vocation* and cf. too C. Rowland, *The Open Heaven*, London 1985, 82ff.; 'Apocalyptic Visions and the Exaltation of Christ in the Letter to the Colossians', *JSNT* 19 (1983), 73–83; McGinn, 'Oracles'.

13 See Groh, 'Utterance and Exegesis', 73ff. and especially 90ff. On

bypassing heavenly intermediaries in the LXX see P. Winter, 'Isa. LXIII,9 (Gk) and the Passover Haggadah', *VT* 4 (1954), 440. Contrast Blanchetière, 'Le Montanisme originel' (1979), 3; Labriolle, *La Crise*, 39; *Les Sources*, 133 n. 88; Bonwetsch, *Montanismus*, 19. On prophets as teachers see D. Hill, 'Christian prophets as teachers or instructors in the Church', in J. Panagopoulos (ed.), *Prophetic Vocation*, 108–30.

14 Origen on Luke 13:33 (in *Comm in Matt.* ser. xxviii) is interesting: Christ would not lie about no prophet being killed outside Jerusalem, though prophets after his day must have suffered so. Phrygian false prophets could not be counted but in any case, he posits, the righteous are by default *in* Jerusalem. I think the Prophets might have agreed.

15 'As the wind moves through the harp and the strings speak, so the Spirit of the Lord speaks through my members, and I speak through his love'(Transl. Aune, 'The Odes of Solomon'. See too *Prophecy*, 296ff.). On the *Odes* and Montanist influence see Charlesworth, *The Odes of Solomon: the Syriac Texts* (corrected edn), Missoula 1977, 31 n. 2. Contrast Aune, 'The Odes of Solomon', 455. Also P. Lejay, 'Le plectre, la lyre et l'Esprit', *BALAC* 2 (1912), 43ff.; Froehlich, 'Montanism and Gnosis', 101; Blanchetière, 'Le Montanisme originel'(1979), 3 ('visiblement inspirée d'Ez., 11:19 et 36:26').

16 O. Michel in *TDNT* iv on *mikros/dikaios* and D. Hill in *NTS* 11 (1965), 296–302; Hill, *Prophecy*, 154f., 170. See too E. Cothenet, 'Les prophètes chrétiens dans l'évangile selon S. Matthieu', in *L'Évangile selon S. Matthieu*, Gembloux 1972, 281–308; E. Schweizer in *NTS* 16 (1969/70), 213–30 and *NTS* 20 (1974), 216ff.; G.N. Stanton, '5 Ezra and Matthean Christianity in the Second Century', *JTS* 28 (1977), 67ff. and Paulsen, 'Bedeutung', 29.

17 Aune, *Prophecy*, 334.

18 So too Labriolle. Cf. also McGinn, 'Oracles'.

19 Other oracles suggest opposition to docetic/Gnostic teaching. See McGinn.

20 Groh, 'Utterance and Exegesis', 94.

21 Blanchetière, 'Le Montanisme originel' (1979) 6.

22 Hill, *Prophecy*, 188. See too Kraft 'Vom Ende der urchristlichen Prophetie', in J. Panagopoulos (ed.), *Prophetic Vocation* 162; Aune, *Prophecy*, 66ff.

23 See Ash, 'Ecstatic prophecy', 236; *Didachē* (final form probably pre 120 CE); Hermas *Man.* xi (Rome in the 140s?). Melito used 'first-person' prophetic rhetoric (*HE* v.24 [Polycrates] and cf. the close of *Hom. Pasch.*), wrote on prophecy and Apocalypse (Tertullian in Jerome *De vir. ill.* xxxiv). See too Justin *Dial.* lxxxii.1 (cf. lxxxvii.6; lxxxviii.1); Irenaeus *Adv. haer.* iii.11,9f.; Hippolytus *Ap. Trad.* xxxv.3; Origen *Contra Celsum* vii.9; *Pap. Ox.* I.5 (combining Hermas *Man.* xi.9f. and what Harnack claimed was a statement from Melito).

24 *Asc. Is.* 3:23ff. (transl M.A. Knibb) in J.H. Charlesworth (ed.), *The Old Testament Pseudepigrapha* ii, London 1985, 161.

25 Significant writers on Christian prophecy include Ellis, Boring, Hill, Dautzenberg, Minear, Cothenet, Müller and Aune. I am using Robeck's modified version (*Prophecy in Carthage*, 4) of Hill's definition of Christian prophetic function: (Christian prophecy is)

divine revelation received by a Christian who functions in the prophetic role, on an occasional, regular or temporary basis, which is then shared in oral or written form with other Christians.

26 ἄδεια in *HE* v.17,2 is freedom from fear (like ἀφοβία following) and not licentiousness, I think, *pace* Lampe, *A Patristic Greek Lexicon*, Oxford 1961.

27 Cf. Jerome, *Comm. in Naum* prol., on Nahum, non-ecstatic prophet who understood all he said. See Labriolle, *Les Sources*, 117; Schepelern, *Montanismus*, 17ff. The 29 LXX references to ἔκστασις translate quite a number of different Hebrew words.

28 Cf. Athenagoras, *Legat.* ix (cf. vii) and Philo *Quis rerum div. heres.* lii–liii; Justin (*Dial.* cxv); *Odes Sol.* vi and Hippolytus *De antichristo* ii. The arguments of A. Daunton-Fear in 'Ecstasies' do not convince.

29 Cf. ἐξίστημι/ἐξιστάω in Matt. 12:23; Luke 24:22; Acts 8:9ff.; 2 Cor. 5:13 (echoed by Didymus and suggesting Paul was charged with losing his senses – which he does not deny); ἔκστασις Mark 5:42; Luke 5:26; Acts 10:10; 11:5; 22:17. See R.P. Spittler on ecstasy in G.F. Hawthorne (ed.), *Current Issues in Biblical and Patristic Interpretation* Grand Rapids 1975, 259–66.

30 See Cyril G. Williams, 'Ecstaticism', on the many pitfalls in study of these phenomena, also ch. 1 of his *Tongues of the Spirit*, Cardiff 1981. Ecstasy, he says (*Tongues*, 30), is much too vague a term to employ 'unless it be abundantly qualified to make clear that there are many degrees of it'. Cf. too Ash, 'Ecstatic Prophecy', 228ff. and Aune in *Prophecy*, 19ff.

31 The debate here is about Peter's experience at the Transfiguration. See also Tertullian *Adv. Marc.* iii.24; *De anima* xlv; *De exhort. cast.* x.5.

32 See Labriolle, *La Crise*, 555ff.; Schepelern, *Montanismus*, 149ff. Against an absolute distinction between 'orthodox' and Montanist prophecy see Turner, *Pattern*, 128f., citing Ritschl and Bardy.

33 Campenhausen, *Ecclesiastical Authority*, 191.

34 Meaning immoderate claims, such as that Jesus had promised their coming (v.16,12)? Or relating to the manner of speech? Was ἀκαίρως directed against *women* Prophets or were all in wrong places and at inappropriate times? Cf. Hermas *Man.* xi and Aune *Prophecy*, 197f., 209f., 218, 226ff.

35 See J.L. Ash, 'Ecstatic Prophecy', 239–43. Accepting that prophecy would continue until the *teleion*, catholics accused when Prophetic succession was not assured. See Heine, *Oracles*, 117, 125; Labriolle, *La Crise*, 562.

36 R.H. Gundry, 'Ecstatic Utterance (N.E.B.)?' *JTS* 17 (1966), 299–307.

37 See H. Bacht, 'Prophetentum', *Biblica* 32 (1951), 237–62; S. Eitrem, *Orakel und Mysterien*, 42 (on pagan parallels with Paul's interpreters of

glossolalia); U.B. Müller, *Prophetie und Predigt im Neuen Testament*, Gütersloh 1975, 31ff.; N.J. Engelsen, 'Glossolalia and Other Forms of Inspired Speech according to 1 Corinthians', Ph.D. dissertation, Yale University 1970. See too W.C. van Unnik, 'The meaning of 1 Cor. 12:31', *NTS* 35 (1993), 142–59.

38 T.W. Gillespie, 'A Pattern of Prophetic Speech ', *JBL* 97 (1978), 74ff.

39 Aune, *Prophecy*, 41: Syrian prophets as 'an amalgam of Christian, Jewish and pagan ingredients'. Cf. too Labriolle, *La Crise*, 95–101; Benko, *The Virgin Goddess*, 140–6. Origen was not describing Prophets.

40 See Schepelern, *Montanismus*, 153ff.; Aune, *Prophecy*, 359 n. 221 on the Origen passage and cf. too T.W. Gillespie, 'A Pattern'. Both sides argued over Paul's witness to such matters. Cf. the introduction to the *Dialexis*. Maximilla was herself an 'interpreter' of sorts (see 4.3.2). *For* glossolalia in the Prophecy: Hilgenfeld *Die Glossolalie in der alten Kirche*, Leipzig 1850, 115–36; Schwegler *Montanismus*, 86; Tabbernee 'Opposition', 97ff.; Goree, 'Cultural Bases', 115ff.; W.G. Murdoch, 'A Study of Early Montanism and its Relation to the Christian Church', Ph.D. Birmingham 1946, 198ff. (which I have not seen).

41 Neither Schepelern nor Aune linked the form of the Prophecy with Phrygian paganism. On 'I' sayings: Hill, *Prophecy*, 160ff.; G.F. Hawthorne, 'The role of Christian Prophets in the Tradition', in Hawthorne and U. Betz, *Tradition and Interpretation in the New Testament* (essays in hon. E.E. Ellis), Grand Rapids 1987, 119–33.

42 Goree, 'Cultural Bases' , 119. He tells of Montanus' 'median position' (124) between the prophetless orthodox church and orgiastic prophecy. 'Developing hierarchy and organizational structure' were foreign to Montanus and his culture. Yet I note he was blamed for loving office and organisation! I have not seen McGinn's Ph.D. dissertation.

43 Contrast Schepelern, *Montanismus*, 157; see Labriolle, *La Crise*, 168ff.

44 H. von Campenhausen, *Ecclesiastical Authority*, 189 and 188.

45 Turner, *Pattern*, 130.

46 See 3.4–3.7. Cf. Turner, *Pattern*, 125 on Montanism as a protest against 'the merciful relaxation of primitive discipline'.

47 P. Brown, *The Making of Late Antiquity*, 67.

48 *NTS* 25 (1978), 113–22. See also 2.2.

49 Boring, 113.

50 Glossolalia, he says, is not in view.

51 Boring defends this with other instances of the prepositions and cases.

52 Boring, 'The Influence of Christian Prophecy', 114.

53 Boring cites a similar 'revelatory chain' at the start of the Apocalypse. Paraclete has replaced *angel* (as figures in the Revelation), demythologising and replacing the figure with the spirit of prophecy (p. 116). See 3.1.2: Montanus says that the Father and not an angel reveals.

54 Later and elsewhere Prophets and catholics had to define the relation of such things to a New Age of the Paraclete. See Turner, *Pattern*, 130.

55 παρακαλεῖν occurs 103 times in the New Testament (54´ in Paul). παράκλησίς occurs 29´ in the New Testament (20 times in Paul): so Schmitz, 'παρακαλεω' in *TDNT* v, 776ff. 'Paraclete' is peculiar to John's Gospel.

56 Schmitz, ibid., about Acts and Paul. For Paul it also encompassed prophetic pastoral exhortation (Rom. 12:8; 1 Cor. 14:3 and 31), consolation and admonition. Contrast Hermas *Man.* viii.10 and *2 Clement* vi.9.

57 See 4.2 for Jensen's case that Montanus was the Advocate (= Paraclete) of the women, who were the *real* Prophets.

58 The catholics denied any prophetic succession on grounds that ancient prophecy and inspiration had not been like that of the Prophets (*HE* v.17,3).

59 On meanings of 'millennialism' see Hill, *Regnum Caelorum*, 1; N. Cohn, *The Pursuit of the Millennium*, 1f.; Daley, *Hope*, 6,17f. *et passim*. See too R. Landes, 'Lest the Millennium be Fulfilled . . .', in W. Verbecke *et. al.* (eds.), *The Use and Abuse of Eschatology in the Middle Ages*, Leuven 1988, 205ff.; Williams, 'Origins', 331ff.; P. Fredriksen, 'Apocalypse and Redemption in Early Christianity . . .', *Vig. Christ.* 45 (1991), 151ff.; R.L. Fox, *Pagans and Christians*, 405f.; Strobel, *Das heilige Land*, 234ff. Critical of typologies of Millenarianism see H. Schwartz in M. Eliade (ed.), *The Encyclopaedia of Religion* New York and London 1987, ix, 521ff.

60 R.L Wilken, 'Early Christian Chiliasm . . .', *HTR* 79 (1986), 298–307; E. Ferguson, 'The Terminology of Kingdom in the Second Century' in E. Livingstone (ed.), *Studia Patristica* xvii, Oxford 1982, 669–76. On Montanism and eschatology see Aland, 'Bemerkungen'.

61 Harnack, 'Millennialism', *Encyclopaedia Britannica*[14], London 1945, xv, 496; F.C. Baur, *Das Christentum und die christliche Kirche der ersten Jahrhunderten*, Tübingen 1855, 247 (transl. A Menzies, Edinburgh 1878–9, ii.2, 45). Cf. also Bonwetsch, *Montanismus*, 78ff.; P. Nagel, *Motivierung* (= TU 95), Berlin 1966, 21f. and many since.

62 See Eusebius *HE* iii.39,13. Apollinarius of Laodicea was accused of chiliastic 'second Judaism'. Contrast Epiphanius *Pan.* lxxvii.36,5.

63 D.E. Aune, *Prophecy*, 316.

64 Charles Hill, 'The marriage of Montanism and Millenialism': paper read at the eleventh International Patristics Congress, Oxford 1991. His views run counter to writers from Schwegler to Frend.

65 Bietenhard, 'The Millennial Hope in the Early Church', *Scottish Journal of Theology* 6 (1953), 12–30; J.D. Moltmann *et al.* 'Doctrines and Dogmas . . . eschatology', in *The New Encyclopaedia Britannica* 1986, xv; J.A. Maculloch, 'Eschatology', in J. Hastings (ed.), *Encyclopaedia of Religion and Ethics* v, 1922, 288.

66 Powell, 'Tertullianists'; Wright, 'Montanists Condemned'; Daley, *Hope*, 18f.; Tabbernee, 'Revelation 21', 52–60; cf. E. Ferguson *et al.* (eds.), *Encyclopaedia of Early Christianity*, Chicago–London 1988, 130.

67 Knox, *Enthusiasm*, 38. Cf. Schneemelcher in *NT Apocrypha* ii, 688 and contrast Goree, 'Cultural Bases', 71ff. Trevett, 'Timetabling'.
68 Epiphanius *Pan.* xlix.1,2. See 4.4.
69 Powell, 'Tertullianists', 45 on the 'ambiguous accusatives and infinitives' of the passage.
70 Cf. Irenaeus *Adv. haer.* v.35,2; Justin *Dial.* lxxx, cf.cxiii; cxxxix; Hippolytus *Ref. omn. haer.* ix.25; Origen *De princ.* ii.11,2 cf. *Comm. Matt.* xvii.35. For Papias, Christ's kingdom would be 'set up' (*HE* iii.39,12) and cf. Cerinthus' presupposed *renewed* Jerusalem (*HE* iii.28,12). See too E. Ferguson, 'The Terminology of Kingdom', 669–76.
71 On Tertullian's *Adv. Marc.* see Barnes, *Tertullian*, 38ff..
72 Contrast Labriolle, *La Crise*, 487 on her Montanism, for Prophets looked *to Pepuza*, he claimed.
73 G. Schöllgen, '"Tempus in collecto est"'; Labriolle, *La Crise*, 331f. See also Fredriksen, 'Apocalypse and Redemption', 155f.
74 Epiphanius *Pan.* xlviii.14,1f.; Powell, 'Tertullianists', 43ff.
75 See too 5.1; Tabbernee, 'Revelation 21', 54f. On Tascodrougites etc.: Trevett, 'Fingers up Noses'. Tabbernee notes that infants might die after baptism *in extremis*. We do not know whether infant baptism was the Montanist norm. Schepelern, *Montanismus*, 122ff. for Phrygian parallels and the Fathers' confused accounts of the religious tattooing.
76 Rev. 7:3; 9:4; 13:16 (of the Beast); 14:1; 20:4: 22:4. σφράγις/σφραγίζω/ κατασφραγίζω occur 32 times in the NT (22 times in the Revelation). The faithful bear forehead marks (cf. Ezek. 9:4ff. and is this presupposed in 1 Kings 20:41?). Note also Isa. 44:3–5: 'I will pour my spirit upon your offspring . . . another shall write the Lord's name on his hand.' Such practice adds to the impression of Montanist open confession of peculiarity (see 5.1).
77 Tabbernee, 'Revelation 21', 54f. On Augustine and abandoning millenarianism: see M. Dulaey, 'L'Apocalypse, Augustine et Tyconius' in A.-M. Bonnardière (ed.), *Saint Augustin et la Bible*, Paris 1986, 369ff.; G. Bonner, 'Augustine and Millenarianism', in R. Williams (ed.), *The Making of Orthodoxy* (essays for Henry Chadwick), Cambridge 1989, 235ff.
78 Campenhausen, *Formation*, 239.
79 C. Rowland, *The Open Heaven*, 228ff., 309ff., 392ff., 398ff. *et passim* and his studies in *JSNT* 19 (1983), 73–83; *JSNT* 24 (1985), 99–110; *NTS* 30 (1984), 498–507. See too F.O. Francis in *Studia Theologica* 16 (1963), 109ff.; A.F. Segal in W. Haase (ed.), *Aufstieg und Niedergang der römischen Welt* II, 23/2, Berlin 1980; J. Maier in *Kairos* 5 (1963).
80 See 1.2. C. Weizsäcker (review in *TLZ* 7 (1882), col. 76) saw 'Jerusalem' as echo of the mother church of Acts (cf. the 'open door' of Rev. 3:8, probably indicating the potential for mission, and 1 Cor. 16:9; 2 Cor. 2:12; Acts 14:27). See too Williams, 'Origins', 343.
81 Cf. R.H. Gundry, 'People as Place'; C. Deutsch, 'Transformation'.

82 Powell, 'Tertullianists': hope of imminent Parousia came with 'failure of the prophetic succession' (43, 50), noting Maximilla's prophecy of the End.

83 C. Rowland, *The Open Heaven*, 106ff., 393f, 396f. on the *Pass. Perp.* iv and xi and Quintilla's vision.

84 Powell, 'Tertullianists', 46; H.B. Swete, *The Holy Spirit in the Ancient Church*, London 1912, 69. The mourning, dishevelled woman of 4 Ezra 9:38 develops a shining face (9:25) and then from invisibility becomes *a city, Zion* (10:27, 44). Was the female Christ who appeared to Quintilla ('thus Jerusalem descends') a vision of its presence?

85 Versions of the *Epistula Apostolorum* vary: M. Hornschuh, *Studien zur Epistula Apostolorum* (PTS 5), Berlin 1965, 117f.; L. Gry, 'La date de la parousie d'après l'Epistula Apostolorum', *Rev. Bib.* 49 (1940), 86ff. Cf. Hill, *Regnum Caelorum*, 101–4 and Schmidt, *Gespräche*.

86 Harnack, *Geschichte der altchristlichen Literatur bis Eusebius²*, ii/2, Leipzig 1952, 249ff.; Labriolle, *Les Sources*, 57ff.; A. d'Alès, *La Théologie de Saint Hippolyte*, Paris 1906, 176f. and see Schöllgen, '"Tempus in collecto est"'. On whether a single 'Hippolytus' wrote all the works contrast especially essays by Loi and Simonetti in *Ricerche su Ippolito, Studia Ephemeridis Augustinianum* xiii, Rome 1977. See too E. Prinzivalli, 'Note sull' escatologia di Ippolito', *Orpheus* (n.s.) 1 (1980), 305ff.; D.G. Dunbar, 'The Delay of the Parousia in Hippolytus', *Vig. Christ.* 37 (1983), 313–27.

87 Aristides *Apol.* xvi.6; Justin *1 Apol.* xxviii.2; *2 Apol.* vii.1 cf. Tertullian *Orat.* v.1ff.; *Apol.* xxx.1; xxxix.2; Hippolytus *Comm. Dan.* iv. 5 and 12.

88 Rev. 2:5; 2:25; 3:11 (to Philadelphia); 22:7 and 20.

89 See (6 Ezra) 15:5,11; 16:22,29 in Hennecke and Schneemelcher (eds.), *NT Apocrypha* ii, 689ff.; *Apocalypse of Peter, NT Apocrypha* ii, 663ff.. On *Apocalypse of Peter* and *Pass. Perp.* see Robeck, 'Prophetic Gifts', 168; Frend, 'Blandina and Perpetua', 172. See too M. Himmelfarb *Tours of Hell. An Apocalyptic Form in Jewish and Christian Literature*, Philadelphia, PA, 1983.

90 Frend, *Martyrdom*, 31–103; Klawiter, 'The New Prophecy', 124. Cf. too Eusebius *HE* v.1,34.

91 See e.g. Bonwetsch *Montanismus*, 121ff., 137ff. On such nineteenth-century interpretation see Klawiter, 'The New Prophecy', 10–20. He wonders (96f.) whether the cultic *Sitz im Leben* of the (presumably Quartodeciman) Prophecy was 'an outgrowth of the enthusiasm associated with . . . the (50-day) Passover-Pentecost festival', during which one anticipated the Parousia and the subsequent ascent of the believer. Cf. *Epist. Apost.* xvii; Melito, *Homily*, c–civ.

92 V.C. de Clercq, 'The expectation of the second coming of Christ in Tertullian', in F.L. Cross (ed.), *Studia Patristica* ix (= TU 108), Berlin 1972, 146–51 and cf. Klawiter, 'The New Prophecy', 15f.

93 Cohn, *Pursuit*, 25; Bray, *Holiness*, 55. Klawiter ('The New Prophecy',

91), like Harnack and Bonwetsch, thinks once the Parousia hope failed Pepuza gatherings became representative assemblies for Montanist delegates. We need not assume the first in order to accept the second.

94 Powell, 'Tertullianists', 43.

95 P. Nagel, *Motivierung*, 21, 25. Cf. Schepelern, *Montanismus*, 92–105.

96 This was additional to the paschal fast. See Hippolytus *Comm. Dan.* iii.20; Labriolle, *Les Sources*, 11f. Jerome said one was at Whitsuntide (*Comm. in Matt.* i.9). Cf. Tertullian *De jej.* i.4; ii.1ff. and xv.2. See J. Schummer, *Die altchristlichen Fastenpraxis. . .*, Münster 1933, 35ff., 227ff.

97 Jerome *Ep.* xli. 3 mentions three *imposed* forty-day fasts annually. He may have exaggerated; cf. Bonwetsch, *Montanismus*, 95.

98 See F. Cardman, 'Tertullian on Doctrine'; G.L. Bray, *Holiness*, 134ff.; Bonwetsch, *Montanismus*, 81–118; V. Morel, 'Le développement de la "Disciplina" sous l'action du Saint-Esprit chez Tertullian', *Rev. d'Hist. Ecclés.* 35 (1939), 243–65; R.P.C. Hanson, *Tradition in the Early Church*, London 1962, 87ff.; Klawiter, 'The New Prophecy', 249ff.; Robeck, *Prophecy in Carthage*, 141ff..

99 See M.E. Stone, *4 Ezra* (Hermeneia series), London 1981, 28ff., 35, 302ff. In 4 Ezra 9:26 Ezra eats plants (cf. 4:23. *Eth.* has 'fruit of the field'). Origen, commenting on the letter to Titus (*PG* xiv.1306; Heine, *Oracles*, 8) described Phrygians as turning to false prophets and claiming Nazirite status – not marrying, drinking wine etc. Like many, I think the oracle is not genuinely Montanist.

100 See 1.2.3.

101 Fox, *Pagans and Christians*, 173f., 205, 396. The light, dry Greek diet favoured visions 'in the days before moussaka' (151). R. Arbesman, 'Fasting and Prophecy in Pagan and Christian Antiquity', *Traditio* 7 (1949–51), 1ff. P. Brown, *The Making of Late Antiquity*, 44f.

102 Sozomen (*HE* vii.19) found Phrygian Montanists had the shortest (two week) Easter fast. Cf. Labriolle, *La Crise*, 110; Turner, *Pattern*, 128.

103 'Station' (*De jej.* x), a term from military discipline, was a fixed time for Christian fasting (*De orat.* xix; *De jej.* i–ii; x in Greek writers only Hermas *Sim.* v.1,1). Prophets took stations beyond 3 p.m. to evening.

104 Carthage and 'mutual accusations of heresy': 'Tertullianists', 36; *De pudic.* i.10; *De monog.* xv.1. On *De jej.* xiii.6ff. and 'concilia' see Fischer, 'Synoden', 258ff..

105 See 4.1.2.

106 In *The Acts of Paul and Thecla* Thecla heard Paul discuss renunciation of marriage and sex. The *Acts* of Thomas, of Andrew and of John are more extreme still in denunciation.

107 P. Nautin, *Lettres*, 16. On celibacy, marriage, clergy etc.: Gryson, *Aux Origines du Célibat ecclésiastique*, Gembloux 1970; M. Crouzel, *Mariage et Divorce, Célibat et Caractère Sacerdoteaux*, Louvain 1982; 'Le celibat et la continence ecclésiastique . . .', in *Sacerdoce et Célibat. Études Historiques et Théologiques*, Louvain 1971, 333ff.; C. Munier, Tertullian *Ad Uxorem* (S.

Chret.), Paris 1980 (esp. Introduction); M. Bevénot, 'Sacerdoce et célibat . . .', *Rev. d'Hist. Ecclés.* 67 (1972), 67–80.

108 The passage was surely important for Prophets' thinking on celibacy.

109 Nagel, *Motivierung*, 34–9. Cf. Tertullian I *Ad uxor.* i and end of *De exhort. cast.*

110 See Fox, *Pagans and Christians*, 308ff.; 352ff.; 368f.; nn. to ch. 6; Harnack, *The Mission and Expansion of Christianity in the First Three Centuries*, 1908 ii, 64–84; R.S. Kraemer 'The Conversion of Women to Ascetic Forms of Christianity', *Signs* 6 (1980), 298–307.

111 Frend, *Rise*, 345.

112 If Callistus was in mind, *De pudic.* would date *c.* 220 CE. Barnes (*Tertullian*, 247) thinks a man of Carthage was in mind. Not so Vokes, 'Penitential', 71–5. See too K.M. Girardet, in *Historia* 26 (1977), 95ff.

113 II *Ad uxor.* conceded the option of remarriage to a Christian. Had Tertullian's wife objected? A work of imaginative reconstruction waits to be written on 'Mrs Tertullian'!

114 Cf. also Irenaeus *Adv. haer.* iii.17,2; Theophilus *Ad Autol.* iii.15.

115 On this passage see J.B. Bauer, 'Was las Tertullian I Kor. 7 39?' *ZNW* 77 (1986), 284ff. Cf. too Ford, 'St Paul the Philogamist (1 Cor. VII in Early Patristic Exegesis)', *NTS* 1(1964), 326–48.

116 See F. Cardman, 'Tertullian on Doctrine'; V. Morel, 'Disciplina, la mot et l'idée . . .', *Rev. d'Hist. Ecclés.* 40 (1944/5), 5–46; Bray, *Holiness*, and cf. D.K. House in *Dionysius* 12 (1988), 29–36. On the *regula fidei*, *traditio* and Scripture in Tertullian see in bibliography F. de Pauw, Robeck, L.W. Countryman, and cf. C. Munier, 'Propagande gnostique et discipline ecclésiale d'après Tertullien', *RScR* 63 (1989), 195–205.

117 *De monog.* justifies the discipline *to* African Montanists and defends it against catholic charges. 'Tradition' was on the Prophecy's side; catholics might be charged with innovation (Barnes, *Tertullian*, 140f. cf. too *De jej.* xiii.1–2). Also A.J. Guerra, 'Polemical Christianity . . .', *The Second Century* 8 (1991), 109ff.; Labriolle, *Les Sources* lviii–lxiv, lxxxix.

118 *De paen.* ix–x: Labriolle, *La Crise*, 407f. Cf. Poschmann, *Paenitentia Secunda* . . ., Bonn 1940; W.P. le Saint, *Tertullian, Treatises on Penance*, London 1959, 179ff.; K. Rahner, 'Zur Theologie der Busse beim Tertullian', *Abhandlungen über Theologie und Kirche* (for K. Adam), 1952, 139ff.; Vokes, 'Penitential', 64f.; Eusebius *HE* v.28,8ff.; Origen *Contra Celsum* vi.15.

119 Cf. Council of Laodicea canons 19, 45, 46 and *De pudic.* xiii. Canons of Elvira 37, 47 for baptism postponed. Cf. G.P. Jeanes, 'How Successful was Baptism in the Fourth Century?', in E. Livingstone (ed.), *Studia Patristica* xx, Leuven 1989, 379–83.

120 Fox, *Pagans and Christians*, 337. Cf. P de Clerck, 'Pénitence seconde et conversion quotidienne . . .', *Studia Patristica* xx, Leuven 1989, 352–74.

121 *De pudic.* xvii.19: Tertullian doubted that Paul pardoned fornication, but in any case it would have been an indulgence of the apostle's time.

122 Campenhausen, *Ecclesiastical Authority*, 215–37 esp. 231.
123 Frend, 'The North African Cult of Martyrs', *Archaeology and History in the Study of Early Christianity*, London 1988, XI. 'Spiritual' and 'elect' Christians and catechumens' study of Daniel, the Apocalypse and *Apocalypse of Peter* furthered African interest in martyrs (156ff.).
124 E. Grässer, 'Die Gemeindevorsteher im Hebräerbrief', in H. Schroer, G. Müller (eds.), *Vom Amt der Laien in Kirche und Theologie*, Berlin–New York 1982, 67–84; Kraft, 'Gemeindeverbanden', 217ff.; Hill, *Prophecy*, 141ff., 178ff. (Hebrews and Barnabas = 'pastoral preaching' of prophets). On Tertullian and Hebrews: J.F. Jansen in *The Second Century* 2 (1982),192f.
125 The oracle reads: 'Potest ecclesia donare delictum, sed non faciam, ne et alia delinquant' (*De pudic.* xxi.7; Heine, *Oracles*, 93). See on this Robeck, *Prophecy in Carthage*, ²7f. ('to supply a policy of deterrence').
126 Cf. *De exhort. cast.* vii.3 on Matt. 18:20, laity, priesthood and remarriage; II *Ad uxor.* viii. Matthew's 'two or three' was important for the Montanist Tertullian, though he had used Matt. 18:16ff. previously. See C. Andresen, '"Ubi tres"'; Robeck, 'Prophetic Gifts', 223ff., 232ff..
127 Klawiter, 'The New Prophecy', 283ff., 298. I am less sceptical than Jensen (*Töchter*, 314) about this item.
128 Contrast W. C. Weinrich, *Spirit*, 200 and J. Hoh, *Die kirchlichen Busse im II Jahrhundert*, Breslau 1932, 102. See too P. Nautin, *Lettres*, 67ff.; Poschmann, *Paenitentia Secunda*, 272; G. Jouassard, 'Le role des Chrétiens comme intercesseurs . . .', *RScR* 30 (1956), 217–29; E. Dassmann, *Sündenvergebung durch Taufe, Busse und Märtyrerfürbitte in den Zeugnissen frühchristlicher Frommigkeit und Kunst*, Münster 1973. In Rome confessors might become presbyters without laying-on of hands (Hippolytus *Trad. Ap.* x and cf. Hermas *Vis.* iii.1,8–iii.3,2 on martyrs and prophet-visionaries). See also 4.6.4.
129 This chapter reminds us of our ignorance about the Asian Prophecy.
130 Cf. Klawiter, 'The New Prophecy', 121f.: first-generation Prophets assumed the power to bind. This was changed at the end of the century.
131 Cf. Dionysius of Corinth to Amastris and to Pontus (Eusebius *HE* iv.23,6f.) and cf. *HE* iv.23,1 and 10.
132 Frend, 'The *Memoriae Apostolorum* in Roman North Africa', *JRS* 30 (1940), 32–49.
133 See 4.6 on Klawiter and the clericalisation of Montanist women because they held the power of the keys.
134 Fox, *Pagans and Christians*, 408f.
135 A. Faggiotto, *L'Eresia*, followed by Piana. Cf. too Carrington on the *Pass. Perp.* in *The Early Christian Church*, London and Cambridge 1957, 427f.
136 Schneemelcher was referring to Epiphanius *Pan.* xl vii.4,1 (the lyre oracle, see 3.1.2); *Pan.* xlviii 10,3 ('righteous and little ones') and Tertullian *De pudic.* xxi.7 (on the Paraclete's refusal to forgive sins).

137 W. Schneemelcher in Hennecke and Schneemelcher (eds.), *NT Apocrypha* ii, 688.
138 Fox, *Pagans and Christians*, 419.
139 Frend, *Martyrdom* (e.g. 9ff.); Barnes, *Tertullian* 143–86; St Croix in *Past and Present* 26 (1963) and J. Perkins, 'The Apocryphal Acts. . .', *Arethusa* 18 (1985), 211–30; M. Sordi, *The Christians*, esp. ch. 13. Important studies of martyrdom include: N. Brox, *Zeuge und Märtyrer* . . ., Munich 1961; Campenhausen, *Die Idee des Martyriums*, Göttingen 1964; T. Baumeister, *Die Anfänge der Theologie des Martyriums*, Münster 1980; B. Dehandschutter, 'Martyr-Martyrium . . .', in G.J.M. Bartelink (ed.), *Eulogia:*(Mélanges A.A.R. Bastiaensen), Steenbrugis 1991, 33–9.
140 R.M. Grant, *Augustine to Constantine*, New York 1970, 90ff..
141 Cf. Rev. 6:9–11; Hermas *Sim.* ix.28; *Pass. Perp.* xiii.8; Tertullian *De anima* lv.5; *De res. mort.* xliii.4. Hill, *Regnum Caelorum*, ch.1, 96ff.; Ferguson, 'Early Christian Martyrdom . . .', *JECS* 1 (1993), 73ff.
142 Criticising those less rigorous about titles? Eusebius *HE* v.2,3–4.
143 Farkasfalvy in *The Second Century* 9 (1992), 3ff.; Bowersock, 253ff.
144 W. Tabbernee, 'Voluntary Martyrdom', 36ff. Cf. on provocation Kötting in A.M. Ritter (ed.), *Kerygma und Logos*, Göttingen 1979, 329ff.
145 Marcionite martyrdoms: *M. Pion.* xxi; Eusebius *HE* vii.12.
146 Tertullian *De fuga* ix (cf. *De cor. mil.* ii; *Ad mart.* i) seems to distinguish between *confession* and martyrdom (contrast *De pudic.* xxii.2). See Labriolle in *BALAC* 1 (19), 50ff.; H. Delehaye in *An Boll.* 39 (1921), 20–49; T.W. Manson in *BJRL* 39 (1957), 463–84; Frend, *Martyrdom*, 14f.; B. Kötting in *JAC* 19 (1976), 7–23.
147 Tabbernee 'Voluntary Martyrdom', 34. See Labriolle, *Les Sources*, 60; contrast Buschmann, 1995.
148 He had 'the apostolic charisma'. Vettius Epagathus, paraclete, took to 'strictness of life' and drew attention to himself (*HE* v.1,9f.). See Tabbernee, 'Voluntary Martydom', 39ff.; Grant, 'Martyrs of Gaul', 129ff.; Kraft, 'Die Lyoner Märtyrer' 233ff.
149 Grant, 'Martyrs of Gaul', 130, on Eusebius' rewriting. Ch. 4 was an interpolation, according to Campenhausen (*Bearbeitungen und Interpolationen des Polykarp-Martyriums*, Heidelberg 1957, 20).
150 Tabbernee, 'Voluntary Martyrdom', 22.
151 Cf. too Eusebius *HE* v.1,45; v.2,5; v.18,6; also *HE* vi.42,5f.; Cyprian *Ep.* xv–xvi; xvii.2; xx–xxiii; xxvii. On volunteers: St Croix, in *HTR* 47 (1954), 83, 93, 101–4; Robeck, *Prophecy in Carthage*, 15, 29 *et passim*; Fox, *Pagans and Christians*, 442f. Bishop Aurelius Cyrenaeus, very much alive, signed himself 'martyr' (*HE* v.19,3).
152 Frend, *Martyrdom* 79f., so assumes. Cf. Barnes, *Tertullian*, 48, 55.
153 On the late second century *Martyrdom of SS Carpus, Papylus and Agathonike*: Tabbernee, 'Voluntary Martyrdom', 40; Cardman, 'Women Martyrs', 144f., 147, 149; Barnes, 'Pre-Decian *Acta*', 514f.; Musurillo,

The Acts of the Christian Martyrs, Oxford 1971, 26ff.; Cf. too Eusebius *HE* vi.41,7; *Passio Pionii* xi.2.

154 Barnes, *Tertullian*, 167.

155 Calder ('Some Monuments', 362f.) writes of 'a community of Montanist fanatics . . . calling upon the God who is over all'. The account need not show dependence on Joel 2 and Acts 2:17–21; Eusebius uses ἐπιβοάω and not ἐπικαλέω as in the LXX and Acts.

156 S. Mitchell, 'St Theodotus' and sources there. See too C. Foss, 'Late Antique and Byzantine Ankara' (VI) in *History and Archaeology of Byzantine Asia Minor* (Variorum reprints), Aldershot 1990, 29–87. 'Galileans' in the *Life* xxxi suggests a date under Julian the Apostate (360–3 CE). Ancyra was a sectarian hotbed: Jerome, *Comm. in Ep. ad Gal.* ii.3 and cf. Filastrius *Div. haer. lib.* lv; lxxiii–lxxvi. Christians of Meiros (edge of the upper Tembris valley) resisted Julian to death (Socrates *HE* iv.28; Sozomen *HE* vii.18).

157 Trophinos, martyr, occurs in a fifth sixth-century inscription from Phrygian Sebaste. Interred in the tomb of Paulinos, Montanist *koinōnos*, he was perhaps a confessor. See Strobel, *Das heilige Land*, 89ff.; F. Halkin in *An. Boll.* 71 (1953), 329; E. Gibson, *Christians*, 137; Tabbernee, 'Remnants', 200; 'Regional Bishops', 269–72.

158 E. Gibbon, *Decline and Fall* ii (ch. 16/iii), London 1853, 128. Ignatius had given himself up: Trevett, *Ignatius*, 56–74.

159 Bray, *Holiness*, 4 (cf. 42ff.). Cf. Barnes, *Tertullian*, 164–86.

160 Barnes, *Tertullian*, 162ff., 26off. Cf. Tertullian *Apol.* xl.1; *M. Pol.* iii.1f.; Eusebius *HE* v.1,7; v.1,15; A. Quacquarelli, 'La persecuzione secundo Tertulliano', *Gregorianum* 31 (1950), 562–89..

161 See Barnes, 'Tertullian's *Scorpiace*', 105ff.; 125f. (*c.* 203–4 CE).

162 So too Fox, *Pagans and Christians*, 407.

163 On Attalus: *HE* v.1,37 and 43f., 50; v.3, 2. The language of v.1,6 does not look to 1 Tim. 3:15, I think. Cf. Bowersock, 'Les Eglises', 252f.

164 Kraft, 'Die Lyoner Märtyrer' 24of., on 'pillar' as a title at the start of the second century. But see Eusebius *HE* vi.41,14.

165 Trevett, *Ignatius*, 187, ch. 5; 'Apocalypse'. On martyrs: H.E. Lona, '"Treu bis zum Tod" . . .' in H. Merklein (ed.), *Neues Testament und Ethik*, Berlin 1989, 442–61.

166 Heine, 'The Role of the Gospel of John', 4ff. On alleged Montanist revisions: C.S.C. Williams, *Alterations to the Text of the Synoptic Gospels*, Oxford 1951, 56; Rendel Harris, *Codex Bezae*, Cambridge 1891, 148ff.

167 Did they associate Gen. 2:23f. with Eph. 5:31f., like Tertullian? (*De anima* xi.4 cf. Epiphanius *Pan.* xlviii.4). Groh, 'Utterance and Exegesis', 84ff.

168 See A.F. Walls, '"Catholic Epistle"', 436ff.; Aland, 'Anonymity', 39ff.; Bauckham, 'Pseudo-Apostolic Letters', *JBL* 107 (1988), 469ff.; Labriolle, *La Crise*, 28. For *Peter* as the apostle concerned: Barns, 'The Catholic Epistle'; for John: Walls and Labriolle.

169 He cites Rev. 22:18f. See van Unnik, 'De la règle', 11f., 25, 35f. and cf. Windisch in *ZNW* 10 (1909), 173.

170 See Hill, *Prophecy*, 140–6. On rejection of Hebrews due to the Prophecy see Lietzmann in *Kleine Schriften* II (TU 68), Berlin 1958, 81ff.

171 Photius *Bibl. cod.* cxxi; ccxxxii; Campenhausen, *Formation*, 232f.: Irenaeus had a 'mediating, wait-and-see attitude towards the Montanists'. See too Labriolle, *La Crise*, 230ff.; Faggiotto, *L'Eresia*, 15ff.

172 *De Trin.* iii.41,3; Jerome *Adv. Jovin.* ii.3; Augustine *Contra Faustum* xxxii.17; Praedestinatus i.26.

173 The Montanist in the *Dialexis*: 'I believe in the Gospels.'

174 Transl. Heine, *Oracles*, 50f. See too in Paulsen, 'Bedeutung', 22ff.

175 Robeck, *Prophecy in Carthage*, 107–45, esp. [3]7ff. Tertullian's use of Scripture and other traditions: see de Pauw, 'La Justification', esp. 12ff.; Campenhausen, *Formation*, 226f.; Jansen, 'Tertullian', 191ff.; Robeck, 'Canon, *Regula Fidei*'.

176 See Harnack in *ZKG* 3 (1879), 358–408; Bludau, *Die ersten Gegner*, 200. Most writers regard the fragment as Roman and of late second- early third-century date, though a fourth-century date is also argued for. It names the Asian Basilides as founder of the Cataphrygians, condemning his 'psalms'. On these see Conybeare in *ZNW* 12 (1911), 71ff. On its date: Campenhausen, *Formation*, 243ff.; A.C. Sundberg, 'Towards a Revised History of the New Testament Canon', *Studia Evangelica* 4 (1968), 452–61; 'Canon Muratori: A Fourth-Century List', *HTR* 66 (1973), 1–41 (from western Syria/Palestine); Ferguson, 'Canon Muratori: Date and Provenance', *Studia Patristica* xvii, Leuven 1982, 677ff. contrast G. Hahneman, 'More on redating the Muratorian Fragment', *Studia Patristica* xix, Leuven 1989, 358ff. The fullest study is Hahneman, *The Muratorian Fragment and the Development of the Canon*, Oxford 1992.

177 Cf. too Theodore of Heraclea *In Johannis* xiv.15 (Heine, *Oracles*, 110); Didymus *De Trin.* iii.41,2–3; Augustine *De agone christiano* xxviii.30 (Heine, *Oracles*, 160); *De haer.* xxvi; *Contra Faustum* xxxii.17 (Heine, *Oracles*, 160f.); Isidore of Pelusium *Ep. libri quinque* i.243 (Heine, *Oracles*, 174, *PG* lxxviii,332f.); Isidore of Spain, *Etym.* xx.8.5,27 (Heine, *Oracles*, 176; *PL* lxxxii, 300). The same thing is being said as late as the twelth century. Cf. also A.H.B. Logan, 'Marcellus of Ancyra and anti-Arian Polemic', *Studia Patristica* xix, Leuven 1989, 194f. See too 5.2.

178 The Paraclete Holy Spirit did not relate to the age of Montanus and *true* prophets were not at odds with the authority of writings old and new. I have not seen K. Sugano, 'Marcella in Rom. Ein Lebensbild', in *Roma Renascens (Festschrift* for I. Opelt), Frankfurt 1988.

179 Heine, 'The Role of the Gospel of John', 13. See too Labriolle, *La Crise*, 34ff.

180 Blanchetière, 'Le Montanisme originel', 126; Vokes, ' Scripture', 319.

181 Aland, 'Anonymity', 47.

182 Walls, '"Catholic Epistle"', 443. See too Paulsen, 'Bedeutung'.
183 Campenhausen, *Formation*, 220f.
184 *Die Entstehung des Neuen Testaments*, Leipzig 1914, 10f. Contrast van Unnik, 'Ή καινή διαθήκη', 215f.; Paulsen, 'Bedeutung', 19ff., 32ff. on earlier German scholars.
185 Rev. is echoing other scriptural passages associated with covenant-making (Deut. 4:2; 12:32; cf. Gal. 3:15).
186 W.C. van Unnik, 'Ή καινή διαθήκη', 218, retracting his earlier view.
187 J. Hoh, *Die Lehre des heiligen Irenaeus über das Neue Testament*, Münster 1919, 1; van Unnik, 'Ή καινή διαθήκη', 210f., 226. Contrast E. Flesseman van Leer, *Tradition and Scripture in the Early Church*, Assen 1953, 132.
188 van Unnik, 'La conception pauliniènne . . .' in *Littérature et Théologie Pauliniènnes* (Recherches biblique v), Bruges 1960, 109–26.
189 D. Hooper, 'Covenant and Promise in Hebrews', unpublished M.Phil. thesis, University of Wales, Cardiff, 1992. More examination of covenantal theology and the Prophecy is needed. See too Klawiter on 'new covenant' and 'one continued time' of the Spirit's activity, 'The New Prophecy', 225–40.
190 On Zahn and Harnack: Paulsen, 'Bedeutung', 20ff. Klawiter, 'The New Prophecy', 30ff., points to Asian (e.g. Irenaeus') flexibility with regard to Christian writing: 'before AD 192–3 the list [of Scripture] was not firmly established'. For Proclus, as for the Anonymous pre-192, new covenant Scriptures could contain both apostolic and post-apostolic works. The threat of the New Prophecy called this principle into question.
191 Campenhausen, *Formation*, 227; Paulsen, 'Bedeutung', 20.
192 Paulsen, 'Bedeutung', 43.
193 Cf. Paulsen on canon and transition from primitive Christianity to early Church: 'Zur Wissenschaft', esp. 208ff.
194 Campenhausen, *Formation*, 220.
195 See E.B. Birks, 'Caius', *DCB* i, 384ff.; Bludau, *Die ersten Gegner*, 40–72.
196 Bludau, *Die ersten Gegner*, 69.
197 Campenhausen, *Formation*, 234ff.: anti-Johannine polemic began in Asia.
198 On the Irenaeus passage and *volunt* emended to *nolunt* see Labriolle, *La Crise*, 233ff.; E. Schwartz, 'Über den Tod der Söhne Zebedaei', *Gesammelte Schriften* v, Berlin 1963, 48–123, esp. 88 (cf. too 'Johannes und Kerinthos', *ibid.*, 170–82). On Gaius in Dionysius bar Salibi's fragments from the debate with Hippolytus see 2.2; 3.9.3; 3.9.6 and the translation in Nautin, *Le dossier d'Hippolyt et de Méliton* (Patristica I), Paris 1953, 144ff. Cf. too, Labriolle, *Les Sources*, lxxi.
199 For Heine the passage is a *testimonium* about Rome: *Oracles*, 52f. Not so Frend, *Rise*, 254. On *Dem.* xcix: J.P. Smith, *Proof of the Apostolic Preaching*, New York 1952, 108f. On Irenaeus: Bludau, *Die ersten Gegner*, 10–39.

200 See Labriolle, *Les Sources*, lxxiif., lxxxi on Gaius and the Alogi of Epiphanius; Quasten, *Patrology* ii, Utrect-Antwerp 1950, 197. Bludau, *Die ersten Gegner*, 150–80 discusses Epiphanius' sources in *Pan*. li (cf. too 120–8) and Klawiter, 'The New Prophecy', excursus II, analyses the evidence.

201 Cf. Bludau, *Die ersten Gegner*, 228f.: Rome was centre for the movement in the beginning of the third century – Asia would not have associated Cerinthus with Johannine writings. See too V. Rose, 'Question johannine . . .', in *Rev. Bib.* 6 (1897), 516–34; Campenhausen, *Formation*, 238ff.

202 Bludau, *Die ersten Gegner*, 221f. See also Campenhausen, *Formation*, 237f. on the work of Schwartz, in particular.

203 Zahn, *Geschichte des neutestamentlichen Kanons* i, Erlangen 1888, 241; Bludau, *Die ersten Gegner*, 27; Paulsen, 'Bedeutung', 25f. Cf. Schmidt, *Gespräche*, 403ff.

204 See 2.2.4. The Gallic martyrs mentioned *paraclete* in writing to Rome and Asia Minor. Irenaeus about *Montanists*: Bludau, *Die ersten Gegner*, 15 (on I. Döllinger, *Hippolytus und Kallistus*, Regensburg 1853, e.g. 292ff., 302).

205 On Alogi see also Schmidt, *Gespräche*, 451f.; Schwartz, 'Söhne Zebedaei', 88ff., 104; Faggiotto, *Diaspora*, 97–103.

206 Labriolle, *La Crise*, 190ff.

207 *La Crise*, 199.

208 H. Chadwick, *The Circle and the Ellipse: Rival concepts of Authority in the Early Church*, Oxford 1959, 12ff. Cf. Tabbernee, 'Trophies'.

209 Cf. the ideas of J.Z. Smith, 'Map is not Territory', in *Map is Not Territory. Study in the History of Religions*, Leiden 1978, 104–28.

210 Trevett, *Ignatius*, chs. 3–5; Klawiter, 'The New Prophecy', 155ff., 164f.

211 J. Daniélou, *The Theology of Jewish Christianity*, London 1964.

212 Cf. Lev. 8:9; Zech. 14:20. This John was teacher and martyr (Eusebius *HE* iii.31,3). In their graves the Three had plates of gold upon the face (see final text and note). This was probably not the petalon.

213 For the likes of Celsus Christianity was peopled by apostate Jews (Origen *Contra Celsum* i.9; ii.2ff.; iii.1; vi.⁴). Cf. Frend, 'Early Christianity and Society', 53ff., 63f.

214 J. Daniélou, *The Origins of Latin Christianity*, London 1977, 17–31 on 5 Ezra and parallel ideas in *The Shepherd*, Revelation and *Pass. Perp.*.

215 Sherman E. Johnson, 'Asia Minor and Early Christianity', 104.

216 We need a full examination of the opposition/dependence/circumstantial relationships between Christianities and their writings in Asia Minor.

217 Asian Christian diversity: Trevett, *Ignatius*, ch. 3; 169–94.

218 Trevett, 'Apocalypse, Ignatius, Montanism'.

219 Cf. Ignatius *Phld.* 6:1 and Rev. 3:12ff., the *styloi stēlai* contrast.

220 *HE* v.1.26 (cf. Acts 15:20): Gallic Christians consumed no blood.

221 J.M. Ford, *Revelation* (Anchor Bible Commentary), New York 1975.

222 On Ramsay (*Cities and Bishoprics of Phoggia*, Oxford 1895, 1897, i/2, 667–73) and Acmoneia, T. Reinach and Apamea.
223 Cf. A. Jaubert, *La Date de la Cêne*, Paris 1957, 111 on Synoptics and John: 'Les deux traditions ne parlent pas de la même Pâque',
224 N. Wieder, *The Judean Scrolls and Karaism*, London 1962, esp. 191f., who posited Jewish influence on Christian 'station days' (see 3.4.5), which suggested *sectarian* Jewish influence to Ford.
225 Radish is indeed found in the Passover *haggadah* and (both long and round) in the Mishnah, *Kil.* 1.5 and 9. Notably radish and cabbage do not differ enough to fall foul of the rules governing 'diverse kinds'.
226 Though G.W.H. Lampe, *A Patristic Greek Lexicon*, Oxford 1961, gives 'oil of radishes' as translation of τὸ ῥανέλαιον.
227 See especially *Ned.* 6 and 7 on vows of abstinence. *M.Nazir* deals specifically with the Nazirite vow. Ford does not cite the questionable 'Nazirite' oracle, Origen *In Ep. ad Titum*.
228 Prophetic continence came from looking to the eschaton and the continence imputed to prophets in intertestamental literature (3.5).
229 Paulsen and Powell reject such views. Ford also traced some of Tertullian's exegesis to Rabbinic influence ('St Paul the Philogamist' *NTS* 11 (1965), 326–48).
230 T.M. Lindsay, *The Church and the Ministry in the Early Centuries*, London 1902, 36. On an edict associating Jews and Montanists see 5.3.2.
231 See D.F. Wright, 'Montanism: A Movement', 19–29.
232 J.L. Ash, 'Ecstatic Prophecy', 234, 250.
233 Trevett, *Ignatius*, ch. 4; Powell, 'Tertullianists', 52. Kraft, 'Gemeindeverbändung', thinks Prophets never accepted rule by bishops.
234 Klawiter, 'The New Prophecy', 164f.: non-opposition to episcopacy.
235 See Origen *Contra Celsum* iii.10f.
236 See Ammianus Marcellinus *Res Gestae* xxii.5,4; cf. Augustine *De civ. Dei*, xviii.51.
237 R.B. Eno, 'Authority and Conflict' 47.

4. MONTANISM AND WOMEN

1 V. Burrus, 'The Heretical woman', 230.
2 *Ibid.*, 243.
3 Quintilla is not another name for Priscilla or Maximilla (Renan, *Marc-Aurèle et la fin du monde antique*, Paris 1891, 215; cf. Kraft, 'Altkirchliche Prophetie', 264 n. 51). Augustine and John of Damascus, dependent on Epiphanius, also mention Quintillians.
4 Labriolle, *Les Sources*, 238.
5 Some more sources on women in early Christianity: J. McNamara, *A New Song: Celibate Women in the First Three Christian Centuries*, New York 1985; D.R. MacDonald, *The Legend and the Apostle: The Battle for Paul in Story and Canon*, Philadelphia 1983; V. Burrus, *Chastity as Autonomy:*

Women in the Stories of the Apocryphal Acts, Lewiston–New York 1987; A. Jensen, 'Thekla, vergessene Verkünderin', in K. Walter (ed.), *Zwischen Ohnmacht und Befreiung. Biblische Frauengestaltung*, Freiburg 1988, 173–9; S.L. Davies, 'Women, Tertullian and the "Acts of Paul"', *Semeia* 38 (1986), 139–43 and the response by T.W. Mackay, 145ff.; K. Aspegren, *The Male Woman: A Feminine Ideal in the Early Church*, Uppsala 1990, 99–114.

6 R.M. Grant, *Second-Century Christianity*, 95.

7 2 Tim. 3:6; Irenaeus *Adv. haer.* i.6,3; i.13,1–7 (Gnostic prophets).

8 R.L. Fox, *Pagans and Christians*, 311.

9 See Aland, 'Bemerkungen', 135. One MS of *HE* v.18,6 (cf.18,3) has the easier reading 'prophet'. Cf what follows on Themiso (v.18,5 and 7ff.).

10 *De iis qui ad ecclesiam accedunt* (*PL* lix, 163–4). Cf. Ps. Gelasius' *Notitia librorum apocryphorum qui non recipiuntur* (*PG* lxxxvi.20) on Montanus and his 'obscenissimis' followers.

11 *De exhort. cast.* x.5 is in the Agobardinus codex only (see 1 Cor. 7:5 and *De exhort. cast.* x.2), with several textual problems. *Concordat* is an accepted reading. This Priscan oracle is usually held to be genuine.

12 Klawiter, 'The New Prophecy', 91f. Cf. S.L. Davies, *The Revolt of the Widows: The Social World of the Apocryphal Acts*, London 1980, 76; Tertullian *De jej.* iii.3–4 and viii.3f. Contrast Jensen, *Töchter*, 316f.

13 Labriolle, *La Crise*, 77f. Jensen, *Töchter*, 316 on critics and the passage. Maximilla's 'wolf' saying also presupposes an evangelist's role.

14 Jensen, *Töchter*, 303, 332 n. 289. For Bauer the Anonymous and Apollonius were 'ugly caricature . . . abusive satires' (*Orthodoxy*, 137, 141). Cyril's 'passionately unreasonable' (Soyres) accusations were written when young. See too A. Henrichs, 'Pagan Ritual and the Alleged Crimes . . .', in P. Granfield, J.A. Jungmann (eds.), *Kyriakon* (J. Quasten *Festschrift*), Münster 1980; Strobel, *Das heilige Land*, 263ff.; Dölger in *Antike und Christentum* 4 (1934), 188ff.

15 Cyril of Jerusalem *Cat.* xvi.8; *De spiritu sancto* i.8.

16 Notably by Jerome *Ep.* xli; *De vir. ill.* xxvi and xl; *Comm. Hab. Prol.*; *Comm. Isa. Prol.* and the seventh-century *Chronicon Paschale* ccxl.

17 Groh, 'Utterance and Exegesis', 78, quoting Campenhausen, 'their utterances make no appeal to Scripture'. On 1 Cor. 2:4 see T.H. Lim, 'Not in Persuasive Words of Wisdom . . .', *Nov. Test.* 29 (1987), 137–49.

18 Hill, *Prophecy*, 91. Lawlor, 'Heresy', 483f.: 'Word, spirit and power' is not 'Monarchian heresy' matched by Montanus' 'Son, Spirit and Father'.

19 Justin *Dial.* lxxxvi; *2 Apol.* vi; Origen *Contra Celsum* i.6; i.25; i.46; iii.24.

20 Cyprian *Ep.* xxiii cf. Firmilian to Cyprian lxxv. Christian exorcism: Dölger, 'Der Exorzismus im altchristlichen Taufritual', in *Studien zur Geschichte und Kultur des Altertums* iii, Paderborn 1909, 1–175; T.A. Finn, 'Ritual Process and the Survival of Early Christianity', *Journal of Ritual Studies* 3 (1989), 69–89; J.Z. Smith, 'Towards Interpreting Demonic

Powers', *Aufstieg und Niedergang* II/16, 1978, 425–39; A. Rouselle, 'Du sanctuaire au Thaumaturge . . .', *Annales: Économies, Sociétés, Civilisations* 6 (1976), 1085–107; MacMullen, *Christianizing*, 35f. and in *Vig. Christ.* 37 (1983).

21 Labriolle, *La Crise*, 20 n.6; *Les Sources*, 103, 160, 170; Klawiter, 'The New Prophecy', 173–6.

22 For Jensen (*Töchter*, 332f.) demonisation is evidence of a growing catholic fear of women.

23 Knox, *Enthusiasm*, 30.

24 Jensen, *Töchter*.

25 Schwegler, *Der Montanismus und die Christliche Kirche des 2. Jahrhunderts*, 1841, 241f.: Montanus' name was used to provide a 'founder' for the sect.

26 See too E.S. Fiorenza, *In Memory of Her; A Feminist Theological Reconstruction of Christian Origins*, London 1983, 300.

27 Jensen, *Töchter*, 306, 340.

28 Dodds, *Pagan and Christian*, 65.

29 Eusebius *HE* v.16,17; Tertullian *De res. mort.* xi.2; *De exhort. cast.* x.5. For Schwegler Montanus was a mythical figure; the women were real.

30 Epiphanius *Pan.* xlviii.4,1; xlviii.10,3; xlviii.11,1 and 9. There is a later *logion* in the *Dialexis* and in Didymus *De Trin.* iii.41,1.

31 It goes too far to suggest Montanus did not prophesy at all (Kraft, 'Altkirchliche Prophetie', 263f.; 'Gemeindeverbänden' 240).

32 Ficker, 'Widerlegung', 456–8; Labriolle, *Les Sources*, 95.

33 Klawiter, 'The New Prophecy', 237; Jensen, *Töchter*, 303f. Hippolytus is imprecise. Cf. x.25: prophetesses and prophet (in that order).

34 Tertullian *De virg. vel.* i.4; xi.1; xiv; *De exhort. cast.* x.

35 Tertullian: 'le premier à avoir réfléchi et systematisé les idées de la "Nouvelle Prophetie" sur le Paraclet' (Blanchetière, 'Le Montanisme originel', 126).

36 Lawlor, 'Montanism', in Hastings (ed.) *Encyclopaedia of Religion* viii, Edinburgh 1915, 282: Matt. 23:34 was taken to include women, John. 14:12–18 was not. While Montanus lived the women had lower status (!).

37 Jensen, *Töchter*, 196. The martyrologist drew parallels with 2 and 4 Maccabees. See also E. Bickerman in *HTR* 42 (1949), 113 n. 27, Weinrich, *Spirit*, 203ff. and M. Lods, *Confesseurs et Martyrs: Successeurs des Prophètes*, Neuchatel 1958, 49f.

38 See 3.4.3 (Aland no. 11).

39 Aland no. 10. J.G. Davies, 'Tertullian *DE RESURRECTIONE*', 91. Cf. Robeck, *Prophecy in Carthage*, 120f. With Jensen I think this looks more of a *bon mot* than an oracle (*Töchter*, 315).

40 J. Stirnimann, *Die Praescriptio Tertullians im Lichte des römischen Rechts und der Theologie*, Hamburg 1949.

41 *De res. mort.* lxiii. The Paraclete plucked out Praxeas' tares (*Adv Prax.* i) and cf. *De monog.* ii; *De virg. vel.* i. Like Davies I think Prophecy was opposed to docetism and Gnosticism. Cf. too Labriolle, *La Crise*,

312–16; Robeck, *Prophecy in Carthage*, 122ff.

42 See 3.8.4.

43 See 3.3.4 and Labriolle, *Les Sources* lv, 77, 116f.

44 Maximilla, not the Spirit, is the 'me'. Cf. John 3:34; 7:16; 12:44.

45 Epiphanius *Pan.* xlviii.13,7.

46 3.3.4. Participial forms and the substantive carry masculine endings, but see Labriolle, *La Crise*, 74ff.

47 R. Heine, 'The Role of the Gospel of John' and 'The Gospel of John and the Montanist Debate'.

48 The 'promises' probably related to the eschaton and the role of the faithful in it (cf. 2 Peter 3:4 and Davies, 'Tertullian, *DE RESURREC-TIONE*', 91f.). I suspect a link to the Abrahamic covenant and Heb. 6:12f.; 9:15 (*HE* v.16,9), but space forbids discussion.

49 See Deutsch, 'Transformation', 118ff.; Fiorenza, *Priester für Gott*, Münster 1972, 120, 361 *et passim*.

50 See 1 Cor. 14:24ff.: interpretation, manifestation of secrets of the heart, teaching and revelation. Contrast Froehlich, 'Montanism', 106f.

51 *Interpretation of Scripture* is the key here. Cf. Eusebius *HE* iii.39,3; ii.39.14–16 (Papias); Ignatius *Phld.* vi,1 on those who 'interpret' Judaism for catholic ears (perhaps Christians who valued the Apocalypse, I have argued); the prophetic *Teacher of Righteousness* was authoritative interpreter (Hill, *Prophecy*, 37ff.). Maximilla 'interpreting the covenant' necessitated comment on Jewish and Christian writings.

52 Contrast Froehlich and J.G. Davies on the influence of Gnosticism.

53 Luke 20:37; John 11:57; Acts 23:30; 1 Cor. 10:28.

54 This was certainly Tertullian's view.

55 She was the most hounded but contrast 4.2 also. Was Maximilla based at Pepuza and Priscilla more peripatetic?

56 See 1.3.3.

57 On the Priscilla–Quintilla passage: Groh, 'Utterance and Exegesis'; Strobel, *Das heilige Land*, 17, 285ff.; Aland, (Montanism/Montanus), in M. Eliade (ed.), *Encyclopaedia of Religion*, New York–London 1987, x, 81f.

58 Basil of Caesarea *Ep.* clxxxviii.11 (Montanus and Priscilla); Augustine *De haer.* xxvii; Praedestinatus i. 27 (the Three and Quintilla).

59 Salmon, 'Montanus', in *DCB* iii, 939.

60 See Tabbernee, 'Revelation 21'; Voigt, *Urkunde des antimontanistischen Kampfes*, Leipzig 1891, 114ff; Trevett, 'Timetabling'.

61 Aland no. 12. Most writers regard the material as authentic.

62 See 3.3.1–2.

63 We may not assume that all later Montanism held the same doctrines.

64 Powell, 'Tertullianists', 44; cf. Groh, 'Utterance and Exegesis', 8of.

65 Cf. too Schepelern, *Montanismus*, 15. Contrast Jensen, *Tochter*, 323ff.

66 See 2.1.1.

67 See 3.3.2.

68 See Jensen on writers' obsession with 'sexual overtones' in this account

(*Töchter*, 319ff.). The Church *casts out* of a woman (Eusebius *HE* v.19,3; Epiphanius *Pan.* xlviii.12,14) but Christ *puts in* wisdom.

69 Schepelern, *Montanismus*, 144f. see too Powell, 'Tertullianists', 46. Benko, *Virgin Goddess* (ch. 4), makes much of the alleged sacred marriage.

70 See Rev. 7:9–17 and cf. 4:4. Cf. also 3:4, 18; 19:14.

71 3.3.2.

72 Frend (*Rise*, 121) dates 2 Clement early, *c.* 100 CE. Contrast Harnack *Die Zeit des Ignatius und die Chronologie der Antiochenischen Bischöfe* i, Leipzig 1878, 438ff. See also Donfried in *HTR* 66 (1973), 487–501.

73 '"She was made . . . that she might save us" is grammatically more probable, but seems to be excluded both by the context and by the history of doctrine' (K. Lake, n. 1 to the passage, Loeb edition, London 1912).

74 Powell, 'Tertullianists', 46, wants a realised eschatological interpretation for the passage.

75 Prov. 1:20; 3:15ff.; 7:4; 8:1; 9:1. Wisdom departing: 2 Bar. 48:33; Isa. 59:14f.; Hill, *Prophecy*, 21, 38ff. The Christ here probably *is* Wisdom.

76 Cf. D. Hill, *Prophecy*, 91f.

77 Carthage was an exception to the general decline of prophetic gifts (see Robeck). Cf. also J.P. Brisson, *Autonomisme et christianisme dans l'Afrique romaine*, Paris 1958; A. d'Alès, in *Rev. d'ascét. et de mystique* 2 (1921), 256ff.; Harnack in *ZNW* 3 (1902), 177–91; Telfer, 'Origins', 512ff. and the essays by Greenslade, Markus and Frend in D. Baker (ed.), *Schism, Heresy and Religious Protest*, Cambridge 1972.

78 See 4.6.1.

79 'Se in Iudaeam et Hierosolymam festinare fingens tamquam inde venisset.'
Was she recruiting for a Montanist 'Jerusalem' community and millenarian Montanist ideas or was pilgrimage to Jerusalem proper intended?

80 There was Montanism in the area. For caution see Lafontaine, *Conditions positives*, 11–12; Labriolle, 'Mulières', 121 n.2; *La Crise*. Jensen, *Töchter*, 352ff. thinks she was a catholic. The period is that of Maximinus Thrax: see A. Belleza, 'Massimino il Trace', *Istit di Storia Antica dell' Universita di Genova* 5 (1964), 122f.; A. Lippold, 'Maximinus Thrax und die Christen', *Historia* 24 (1975), 479ff.

81 Cotiaeon had a Novatianist bishop in 368 CE (Socrates *HE* iv.28) and Novatianism appeared where Montanism had been (see 5.2.2). See too Buckler, Calder, Cox, 'Asia Minor 1924: Monuments from Cotiaeum', *JRS* 15 (1925), 141–75; Gibson *Christians*, 5ff., 141f.

82 For the inscription see Haspels, *Highlands* i, 338f. no. 107, Pl. 630. Cf. also E. Gibson in *GRBS* 1975, 433–42, contrast Fox, *Pagans and Christians*, 747 n. 11.

83 See Tabbernee, 'Remnants', 199f.; Gregoire, 'Epigraphie chrétienne', *Byzantion* 1 (1924), 708.

84 E. Gibson, *Christians*, 103f., 132: her name and 'spiritual' status made her a Montanist. Contrast Schepelern, *Montanismus*, 80ff.

85 S. Mitchell, 'The Life of St Theodotus', 92ff. Contrast Delehaye in *An. Boll.* 22 (1903), 320–8. Montanism was early in Ancyra (*HE* v.16,4).

86 Origen *Contra Celsum* vii.5f. is not clearly about Montanists: Klawiter, 'The New Prophecy', 169f.; Chadwick (ed.), *Contra Celsum*, Cambridge 1965, xxivff., 402f.; Labriolle, *La Crise*, 95ff. n. 6.

87 The *nos* (i) 'we Montanists' generally (and see xlviii,4); or (ii) a wholly 'orthodox' North African Christian congregation; or (iii) the Tertullianist *ecclesiola in ecclesia* (Powell, 'Tertullianists', 38). Cf. Tabbernee, 'Opposition', 77; Robeck, *Prophecy in Carthage*, 128ff.

88 A.J. Guerra, 'Polemical Christianity', *The Second Century* 8 (1991), 121: 'committees comprised ostensibly of spiritual elders functioned as review boards'.

89 Knox, *Enthusiasm*, 34. See too Tabbernee, 'Opposition', 143 and the balanced discussion in Robeck, *Prophecy in Carthage*, 131;

90 Conservatism about veils: cf. P. Brown, *The Body and Society*, 82; Robeck, *Prophecy in Carthage*, 135ff.

91 See Labriolle, 'Mulières', 103–4.

92 Origen was sometimes amenable towards New Testament women: *Ep. ad Rom.* x.17. For the *catena* see C. Jenkins in *JTS* 10 (1909), 29–51, esp. 41f. Cf. too Faggiotto in *Diaspora*, 31ff.

93 Trevett, *Women and Quakerism in the Seventeenth Century*, York 1991 for the same phenomenon.

94 Cf. *De bapt.* i,3: a woman had no right to teach, even correctly.

95 Eve in the Apocryphal *Acts*: Davies, *The Revolt of the Widows*, 114ff.; Aspegren, *The Male Woman*, ch. 8.

96 Labriolle, 'Mulières', 112f. cf. Fiorenza, *In Memory*, 307ff.

97 John Chrysostom said only 'angelic condition' granted the first Christian women's ministries and travels (*Hom.* iii on Acts, i; *Hom.* lxxiii Matt. 3–4). Contrast women of his own day (*Salut. Prisc. et Aqu.* i,3).

98 Virginia Burrus, 'The Heretical Woman'.

99 Robeck, 'Prophetic Gifts', 30ff., 176–83 and *Prophecy in Carthage* 16f. on (R[Pass]). For Tertullian as R[Pass] see d'Alès, 'L'auteur', *Rev. d'Hist. Ecclés.* 8 (1907), 5–18; A.G. Amatucci, in *Studi in onore di A. Calderini and R. Paribeni* i, Milan 1956, 363–7. For a disciple of Tertullian as R[Pass]: Campos 'El autor', *Helmantica* 10 (1959), 357–81; Barnes, 'Pre Decian Acta', 522; *Tertullian*, 79f., 263ff. Arguments *against* Tertullian as R[Pass] included different use of Joel 2:28ff./Acts 2:17, Tertullian's alleged hostility to pregnancy, his reference to the wrong martyr's vision in *De anima* lv,4 (cf. *Pass. Perp.* xi,1 and 9) and the absence of his brash style. On style, authorship and the *Passio*'s importance see J. Armitage Robinson, *The Passion of S. Perpetua*, Cambridge 1891, 47ff.; Braun in *Rev. des Etudes Latines* 33 (1955), 79–81 and *Vig. Christ.* 33 (1979), 105–17; L. Robert, 'Une vision de Perpetue', *Académie des Inscriptions et*

Belles Lettres, Comptes rendus, Paris 1982, 229–76; J. Amat, 'L'authenticité des songes . . .', *Augustinianum* 29 (1989), 177–91. I think Tertullian was not R^{Pass} but he did not necessarily cite the wrong vision in *De anima* lv,4: see Waszink, *Quint. Sept. Fl. Tertulliani 'De Anima'*, Amsterdam 1947, 561f.; Bastiaensen, 'Tertullian's reference to the *Pass. Perpetuae* . . .', in Livingstone (ed.), *Studia Patristica* xvii, 1982, 190–5. For overview: J.W. Halporn, 'Literary history and generic expectations in the *Passio* and *Acta Perpetuae*', *Vig. Christ.* 45 (1991), 223–41.

100 Its historicity and Montanism: Delehaye, *Les Passions des Martyrs et les Genres Litteraires*, Brussels 1921, 63ff.; Labriolle, *La Crise*, 220ff.

101 Atkinson, 'Joel 2:28', 11–16: in the *Passio* the Joel passage is more developed. The Spirit *in omnem carnem* was too universal an idea for the Montanist Tertullian.

102 Curds/cheese and Montanism: compare and contrast J. Campos, 'El autor', 367; Labriolle, *La Crise*, 344; Robeck, 'Prophetic Gifts', 68ff.; Soyres, *Montanism and the Primitive Church*, Cambridge 1878, 140; d'Alès, 'L'auteur', 16ff.; H. Leclercq, 'Perpetue et Felicité', *Dict. d'Arch. Chrét.et de Liturgie* xiv, Paris 1939, cols. 403f.

103 Tertullian *De cor. mil.* iii.3 cf. *Adv. Marc.* i.14,3; *De. pudic.* x.12.

104 Musurillo (*The Acts of the Christian Martyrs*, Oxford 1971, 111ff.) made *caseo* = 'milk' and *manducavi* = receiving hands 'cupped', rather than folded – it would be an unusual usage.

105 Jensen, *Töchter*, 209, 213–19, here 214. Cf. too A. Pettersen, 'Perpetua, Prisoner of Conscience', *Vig. Christ.* 41 (1987), 139–53.

106 There is considerable literature, including Weinrich, *Spirit*, 227 *et passim*; Dassmann, *Sündenvergebung durch Taufe*, Münster 1973, 153ff. On Perpetua and Dinocrates see Robeck, 'Prophetic Gifts', 88ff.; *Prophecy in Carthage*, 42–56; A. de Waal, 'Der leidende Dinocrates . . .', *RQCAK* 17 (1903) 338f.; Dölger, 'Antike Parallelen zum leidenden Dinokrates', *Antike und Christentum* 2 (1930), 1–40; 'Tertullian über die Bluttaufe', *Antike und Christentum* 2, 1930, 117–41 and cf. E. Corsini, 'Proposte per una Lettura della "Passio Perpetuae"' in *Forma Futuri: Studi in onore del. Card. M. Pellegrino*, Turin 1975, 499–505 (critical of Meslin); D. Devoti, 'La Passion de Perpetue: un noeud familial', in E. Livingstone (ed.), *Studia Patristica* xxi, Leuven 1989, 66–72; Barnes, *Tertullian* 77f.

107 The Paraclete enabled people to face martyrdom (*De anima* lviii.8; *De res. mort.* lxiii.7ff.; *De fuga* xiv.3 cf. Luke 12:11f.).

108 Robeck, 'Prophetic Gifts', 46–75, 129f., 152–68; cf. *Prophecy in Carthage* 22f.; 30f.; 76f.; 85f. *et passim* on Perpetua's circle and apocalyptic sources. There may be parallels with the *Apocalypse of Peter*, *The Shepherd*, Enoch literature, Ezra apocalypse and perhaps the *Asc. Isa.* as well as the Revelation, cf. too Lawlor in *J. of Philology* 49 (1897), 210; Robinson, *The Passion*, 26–43; Frend, 'Blandina and Perpetua', 172; R. Petraglio, 'Des influences de l'Apocalypse dans la "Passio Perpetuae" 11–13' in Petraglio *et al.* (eds.), *L'Apocalypse de Jean: Traditions exégétiques*

et iconographiques IIIe–XIIIe Siècles, Geneva 1979, 15ff.; J. Fontaine, 'Tendances et difficultés. . .', *Aspects et problèmes de la prose d'art latine au IIIe siècle*, Lezioni Augusto Rostagni 4, Turin 1968, 69–97.

109 Tertullian was Montanist by 207 CE. I think the martyrs were Montanists. Contrast Labriolle, *La Crise*, 341ff.; d'Alès, 'L'auteur'.

110 There were two towns called Thuburbo 35 + miles from Carthage (cf. *Pass. Perp.* ii,1). The Monte Cassino codex, longer Latin form, mentions no city. Perhaps Thuburbitan martyrs *were* examined in Carthage or there may have been confusion with later Thuburbitan virgin-martyrs.

111 See 2.3.4.

112 Augustine (*Sermons* cclxxx–cclxxxii); Tertullian *De anima* lv.4 . See W.H. Shewring, *The Passion of SS Perp. and Fel. MM together with the sermons of St Augustine upon these Saints*, London 1931. Third-century Pontius (*Vit. Cyp.* i) may have meant Perpetua and Felicitas when complaining of recorded deeds of 'plebeians and catechumens who have been martyred'.

113 In the fourth century a church was dedicated to Perpetua. See Victor Vitensis, after the onslaught of the Vandals (*Vict. Vit.* i.3,9); also Duval, *Loca Sanctorum Africae* (CEFR 58, 2 vols.) i, 13–16, Rome 1982, 682ff. The 'Tertullianists' basilica was transferred to the catholics in bishop Aurelius' day (Augustine *Haer.* lxxxvi; Praedestinatus *Haer* i.86).

114 Conversions to Christianity had been numerous (Tertullian *Ad nat.* i.14; cf. *Apol.* xviii.4), penalties heavy for not conforming to the edict. See Robeck, 'Prophetic Gifts', 10ff., 22ff.; L. Duchesne, *Early History of the Christian Church*, i, London 1909, 262f.; Frend, 'Open questions', *JTS* 25 (1974), 340–3 and 'A Severan Persecution?' in *Forma Futuri: Studi in onore del Card. M. Pellegrino*, Turin 1975, 470–80 (and also in *Town and Country*, Variorum reprints, London 1980); Sordi, *The Christians*, 79ff.; P. Keresztes in *Historia* 9 (1970), 565ff. See Eusebius *HE* vi.1,1 and 6; vi.1,3. Cf. Hippolytus *Comm. Dan.* i.20,2f.; Tertullian *Ad Scap.* i and iv and Barnes, *Tertullian*, 31; *JRS* 58 (1968), 40f.; *JTS* 19 (1968), 526f. and *JTS* 20 (1969), 130f.; *Harvard Studies* 74 (1970), 313ff.

115 *De bapt.* viii; xx, though Harnack believed the 'distributiones charismatum subiacere' of this passage was a gloss.

116 The literature is extensive: Robeck, 'Prophetic Gifts', ch. 5; *Prophecy in Carthage* 57ff.; Robinson, *The Passion*, 130ff.; Dölger, 'Der Kampf mit dem Ägypter', *Antike und Christentum* 3 (1932), 177–88; 'Gladiatorenblut und Märtyrerblut', *Vortrage der Bibliothek Warburg* 1923/4, 196–214; K. Aspegren, *The Male Woman*, 138–43 (I have not seen P. Habermehl, *Perpetua und der Ägypter oder Bilder des Bösen im frühen afrikanischen Christentum* (TU 140), Berlin 1992; M.L. Robert, 'Une vision de Perpetue', 272; M.A. Rossi, 'The Passion of Perpetua. Everywoman of Late Antiquity', in R.C. Smith and J. Lounibos (eds.), *Pagan and Christian Anxiety. A Response to E.R. Dodds*, New York–London 1984, 53–86. For a psycho-historical approach, M. Lefkowitz in *JAAR* 44

(1976), 419f.; M.L von Franz, 'Die Passio Perpetuae', in C.J. Jung *Aion* (vol. ii of *Gesammelte Werke*, Zurich 1951; essay only in this German edition), 393–495. For other Jungian insights see Dodds, Meslin, Amat, *Songes et Visions. L'au-delà dans la littérature latine tardive*, Paris 1985. 'Becoming male': Robeck, 'Prophetic Gifts', 129f.; *Prophecy in Carthage*, 64f. (Gnostic parallels and the influence of the Gospel of Thomas) contrast Frend, 'Blandina and Perpetua', 173. Augustine discussed the matter, *De anima* iv.26.

117 Cf. Ignatius *Magn.* i.2; *Trall.* iv.2; *Rom.* vii.1–2; Eusebius *HE* v.1,42; Papylos in *Acts of Carpus, Papylus and Agathonike*; Celerinus in Cyprian *Ep.* xxi and xxxix; Tertullian *De scorp.* v.6ff.; *De fuga* ii.1ff.

118 For other writers see Jensen, *Töchter*, 225f.

119 Cf. *M. Pionius* xxi.22; *M. Lyons* in *HE* v.1,19 (Blandina); v.1,42.

120 This is most writers' view. See too J. van Boeft, 'Are you their teacher?', in Livingstone (ed.), *Studia Patristica* xxi, Leuven 1989, 60–5.

121 Cardman, 'Acts', 148; Cf. Lefkowitz in *JAAR* 44 (1976), 418: 'explicit bodily torture and savage male accusers'; Jensen, *Töchter*, 194 *et passim*.

122 A. Pettersen, 'Perpetua', 149. Contrast L.F. Pizzolato, 'Note alla Passio Perpetuae', *Vig. Christ.* 34 (1980) 105–19 (Perpetua and Stoicism).

123 Cardman, 'Acts', 146.

124 *Pass. Perp.* vii.4, 10 for the date 7 March 202–3, birthday of Geta, Septimius Severus' son. See Barnes, 'Pre-Decian Acta', 522ff.

125 See E. Corsini, 'Proposte per una Lettura della "Passio Perpetuae"'.

126 See Schöllgen, *Ecclesia Sordida*, 248f.

127 Gen. 28. Quintilla also heard that 'this place is sacred' (Epiphanius *Pan.* xlix.1,3). Cf. 'sign of Jacob' in the Carthaginian *Acts of Montanus and Lucius* vii. On ladder, serpent and apocalyptic imagery see Robeck, 'Prophetic Gifts', 153ff.; M.L. von Franz, 'Die Passio Perpetuae', 412–19.

128 See 1.2.3.

129 Lefkowitz: 'more a-sexual, fraternal relationships between men and women' in Perpetua's religion.

130 *Pan.* xlix. N.b. Rom. 10:12 cf. Gal. 3:28 from Quintillianists about female clergy (4.6.1). Florilegia of such passages were surely compiled for Prophetic defence.

131 Cardman, 'Acts', 147 on *domina*, citing also Jan dan Boeft and Jan Bremmar in *Vig. Christ.* 36 (1982), 387f.

132 Cf. Rev. 2:3; Eusebius *HE* v.1,42; Augustine *Sermons* cclxxx.

133 Cardman, 'Acts', 147. See too R. Rader, 'The Martyrdom of Perpetua: A Protest Account', in P. Wilson-Kastner (ed.), *A Lost Tradition: Women Writers . . .*, Washington DC 1981, 1–32 and her *Breaking Boundaries: Male/Female Friendship in Early Christian Communities*, New York 1983.

134 See Fiorenza, *In Memory*, esp. ch. 8; E.A. Clark, *Women in the Early Church*, Wilmington DE 1983, ch. 2, 77f.; Ruether, 'Mothers of the Church', in Ruether and E. McLaughlin (eds.), *Women of Spirit: Female Leadership*, New York 1979, 71–98; 'Misogynism and Virginal Femin-

ism', in Ruether (ed.), *Religion and Sexism*, New York 1974, 150–83.

135 African Christianity was determinedly 'different . . . an uncompromising rejection of an alien world' (Barnes, *Tertullian*, 62).

136 Klawiter, 'The New Prophecy', 27. Schepelern, *Montanismus*, 127f. (cult of Attis-Cybele parallels). Contrast Powell, 'Tertullianists', 47.

137 E. Gibson, 'Uşak', 437f.; *Inscriptiones Bureschianae*, Greifswald 1902, 31 no. 55; Gibson, *Christians*, 136: this inscription lacks the cross or communion paten above a table, which is in others of the group. 'Celebration of the Eucharist was not one of her activities; hers showing merely feminine domestic objects.' See Tabbernee, 'Regional Bishops', 250f.

138 Hefele, *A History of the Christian Councils* i/1 Edinburgh 1871, 303 (cf. 295, 305), Laodicean gathering 343–81 CE (i/II 298). See Gryson, *Ministry*, 53f.

139 N. Afanasiev, 'Presbytides or female presidents', in T. Hopko (ed.), *Women and the Priesthood*, New York 1983, 61–74. Cf. Hefele's meandering dismissal in *Councils* i/II, 305f. and see also M.A. Rossi, 'Priesthood, Precedent and Prejudice', *JFemSR* 7 (1991), 73–93.

140 See also discussion in Jensen, *Töchter*, 331f.; Ysebaert, 427ff.

141 Labriolle, *Les Sources*, 226–30, and especially J. Friedrich, 'Ueber die Cenones der Montanisten bei Hieronymus', *SBAW* 26 (1895), 207–21 (similar dates for the *Epistula* and Jerome's writing). Contrast Hilgenfeld in *ZWT* 3 (1895), 635ff.; Schepelern, *Montanismus*, 39ff., 173; Jülicher, 'Ein Gallisches Bischofschreiben des 6 Jahrhunderts', *ZKG* 16 (1896), 664ff.; Labriolle, *La Crise*, 506–12; Tabbernee, 'Regional Bishops', 260f.

142 See 4.4. Jensen, *Töchter*, 352–8, makes a good case for demonisation but says the woman was not a Montanist.

143 See Labriolle, 'Mulières. . .', 121 n. 1 on the text. A negative needs to be added. Firmilian's point is that she performed the rite correctly.

144 Robeck, *Prophecy in Carthage*, 82. Grant is right (*CH* 62 (1993), 378f): Robeck underplays the fights and makes catholics 'spiritual' and well-mannered.

145 Tertullian was not a presbyter: Barnes, *Tertullian*, ch. 3. Cf. too U. Neymeyr, *Die christlichen Lehrer*, 107–12 and the literature there.

146 Barnes, *Die Christlichen Tertullian*, 78f. ('a subversive attitude towards the clergy'); Neymeyr, *Die Christlichen Lehrer* 118f.; J.W. Trigg, 'Martyrs and churchmen', in *Studia Patristica* xv, 1984, 242–6. Contrast Weinrich, *Spirit*, 227f.

147 Klawiter, 'The New Prophecy', 188 cf. 3 John 9.

148 Barnes, *Tertullian*, 222, 141: he 'resented the strengthening of episcopal control . . . against Montanism'. Labriolle, *La Crise*, 294ff. on his dilemma.

149 No Montanist clerical orders in the early sources but see Jerome *Ep.* xli; *Cod. Just.* i.5.20.3. The 'companion' has an echo in *M. Pol.* vi.2; xvii.3 and in a sixth century inscription. See Leclercq, 'Montaniste (Epigraphie)' in *Dict. d'Arch. Chrét. et de Liturgie* xi/2, Paris 1924, 2542 n. 20

and Gregoire, 'Du nouveau', 329ff.; Aland, 'Augustin', 158f.
150 Klawiter, 'Martyrdom and Persecution', 254.
151 *Ibid.* 254f. Cf. also *Apost. Const.* viii.23.
152 Klawiter, 'The New Prophecy', 120. Roman confessors and clergy rank: Hippolytus *Trad. Ap.* x and J.E. Stamm, 'Charismatic Theology in the *Apostolic Tradition of Hippolytus*' in G.F. Hawthorne (ed.), *Current Issues in Biblical and Patristic Interpretation*, Grand Rapids 1975, 267–76, 274f. See too the interesting Hermas *Vis.* iii.
153 Cf. Matt. 20:27; 23:6.
154 Tertullian and laicisation: Andresen,'"Ubi tres" '. On *De exhort. cast.* vii.2–4 cf. also M. Jourjon, 'Les premiers emplois du mot laic', *LV* 65 (1963), 37–42; G. Otranto, 'Nonne et laici sacerdotes sumus? (*Exh. cast.* 7,3)', *Vet. Chr.* 8 (1971), 27–47; A. Vilela, *La condition collégiale des prêtres au IIIe siècle*, Paris 1971, 243ff.; M. Bevénot, 'Tertullian's thoughts about the Christian "Priesthood"' in A.J. Smedt, P. de Cloedt (eds.), *Corona Gratiarum: Miscellanea patristica, historica et liturgica E. Dekkers XII lustra complenti ablata* i, Brugge 1975, 125–37. Tertullian's thought on the matter did not change greatly: J.I. Rankin, 'Tertullian's consistency of thought on ministry' in E. Livingstone (ed.), *Studia Patristica* xxi, Leuven 1989, 276.
155 *De bapt.* xvii.4f. (textually troublesome); *De virg. vel.* ix.1; *Adv. Marc.* iii.22,6; iv.1,8.
156 I am indebted to M. Bevénot. See also C. Andresen, '"Ubi tres"'.
157 Klawiter, 'Martyrdom and Persecution', 261. Cf. too Weinrich, *Spirit*, 202ff. and K. Delehaye, 'Ecclesia Mater chez les Pères. . .', *Unam Sanctam* 46, Paris 1964.
158 Klawiter, 'Martyrdom and Persecution', 254; 'The New Prophecy', 178ff. and ch. 3.
159 W. Tabbernee, 'Voluntary Martyrdom', 33–44.
160 'The New Prophecy', 172f.
161 Klawiter, 'Martyrdom and Persecution', 261. *Pace* Ramsay, Montanist women's position did not come from 'the tone' of Asian society (*The Church in the Roman Empire*, 162, 437f.) rather than any essential principle in Montanism. A Maximilla could not have arisen in Polycarp's congregation, I think.
162 The Joel passage in Tertullian shows the achieved transition from the age of the Law to that of the Gospel (*Adv. Marc.* v.4,2ff.; v.11,4; v.17,4; *De fuga* vi.4). It is used in relation to dreams (*De anima* xlvii.2), Pentecost (cf. *Adv. Marc.* v.8,6; *De res. mort.* x.2; lxiii.7) and just once as proof of the Prophecy's validity (*De res. carn.* lxiii.7).

5. THE FATE OF MONTANISM

1 Trevett, 'Fingers up noses'.
2 I think they bore distinguishing marks. Schepelern, *Montanismus*, 122f. on Phrygian pagan initiatory marking and possible Christian equivalent.

3 The *Panarion* lists many groups with odd customs, some with names akin to those mentioned in this chapter. We should not assume their Montanism.

4 H. Taylor discussed in Frend, 'Montanism: A Movement', 32.

5 Tabbernee, *Montanist Inscriptions and Testimonia*: see too Ferrua, 'Una nuova iscrizione', 98f.; 'Comunità Montanista' (Galatian Ablabēs at Rome). Gibson thought such Italian epitaphs were Montanist: *Christians*, 138.

6 Orthography: Tabbernee, 'Christian Inscriptions', 129f. and cf. Gibson, *'Christians'* 16f.

7 *MAMA* i, 171 from Laodicea refers to a 'spiritual' shepherd (bishop).

8 Calder, 'New Jerusalem', 423; *MAMA* iv, 1933, no. 321 plate 65. Bekilli region provides epigraphy for a *hegoumenē*, not certainly Montanist. See I.W. Macpherson, 'New Evidence for the Historical Geography of Galatia', D.Phil. thesis, Cambridge 1958. See no. 243 plate 59.

9 See M. Waelkens in *Ancient Society* 8 (1977), 277–315.

10 Gibson, *'Christians'*, 24 and plate XI: with motifs including a wreath (cross inset), grapes, spindles and distaffs, combs, a basket and ploughing oxen. Without evidence of rigorous lifestyle Schepelern thought these were *not* Montanist (*Montanismus*, 82). On Gibson nos. 19 and 5 (indicative of endogamy) see Tabbernee 'New Documents', 128ff.

11 Gibson, *'Christians'*, 4. Dated *Eumeneian formula* examples place most in the late third century. 'He shall be answerable to God' was used by Jews and Christians alike. Cf. Tabbernee, 'Christian Inscriptions', 136ff.

12 A change of mind: cf. 491, 537 in Ramsay, *Cities and Bishoprics of Phrygia*, Oxford 1895, 1897.

13 J.G.C. Anderson, 'Paganism in Northern Phrygia', 201; Labriolle, *La Crise*, 489.

14 For Gibson Calder had in mind 'an isolated brotherhood' (*'Christians'*, 135 n.2). See discussion in Schepelern, *Montanismus*, 79ff.

15 Anderson, 'Paganism in Northern Phrygia', 188ff.; J. Strubbe, 'A Group of Imperial Estates in Central Phrygia', *Ancient Society* 6 (1975), 228–36.

16 *'Christians'*, 136; and 'Montanist Epitaphs', *GRBS* 16 (1975), 433–42.

17 *'Christians'*, 140.

18 This was in Cotiaeon. See Ramsay, 'Phrygian Orthodox', 12.

19 Frend, 'Montanism: Research', 534; Strobel, *Das heilige Land*, 104–12.

20 Tabbernee, 'Christian Inscriptions', 132: the *nomen* Aurelia is no good indicator of date. Even post-Constantinian inscriptions bear the letters.

21 Frend, 'Montanismus', in G. Müller *et. al.*, *Theologische Realenzyklopädie*, 1993 (I have used the pre-publication English text).

22 Strobel, *Das heilige Land*, 117; Tabbernee, 'Christian Inscriptions', 135.

23 Trombley (*Hellenic Religion* i, 75) on survival of 'a strong pre-Christian stratum of religious belief and behavior'. Though Christian, the Prophecy's first adherents would have been recognisably *Phrygian*.

24 Later imperial legislation: Tabbernee, 'Opposition', 418–55.

25 Tabbernee, 'Regional Bishops', 250.

26 Pacian of Barcelona: some 'Phrygians' traced their line of tradition via Proclus (*Ep. I ad Sympronianum*).

27 Vokes, 'Montanism and the Ministry', 309f. Tabbernee, 'Regional Bishops', 250f. suspects as Montanist the early third-century Temenothyrai inscriptions (North Phrygia, with a female presbyter and two male bishops).

28 'Regional Bishops', 25; but cf. Kraft, 'Altkirchliche Prophetie', 268f.

29 Mitchell, 'The *Life* of St Theodotus', 105.

30 E. Seckel, 'Die karthagische Inschrift CIL VIII 25045 – ein kirchenrechtliches Denkmal des Montanismus?', *SPAW* 54 (1921), 989–1017.

31 Tabbernee, 'Regional Bishops', 257. See too 3.5.4.

32 Note Ignatius *Philadelphians* (!) ix. He had employed prophecy (vii), countered disagreement about use of the Scriptures (viii.2) and in ix wrote of priests, prophets, apostles and Abraham, Isaac and Jacob (the patriarchs). Were priesthood, apostolate, prophetic status and the patriarchate being debated already in Philadelphia? Cf. Trevett, 'Apocalypse, Ignatius, Montanism' for other examples.

33 'Regional Bishops', 275f.

34 Contrast Hilgenfeld, *ZWT* 3 (1895), 635ff.; Jülicher, *ZKG* 16 (1896), 664f.; Schepelern, *Montanismus*, 39f. and discussion in Tabbernee, 'Regional Bishops', 260f.

35 Cf. A. Hauck, 'κοινωνός/κοινός', *TDNT* iii, 801f. on *koinōnos* as possible equivalent of חברים (*Haverîm*) in the Rabbis. Vokes and Strobel hold the 'financial officer' theory, Tabbernee rejects ('Regional Bishops', 258f.). The word has a range of meanings, as he notes.

36 Lampe, *A Patristic Greek Lexicon*, Oxford 1961, 'κοινωνία'; F. Hauck, 'κοινωνός', *TDNT* iii, 789–809.

37 'Regional Bishops', 263. Klawiter's view lacks precision, I think.

38 The third inscription concerns *hagios* Paulos. The language is ambiguous. It comes from Lydia, where the town of Güre now stands, on a route between Temenothyrai (east) and Philadelphia (75 km. to the west). Tabbernee thinks it indicates a regional (Philadelphia) bishop (*koinōnos*). But Paulos may have been a native Philadelphian. He may indeed have been *koinōnos* in an area close to Philadelphia itself but for unknown reasons his epitaph was set up in Lydia.

39 Cf. Pelikan, 'Trinitarian', 99ff., citing other writers. On Tertullian and Trinity see Moingt's monumental *Théologie trinitaire de Tertullien* i, Paris 1966; Daniélou, *Latin Christianity*, 361ff.; Sider, 'Approaches', 251f.

40 Pelikan (103ff.): Montanism had no *major* significance in the evolution of the Trinity doctrine, noting the high incidence of textual variants in Tertullian passages about christology and Trinity. On *Adv. Prax.* viii.5: Robeck, *Prophecy in Carthage*, 124–7 (Johannine and Heb. 1:3 influence); contrast Aland 'Bemerkungen', 147; Labriolle, *La Crise*, 56.

41 D.F. Wright, 'Montanists Condemned?', 16.

42 Wright, ibid. and 21.

43 J. Pelikan, 'Trinitarian' 102f.
44 Tertullian did not identify Montanus *as* the Paraclete. *Paracletus* appears 11 times in *Adv. Prax.*, as Holy Spirit in the Trinity and as the prophetic Spirit in the Prophets.
45 See Aland, 'Augustin', 150ff., 154f., Labriolle, *Les Sources*, xcviiiff.
46 Heine, *Oracles*, 113–17. In 342–3 the (Eastern) Council of Sardica (Sofia) housed those who refused contact with Athanasius or Marcellus of Ancyra. It accused Marcellus of theology tainted with the thought of Sabellius, Paul of Samosata *and Montanus*, the *dux* of all heretics. See A.H.B. Logan, 'Marcellus of Ancyra and anti-Arian Polemic', *Studia Patristica* xix, Leuven 1989, 189–97.
47 *CIL* viii.1, 1881, 252 no. 2272. Heine, *Oracles*, 164. Labriolle, *La Crise*, 525ff.; Schepelern, *Montanismus* 42ff.; Pelikan, 'Trinitarian', 103f. The accusation recurs in (eleventh century) Theophylactus *Enarr. in Euang. Luc.* xxiv (*PG* cxxiii.1124; Labriolle, *Les Sources*, 253).
48 *CIL* viii, 2272 and 950. Pelikan, 'Trinitarian', 104. See for literature Ferrua in 'Communità Montanista', 221f.
49 Novatian wrote an orthodox work on the Trinity. Opposition to the election of Cornelius as bishop of Rome (251 CE) derived from dislike of concessions to the lapsed. See e.g. M. Simonetti, 'Alcune osservazione', in *Studi in onore di Angelo Monteverdi*, ii, Modena 1959, 771–83; d'Alès, *Novatien: étude sur la théologie romaine*, Paris 1924. On Novatianism in Africa: Frend, *The Donatist Church*, Oxford 1952, 128ff., 319.
50 Novatianists and Donatists persisted in pockets, the former into the fifth century at least. Fourth-century Donatism was sullied by association with the Circumcellians. Optatus, *De schism. Donat.* iii.4; Augustine, *Contra Gaudentium* i.28,32; *Enarratio in Ps.* cxxxii.3,6; *De opere monachorum* xxviii.36. See Frend in *JTS* 3 (1952), 87ff.; *JTS* 20 (1969), 542–9.
51 Socrates *HE* iv.28; Sozomen *HE* vii.9,2. See Schepelern, *Montanismus*, 175f. Myloukomē (15 km. from Philadelphia) appears in the Praÿlios the Montanist *koinōnos* inscription (Tabbernee, 'Regional Bishops', 273f.). The date is 514–5. Possibly the birthplace of Ablabēs, the *pneumatikos* known in Rome (see 5.3.1; *CIG* iv (1977), 9578).
52 Frend, *The Donatist Church*, 86, 139, 334 cf. Epiphanius *Pan.* lix.13. See too A.H.M. Jones in *JTS* 10 (1959), 280–98.
53 *ibid.* See too Schepelern, *Montanismus*, 101ff. on the decline of Phrygian cults and Ramsay, *Cities and Bishoprics* i, 148.
54 *The Donatist Church*, 124.
55 Heine, *Oracles*, 173. But see Aland, 'Augustin', 162f. and 5.3.
56 C. Cecchelli, *Monumenti*, 92ff. Contrast Frend, *Rise*, 280f. and literature there. Irenaeus *Adv. haer.* i.29,4; i.30,7.
57 See Dölger, 'Die eigenartige Marienverehrung der Philomarioniten . . .', *Antike und Christentum* 1 (1929), 107–40. Some of the sectarians originated in Thrace which Montanism reached at an early stage (see 2.1.3). Benko sees Montanism as a catalyst for the rise of Mariology.

58 In light of *Pan.* xlix.2.2 Benko suggests 'Montanist devotion to Eve' influenced early apologists (see n. 61 and Benko, 169). The source (on Quintillianists) is late. See J.A. Cerrato, 'Hippolytus'.

59 Contemporary of Henana's disciple at Nisibis, of the same name. 'Abdiso' of Nisibis mentions him in *Catalogus Librorum* ch. xciii (Assemani, *Bibliotheca Orientalis* III.i, 169). He wrote *History of the Holy Fathers which were Persecuted.* . . . : Labriolle, *Les Sources*, no. 197, p. 239 and refers to *Mountianoi* (*sic*).

60 Maruta bishop of Maipherqat, friend of John Chrysostom: see *De Sancta Synodo Nicaena* (Harnack, TU 19 (1899), 17, Latin recension from Arabic), Labriolle, *Les Sources*, 194f.

61 Benko, *Goddess*, 168 thinks the *Eva–Maria* parallelism in Justin and Irenaeus came from exposure to Montanism (Justin Martyr?!). I do not. Cf. 'the significance of Eve was discovered by the Montanists' (p. 195).

62 S. Benko, *Goddess*, 163. Cf. too 168.

63 Aland, 'Augustin', 149f. cf. 'Montanism' in M. Eliade (ed.), *Encyclopaedia of Religion*, New York–London 1987, x, 81. Labriolle (*Les Sources*, xc) notes Augustine's use of John 14:17; 16:13 and 1 Cor. 13:9 in *Contra Faustum* xxxii.17.

64 Pacian: see Labriolle, *Les Sources*, xcix, 144f.; Aland, 'Augustin', 149f.; Heine, *Oracles*, 136f. (partial refs. only).

65 Text of Praedestinatus: Labriolle, *Les Sources*, 216ff. (*PL* liii.617). The account refers also to martyrs.

66 See Aland, 'Augustin', 149–51 (doubting its authenticity); Heine, *Oracles*, 160; Labriolle, *Les Sources*, 183f.

67 M.A. Boldetti, *Osservazioni sopra i cimiteri de' santi Martiri, ed antichi Cristiani di Roma*, Rome 1720, 539. On the inscription: Ferrua, 'Comunità Montanista', 216–22 (not catholic or Gnostic). For the Alexander (Ἀλέξανδρος ἰατρός) inscription see *CIG* 9792. Documentation of the Council of Rome of 368 CE does not mention Montanists.

68 Scant evidence for Montanism in the West: Aland, 'Augustin', 151ff.

69 M.R. Salzman, 'The Evidence for the Conversion of the Roman Empire to Christianity in Book 16 of the *Theodosian Code*', *Historia* 41 (1993), 362–378, esp. 363.

70 For the East, Ramsay, 'Phrygian Orthodox': Hierapolis (north of Laodicea) was a fifth–sixth century rallying-point for heretics, with little evidence for orthodox bishoprics in Ancyra, Aezani and other places adjoining the Tembris valley region 'where Montanism was strong' (pp. 11f).

71 See 5.1. Ramsay (*Cities and Bishoprics*, ii. chs. 12 and 17, esp. 501ff.) tells of good pagan–Christian relations and few Phrygian martyrdoms.

72 See 3.8. The *Acts of Achatius*, of course, do claim that on one occasion, at least, Cataphrygians had committed apostasy.

73 Salzman, 'The Evidence', 364ff. *et passim*. The synods of Gagra (in the 340s), Laodicea (Canon 8) and Ps.-Canon 7 of Constantinople demanded

that Montanists (Sabellian in doctrine) be rebaptised.

74 Salzman, 'The Evidence', 364ff.; Labriolle, *Les Sources*, nos. 188–91. *Cod. Just.* i.5,18 and 21 treats of Montanists, Manichaeans and Ophites together. This does not mean that Montanists were (or ever had been) of like mind with these groups. *Cod. Theod.* xvi.5.40 treats Pepuzites with Manichaeans. Such listings are for 'administrative convenience', so Vokes, 'Opposition'.

75 Trombley, 'Paganism in the Greek World'.

76 *Chronicle (Chronographia)* of Michael the Syrian, ii, 269f. See also Gero, 'Syriac Source', 520–4. But Montanists existed under Justin II (565–78, CE) and Tiberius (d. 582). See John of Ephesus *HE* iii.20 and 32.

77 Salzman, 'The Evidence', 365ff.,368f.

78 Aland, 'Augustin', 152.

79 Procopius *Hist. Arc.* xi.13ff., 23 (showing that Montanists were not all poor, despite the authorities' efforts); Labriolle, *La Crise*, 528ff.

80 See A. Scharf, 'The Jews, the Montanists and Emperor Leo III'.

81 On Montanism as 'Jewish Christianity' see 3.10.2.

82 οἱ δὲ Μοντανοὶ διαμαντεύσαντες ἑαυτοῖς καὶ ὁρίσαντες ἡμέραν εἰσῆλθον εἰς τοὺς ὡρισμένους οἴκους τῆς πλάνης αὐτῶν καὶ κατέκαυσαν ἑαυτούς.

83 Martin, *A History of the Iconoclastic Controversy*, London 1932, 26.

84 Scharf, 'The Jews', 46 cf. John 16:13ff.: their leaders 'harbingers of the physical establishment of the New Jerusalem'; Pepuza was 'promised land' of an elect which tolerated 'no external earthly rule'. Cf. too E. Stein, *Histoire du Bas-Empire* ii, Paris 1949, 373ff.

85 S. Gero, 'Syriac Source', 520–4.

86 Schepelern (*Montanismus*, 122f.) cited pagan Phrygian parallels for initiatory tattooing and quoted Prudentius' *Peristephanon*. In the same Prudentius passage sheets/plates covered in gold leaf were laid on parts of corpses, which Schepelern did not note. Cf. also 3.10.2 and n. 212. Gold mouth-coverings were known in the Greek world from pre-Christian times.

Select bibliography

Readers should consult the Index of scholars' names for further writings by people named below and for other works cited in this study.

Aland, K., 'Der Montanismus und die kleinasiatische Theologie' *ZNW* 46 (1955), 109–16.
  'Bemerkungen zum Montanismus und zur frühchristlichen Eschatologie', 105–48; 'Augustin und der Montanismus', 149–64; both in Aland, *Kirchengeschichtliche Entwürfe*, Gütersloh, 1960.
  'The problem of Anonymity and Pseudonymity in Christian Literature of the First Two Centuries', *JTS* 12 (1961), 39–49.
  'Noch einmal: Das Problem der Anonymität und Pseudonymität in der christlichen Literatur', in *Pietas* (B. Kötting *Festschrift*), *JAC* Suppl. 8, Münster 1980, 121–9.
Anderson, J.G.C., 'Paganism and Christianity in the Upper Tembris Valley', in W.M. Ramsay (ed.), *Studies in the Eastern Provinces*, London 1906, 193–201.
  'Paganism and Christianity in Northern Phrygia', in W.M. Ramsay (ed.), *Studies in the History and Art of the Eastern Provinces of the Roman Empire*, Aberdeen 1906, 183–227.
Andresen, C., '"Ubi tres, ecclesia est, licet laici". Kirchengeschichtliche Reflexionen zu einem Satz des Montanisten Tertullian Matt. 18,20', in H. Schroer (ed.), *Vom Amt des Laien in Kirche und Theologie*, Berlin 1982, 103–21.
Ash, J.L., 'The Decline of Ecstatic Prophecy in the Early Church', *ThSt* 37 (1976), 227–52.
Atkinson, P.C., 'Joel 2:28 (LXX 3:1,2)', in E.A. Livingstone (ed.), *Studia Evangelica* vii (TU 126), Berlin 1982, 11–16.
Aune, D.E., *Prophecy in Early Christianity and the Ancient Mediterranean World*, Grand Rapids 1983.
  'The Odes of Solomon and Early Christian Prophecy', *NTS* 28 (1982), 435–60.
Bacht, H., 'Die prophetische Inspiration in der kirchlichen Reflexion der vormontanistischen Zeit', *ThQ* 125 (1944), 1–18.
  'Wahres und falsches Prophetentum. Ein kritischer Beitrag zur religion-

sgeschichtlichen Behandlung des frühen Christentums', *Biblica* 32 (1951), 237–62.

Bardy, G., *La Vie Spirituelle d'Après les Pères des Trois Premiers Siècles*, Tournai 1968.

Barnes, T.D., 'The Pre-Decian *Acta Martyrum*', *JTS* 19 (1968), 509–31.
'Tertullian's *Scorpiace*', *JTS* 20 (1969), 105–32.
'The Chronology of Montanism', *JTS* 21 (1970), 403–8.
Tertullian: A Historical and Literary Study, Oxford 1971.
'Eusebius and the Date of the Martyrdoms', *Les Martyrs de Lyon* (Edits. CNRS), Paris 1978, 137–41.
'Tertullian the Antiquarian', *Early Christianity and the Roman Empire* (Variorum reprints), London 1984.

Barns, T., 'The Catholic Epistle of Themison: a Study in 1 and 2 Peter', *The Expositor* 3rd series viii (1903), 40–62; ix (1904), 369–93.

Bauer, W., *Orthodoxy and Heresy in Earliest Christianity*, Philadelphia 1971.

Benko, S., *The Virgin Goddess: Studies in the Pagan and Christian Roots of Mariology*, Leiden 1993.

Bickel, E., 'Protogamia', *Hermes* 58 (1923), 426–40.

Blanchetière, F., 'Le Montanisme originel', *RScR* 52 (1978), 118–34; 53 (1979), 1–22.

Bludau, A., *Die ersten Gegner der Johannesschriften* (Bib. St. 22), Freiburg 1925.

Bonwetsch, N., in Lietzmann, H. (ed.), *Kleine Texte zur Geschichte des Montanismus* (Kleine Texte 129), Bonn 1914

Boring, M.E., 'The Influence of Christian Prophecy on the Johannine Portrayal of the Paraclete and Jesus', *NTS* 25 (1978), 113–22.
Sayings of the Risen Christ: Christian Prophecy in the Synoptic Tradition, SNTSMS 46, Cambridge 1982.

Bowersock, G.W., 'Les Eglises de Lyon et de Vienne: relations avec L'Asie', in *Les Martyrs de Lyon* (Edits. CNRS), Paris 1978, 249–55.

Bray, G.L., *Holiness and the Will of God: Perspectives on the Theology of Tertullian*, Atlanta 1979.
'The Relationship Between Holiness and Chastity in Tertullian', in E.A. Livingstone (ed.), *Studia Patristica* xvi (TU 129), Berlin 1985, 132–5.

Brown, P., *The Making of Late Antiquity*, Cambridge MA 1978.
Society and the Holy in Late Antiquity, London 1982.
The Body and Society: Men, Women and Sexual Renunciation in Early Christianity, London 1988.

Buckler, W.H., See CALDER

Burghardt, W.J.,. 'Primitive Montanism: Why Condemned?' in D. Hadidian (ed.), *From Faith to Faith* (essays in hon. D.G. Miller), Pittsburgh 1979, 339–56.

Burrus, V., 'The Heretical Woman as Symbol in Alexander, Athanasius, Epiphanius and Jerome', *HTR* 84 (1991), 230ff.

Buschmann, G., 'Martyrium Polycarpi 4 und der Montanismus', *Vig. Christ.* 49 (1995), 105–45

'Martyrium Polycarpi. Eine formkritische Studie. Ein Beitrag zur Frage nach der Entstehung der Gattung Martyrerakte', *BZNW* 70, Berlin, 1994.

Calder, W.M., 'Philadelphia and Montanism', *BJRL* 7 (1923), 309–53.

'The Epigraphy of the Anatolian Heresies', in *Anatolian Studies* (W.M. Ramsay *Festschrift*), Manchester 1923, 59–91.

'Some Monuments of the Great Persecution', *BJRL* 8 (1924), 345–64.

'Leaves from an Anatolian Notebook', *BJRL* 13 (1929), 254–71.

'The New Jerusalem of the Montanists', *Byzantion* 6 (1931), 421–5.

'Early Christian Epitaphs from Phrygia', *Anatolian Studies* 5 (1955), 25–9.

and Buckler, W.H. (eds.), *Anatolian Studies Presented to Sir W.H. Ramsay*, Manchester 1923.

Campenhausen, H. von., *Ecclesiastical Authority and Spiritual Power in the Church of the First Three Centuries*, London 1969.

The Formation of the Christian Bible, Philadelphia 1972.

Cardman, F., 'Tertullian on Doctrine and the Development of Discipline', in E. A. Livingstone (ed.), *Studia Patristica* xvi (TU 129), Berlin 1985, 136–42.

'Acts of the Women Martyrs', *ATR* 70 (1988), 144–150.

Cecchelli, C., *Monumenti Cristiani-Eretici di Roma*, Rome 1944.

Cerrato, J.A., 'Hippolytus *On the Song of Songs* and the New Prophecy', forthcoming in *Studia Patristica*, Peeters Press, Leuven (Proceedings of the 12th International Congress on Patristic Studies, Oxford 1995).

Cohn, N., *The Pursuit of the Millennium*, Harmondsworth 1970 first publ. 1957.

Connolly, R.H., 'The Didachē and Montanism', *Down. Rev.* 55 (1937), 339–47.

Conybeare, F.C., 'The Odes of Solomon: Montanist', *ZNW* 12 (1911), 70–5.

Countryman, L.W., 'Tertullian and the Regula Fidei', *The Second Century* 2 (1982), 208–27.

Daley, B., *The Hope of the Early Church*, Cambridge 1991.

Daunton-fear, A., 'The Ecstasies of Montanus', in E.A. Livingstone (ed.), *Studia Patristica* xviii, Oxford 1982, 648–51.

Davies, J.G., 'Tertullian, *DE RESURRECTIONE CARNIS* LXIII: A Note on the Origins of Montanism', *JTS* 6 (1955), 90–4.

Dehandschutter, B., 'The Martyrium Polycarpi; a century of research', *ANRW* II.27,1, Berlin 1993, 485–522.

Deutsch, C., 'Transformation of Symbols: the New Jerusalem in Rev. 21.1–22.5', *ZNW* 78 (1987), 106–26.

Dodds, E.R., *Pagan and Christian in an Age of Anxiety*, Cambridge 1965.

Eitrem, S., *Orakel und Mysterien am Ausgang der Antike*, Zurich 1947.

Ellis, E.E., *Prophecy and Hermeneutic in Early Christianity*, Grand Rapids 1980.

Eno, R.B, 'Authority and Conflict in the Early Church', *Eglise et Théologie* 1 (1976), 41–60.

Evans, E., *Tertullian's Treatise Against Praxeas*, London 1948.

Faggiotto, A., *L'Eresia dei Frigi. Fonti e Frammenti* (Scrittori Cristiani Antichi

9), Rome 1924.

La Diaspora Catafrigi, Rome 1924.

Ferrua, A., 'Di una comunità Montanista sull' Aurelia alla fine dell' IV secolo', *Civ. Catt.* 87 (1936), 216–27.

'Questioni di epigrafia eretica romana', *RivAC* 21 (1945), 165–221.

'Una nuova iscrizione Montanista', *RivAC* 31 (1955), 97–100

Ficker, G., 'Widerlegung eines Montanisten', *ZKG* 26 (1905), 447–63.

Fischer, J.A., 'Die antimontanistischen Synoden des 2 u. 3 Jahrhunderten', *Annuarium Historiae Conciliorum* 6 (1974), 241–73.

Ford, J. Massingberd, 'Was Montanism a Jewish Christian Heresy?', *JEH* 17 (1966), 145–58.

'A Note on Proto Montanism in the Pastoral Epistles', *NTS* 17 (1970–1), 338–46.

Fox, R.L., *Pagans and Christians in the Mediterranean World*, Harmondsworth 1986.

Fredouille, J.-C., *Tertullien et la conversion de la culture antique*, Paris 1972.

Freeman, G, 'Montanism and the Pagan Cults of Phrygia', *Dominican Studies* 3 (1950), 297–316.

Freeman-Grenville, G.S.P., 'The Date of the Outbreak of Montanism', *JEH* 5 (1954), 7–15.

Frend, W.H.C., 'Note on the Chronology of the Martyrdom of Polycarp and the Outbreak of Montanism', in J. Courcelle *et al.* (eds.), *Oikoumene: Studi Paleocristiani*, Rome 1964, 499–506.

Martyrdom and Persecution in the Early Church, Oxford 1965.

'Blandina and Perpetua: Two Early Christian Martyrs', in *Les Martyrs de Lyon* (Edits. CNRS), Paris 1978, 167–75.

'Early Christianity and Society: A Jewish Legacy in the Pre-Constantine Era', no. 5 in *Archeology and History in the Study of Early Christianity* (Variorum reprints), London 1988, and in *HTR* 76 (1983), 53–71.

The Rise of Christianity, London 1984.

'Montanism: Research and Problems' no. 6 in *Archaeology and History in the Study of Early Christianity* (Variorum reprints), London 1988.

'Montanism: A Movement of Prophecy and Regional Identity in the Early Church', *BJRL* 70 (1988), 25–34.

Fries, S.A., 'Die Oden Salomos. Montanistische Lieder aus dem 2. Jahrhundert', *ZNW* 12 (1911), 108–25.

Froehlich, K., 'Montanism and Gnosis', *Orientalia Christiana Analecta* 195 (1973), 91–111 and in D. Neiman, M. Scatkin (eds.), *The Heritage of the Early Church* (essays for L.G.V. Florovsky), Rome 1973, 91ff.

Georgi, D., 'Die Visionen vom himmlischen Jerusalem', in D Lührmann, G. Strecker (eds.), *Kirche* (G. Bornkamm *Festschrift*), Tübingen 1980, 351–72.

Gero, S., 'Montanus and Montanism according to a Medieval Syriac Source', *JTS* 28 (1977), 520–4.

Gibson, E., 'Montanist Epitaphs at Uşak', *GRBS* 16 (1975), 433–42.

284 *Select bibliography*

The *'Christians for Christians' Inscriptions of Phrygia* (Harvard Theological Studies 32), Missoula MT 1978.

Goree, B., 'The Cultural Bases of Montanism' unpublished Ph.D. dissertation, Baylor University, Waco TX 1980.

Grant, R.M., *Second Century Christianity: A Collection of Fragments*,[2], London 1957.

'Eusebius and the Martyrs of Gaul', *Les Martyrs de Lyon* (Edits. CNRS), Paris 1978, 129–36.

Eusebius as Church Historian, Oxford 1980.

Gregoire, H., 'Épigraphie chrétienne: I. Les inscriptions hérétiques d'Asie Mineure', *Byzantion* 1 (1924), 695–710.

'Du nouveau sur la hierarchie de la secte Montaniste, d'après une inscription grecque. . .', *Byzantion* 2 (1925), 329–35.

'Un nouveau κοινωνος montaniste', *La Nouvelle Clio* 4 (1952), 314.

and Orgels, P. *Les Persécutions dans l'Empire Romain*[2] (Memoires de l'Acad. Roy. de Belgique, Lettres et des Sciences Morales lvi/5) 1964.

Groh, D.E., 'Utterance and Exegesis: Biblical Interpretation in the Montanist Crisis', in D.E. Groh and R. Jewett (eds.), *The Living Text*, New York 1985, 73–95.

Gryson, R., *The Ministry of Women in the Early Church*, Collegeville 1976.

Gundry, R.H., 'People as Place Not Place for People', *Nov. Test.* 29 (1987), 254–64.

Haspels, C.H.E., *The Highlands of Phrygia: Sites and Monuments*, Princeton 1971.

Hawthorne, J.F.(ed.), *Current Issues in Biblical and Patristic Interpretation* (Studies for M.C. Tenney), Grand Rapids 1975.

Heine, R.E., 'The Role of the Gospel of John in the Montanist Controversy', *The Second Century* 6 (1987), 1–19.

The Montanist Oracles and Testimonia, Macon GA 1989

'The Gospel of John and the Montanist Debate at Rome', in E.A. Livingstone (ed.), *Studia Patristica* xxi, Leuve 1989, 95–100.

Hennecke, E., and Schneemelcher, W. (eds.), *New Testament Apocrypha*, ii, London 1965, 686f.

Hill, C., *Regnum Caelorum: Patterns of Future Hope in Early Christianity*, Oxford 1992.

Hill, D., *New Testament Prophecy*, London 1979.

Holl, K., 'Das Fortleben der Volkssprachen in Kleinasien in nachchristlicher Zeit', *Hermes* 43 (1908), 240–54.

Epiphanius Werke, Leipzig 1922.

Jansen, J.F., 'Tertullian and the New Testament', *The Second Century* 2 (1982), 191–207.

Jensen, A., *Gottes selbstbewusste Töchter: Frauenemanzipation im frühen Christentum?*, Freiburg 1992.

Johnson, S.E., 'Unsolved Questions about Early Christianity in Anatolia', in *Studies in New Testament and Early Christian Literature (Festschrift for A.P. Wikgren)*, Leiden 1972, 181–93.

'Asia Minor and Early Christianity', in *Christianity, Judaism and other Greco-Roman Cults (Festschrift* for Morton Smith), Leiden 1975, 77–145.

Jones, A.H.M., *Cities of the Eastern Roman Empire*, Oxford 1937.

Klawiter, F.C., 'The New Prophecy in Early Christianity: The Origin, Nature and Development of Montanism AD 165–220', unpublished Ph.D. dissertation, University of Chicago 1975.

'The Role of Martyrdom and Persecution in Developing the Priestly Authority of Women in Early Christianity: A Case Study of Montanism', *CH* 49 (1980), 251–61.

Knox, R., *Enthusiasm*, Oxford 1950.

Kraft, H., 'Die altkirchliche Prophetie und die Entstehung des Montanismus', *ThZ* 11 (1955), 249–71

'Die Lyoner Märtyrer und der Montanismus', *Pietas (B. Kötting Festschrift)*, *JAC* Suppl. 8, Münster 1980, 250–7 and in *Les Martyrs de Lyons* (Edits. CNRS), Paris 1978, 233ff.

'Die Entstehung von Gemeindeverbänden', in W. Schrage (ed.), *Studien zum Text und zur Ethik des Neuen Testaments*, Münster 1986, 217–41.

Kühnert, W., 'Der antimontanistische Anonymus des Eusebius', *ThZ* 5 (1949), 436–46.

Labriolle, P. de, 'Mulières in ecclesia taceant. Un aspect de la lutte antimontaniste', *BALAC* 1 (1911), 1–24; 103–22, 292–98.

La Crise Montaniste, Paris 1913.

Les Sources de l'Histoire du Montanisme: textes grecs, latins, syriaques (Collecteanea Friburgensia 24), Paris 1913

History and Literature of Christianity from Tertullian to Boethius, London 1924.

Lawlor, H.J., 'The Heresy of the Phrygians', *JTS* 9 (1908), 481–99 and in Lawlor, *Eusebiana*, Oxford 1912.

Lof, L.J.van, 'The Plebs of the Psychici: are the Psychici of De Monogamia Fellow-Catholics of Tertullian?' in G.J.M. Bartelink et al., *Eulogia (Mélanges à A.A.R. Bastiaensen)*, The Hague 1991, 353–64.

McGinn, S.E., 'The New Prophecy in Asia Minor and the Rise of Ecclesiastical Patriarchy in Second-Century Pauline Tradition', Ph.D. dissertation, Northwestern University, Evanston IL, 1989.

'The "Montanist" Oracles and Prophetic Theology', forthcoming in *Studia Patristica*, Peeters Press, Leuven.

Macmullen, R., *Christianizing the Roman Empire*, New Haven and London 1984.

Magie, D., *Roman Rule in Asia Minor*, 2 vols, Princeton 1950.

Maino, G.B., 'Il Montanismo e le tendenze separatiste della chiese dell' Asia Minore', *Il Rinnovamento* 5 (1909), 108–22.

Markschies, C., 'Nochmals: Wo lag Pepuza? Wo lag Tymion?', *JAC* 37 (1994), 7–28.

Mitchell, S., 'The Life of St Theodotus of Ancyra', *Anatolian Studies* 32 (1982), 93–113.

Anatolia, 2 vols., Oxford 1993.

Monceaux, P., *Histoire Littéraire de l'Afrique Chrétienne depuis les Origines jusqu'à l'Invasion Arabe*, Paris 1901.

Nagel, P., *Die Motivierung der Askese in der alten Kirche und der Ursprung des Mönchtums* (TU 95), Berlin 1966.

Nautin, P., *Lettres et Écrivains Chrétiens des iie et iiie Siècles*, Paris 1961.

Neymeyr, U., *Die christlichen Lehrer im zweiten Jahrhundert*, Suppl. *Vig. Christ.* 4, Leiden 1989.

Panagopoulos, J.(ed.), *Prophetic Vocation in the New Testament and Today*, Leiden 1977.

Paulsen, H., 'Zur Wissenschaft vom Urchristentum und der alten Kirche – ein methodischer Versuch', *ZNW* 68 (1977), 200–30.

'Die Bedeutung des Montanismus für die Herausbildung des Kanons', *Vig. Christ.* 32 (1978), 19–52.

'Papyrus Oxyrhyncus I.5 und die ΔΙΑΔΟΧΗ ΤΩΝ ΠΡΟΦΗΤΩΝ', *NTS* 25 (1979), 443–53.

Pauw, F. de, 'La Justification des Traditions Non Écrits chez Tertullien', *Ephemerides Theologicae Lovaniensis* 19 (1942), 5–46.

Pelikan, J., 'Montanism and its Trinitarian Significance', *CH* 25 (1956), 99–109.

Peterson, E., 'Zwei angeblich montanistische Inschriften', *RQ* 2 (1934), 173–6.

Piana, G. La *Il Problema della Chiesa Latina in Roma*, Rome 1922.

'The Roman Church at the End of the Second Century', *HTR* 18 (1925), 201–77.

Powell, D., 'Tertullianists and Cataphrygians', *Vig. Christ* 29 (1975), 33–54.

Preuschen, E., 'Ardaf IV Esra 9,26 und der Montanismus', *ZNW* 1 (1900), 265f.

Rader, R., 'The Martyrdom of Perpetua: A Protest Account of Third-Century Christianity', in P. Wilson-Kastner (ed.), *A Lost Tradition: Women Writers in the Early Church*, Washington DC 1981, 1–17.

Ramsay, W.M., *The Church in the Roman Empire to 170 AD*[12], London 1912.

'Phrygian Orthodox and Heretics', *Byzantion* 6 (1931), 1–35.

Robeck, C.M. 'The Role and Function of Prophetic Gifts for the Church at Carthage AD 202–58', Doctoral Dissertation Fuller Theol. Seminary, 1984.

'Canon, *Regula Fidei* and Continuing Revelation in the Early Church', in J.E. Bradley and R.A. Muller (eds.), *Church, Word and Spirit* (essays in hon. G.W. Bromiley), Grand Rapids 1987, 65–91.

Prophecy in Carthage, Cleveland OH 1992.

Rowland, C., *The Open Heaven: A Study of Apocalyptic in Judaism and Early Christianity*, London 1985.

Saxer, V., *Morts, Martyrs, Reliques en Afrique Chrétienne aux Trois Premiers Siècles*, Paris 1981.

Scharf, A., 'The Jews, the Montanists and Emperor Leo III', *Byzantinische Zeitschrift* 59 (1966), 37–46.

Schepelern, W., *Der Montanismus und die phrygischen Kulte*, Tübingen 1929.
Schmidt, C., *Gespräche Jesu mit seinen Jüngern nach der Auferstehung* (TU 13), Leipzig 1919.
Schöllgen, G, *Ecclesia Sordida*, Münster 1984.
'"Tempus in collecto est". Tertullian, der frühe Montanismus und die Naherwartung ihrer Zeit', *JAC* 27/28 (1984–5), 74–96.
Selwyn, E.C., *The Christian Prophets and the Prophetic Apocalypse*, London 1900.
Sider, R.D., 'Approaches to Tertullian: A Study of Recent Scholarship', *The Second Century* 2 (1982), 228–60.
Sordi, M., 'La ricerca d'ufficio nel processo del 177', *Les Martyrs de Lyon* (Edits. CNRS), Paris 1978, 179–85.
The Christians and the Roman Empire, London 1983.
Speigl, J., *Der römische Stadt und die Christen*, Amsterdam 1970.
Strobel, A., *Ursprung und Geschichte des frühchristlichen Osterkalenders* (TU 121), Berlin 1977.
Das heilige Land der Montanisten. Eine religions-geographische Untersuchung, Berlin 1980.
Tabbernee, W., 'The Opposition to Montanism from Church and State', unpublished Ph.D. thesis, University of Melbourne 1978.
'Christian Inscriptions from Phrygia', in G.H.R. Horsley (ed.), *New Documents Illustrating Early Christianity* iii, Sydney 1983, 128–39.
'Early Montanism and Voluntary Martyrdom', *Colloquium* 17 (1985), 33–44.
'Revelation 21 and the Montanist New Jerusalem', *ABR* 37 (1989), 52–60.
'Remnants of the New Prophecy: Literary and Epigraphal Sources of the Montanist Movement', in E. Livingstone (ed.), *Studia Patristica* xxi, Leuven 1989, 193–201.
'Montanist Regional Bishops: New Evidence from Ancient Inscriptions', *JECS* 1 (1993), 249–280.
Montanist Inscriptions and Testimonia: Epigraphic Sources Illustrating the History of Montanism, Macon GA (forthcoming 1996).
'"Our Trophies are Better than your Trophies": The Appeal to Tombs and Reliquaries in Montanist–Orthodox Relations', forthcoming in *Studia Patristica*, Peeters Press, Leuven (Proceedings of the 12th International Congress on Patristic Studies, Oxford 1995).
Telfer, W., 'The Origins of Christianity in Africa', in F.L. Cross (ed.), *Studia Patristica* iv (TU 79), Berlin 1961, 512–17.
Trevett, C., 'Prophecy and Anti-Episcopal Activity: A Third Error Combated by Ignatius?', *JEH* 34 (1983), 1–18.
'Apocalypse, Ignatius, Montanism: Seeking the Seeds', *Vig. Christ.* 43 (1989), 313–38.
'The Other Letters to the Churches of Asia: Apocalypse and Ignatius of Antioch', *JSNT* 37, Festschrift for David Hill (1989), 117–35.
A Study of Ignatius of Antioch in Syria and Asia, Lewiston–New York 1992.
'Fingers up Noses and Pricking with Needles: Possible Reminiscences of

the Revelation in Later Montanism', *Vig. Christ.* 46 (1995), forthcoming.
'Eschatological Timetabling and the Montanist Prophet Maximilla',
forthcoming in *Studia Patristica*, Peeters Press, Leuven (Proceedings of
the 12th International Congress on Patristic Studies, Oxford 1995).

Trombley, F.R., *Hellenic Religion and Christianization c. 370–529* vol. ii, Leiden
1993.
'Paganism in the Greek World at the End of Antiquity', *HTR* 78 (1985),
327–52.

Turner, H.E.W., *The Pattern of Christian Truth*, London 1954.

Unnik, W.C. van, 'De la règle ΜΗΤΕ ΠΡΟΣΘΕΙΝΑΙ ΜΗΤΕ ΑΤΕΛΕΙΝ dans
l'histoire du canon', *Vig. Christ.* 3 (1949), 1–36.
'Ἡ καινή διαθήκη: a Problem in the Early History of the Canon', F.L.
Cross (ed.), *Studia Patristica* iv (TU 79), Berlin 1961, 212–27.

Vokes, F.E., 'The Opposition to Montanism from Church and State in the
Christian Empire', F.L. Cross (ed.), *Studia Patristica* iv (TU 79), Berlin
1961, 512–17.
'Montanism and the Ministry', in F.L. Cross (ed.) *Studia Patristica* ix (TU
94), Berlin 1966, 306–15.
'The Use of Scripture in the Montanist Controversy', *Studia Evangelica* v
(TU 103), Berlin 1968, 317–20.
'Penitential Discipline in Montanism', in E.A. Livingstone (ed.), *Studia
Patristica* xiv, 1976, 62–76.

Waelkens, M., *Die kleinasiatischen Türsteine*, Mainz 1986.

Walls, A.F., 'The Montanist "Catholic Epistle" and its New Testament
Prototype', *Studia Evangelica* iii (TU 88), Berlin 1964, 436–46.

Waszink, J.H., *Tertullian, De Anima*, Amsterdam 1947.

Weinrich, W.C., *Spirit and Martyrdom*, Washington DC 1981.

Whale, J.S., 'Montanus', *Exp. T.* 45 (1934), 496–500.

Williams, C.G., 'Ecstaticism in Hebrew Prophecy and Christian Glossolalia',
Study of Religions 3 (1974), 320–38.

Williams, D.H., 'The Origins of the Montanist Movement: a Sociological
Analysis', *Religion* 19 (1989), 331–51.

Wischmeyer, W., *Griech. u. lat. Inscriptionen zur Sozialgeschichte der alten Kirche*,
Gütersloh 1982.

Wright, D.F., 'Why were the Montanists Condemned?' *Themelios* 2 (1970),
15–21.
'Montanism: A Movement of Spiritual Renewal?', *Theological Renewal* 22
(November 1982), 19–29.

Ysebaert, J., 'The Deaconesses in the Western Church of Late Antiquity and
their Origin', in G.J.M. Bartelink et al., *Eulogia (Mélanges à A.A.R.
Bastiaensen)*, The Hague 1991, 421–36.

Index of scholars' names

Index of subjects, ancient names and places